Weekly Timetable

	Mon	Tues	Wed	Thurs	Fri	Sat	Sun
6–7 AM							
7–8 AM							
8–9 AM							
9–10 AM							
10–11 AM							
11–12 AM							
12 (noon)–1 PM							
1–2 PM							
2–3 PM							
3–4 PM							
4–5 PM							
5–6 PM							
6–7 PM							
7–8 PM							
8–9 PM							
9–10 PM							
10–11 PM							
11 PM–12 (midnight)							

Annotated Instructor's Edition

POWER

Learning

Strategies
for
Success
in College
and Life

Robert S. Feldman
University of Massachusetts—Amherst

McGraw Hill

Boston   Burr Ridge, IL   Dubuque, IA   Madison, WI   New York   San Francisco   St. Louis
Bangkok   Bogotá   Caracas   Lisbon   London   Madrid
Mexico City   Milan   New Delhi   Seoul   Singapore   Sydney   Taipei   Toronto

McGraw-Hill Higher Education

*A Division of The **McGraw-Hill** Companies*

P.O.W.E.R. LEARNING: STRATEGIES FOR SUCCESS IN COLLEGE AND LIFE

This book is printed on acid-free paper.

2 3 4 5 6 7 8 9 0 VNH/VNH 9 0 9 8 7 6 5 4 3 2 1 0

ISBN 0-07-365505-8

Editorial director: *Phillip A. Butcher*
Sponsoring editor: *Sarah Touborg Moyers*
Senior developmental editor: *Rhona Robbin*
Editorial assistant: *Bennett Morrison*
Director of marketing: *Margaret Metz*
Marketing manager: *David Patterson*
Senior project manager: *Denise Santor-Mitzit*
Production supervisor: *Kari Geltemeyer*
Senior designer: *Jennifer McQueen Hollingsworth*
Cover photographer: *Sharon Hoogstraten*
Senior photo research coordinator: *Keri Johnson*
Photo researcher: *Elyse Rieder*
Supplement coordinator: *Carol Loreth*
Compositor: *ElectraGraphics, Inc.*
Typeface: *10.5/13 Palatino*
Printer: *Von Hoffmann Press, Inc.*

Library of Congress Cataloging-in-Publication Data

Feldman, Robert S. (Robert Stephen)
   P.O.W.E.R. learning : strategies for success in college and life /
Robert S. Feldman.
     p.   cm.
   Includes bibliographical references (p.   ) an index.
   ISBN 0-07-365505-8 (softcover)
   1. College student orientation.   2. Study skills.   3. Life skills.
4. Success.   I. Title.   II. Title: POWER learning.
LB2343.3.F44   2000
378.1'98—dc21   99-39465

http://www.mhhe.com

To my students, who make teaching a joy.

About the Author

Robert S. Feldman is a professor of psychology at the University of Massachusetts at Amherst, where he is Director of Undergraduate Studies and recipient of the College Outstanding Teacher Award. He has also taught courses at Mount Holyoke College, Wesleyan University, and Virginia Commonwealth University. As Director of Undergraduate Studies, he initiated the Minority Mentoring Program. He teaches the first-year experience course and in the Talent Advancement Program for new students.

A graduate of Wesleyan University and the University of Wisconsin—Madison, Professor Feldman is a fellow of both the American Psychological Association and the American Psychological Society. He is a recipient of a Fulbright Senior Research Scholar and Lecturer award and has written some 100 scientific articles, book chapters, and books. His books, some of which have been translated into Spanish, French, Portuguese, and Chinese, include *Fundamentals of Nonverbal Behavior, Development of Nonverbal Behavior in Children, Understanding Psychology, Social Psychology, and Development Across the Life Span.* His research interests encompass the development of nonverbal behavior in children and the social psychology of education, and his research has been supported by grants from the National Institute of Mental Health and the National Institute on Disabilities and Rehabilitation Research.

Professor Feldman's spare time is most often devoted to serious cooking and earnest, but unpolished, piano playing. He lives with his wife, a psychologist, in a home overlooking the Holyoke mountain range in Amherst, Massachusetts, and has three children.

Brief Contents

Contents

Part One
Getting Started

1 P.O.W.E.R. Learning: Becoming a Successful Student — 1

2 Making the Most of Your Time — 25

3 Recognizing How You Learn, Who You Are, and What You Value 53

Part Two
Using P.O.W.E.R. in the Classroom

 Finding and Using Information 83

 Taking Notes 113

6 Taking Tests   139

Part Three
P.O.W.E.R. Foundations of Success

7 Building Your Reading and Listening Skills 167

8 Writing and Speaking 193

9 Improving Your Memory   221

Part Four
Life Beyond the Classroom

 10 Making Decisions That Are Right for You **243**

 11 Choosing Your Courses and Major **267**

12 Getting Along with Others 293

13   Money Matters   321

14   Enjoying Health and Wellness   349

Preface

He doesn't know it, but Mark Johnson provided the impetus for this book.

Mark was an enigma when I first met him some two decades ago, soon after I first began college teaching. Enrolled in my introductory psychology class, he was a quiet, good-natured student. His attendance was sporadic, but he passed the tests, although just barely. For most of the semester, he managed to squeak by, a pattern, I would learn, that was typical for him and for other students like him.

Then, on the day that term papers were due, Mark came up to me after class and offered up a lengthy list of reasons why he was unable to complete his paper on time. The paper due date could hardly have sneaked up on him—we had been talking about it in class for several weeks. Yet Mark had managed to put himself in a situation that ensured he would fall short of what was required.

What puzzled me about Mark was that he was smart, articulate, and eager to succeed. He certainly wanted to do well, and seemed every bit as capable as those students who were doing quite well in class. Why, then, was Mark a marginal student, and what didn't he know that his more successful classmates did? Over the years, I encountered other students like Mark, and I wondered: Was there a way to teach *every* student how to succeed, both academically and beyond the classroom?

P.O.W.E.R. Learning embodies the answers to these questions. Based on the conviction that *good students are made, not born,* the central message of *P.O.W.E.R. Learning* is that students can be successful in college if they follow the basic principles and strategies presented in this book. Once mastered, these principles and strategies can help students to maximize their accomplishments, both in and out of the classroom.

Introducing *P.O.W.E.R. Learning: Strategies for Success in College and Life*

This text is designed to be used by students in first-year experience courses. For many students, the first-year experience course is a literal lifeline. It provides the means to learn what it takes to achieve academic success and to make a positive social adjustment to the campus community. If students learn how to do well in their first term of college, they are building a foundation that will last a lifetime.

I wrote *P.O.W.E.R. Learning* because no existing text provides a systematic framework to help students develop learning and problem-solving strategies that will be effective both in and out of the classroom. The book is an outgrowth of my experience as a college instructor—most of it involving first-year students—combined with my research on the factors that influence learning.

P.O.W.E.R. Learning provides a framework that students can begin to use immediately to become more effective students. Having taught first-year-experience courses many times, I knew this framework had to meet several important criteria. Specifically, it had to be:

- Clear, easy-to-grasp, logical, and compelling, so that students could readily see its merits.

- Effective for a variety of student learning styles—as well as a variety of teaching styles.

- Workable within a variety of course formats.

- Transferable to settings ranging from the classroom to the dorm room to the board room.

- Effective in addressing both the mind *and* the spirit, presenting cognitive strategies and skills, while engaging the natural enthusiasm, motivation, and inclination to succeed that students carry within them.

Based on comprehensive, detailed feedback obtained from both instructors and students, *P.O.W.E.R. Learning: Strategies for Success in College and Life* meets these criteria. The book will help students confront and master the numerous challenges of the college experience through use of the P.O.W.E.R. learning approach, embodied in the five steps of the acronym *P.O.W.E.R.* (*Pre*pare, *O*rganize, *W*ork, *E*valuate, and *R*ethink). Using simple—yet effective—principles, *P.O.W.E.R. Learning* teaches the skills needed to succeed in college and careers beyond.

Developing *P.O.W.E.R. Learning*

P.O.W.E.R. Learning: Strategies for Success in College and Life has undergone the most extensive pre-publication development of any book published for the first-year-college experience course. The input of literally hundreds of instructors and students in face-to-face focus groups and conferences, manuscript reviews (through several drafts), questionnaires, and surveys, contributed significantly to the development of the book. The material has been thoroughly class-tested, aggressively critiqued by dozens of students taking their own first-year experience college success course, and revised on the basis of this student feedback.

What did instructors and students say? Several key examples illustrate what I learned and how I responded. First, both groups found the *P.O.W.E.R. Learning* framework easy to grasp, useful, and likely to provide substantial benefits, both in and out of the classroom. They asked for more hands-on and group learning activities than they found in existing texts. In response to this feedback, the ratio of exercises-to-text shifted substantially in terms of increased exercises in later drafts. Finally, it became clear that the World Wide Web was playing an increasingly large role in instruction and students' lives. Consequently, not only did I add material and exercises on using the Web in every chapter, but there is an interactive Web site for readers of *P.O.W.E.R. Learning.* (Visit it at http://www.mhhe.com/power and see for yourself!)

Furthermore, a review of the scientific literature (summarized in the *Instructor's Manual*) confirmed that the principles guiding the development of the *P.O.W.E.R.* framework are supported by extensive research in educational psychology. In short, the result of this thorough pre-publication development and testing is a book and supplements package that both author and publisher are confident will meet the needs of those who teach the course and those who take it. *No other book more closely reflects what instructors and students say they want in a first-year-experience text.*

The Goals of the Book

P.O.W.E.R. Learning: Strategies for Success in College and Life addresses five major goals.

1. **To provide a systematic framework for organizing the strategies that lead to success.** First and foremost, the book provides a systematic, balanced presentation of the skills required to achieve student success. Using the *P.O.W.E.R.* framework and relying on proven strategies, *P.O.W.E.R. Learning* provides specific, hands-on techniques for achieving success as a student.

2. **To offer a wide range of skill-building opportunities.** *P.O.W.E.R. Learning* provides a wealth of specific exercises, diagnostic questionnaires, case studies, and journal writing activities to help students to develop and master the skills and techniques they need to become effective learners and problem solvers. *Readers learn by doing.*

3. **To demonstrate the connection between academic success and success beyond the classroom.** Stressing the importance of *self-reliance* and *self-accountability*, the book demonstrates that the skills required to be a successful student are tied to career and personal success as well.

4. **To develop critical thinking skills.** Whether to evaluate the quality of information found on the Internet or in other types of media, or to judge the merits of a position taken by a friend, colleague, or politician, the ability to think critically is more important than ever in this age of information. Through frequent questionnaires, exercises, journal activities, and guided group work, *P.O.W.E.R. Learning* helps students to develop their capacity to think critically.

5. **To provide an engaging, accessible, and meaningful presentation.** The fifth goal of this book underlies the first four—to write a student-friendly book that is relevant to the needs and interests of its readers and that will promote enthusiasm and interest in the process of becoming a successful student. Learning the strategies needed to become a more effective student should be a stimulating and fulfilling experience. Realizing that these strategies are valuable outside the classroom as well will provide students with an added incentive to master them.

In short, *P.O.W.E.R. Learning: Strategies for Success in College and Life* is designed to give students a sense of mastery and success as they read the book and work through its exercises. It is meant to engage and nurture students' minds and spirits, stimulating their intellectual curiosity about the world and planting a seed that will grow throughout their lifetime.

Achieving the goals of the book

The goals of *P.O.W.E.R. Learning: Strategies for Success in College and Life* are achieved through a consistent, carefully devised set of features common to every chapter. Students and faculty endorsed each of these elements. They include the following:

- *Chapter-opening scenarios.* Each chapter begins with a short vignette, describing an individual grappling with a situation that is relevant to the subject matter of the chapter. Readers will be able to relate to these vignettes, which feature students running behind schedule (Chapter 2), figuring out a way to keep with a reading assignments (Chapter 7), or facing a long list of French vocabulary words to memorize (Chapter 9).

- *Looking Ahead* sections. These sections provide a bridge between the opening vignettes and the remainder of the chapter and include orienting questions that lay out the chapter's objectives.

- *P.O.W.E.R. Plan.* Every chapter includes a figure that summarizes the key activities related to each step of the P.O.W.E.R. process for the major topic discussed in the chapter. The P.O.W.E.R. Plan figures are especially helpful to visually oriented learners.

- *Try It* activities. These sections, interspersed throughout the chapter, include written exercises of all types. These activities are keyed to one or more of the steps of P.O.W.E.R.; the relevant steps are indicated by highlighted letters at the top of each Try It. There are at least five *Try It* activities in every chapter, and at least one of these is designated as an in-class, group exercise. Examples of *Try It* exercises include "Assess Your Learning Style" (Chapter 3), "Identify Course Goals" (Chapter 5), "Discover Your Attention Span" (Chapter 7), and "Use Freewriting" (Chapter 10).

- *Journal Reflections.* This feature provides students with the opportunity to keep an ongoing journal, making entries relevant to the chapter content. Students are asked to reflect and think critically about related prior experiences. For example, the Journal Reflections in Chapter 4, "Finding and Using Information," asks for students' reactions to computers, and the one in Chapter 8, "Writing and Speaking," asks students to reflect on their feelings about the writing process.

- *Speaking of Success.* Every chapter includes interviews with individuals who exemplify academic success. Some of these individuals are well-known figures such as Bill Cosby, Rebecca Lobo, and Colin Powell; others are current students or recent graduates. Many of these individuals have struggled to overcome difficulties in their personal lives or in school before achieving academic or career success. Students will be able to relate to or identify with the stories told by the people profiled in these sections; some accounts may inspire readers to realize their goals and aspirations.

- *Career Connections.* This feature links the material in the chapter to the world of work, demonstrating how the strategies discussed in the chapter are related to career choices and success in the workplace. Topics addressed in these sections include narrowing career choices, applying for jobs, and developing workplace listening skills.

- *Running Glossary.* Key terms appear in boldface in the text and are defined in the margins. In addition, they are listed in a Key Terms and Concepts section at the end of the chapter, with accompanying page references. Key terms are highlighted in color in the index.

- *End-of-chapter material.* Each chapter ends with a summary (Looking Back), organized around the orienting questions featured in the Looking Ahead section; a list of key terms and concepts with page references; and an annotated list of student resources. These resources include campus offices, relevant supplemental readings, and World Wide Web sites and exercises (Taking It to the Net) that require use of the Web. This material helps students study and retain important concepts presented in the chapter, as well as guiding future inquiry.

- *Case Study.* Each chapter ends with a case study (The Case of . . .) to which the principles described in the chapter can be applied. Case studies are based on situations that students might themselves encounter. For instance, the case study in the note-taking chapter describes the difficulties experienced by a student who writes down the instructor's every word ("The Case of . . . The Human Dictation Machine"), and the case study in the decision-making chapter describes a problem involving an apartment lease and roommates ("The Case of . . . Left Holding the Lease"). Each case provides a series of questions that encourage students to consider what they've learned and to use critical thinking skills in responding to these questions.

P.O.W.E.R. Tools for Instructors and Students

The same philosophy and goals that guided the writing of *P.O.W.E.R. Learning: Strategies for Success in College and Life* have informed the development of a *comprehensive, first-rate* set of teaching aids. Through a series of focus groups, questionnaires, and surveys, we asked instructors what they needed to optimize their courses. We also analyzed what other publishers provided in the way of teaching aids to make sure that the ancillary materials accompanying *P.O.W.E.R. Learning* would surpass the level of support to which instructors are accustomed.

As a result of the extensive research that went into devising the teaching aids, we are confident that whether you are an instructor with long experience, or are teaching the course for the first time, this book's instructional package will enhance classroom instruction and provide guidance as you prepare for and teach the course.

Print Resources

Annotated Instructor's Edition (AIE) (0-07-233724-9)
The AIE contains the full text of the student edition of the book with the addition of marginal notes providing a rich variety of teaching strategies, discussion prompts, and helpful cross-references to the Instructor's Resource Manual. Prepared by Cindy Wallace and Joni Webb Petschauer of Appalachian State University.

Instructor's Resource Manual and Testbank (0-07-234372-9)
Written by Cindy Wallace, Joni Webb Petschauer, and Don Friedman of Appalachian State University, with additional contributions from experienced instructors across the country, this manual provides specific

suggestions for teaching each course topic in the text, tips on implementing a first-year experience program, handouts to generate creative classroom activities, transparency masters, audiovisual resources, sample syllabi, tips on incorporating the Web into your course, and a bank of chapter quizzes.

Custom Options   P.O.W.E.R. Learning can be customized for brevity in shorter courses and can be expanded to include semester schedules, campus maps, and other materials specific to your course. Please contact your McGraw-Hill representative for details.

Human Resources

Workshops with Author and Author Team   A variety of workshops are available on topics such as teacher training and using technology in the first-year seminar. Please ask your McGraw-Hill representative for details.

Digital Resources

P.O.W.E.R. Learning CD-ROM   (0-07-234375-3)   This CD-ROM provides students with a rich multimedia extension of the text's content. Each module of the CD-ROM is tied to a chapter of the text, featuring interactive self-assessments, simulations, video and audio clips, crossword puzzles, Web links, journal activities, and an Internet primer. Available in both Windows and Mac for free when packaged with the text.

Health Quest CD-ROM   This interactive program features an array of dynamic simulations and assessment activities to help students make responsible decisions about all aspects of their health and wellness, including stress, nutrition, alcohol and drug use, and sex. Available in both Windows and Mac for a nominal fee, packaged with the text.

P.O.W.E.R. Learning Website   (0-07-233723-0)   Look to us for online teaching and learning tools at www.mhhe.com/power. Instructors and students will find downloadable resources, demonstrations of all of our software programs, opportunities for online discussion, e-mail access to the author and project contributors, Web exercises, and a rich bank of links for college success.

PageOut: The Course Website Development Center   Let us help build your own course Web site. PageOut lets you offer students instant access to your syllabus, lecture notes, original material, recommended Web site addresses, and material from the *P.O.W.E.R. Learning* Web site. Students can even check their grades online. PageOut also provides a discussion board where you and your students can exchange questions and post announcements, as well as an area for students to build personal Web pages.

   To find out more about PageOut: The Course Website Development Center, ask your McGraw-Hill representative for details, or fill out the form at www.mhhe.com/pageout.

PowerPoint Slides (0-07-234373-7) These slides, drawn from the book's graphics and other sources, offer a variety of electronic options to enhance instructor and student presentations.

Study Smart (0-07-552888-6) This innovative study skills tutorial for students is an excellent resource for the learning lab. Teaching students note-taking methods, test-taking strategies, and time management secrets, Study Smart operates with a sophisticated answer analysis that students will find motivational. Available for individual purchase and site license adoption.

Video Resources (0-07-236710-5) *Real People Talk About Real Success.* Filmed expressly for *P.O.W.E.R. Learning* on various campus locations and "real-world" settings, this documentary-style video features a variety of inspiring people, both professional and student, describing life challenges and how the elements of the *P.O.W.E.R.* framework help them achieve success. Designed for use during the early part of the semester, this video is ideal for helping break the ice and stimulating discussion. Ask your McGraw-Hill representative for details.

Start Right Video Series Produced in conjunction with the National Orientation Directors Association, this program consists of six videos (approximately 20 minutes each) on diversity, residential life, academic success, wellness, alcohol, and money. The series is supported by an instructor's guide by Nancy Hunter Denny, including discussion questions, handouts and worksheets, and student exercises. An additional hour-long program, *The Facilitator's Training Video,* illustrates effective methods and strategies for peer discussion leaders. Ask your McGraw-Hill representative for details.

Additional Value-Added Packaging Options

The McGraw-Hill Guide to Electronic Research and Documentation (0-07-069027-8) Written by Diana Roberts Wienbroer of Nassau Community College, this 60-page booklet will help students in all of their cross-curricular endeavors. It is available at no charge when packaged with the text.

Random House Webster's College Dictionary (0-07-366069-8) Updated for the 21st century, this dictionary is available for a nominal cost when packaged with the text.

To the Student

Using *P.O.W.E.R. Learning: Strategies for Success in College and Life*

Do you find that there's not enough time to accomplish all the things you want to do? Do you put off studying for tests until the last minute? Do you sometimes have trouble making decisions?

If so, you're not alone. *Every* first-year college student encounters challenges such as these, and many others. That's where *P.O.W.E.R. Learning: Strategies for Success in College and Life* comes in. It is designed to help you to master the challenges you'll face in college as well as in life after college. The *P.O.W.E.R.* framework—which is based on five key steps embodied in the word *P.O.W.E.R.* (Prepare, Organize, Work, Evaluate, and Rethink)—teaches strategies that will help you become a more successful student and that will give you an edge in attaining what you want to accomplish in life.

But it's up to you to make use of the book. By familiarizing yourself with its features and using the built-in learning aids, you'll maximize it usefulness and be more likely to get the most out of it.

Familiarize yourself with the scope of *P.O.W.E.R. Learning*

Begin by skimming the table of contents, which provides an overview of the book. By reading the chapter titles, you'll get a sense of the topics that are covered and the logic of the sequence of chapters.

Then, take some time to flip through the book. Choose a chapter that sounds interesting to you, skim a few pages, and see for yourself the kinds of practical information the book provides.

Note that every chapter has the same diamond-shaped pattern:

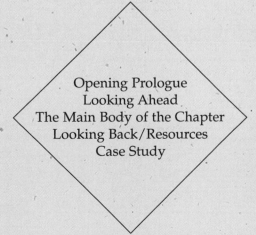

Opening Prologue
Looking Ahead
The Main Body of the Chapter
Looking Back/Resources
Case Study

Use the built-in learning aids

Now that you have a broad overview of *P.O.W.E.R. Learning,* you're ready to consider each of the book's different components. What follows is a visual guide.

Opening Prologue This is a brief account of a student confronting a challenge, of the kind you are likely to face, that is relevant to the chapter topic.

Looking Ahead This opening section orients you to the topics covered in each chapter, providing a link between the opening situation and the rest of the chapter. It also includes a list of key questions that are addressed—and answered—within the chapter.

Journal Reflections This feature allows you to keep an ongoing journal, making entries relevant to the chapter content.

Try It Every chapter offers at least five opportunities for you to gain hands-on experience with the material covered in the chapter. These activities include questionnaires, self-assessments, and group exercises that you can do with your classmates. The name says it all: Try It!

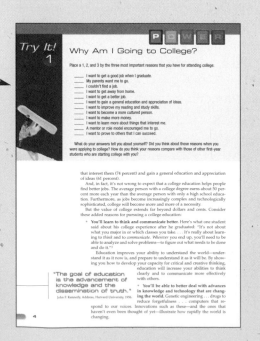

P.O.W.E.R. Plan Every chapter includes a figure that summarizes the key activities related to each step of the P.O.W.E.R. process for the major topic discussed in the chapter. The P.O.W.E.R. Plan figures are especially helpful to visually oriented learners.

Speaking of Success Every chapter includes an interview with someone who has achieved academic success. Some of these people are well-known individuals, whereas others are current students or recent graduates who have overcome academic difficulties to achieve success.

Career Connections Linking college success strategies to the workplace, Career Connections boxes illustrate how the strategies and skills discussed in the chapter can help you on-the-job—and to find a job in the first place.

Running Glossary Key terms appear in boldface in the text and are defined in the margins. In addition, they are listed in a Key Terms and Concepts section at the end of the chapter, where they are referenced by page number, and identified in the index in color.

Looking Back Looking Back is a summary organized around the questions featured in the Looking Ahead section that lists the key points discussed in the chapter.

Key Terms and Concepts This list of important terms you should know is alphabetized, and the page numbers refer back to the point in the chapter where the term was introduced.

Resources Every chapter includes a list of the three types of resources that can help you find information relevant to the chapter: a list of on-campus resources; books; and websites. There are also exercises in using the web, called Taking It to the Net.

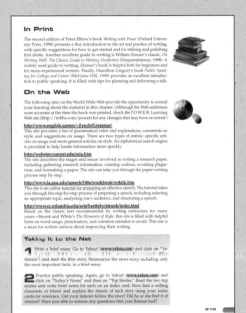

Case Study Every chapter ends with a case study (The Case of . . .) and accompanying questions. These cases are designed to provide you with an opportunity to apply the principles in the chapter.

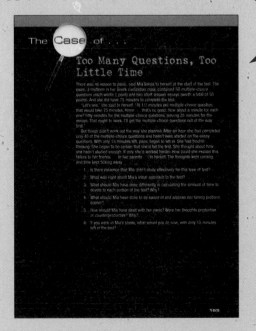

Every chapter contains these features, which will serve as familiar guideposts as you make your way through the book. The structure will help you in organizing the book's content, as well as in learning and remembering the material.

Get in touch

I welcome your comments and suggestions about *P.O.W.E.R. Learning*, as well as the Web site and CD-ROM that accompany the book. You can send letters to me at the Department of Psychology at the University of Massachusetts, Amherst, Massachusetts 01003. Even easier, send me an e-mail message at feldman@psych.umass.edu. I will write back!

A final word

P.O.W.E.R. Learning presents the tools that can maximize your chances for academic and life success. But remember that they're only tools, and their effectiveness depends on the way in which they are used. Ultimately, you are the one who is in charge of your future.

The start of college offers a wonderful point of departure. Make the journey a rewarding, exciting, and enlightening one!

Acknowledgments

I am indebted to the many reviewers of *P.O.W.E.R. Learning* who provided input at every step of development of the book. These dedicated instructors and administrators provided thoughtful, detailed advice, and I am very grateful for their help and insight. They are listed on p. xxv.

I extend a special thanks to those reviewers who participated in a two-day focus group directed at fine-tuning the manuscript. Providing a wealth of ideas and strategies, they gave unstintingly of their time, and they helped shape many aspects of this volume. They include: Elizabeth Boucher, Tennessee Technological University; Deborah Kimbrough-Lowe, Nassau Community College; Michaeline Laine, University of Cincinnati; Evelyn Love, Cuyahoga Community College; Karen Patterson, Central Missouri State University; Jane Sarber, University of Oklahoma; and Cindy Wallace, Appalachian State University.

I also appreciate the contributions of the members of a second focus group; their insights helped us to fine-tune the design for the book and its cover and to refine our plans for the ancillary materials. They include: Dee Bostick, Midlands Technical College; Elizabeth Boucher, Tennessee Technological University; Leslie Chilton, Arizona State University; Joni Webb Petschauer, Appalachian State University; John Pigg, Tennessee Technological University; Sara Stensgaard, SUNY-Buffalo; and Cindy Wallace, Appalachian State University.

A focus group composed of students was particularly helpful to the development of the book. These students, who were either currently enrolled in a first-year-experience course or who worked as peer tutors, contributed a student's-eye-view of the *P.O.W.E.R.* framework and the book. I appreciate their input. The students, who attend Delaware County Community College, Gloucester County Community College, Montgomery County Community College, and Temple University, include: Joseph Albertson, Roy Burton, Matthew DiGregorio, Chanell Gormany, Adrienne Hetward, Leslie Ann Jeffreys, Annamaria Mebbitt, Brant Rider, Abraham Sunny, and Jacqueline Wisniewski.

The students in my own first-year experience course in the spring term of 1999 provided thoughtful and wise advice as they were using the manuscript that was to become *P.O.W.E.R. Learning.* I thank them for their enthusiasm and willingness to participate in the development process.

Professors Cindy Wallace and Joni Webb Petschauer of Appalachian State University wrote the *Instructor's Resource Manual and Test Bank* and provided marginal notes and tips for the *Annotated Instructor's Edition.* I thank both of them for their good ideas, creativity, and dedication. I also thank Dan Friedman of Appalachian State University for writing the test items for the manual.

Edward Murphy, an educational testing expert, helped develop the exercises in the book, and editor Leslie Carr made many creative contributions and stylistic improvements to the text. I'm grateful to both of them for their superb work.

John Graiff participated in every aspect of putting this book together. He was a great help on every level, and I thank him for his willingness to go the extra mile. I could not have written this book without his unflagging support.

I am proud to be part of an extraordinary McGraw-Hill editorial team. Sarah Moyers, sponsoring editor, provided continuing inspiration for the book, and I am grateful for her unwavering support, enthusiasm, and good ideas. Rhona Robbin, senior developmental editor, taught me much of what I know about good writing, and she pored over every word of the text, giving unstintingly of her expertise and support. It was also terrific to be back in Editorial Director Phil Butcher's fold, and I thank him for his support not only on this book, but also on other projects throughout the years. Vice President and Editor-in-Chief Thalia Dorwick gave extraordinarily of her time and wisdom. I value her above-and-beyond-the-call-of-duty contributions immensely. There is, without a doubt, no better editorial group in the business, and I count myself extremely lucky not only to have found myself a part of this world-class team, but to count each of them as friends.

Burrston House, personified by Glenn and Meg Turner, provided editorial and marketing advice at an extraordinary level. I thank them for their good ideas, creativity, constant prodding, and careful calculation of grade point averages. I am also grateful to photo researcher Elyse Rieder and text permissions editor Elsa Peterson. Finally, I am planning to be indebted to David Patterson, marketing manager *par excellence,* into whose capable hands I place ***P.O.W.E.R. Learning,*** and on whose skills I'm counting.

I am also deeply appreciative of the efforts of the fine production team who worked on the book. Senior Project Manager Denise Santor-Mitzit overcame obstacles with grace and good cheer. Designer Jennifer Hollingsworth created the beautiful design for the book, under the direction of Art Director Keith McPherson. These professionals worked under the stewardship of Vice President of Editing, Design, and Production, Merrily Mazza, who was gracious and helpful from the very start of the project.

In the end, I am eternally indebted to my family, both extended and immediate. Sarah, Josh, and Jon, and of course Kathy, thank you for everything.

Reviewers

Bernadette Archer
Fullerton College

J. D. Beatty
Iowa State University

LaVerne Blagmon-Earl
University of District of Columbia

Dee Bostick
Midlands Technical College

Elizabeth Boucher
Tennessee Technological University

Marilyn Bowers
Walters State Community College

Lanny R. Bowers
Northeast State Technical Community College

Tina Brooks
Del Mar College

Elaine Byrd
Utah Valley State College

Leslie Chilton
Arizona State University

Mark Costello
Drexel University

Brian Doyle
Humber College

Linda Dunham
Central Piedmont Community College

Jana Flowers
Richland College

Glenn Graham
Columbia College

Kathy Griffith Fish
Cumberland College

Patricia Hayter-Hall
Richland College

Dawn Hayward
Central Piedmont Community College

Eileen Hewitt
University of Scranton

Lee Brewer Jones
Georgia Perimeter College

Michaeline Laine
University of Cincinnati

Deborah Kimbrough-Lowe
Nassau Community College

Evelyn Love
Cuyahoga Community College

Judy Lynch
Kansas State University

Paul Martin
Pasadena City College

Nancy McCarley
Mississippi State University

Linda Patterson
Middle Tennessee State University

Karen Patterson
Central Missouri State University

Brian A. Richardson
Arizona State University

Jane Sarber
University of Oklahoma

Anna Shiplee
University of West Florida

Margaret Sims
Midlands Technical College

Sara Stensgaard
SUNY Buffalo

Sharon Wagner
Missouri Western State College

Cindy Wallace
Appalachian State University

Gina Walls
Parkland College

Don Williams
Grand Valley State University

Anthony Zoccolillo
Seton Hall University

P.O.W.E.R. Learning: Becoming a Successful Student

1

The day has started off with a bang. Literally. Jessie Trevant's alarm has gone off at 8:35 A.M., rousing her from a deep sleep. As she struggles, eyes closed, to turn off the clock radio's incessant electronic pinging, Jessie knocks it off the desk next to her bed, and it falls to the floor. The bang as it hits not only wakes her fully, but also rouses her roommate, normally a deep sleeper.

Jessie is distressed. Although she and her roommate, squeezed into a room designed originally as a single, have gotten along pretty well for the first two weeks of the term, their relationship is still shaky. Jessie wonders how her roommate will react to being awakened so early.

Struggling out of bed, Jessie reflects on the day ahead. It's one of her most intense class days—four different classes, scattered across the campus. She also must put in several hours of work in the college bookstore, where she has a 15-hour-a-week job, and she knows she better get started on her history paper, which is due next week.

But her major concern is the biology test she must take during her first class of the day. She studied until 2:00 in the morning, leaving precious little time for sleep, but she still could have used more study time. It is her first test in college, and there is so much material to remember. In some irrational way, she feels her performance will signal how successful her entire college career will be, and she wants to make sure she does well on the test.

After a quick shower, Jessie joins a flood of students making their way to classes. She glances at her biology textbook and feels a wave of anxiety flood over her, raising the same questions that have dogged her since she started college: Will I do well in my classes? How can I manage to hold down a job and have enough time to study? Will I make friends and become part of the college community? Can I live up to my family's expectations? . . . And underlying them all is a single challenge: *Will I be successful in college?*

Looking *Ahead*

Whether academic pursuits are a struggle or come easily to you . . . whether you live on campus or commute . . . whether you are fresh out of high school or are returning to school many years after high school graduation—college is a challenge. Every one of us has doubts of one sort or another about our capabilities and motivation, and new situations—like starting college—make us wonder how well we'll succeed.

That's where this book comes in. It is designed to help you learn the most effective ways to approach the challenges you encounter, not just in college, but outside the classroom, too. It will teach you practical strategies, hints, and tips that can lead you to success, all centered around an approach to achieving college success: P.O.W.E.R. Learning.

This book is designed to be useful in a way that is different from other college texts. It presents information in a hands-on format. It's meant to be *used*—not just read. Write on it, underline words and sentences, use a highlighter, circle key points, and complete the questionnaires right in the book. The more exercises you do, the more you'll get from the book. Remember, this is a book to help you with your course work throughout college. It's a good idea to invest your time here and now. If the learning techniques you master here become second nature, the payoff will be enormous.

This first chapter lays out the basics of P.O.W.E.R. Learning. By the time you finish this chapter, you'll be able to answer these questions:

- **What are the benefits of a college education?**

- **What are the basic principles of P.O.W.E.R. Learning?**

- **How do expert students use P.O.W.E.R. Learning?**

Why Go to College?

Congratulations. You're in college.

Why?

Although it seems as if it should be easy to say why you're continuing your education, for most students it's not that simple. The reasons that people go to college vary from the practical ("I want to get a good job"), to the lofty ("I want to learn about people and the world"), to the unreflective ("Why not?— I don't have anything better to do"). Consider your own reasons for attending college, as you complete Try It 1 on page 4.

Surveys of first-year college students show that almost three-quarters say they want to get a better job and make more money (see Figure 1.1).[1] But most students also have additional goals in mind: They want to learn about things

Teaching Tip: Starting on the first day of class, you will be asking students to reveal personal information. Intentionally set the stage for students to respect one another. One way to encourage confidentiality during such discussions is to shut the classroom door.

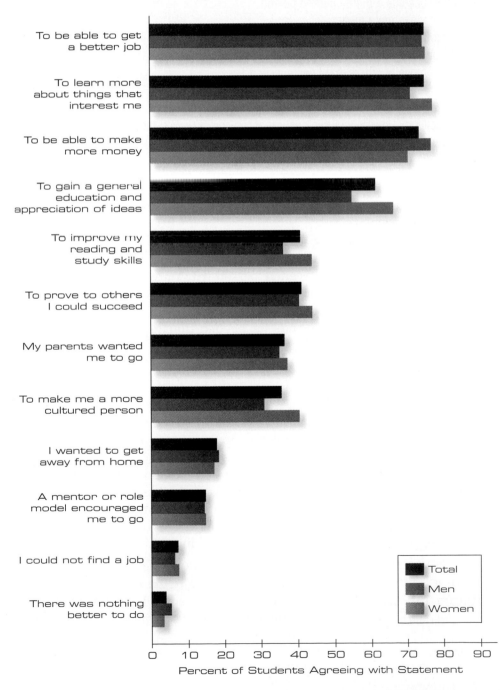

Figure 1.1

Choosing College

These are the most frequently-cited reasons that first-year college students gave for why they enrolled in college when asked in a national survey.[2]

Try It!

1

Why Am I Going to College?

Place a 1, 2, and 3 by the three most important reasons that you have for attending college:

_____ I want to get a good job when I graduate.
_____ My parents want me to go.
_____ I couldn't find a job.
_____ I want to get away from home.
_____ I want to get a better job.
_____ I want to gain a general education and appreciation of ideas.
_____ I want to improve my reading and study skills.
_____ I want to become a more cultured person.
_____ I want to make more money.
_____ I want to learn more about things that interest me.
_____ A mentor or role model encouraged me to go.
_____ I want to prove to others that I can succeed.

What do your answers tell you about yourself? Did you think about these reasons when you were applying to college? How do you think your reasons compare with those of other first-year students who are starting college with you?

Teaching Tip: This is the point at which your students will begin to reveal their personalities. How are your students alike? How are they different? Begin to build community.

that interest them (74 percent) and gain a general education and appreciation of ideas (61 percent).

And, in fact, it's not wrong to expect that a college education helps people find better jobs. The average person with a college degree earns about 50 percent more each year than the average person with only a high school education. Furthermore, as jobs become increasingly complex and technologically sophisticated, college will become more and more of a necessity.

But the value of college extends far beyond dollars and cents. Consider these added reasons for pursuing a college education:

Student Alert: Your students' goals for being in college will likely be different than yours are for them. Be prepared to start where they are and to take them where you want them to go.

- **You'll learn to think and communicate better.** Here's what one student said about his college experience after he graduated: "It's not about what you major in or which classes you take. . . . It's really about learning to *think* and to *communicate. Wherever* you end up, you'll need to be able to analyze and solve problems—to figure out what needs to be done and do it."[3]

Education improves your ability to understand the world—understand it as it now is, and prepare to understand it as it will be. By showing you how to develop your capacity for critical and creative thinking, education will increase your abilities to think clearly and to communicate more effectively with others.

> "The goal of education is the advancement of knowledge and the dissemination of truth."
>
> John F. Kennedy, Address, Harvard University, 1956.

- **You'll be able to better deal with advances in knowledge and technology that are changing the world.** Genetic engineering . . . drugs to reduce forgetfulness . . . computers that respond to our voices. Innovations such as these—and the ones that haven't even been thought of yet—illustrate how rapidly the world is changing.

No one knows what the future will hold. But education can provide you with the intellectual tools that you can apply regardless of the specific situation in which you find yourself. You can't anticipate what the future holds, but you can prepare for it through a college education.

- **You'll be better prepared to live in a world of diversity.** The United States is changing rapidly. In fact, by the middle of the twenty-first century, non-Hispanic whites will become a minority group. You'll be working and living with people whose backgrounds, lifestyles, and ways of thinking may be entirely different from your own.

  The greater diversity of the United States, along with the fact that we live in a global society, necessitates a deeper understanding of other cultures. Culture provides a lens through which people view the world. You won't be prepared for the future unless you understand others and their cultural backgrounds—as well as how your own cultural background affects you.

- **You'll make learning a lifelong habit.** Higher education isn't the end of your education. If you make the most of college, you will develop a thirst for more knowledge, a lifelong quest that can never be fully satisfied. Education will build upon your natural curiosity about the world, and it will make you aware that learning is a rewarding and never-ending journey.

- **You'll understand the meaning of your own contributions to the world.** No matter who you are, you are poised to make your own contributions to society and the world. Higher education provides you with a window to the past, present, and future, and it allows you to understand the significance of your own contributions. Your college education provides you with a compass to discover who you are, where you've been, and where you're going.

Journal Reflections

My School Experiences

Throughout this book, you will be given opportunities to write down your thoughts. These opportunities—called Journal Reflections—will permit you to record your reactions to what you have read, your ideas, notes, questions, and concerns. Above all, be honest in your reactions. If you save these entries and return to them later, you may be surprised at the changes they record over the course of the term.

1. Describe one of the successful experiences you've had so far in your years in school.

2. What made the experience successful? Think of the teacher's methods, the subjects you were studying, how you did your work, interactions you had with others, and other elements of the experience.

3. What did you learn from it?

4. Did you ever have a "light bulb" experience—in which you suddenly "saw the light" about something that had seemed beyond understanding before? If so, how did it happen?

5. Describe an unsuccessful experience or failure you had in school.

6. Why did it occur? What choices did you make to contribute to it?

7. What did you learn from it?

8. What other comments do you have?

Now it's time to introduce you to a process that will help you achieve your goal of attaining a college education, as well as succeeding in life beyond college: P.O.W.E.R. Learning.

P.O.W.E.R. Learning: The Five Key Steps to Achieving Success

P.O.W.E.R. Learning

A system designed to help people achieve their goals, based on five steps: *Prepare, Organize, Work, Evaluate,* and *Rethink*

P.O.W.E.R. Learning itself is merely an acronym—a word formed from the first letters of a series of steps (see the P.O.W.E.R. Plan below) that will help you take in, process, and make use of the information you'll be exposed to in college. It will help you to achieve your goals, both while you are in college and later after you graduate. The steps in P.O.W.E.R. Learning serve as a strategy for accomplishing what you wish to—and sometimes have to—accomplish.

Prepare, Organize, Work, Evaluate, and **Rethink.** That's it. It's a simple framework, but an effective one. Using the systematic framework that P.O.W.E.R. Learning provides will increase your chances of success at any task, from writing a college paper to purchasing the weekly groceries.

Keep this in mind: P.O.W.E.R. Learning isn't a product that you can simply pull down off the bookshelf and use without thinking. P.O.W.E.R. Learning is a *process*, and *you* are the only one who can make it succeed. Without your personal investment in the process, P.O.W.E.R. Learning consists of just words on paper. You will have to supply the effort and practice to make it work for you.

Relax, though. You already know each of the elements of P.O.W.E.R. Learning. You've graduated from high school and been accepted into college. You've also probably held down a job, had a first date, and registered to vote. Each of these accomplishments required that you use strategies of P.O.W.E.R. Learning. What you'll be doing throughout this book is becoming more aware of these strategies and how they can be used to help you in situations you will encounter in college and beyond.

P repare

Chinese philosopher Lao Tzu said that travelers taking a long journey must begin with a single step.

PREPARE

ORGANIZE

WORK

EVALUATE

RETHINK

P.O.W.E.R Plan

But before they even take that first step, travelers need to know several things: what their destination is, how they're going to get there, how they'll know when they reach the destination, and what they'll do if they have trouble along the way.

In the same way, you need to know where you're headed as you embark on the intellectual journeys involved in college. Whether it be a major, long-term task, such as college attendance, or a more limited activity, such as getting ready to complete a paper due in the near future, you'll need to prepare for the journey. To see this for yourself, complete Try It 2, "How I Enrolled in College."

Setting Goals Before we seek to accomplish any task, all of us do some form of planning. The trouble is that

Try It! 2

How I Enrolled in College

Academic journeys are similar to other major trips you may have taken, and they require the same sort of preparation. Consider, for instance, the steps you needed to take in order to enroll in the college you're now attending. Think back to how you proceeded, and in the spaces provided below write as many of the preparatory steps as you can think of, in the order you did them:

_____

_____

_____

_____

_____

_____

_____

_____

_____

_____

_____

_____

_____

_____

_____

_____

_____

_____

Now go back and number the steps in the most ideal, logical order. How closely does this numbering match the order in which you actually accomplished them? If you actually did some of the steps in a less-than-ideal order, how did it hinder or help your attainment of the goal of enrolling in college? **Working in a Group:** Compare the steps you followed with those of other students. What steps are universal, and which ones were unique to you?

most of the time such planning is done without conscious thinking, as if we are on autopilot. However, the key to success is to make sure that planning is systematic.

The best way to plan systematically is to use *goal-setting strategies*. In many cases, goals are clear and direct. It's obvious that our goal in washing dishes is to have the dishes end up clean and dry. We know that our goal at the gas

Student Alert: Some of your students will report that they have done goal setting before. Encourage your students to plan anew as they begin their college experience.

Try It! 3

Course Goals

Think about one of the classes that you are taking this term. List as many goals as you can think of for taking the class:

_____

_____

_____

_____

_____

_____

_____

_____

_____

The goals you've listed most likely range from the specific ("passing the class with a good grade") to the more general and vague ("becoming educated in the subject matter of the class").

Now, rank order them to determine which are the most important to you. Note that some of these goals may be short-term goals ("get a decent grade") and some represent longer-term goals ("complete all college requirements"). In addition, your goals may be specific ("get an A in the course") or relatively vague ("do well in the class").

What is the difference between those goals that are most important to you and those least important to you? Are your goals mostly short-term or long-term? How specific are your goals? What implications might your different goals have for your future success in the course?

Working in a Group: Compare *your* goals for the course with those of other students and consider the similarities and differences.

Long-term goals
Aims relating to major accomplishments that take some time to achieve

Short-term goals
Relatively limited steps toward the accomplishment of long-term goals

station is to fill the car's tank with gas. We go to the post office to buy stamps and mail letters.

Other goals are not so clear-cut. In fact, often the more important the task, the less obvious are our goals.

Let's consider taking a college course, for example. You probably have several goals for each course you are taking this term. To see this, carry out the activity in Try It 3.

What's the best way to set appropriate goals? Here are some guidelines:

- **Set both long-term and short-term goals. Long-term goals** are aims relating to major accomplishments that take some time to achieve. **Short-term goals** are relatively limited steps you would take on the road to accomplishing your long-term goals. For example, one of the primary reasons you're in college is to achieve the long-term goal of getting a degree. But in order to reach that goal, you have to accomplish a series of short-term goals, such as completing a set of required courses, taking a series of elective courses, and choosing a major. Furthermore, even these short-term goals can be broken down into shorter-term goals. In order to complete a required course, for instance, you have to accomplish short-term goals, such as completing a paper, taking several tests, and so on.

IM Link: "Teaching the Text" Chapter 1—Section III; questions 1–3 are relevant here.

- **Recognize that who you are determines your goals.** Goal setting starts with knowing yourself. As you'll see when we focus on understanding yourself in Chapter 3, it is self-knowledge that tells you what is and is not important to you, and this knowledge will help you keep your goals in focus and your motivation up when things get tough.

- **Make goals realistic and attainable.** Someone once said, "A goal without a plan is but a dream." We'd all like to win gold medals at the Olympics or star in rock videos or write best-selling novels. Few of us are likely to achieve such goals.

  Be honest with yourself. There is nothing wrong with having big dreams. But it is important to be realistically aware of all that it takes to achieve them. If our long-term goals are unrealistic and we don't achieve them, the big danger is that we may wrongly reason that we are inept and lack ability and use this as an excuse for giving up. Instead, we should have realized that the problem has less to do with our abilities than with poor goal-setting strategies. If goals are realistic we can develop a plan to attain them, spurring us on to attain more.

  > "Goal setting, as far as I can see it, is simply a state of mind, a way of thinking about things. A goal setter makes sure he accomplishes what he needs to accomplish."
  >
  > Greg Gottesman, student, Stanford University.[4]

- **State goals in terms of behavior that can be measured against current accomplishments.** Goals should represent some *measurable* change from a current set of circumstances. We want our behavior to change in some way that can usually be expressed in terms of numbers—to show an increase ("raise my grade point average 10 percent") or a decrease ("reduce wasted time by two hours each week"); or to be maintained ("keep in touch with my out-of-town friends by writing four e-mail messages each month"), developed ("participate in one workshop on critical thinking"), or restricted ("reduce my phone expenses 10 percent by speaking less on the telephone").

Student Alert: Students have difficulty writing specific, measurable goals. Give them feedback on their statements.

- **Goals should involve behavior over which you have control.** We all want world peace and an end to poverty. Few of us have the resources or capabilities to bring either about. On the other hand, it is realistic to want to work in small ways to help others, such as by becoming a Big Brother or Big Sister or by volunteering at a local food bank.

- **Take ownership of your goals.** Make sure that the goals you choose are *your* goals, and not the goals of your parents, teachers, brothers and sisters, or friends. Trying to accomplish goals that "belong" to others is a recipe for disaster. If you're attending college only because others have told you to, and you have no commitment of your own, you'll find it hard to maintain the enthusiasm—not to mention the hard work—required to succeed.

Teaching Tip: Reinforce this idea by asking students to use "I" statements during class discussions.

Try It! 4

Course Goals, Revisited

Given the goal-setting guidelines we've discussed, let's revisit the goals that you listed earlier regarding a specific course in which you are enrolled. Rewrite each of those goals in terms that are realistic, measurable, and under your control.

_____

_____

_____

_____

_____

_____

_____

_____

_____

_____

_____

Do the goals, as restated, seem more or less attainable? Do the restated goals help provide you with greater clarity in how you can achieve them? Are there any goals that now seem unattainable? **Working in a Group:** Exchange your list of goals with your classmates and ask them to critique them, based on the criteria of realism and measurability.

- **Identify how your short-term goals fit with your long-term goals.** Your goals should not be independent of one another. Instead, they should fit together into a larger dream of who you want to be. Every once in a while step back and consider how what you're doing today relates to the kind of person that you would ultimately like to be.

O rganize

By determining where you want to go and expressing your goals in terms that can be measured, you have already made a lot of progress. Having a distinct destination will make clearer the various options you have for reaching it and will also help you know when you've arrived. You might think you're now ready to head out and begin the intellectual trip to student success. But there's still another step you must take before you get going. You now have to *organize* the resources you'll need in order to reach your goal.

The second step in P.O.W.E.R. Learning is to *organize* the tools you'll need to accomplish your goals. Building upon the goal-setting work you've undertaken in the *preparation* stage, it's time to determine the best way to accomplish the goals you've identified.

How do you do this? Suppose you've decided to build a set of bookshelves for one room in your house. Let's say that you've already determined the kind of bookshelves you like and figured out the basic characteristics of the ones you will build (the preparation step in P.O.W.E.R. Learning). The next stage involves gathering the necessary tools, buying the wood and other building materials, sorting the construction supplies, and preparing the room for the shelving project—all aspects of organizing for the task.

Similarly, your academic success will hinge to a large degree on the thoroughness of your organization for each academic task that you face. In fact, one of the biggest mistakes that students make in college is plunging into an academic project—studying for a test, writing a paper, completing an in-class assignment—without being organized.

There Are Several Kinds of Organization

On a basic level is organization involving the *physical aspects* of task completion. For instance, you need to ask yourself if you have the appropriate tools, such as pens, paper, and a calculator. If you're using a computer, do you have access to a printer? Is the printer working? Do you have disks to back up your files? Do you have the books and other materials you'll need to complete the assignment? Will the campus bookstore be open if you need anything else? Will the library be open when you need it?

Intellectual organization is even more critical. Intellectual organization is accomplished by considering and reviewing the academic skills that you'll need to successfully complete the task at hand. You are an academic general in command of considerable forces; you will need to make sure your forces—the basic skills you have at your command—are at their peak of readiness.

For example, if you're working on a math assignment, you'll want to consider the basic math skills that you'll need and brush up on them. Just actively thinking about this will help you organize intellectually. Recalling and reviewing fundamental math skills, such as how to figure percentages and use decimals, will organize your thinking when you begin a new assignment. Similarly, you'd want to mentally review your understanding of the causes of the American Civil War before beginning an assignment on the Reconstruction period that followed the war.

Why does creating an intellectual organization matter? The answer is that it provides a context for when you actually begin to work. Organizing in advance paves the way for better subsequent learning of new material. The better your intellectual (as well as physical) organization for a task, the more successful you'll be.

Too often students are in a hurry to meet a deadline and figure they better just dive in and get it done. Organizing in advance can actually *save* you time, because you're less likely to end up losing your way as you work to complete your task.

Much of this book is devoted to strategies for determining—*before* you begin work on a task—how to develop the intellectual tools for completing an assignment. However, as you'll see, all of these strategies share a common

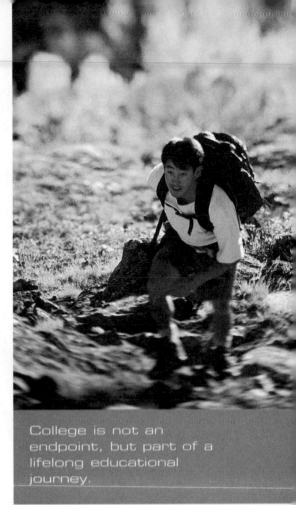

College is not an endpoint, but part of a lifelong educational journey.

theme: that success comes not from a trial-and-error approach, but from following a systematic plan for achievement. Of course, this does not mean that there will be no surprises along the way, nor that sheer luck is never a factor in great accomplishments. But it does mean that we often can make our own luck through careful preparation and organization.

W ork

You're ready. The preliminaries are out of the way. You've *prepared* and you've *organized*. Now it's time to get started actually doing the work.

In some ways *work* is the easy part, because—if you conscientiously carried out the preparation and organization stage—you should know exactly where you're headed and what you need to do to get there.

It's not quite so easy, of course. How effectively you'll get down to the business at hand depends on many factors. Some may be out of your control. There may be a power outage that closes down the library or a massive traffic jam that delays your getting to campus. But most factors are—or should be—under your control. Instead of getting down to work, you may find yourself thinking up "useful" things to do—like finally hanging that poster that's been rolled up in a corner for three months—or simply sitting captive in front of the TV. This kind of obstacle to work relates to motivation.

Finding the Motivation to Work   "If only I could get more motivated, I'd do so much better with my _____" (insert *schoolwork, diet, exercising,* or the like—*you* fill in the blank).

All of us have said something like this at one time or another. We use the concept of **motivation**—or its lack—to explain why we just don't work hard at a task. But when we do that, we're fooling ourselves. We all have *some* motivation, that inner power and psychological energy that directs and fuels our behavior and allows us to persist, even when the going gets rough. Without any motivation, we'd never get out of bed in the morning and accomplish anything.

We've all seen evidence of how strong our motivation can be. Perhaps you're an avid runner and you love to jog in the morning and compete in weekend races. Or maybe your love of music helped you learn to play the guitar, making practicing for hours a pleasure rather than a chore. Or perhaps you're a single mother, juggling work, school, and family, and you get up early every morning to make breakfast for your kids before they go off to school.

All of us are motivated. The key to success in and out of the classroom is to tap into, harness, and direct that motivation.

Thought of in this way, motivating ourselves becomes a little less intimidating. If we assume that we already have all the motivation we need, P.O.W.E.R. Learning becomes a matter of turning the skills we already possess into a habit. It becomes a matter of redirecting our psychological energies toward the *work* we wish to accomplish.

Most of us have to learn how to do this, and that's where this book comes

Motivation
The inner power and psychological energy that directs and fuels behavior

Teaching Tip: Ask students to think about an activity they felt motivated to carry out. Have them share with another student what it was like to "feel motivated."

in. In a sense, everything you'll encounter in this book will help you to improve your use of the motivation that you already have. But there's a key concept that underlies the control of motivation—viewing success as a result of effort:

Effort is the cause of success.

Suppose, for example, you've gotten a good grade on your midterm. The instructor beams at you as she hands back your test. How do you feel?

You will undoubtedly be pleased, of course. But at the same time you might think to yourself, "Better not get a swollen head about it. It was just luck. If she'd asked other questions I would have been in trouble." Or perhaps you explain your success by thinking, "Pretty easy test."

If you often think this way, you're cheating yourself. Using this kind of reasoning when you succeed, instead of patting yourself on the back and thinking with satisfaction, "All my hard work really paid off," is sure to undermine your future success. A great deal of psychological research has shown that thinking you have no control over what happens to you sends a powerful and damaging message to your self-esteem—that you are powerless to change things. Just think of how different it *feels* to say to yourself, "Wow, I worked at it and did it," as compared with "I lucked out" or "It was so easy that anybody could have done well."

In the same way, we can delude ourselves when we try to explain our failures. People who see themselves as the victims of circumstance may tell themselves, "I'm just not smart enough" when they don't do well on an academic task. Or they might say, "Those other students don't have to work five hours a day." By making these kinds of excuses, they have disconnected themselves from their own motivation to do better.

Discussion Prompt: W.E.B. DuBois's quote on this page reflects the essence of being involved in an academic community. Spend time discussing this idea.

"The function of the university is not simply to teach bread-winning, or to furnish teachers for the public schools or to be a center of polite society; it is, above all, to be the organ of that fine adjustment between real life and the growing knowledge of life, an adjustment which forms the secret of civilization."

W.E.B. DuBois, *The Souls of Black Folk* (1903).

The way in which we view the cause of success and failure is, in fact, directly related to our success. Students who generally see effort and hard work as the reason behind their performance usually do better in college. It's not hard to see why: When they are working on an assignment, they feel that the greater the effort they put forth, the greater their chances of success. So they work harder. They are positive thinkers, believing that they have control over their success. If they fail, they believe they can do better in the future. Failure just makes them try harder.

Here are some tips for keeping your motivation alive, so you can *work* with your full energy behind you:

- **Take responsibility for your failures—and successes.** When you do poorly on a test, don't blame the teacher, the textbook, or a job that kept you from studying. Analyze the situation, and see how you could have changed what you did to be more successful in the future. At the same time, when you're successful, think of the things you did to bring about that success.

Teaching Tip: In teaching this chapter, you will establish the patterns of communication between your students and you. If you want students to talk, make certain you give them time to think and a chance to speak.

Chapter 1 P.O.W.E.R. Learning: Becoming a Successful Student

- **Think positively.** Assume that the strengths that you have will allow you to succeed and that, if you have difficulty, you can figure out what to do. The more effectively you work, the greater the success you'll experience.

- **Accept that you can't control everything.** Sometimes things are out of your control. Seek to understand which things can be changed and which cannot. You might be able to get an extension on a paper due date, but you are probably not going to be excused from a collegewide requirement.

To further explore the causes of academic success, consider the questions in Try It 5, discussing them with your classmates.

 valuate

"Great, I'm done with the work. Now I can move on."

It's natural to feel relief when you've finished the work necessary to fulfill the basic requirements of an assignment. After all, if you've written the five double-spaced pages required for an assignment, why shouldn't you heave a sigh of relief and just hand your paper in to the instructor?

The answer is that if you stop at this point, you'll almost be guaranteed a mediocre grade. Did Shakespeare dash off the first draft of *Hamlet* and, without another glance, send it off to the Globe Theater for production? Do professional athletes just put in the bare minimum of practice to get ready for a big game? Think of one of your favorite songs. Do you think the composer wrote it in one sitting and then performed it in a concert?

In every case, the answer is no. Even the greatest work does not spring forth as the embodiment of perfection, immediately meeting all the goals of its producer. In fact, the ultimate success of an activity is based on how closely it matches what it was intended to be.

Consequently, the fourth step in the P.O.W.E.R. process is **evaluation,** which consists of determining how well the work we have produced matches our goals for it. Let's consider some steps that it makes sense to follow in evaluating what you've accomplished:

- **Take a moment to congratulate yourself and feel some satisfaction.** Whether it's been studying for a test, writing a paper, preparing a review sheet, or reading an assignment, you've done something important. You've moved from ground zero to a spot that's closer to your goal. Maybe you've reached the midpoint of your journey; maybe you're three-quarters of the way there. In fact, maybe you're just about where you want to be. Whatever the specific spot you've reached, the fact that you've already *prepared, organized,* and done the *work* means that you've navigated through many difficulties and completed the greater part of the journey.

- **Compare what you've accomplished with the goals you're seeking to achieve.** Think back to the goals, both short-term and long-term, that you're seeking to accomplish. How closely does what you've done match what you're aiming to do? Zero in on your short-term goal for the task, and see how close you've come. For instance, if your short-term goal is to complete a statistics problem set with no errors, you'll

Student Alert: Freshmen need feedback early and frequently. They need to understand how college grades and evaluation are different from what they have experienced in high school.

Evaluation

An assessment of the match between a product or activity and the goals it was intended to meet

Try It! 5

Working in a Group: Examine the Causes of Success and Failure

Consider, in a group, the following situations:

1. Although he studied for a few hours the night before the test, Jack gets a D on a midterm. When he finds out his grade, he is disgusted and says to himself, "I'll probably never do any better in this course. I better just blow it off for the rest of the term and put my energies into my other classes."

2. Anne receives an A– on her history exam. She is happy, but when her instructor tells the class that they did well as a group and that the average grade was B+, she decides that she did well only because the exam was so easy.

3. Chen gets a C on his first math quiz. Because he didn't do as well as he expected, he vows to perform better the next time. He doubles the amount of time he studies for the next quiz, but still his grade is only slightly higher. Distressed, he considers dropping the class because he thinks that he'll never be successful in math.

In a group, consider the following questions about each of the situations:

1. What did each student conclude was the main cause of his or her performance, and what effect will this conclusion probably have on the student?

2. Taking an outsider's point of view, what would *you* think was probably the main cause of the student's performance?

3. What advice would you give each student?

Now consider these broader questions:

1. What are the most important reasons some students are more academically successful in college than others?

2. How much does ability determine success? How much does luck determine success? How much do circumstances determine success?

3. If someone performs poorly on an exam, what are the possible reasons for his or her performance? If someone performs well on an exam, what are the possible reasons for his or her performance? Why is it harder to find reasons for good compared with poor performance?

need to check over the paper carefully to make sure you've made no mistakes.

- **Have an out-of-body experience: Evaluate your accomplishments as if you were a respected teacher from your past.** If you've written a paper, reread it from the perspective of that teacher. If you've completed a worksheet, think about what comments you'd write across the top if you were that teacher. Remember, you're no longer you, assessing something you've accomplished, but a demanding (though fair) teacher evaluating someone else's work.

Try It! 6

The Good and the Bad

Suppose your instructor asked you to write a paragraph stating your best and worst moments in college so far. Write a first draft of that paragraph below.

_____
_____
_____
_____
_____
_____
_____

Now, evaluate the paragraph you've written. Is the grammar correct? Is every word spelled correctly? Does the paragraph flow nicely? Did you use vivid language? Do you think your instructor will find it acceptable?

When you consider all these factors, you'll probably find the paragraph falls short of what you'd like it to be. Consequently, rewrite it below, trying to make it conform more closely to your ideal.

_____
_____
_____
_____
_____
_____
_____

What things did you learn from the evaluation step that you didn't know before you did it? Does evaluation get you closer to the goal of perfecting the paragraph? **Working in a Group:** Have a classmate evaluate your initial paragraph. How does your classmate's evaluation compare to your own?

- **Evaluate what you've done as if you were your current instructor.** Now exchange bodies and minds again. This time, consider what you're doing from the perspective of the instructor who gave you the assignment. How would he or she react to what you've done? Have you followed the assignment to the letter? Can you figure out which aspects of your work are particularly important? Is there anything you've missed?

- **Be fair to yourself.** The guidelines for evaluation will help you to determine just how much further work is necessary and, even more important, *what* work is necessary. But don't go too far: It's as counterproductive to be too hard on yourself as it is to be too easy. Stick to a middle ground, always keeping your final goal in mind.

- **Based on your evaluation, revise your work.** If you're honest with yourself, it's unlikely that your first work will satisfy you. None of us can produce our best work initially. So go back to *Work* and revise what you've done. But don't think of it as a step back: Revisions you make as a consequence of your evaluation bring you closer to your final goal. This is a case where going back moves you forward.

R ethink

They thought they had it perfect. But they were wrong.

In fact, it was a 1.5 billion dollar mistake—a blunder on a grand scale. The finely ground mirror of the Hubble space telescope, designed to provide an unprecedented glimpse into the vast reaches of the universe, was not so finely ground after all.

Despite an elaborate system of evaluation designed to catch any flaws, there was a tiny blemish in the mirror that was not detected until the telescope had been launched into space and started to send back blurry photographs. By then, it seemed too late to fix the mirror.

Or was it? NASA engineers rethought the problem for months, devising, and discarding, one potential fix after another. Finally, after bringing a fresh eye to the situation, they formulated a daring solution that involved sending a team of astronauts into space. Once there, a space-walking Mr. Goodwrench would install several new mirrors in the telescope, which could refocus the light and compensate for the original flawed mirror.

Although the engineers could not be certain that the $629 million plan would work, it seemed like a good solution, at least on paper. It was not until the first photos were beamed back to earth, though, that NASA knew their solution was A-OK. These photos were spectacular.

The daring mission to repair the Hubble Space Telescope was the culmination of months of rethinking the problem of how to fix the flaw in the telescope's mirror. It worked: A new time-lapse movie of images taken by the telescope showed the seasonal changes taking place on Uranus.

It took months of reconsideration before NASA scientists could figure out what went wrong and devise a solution to the problem they faced. Their approach exemplifies—on a grand scale—the final step in P.O.W.E.R. Learning: rethinking.

To *rethink* what you've accomplished earlier means bringing a fresh eye to what you've done. It involves using **critical thinking**, thinking that involves reanalyzing, questioning, and challenging our underlying assumptions. While evaluation means considering how well what we have done matches our initial goals, rethinking means reconsidering not just the outcome of our efforts, but the ideas and the process we've used to get there.

We'll be considering critical thinking throughout this book, examining specific strategies in every chapter. For the moment, the following steps provide a general framework for using critical thinking to rethink what you've accomplished:

- **Reanalyze, reviewing how you've accomplished the task.** Consider the approach and strategies you've used. What seemed to work best? Do they suggest any alternatives that might work better the next time?

- **Question the outcome.** Take a "big picture" look at what you have accomplished. Are you pleased and satisfied? Is there something you've somehow missed?

- **Identify your underlying assumptions; then challenge them.** Consider the assumptions you made in initially approaching the task. Are these

Critical thinking
A process involving reanalysis, questioning, and challenging of underlying assumptions

Student Alert: Your students will probably not have experienced "rethinking" their opinions, papers, or any part of the academic process. They may have done it in their personal life (*i.e.*, "If only I hadn't said this . . ."; "I think I would have looked better if I had worn the green shirt. . . ."). Most students need assistance in applying this idea to the learning process.

Career Connections

P.O.W.E.R. Learning Meets the World of Work

Although the focus of the P.O.W.E.R. Learning system is on developing school success, its applications extend well beyond the classroom. In particular, the principles of P.O.W.E.R. Learning are useful in the world of work, and your ability to use them will provide you with keys to success in the workplace.

Skeptical? In *Career Connections* boxes in future chapters we'll explore how the principles we're discussing can help you choose an appropriate career and excel in the workplace. For now, though, take a look at the following "help wanted" advertisements, which illustrate the importance of the components of P.O.W.E.R. Learning in the workplace.

underlying assumptions reasonable? If you had used different assumptions, would the result have been similar or different?

- **Consider alternatives rejected earlier.** You've likely discarded possible strategies and approaches prior to completing your task. Now's the time to think about those approaches once more and determine if they might have been more appropriate than the road you've followed. It's still not too late to change course.

Completing the Process The rethinking step of P.O.W.E.R. Learning is meant to help you understand your process of work and to improve the final product if necessary. But mostly it is meant to help you grow, to become better at whatever it is you've been doing. Like a painter looking at his or her finished work, you may see a spot here or there to touch up, but don't destroy the canvas. *Perfectionism can be as paralyzing as laziness.* Keep in mind these key points:

- **Know that there's always another day.** Your future success does not depend on any single assignment, paper, or test. Don't fall victim to self-defeating thoughts such as "If I don't do well, I'll never graduate" or "Everything is riding on this one assignment." Nonsense. There is almost always an opportunity to recover from a failure.

- **Realize that deciding when to stop work is often as hard as getting started.** For some students, knowing when enough is enough is as hard as taking the first step on an assignment. Knowing when you have put in enough time studying for a test, have revised a paper sufficiently, or have reviewed your answers adequately on a worksheet is as much a key to success as properly preparing. If you've carefully evaluated what you've done and seen that there's a close fit between your goals and your work, it's time to stop work and move on.

Are You Ready to Become a P.O.W.E.R. Learner?

It's a bother. You've done things a certain way all your life, and it's worked reasonably well. It won't matter in the long run.

Are such excuses running through your head as you contemplate P.O.W.E.R. Learning? Are you thinking to yourself that P.O.W.E.R. Learning doesn't seem worth the effort and, even if it works with other people, it probably won't work with you?

Such thoughts are a natural reaction to being challenged. For most of us, change is uncomfortable, and when we're confronted with new ways of doing things, we may react with anxiety, defensiveness, fear, or even anger. Why? Because we're creatures of habit, and the feeling of familiarity we get from our routine style of doing things is as comforting as an old, worn bathrobe.

Ironically, sometimes we may reject change because it can bring about more success than we're ready to handle. Some people have a **fear of success,** in which they are reluctant to excel and thus actively avoid getting into situations in which success is likely. (To determine if you have a fear of success, complete Try It 7 on page 20.)

If you do fear success to some degree, you're not alone. Many people feel they don't deserve to do well. And even some people who have already achieved success don't feel they deserve it; instead, they believe their success was unearned or unwarranted.

However, such negative thinking is inappropriate, and you need to overcome the thought that somehow you are unworthy of success. Becoming an accomplished student depends on your willingness to accept wholeheartedly the possibility of change in yourself and to embrace success. The techniques for doing this are in this book, but only you can implement them. The road to success may not be simple or direct (see the *Speaking of Success* interview with Normaris Gonzalez for a glimpse of one student's travels), but there are few goals that are more important in life than attaining a college education.

Teaching Tip: Acknowledge the P.O.W.E.R. Learning acronym. Students might tell you that it is artificial, but they will use it and benefit from it if you make it a positive framework for understanding information in this class.

Fear of success
Reluctance to excel and avoidance of situations in which success is likely

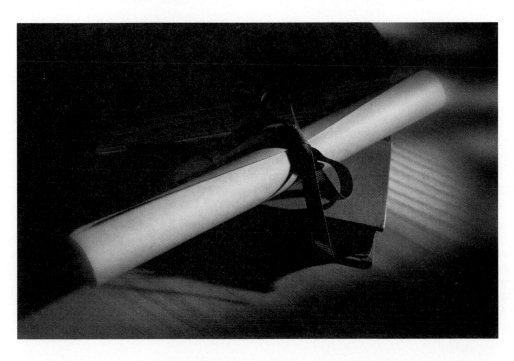

Are You Afraid of Success?

Answer each of the following true/false questions:[5]

1. I am sometimes afraid to do things as well as I know I could. _____ True _____ False

2. I never worry about the possibility of being disliked by others for doing well at something. _____ True _____ False

3. I sometimes do less than my very best so that no one will be threatened. _____ True _____ False

4. I often worry about the possibility that others will think I am a "showoff." _____ True _____ False

5. I never worry abut the possibility that others may think I work too hard. _____ True _____ False

6. I would find it nerve-wracking to be regarded as one of the best in my field. _____ True _____ False

7. I seem to be more anxious after succeeding at something than after failing at something. _____ True _____ False

8. I do not like competing with others if there is a possibility that hard feelings toward me may develop. _____ True _____ False

9. If I were outstanding at something, I would worry about the possibility of others making fun of me behind my back. _____ True _____ False

10. I worry that I may become so knowledgeable that others will not like me. _____ True _____ False

Scoring: Use the key below to score the assessment. Give yourself one point for each "correct" answer.
1. True; 2. False; 3. True; 4. True; 5. False; 6. True; 7. True; 8. True; 9. True; 10. True.

If you scored 5 or below, you have little fear of success and are ready to move toward becoming a more successful student. However, if your total score is greater than 5, you have some degree of anxiety about success.

Does your score surprise you? Do you think your fear of success may have hindered you in the past? How might your fear of success have developed during earlier stages of life? Can you speculate on ways that you might overcome your fear of success?

Student Alert: This is a telling exercise. In the beginning of the first year in college, your students are extremely hopeful and optimistic AND they are also very fearful. Teaching Tip: Read Art Levine's book, *Where Hope and Fear Collide.*

Speaking of Success

Name: *Normaris Gonzalez*
Education: *University of Massachusetts at Amherst, B.A. in psychology; State University of New York at Albany, currently enrolled in counseling psychology doctoral program*
Home: *Albany, New York*

For Normaris Gonzalez, college success did not come easily. The first member of her family to attend college, she faced the typical challenges confronting college students. In addition, her English language skills were not good at first. But through hard work and strong self-motivation, she was able to develop techniques that helped propel her through college and, ultimately, into a doctoral program, where she is studying to become a psychologist.

"It was hard," Gonzalez says about her start in college. "Initially, I had no clue what my instructors were speaking about," she says. "I found myself writing down so many words that I didn't know. It made me anxious not knowing what was going on."

To train herself to understand the unfamiliar words, Gonzalez made constant use of a dictionary, and she also sought out other students to help her along.

"I would meet with my friends and ask not only about the meanings of words, but also about what went on in their classes and what was being taught. I found this sort of buddy system to be very helpful," she explains.

In addition, Gonzalez would frequently visit her instructors outside of class. Not only did this permit them to get to know her, but it helped her understand what they were presenting in class.

"In some classes I would go to the professor at least once a week and talk about what was going on in the course," Gonzalez explains. "I always made it clear that I was personally having difficulty, but that I didn't want to be treated differently. It helped open up contact and also made myself noticeable to them."

Being the first of her family to go to college and now to pursue a doctorate is her prime motivation to continue to excel in her studies.

"If there was anyone who motivated me, it was me," she says. "I've always looked within myself to get motivated. I think self-motivation is the rule in college, where you are on your own and have to make many decisions for yourself.

"No one in my family ever went to college. I'm the first to graduate and go to graduate school. I'm also motivated to be a role model. I want to give something to my culture, and allow younger kids to look up to me and say, 'She's Hispanic and she's doing it, so I can too.' "

What are the benefits of a college education?

- The reason first-year college students most often cite for attending college is to get a better job, and college graduates do earn more on average than nongraduates.

- College also provides many other benefits. These include becoming well-educated, understanding the interconnections between different areas of knowledge and our place in history and the world, and understanding diversity.

What are the basic principles of P.O.W.E.R. Learning?

- P.O.W.E.R. Learning is a systematic approach people can easily learn, using abilities they already possess, to acquire successful habits for learning and achieving personal goals.

- P.O.W.E.R. Learning involves preparation, organization, work, evaluation, and rethinking.

Teaching Tip: Use these questions as an open-ended review of the chapter. Ask students how this information might be used in a testing situation.

How do expert students use P.O.W.E.R. Learning?

- To *prepare,* learners set both long-term and short-term goals, making sure their goals are realistic, measurable, and under their control and will lead to their final destination.

- They *organize* the tools they will need to accomplish those goals.

- They get down to *work* on the task at hand. Using their goals as motivation, expert learners also understand that success depends on effort.

- They *evaluate* the work they've done, considering what they have accomplished in comparison with the goals they set for themselves during the preparation stage.

- Finally, they *rethink,* reflecting on the process they've used and taking a fresh look at what they have done.

Key Terms and Concepts

Critical thinking (p. 17)
Evaluation (p. 14)
Fear of success (p. 19)
Long-term goals (p. 8)

Motivation (p. 12)
P.O.W.E.R. Learning (p. 6)
Short-term goals (p. 8)

Resources

On Campus

If you are commuting to school, your first "official" encounters on campus are likely to be with representatives of the college's Student Affairs Office or its equivalent. The Student Affairs Office has the goal of maintaining the quality of student life, helping to ensure that students receive the help they need.

If you are living on campus, your first encounter will more likely be with representatives of the dormitory system, often called the Residential Life Office. Their job is to help you settle in and orient you to campus. Your dormitory also probably has student residential advisors living on every floor; they can give you an insider's view of college life.

During your first days of college, don't feel shy about asking whatever college representative you encounter questions regarding what you may expect, how to find things, and what you should be doing.

You'll find specific information about which college officials you should turn to in future chapters. Be sure to seek them out if you are experiencing any difficulties. They are there to help you get the most out of college.

In Print

In *The Art of Academic Finesse: How Ordinary Students Achieve Extraordinary Grades* (Nova Press, 1998), Eric Evans provides a first-person account of his journey through college, beginning his career with little promise and ending as an honors graduate.

Melanie and Joseph Sponholz offer a wealth of information on college life from a student's vantage point in *College Companion: Real Students True Stories Good Advice* (Random House, 1996).

On the Web

The following sites on the World Wide Web provide the opportunity to extend your learning about the material in this chapter. (Although the Web addresses were accurate at the time the book was printed, check the P.O.W.E.R. Learning Web site [http://mhhe.com/power] for any changes that may have occurred.)

http://eric-web.tc.columbia.edu/families/preparing/general.html
This site offers answers to questions such as "Why attend college?" and "What kinds of jobs are available to college graduates?"

http://www.aboutcollege.com/index.htm
This site bills itself as a "complete guide to everything you ever wanted to know about college but didn't know whom to ask."

Taking It to the Net

1 Find out what percent of the population of the United States has received an undergraduate degree. (If you've never used the Internet, see Chapter 4 for suggestions that will get you started.) Go to Yahoo! (**www.yahoo.com**) and click on the category "Reference." From there, click on "statistics" and then again on "education@." From there, click on "Education census" and then again on "Educational attainment." Click on "Preliminary data" and examine the chart. How many men have received a bachelor's degree? How many women?

2 Consider the reasons for going to college. Go to the Website **http://www.ed.gov/offices/OPE/thinkcollege/** and identify the various rationales for continuing your education beyond high school. Were you aware of them prior to your enrollment in college?

The Case of . . .

Clueless in Seattle

It was during the second week of classes that the questioning started. Until then, Roger hadn't thought much about his decision to attend a large state college in a Seattle suburb. It had seemed like a good idea, and he was excited when he was accepted, but he couldn't really pinpoint why he was there.

And that was becoming a problem. As he was walking to class, he began to think about all that had happened to him in the last few weeks. First-year orientation . . . . meeting his roommate, and trying to deal with his odd neatness . . . enrolling for classes . . . finding his way around campus . . . meeting an overwhelming number of new people and trying to figure out where he fit in. Everyone else seemed to know what they were doing. Why didn't he?

It was overwhelming. He wanted to run that minute and call his parents and tell them to come pick him up. He needed to sit on the porch where it was familiar and comfortable and not overwhelming and try to figure out what he should do. Nothing seemed to make sense. He began to question his decision to attend college. What was he going to do with his life? The question made him feel even more overwhelmed. Did he really need a college degree? With his computer skills, he could probably get a job right away. Hadn't his father's friend told him that he had a job waiting for him whenever he wanted it? At least then he'd be making money.

"Why bother," he thought to himself. "What an expense, and what a hassle. For what?" He realized, to his surprise, he had no real clue as to why he was in college.

1. What arguments could you provide Roger as to the value of a college education?

2. Do you think that Roger's doubts are common? Do people often attend college without thinking about it very much?

3. What might you suggest that Roger do to help deal with his doubts about the value of college?

4. Why might a student's doubts about the value of college be especially strong during the beginning weeks of college?

5. Do you share any of Roger's concerns about the value of a college education? Do you have additional ones? Did you think carefully about the reasons for attending college before you enrolled?

Making the Most of Your Time

2

As Samantha Liccardelli stands in the surprisingly long line at the Dining Commons, waiting to grab a bite of breakfast, she mentally goes over the things she needs to get done during the day: *Review notes for the 8:30 A.M. management quiz . . . work on philosophy paper after class . . . computer sci class at 11:15 A.M. . . . . pick up ticket receipts from last night's game after class . . . get to work at student affairs office by 1:00 P.M. . . . go to library to work on philosophy paper.* She has the nagging feeling that there's something else she needs to do, but she can't put her finger on it.

After waiting in line far longer than she expected, she finally gets to the head of the line with her bagel, eating it as she pays. Glancing at a clock as she leaves the Dining Commons, she gives up the thought of getting in some last-minute studying for her management quiz. It will be a minor miracle if she even makes it to class on time.

She's been up less than an hour, and already Samantha is running behind schedule.

Are your days like Samantha's? Are you constantly trying to cram more activities into less time? Do you feel as if you never have enough time? Or do you feel overwhelmed and paralyzed by all you know you have to do?

You're not alone: Most of us wish we had more time to accomplish the things we need to do. However, some people are a lot better at juggling their time than others. What's their secret?

There is no secret. No one has more than 168 hours a week, no matter how industrious they may be. Instead, it comes down to figuring out our priorities and using our time better.

This chapter will give you strategies for improving your time management skills. After first helping you learn to account for the ways you currently use—and misuse—time, it gives you strategies for planning your time, including some ways to deal with the inevitable interruptions and counterproductive personal habits that can sabotage your best intentions.

We also consider techniques for dealing with competing goals. There are special challenges involved in juggling the priorities of college work with other aspects of life, especially when they include child rearing or holding a job.

After reading this chapter, you'll be able to answer these questions:

- **How can I manage my time most effectively?**

- **How can I deal better with surprises and distractions?**

- **How can I balance competing priorities?**

Time for Success

Without looking up from the page, answer this question: What time is it?

You've probably got some idea of the current time. In fact, most people are pretty accurate in their answer. And if you don't know for sure, it's very likely that you can find out. There may be a watch on your wrist; there may be a clock on the wall, desk, or computer screen; or maybe you're riding in a car that has a clock in the dashboard.

Even if you don't have a timepiece of some sort nearby, your body keeps its own beat. We humans, like members of most other species, have an internal clock that regulates the beating of our heart, the pace of our breathing, the discharge of chemicals within our bloodstream, and myriad other bodily functions.

Time is something from which we can't escape. Even if we ignore it, it's still going by, ticking away, second by second, minute by minute, hour by hour. Our lives are moving forward in time whether we choose to pay attention to it or not. So the main issue in using your time well is, "Who's in charge?" We can allow time to slip by and let it be our enemy. Or we can take control of it and make it our ally.

By taking control of how you spend your time, you'll increase your ability to do the things you must do to be successful as a student. More than that, the better you are at managing the time you devote to your studies, the more time you will have to spend on pursuing your interests.

We all know people who seem to be able to find time to do everything. Successful time managers make conscious choices about how they spend their time. Being in control of their time enables them to shape their future in the way *they* want, rather than feeling they are running around trying to keep up with a timetable set by others or by circumstance.

The goal of time management is not to schedule every moment so we become pawns of a timetable that governs every waking moment of the day. Instead, the goal is to permit us to make informed choices as to how we use our time. Rather than letting the day slip by, largely without our awareness, the time management procedures we'll discuss can make us more aware of time's passage and better able to harness time for our own ends.

Prepare: Learning Where Time Is Going

Before you get somewhere, you need to know where you're starting from and where you want to go. So the first step in improving your time management skills is figuring out how you're managing your time now.

Here are some ways to figure out how you are now spending your time:

Create a Time Log "Where did the day go?" If you've ever said this to yourself, one way of figuring out where you've spent your time is to create a **time log.** A time log is the most essential tool for improving your use of time.

Discussion Prompt: Ask students to share phrases they associate with the use of time (i.e.; "24-7"; "time flies when you're having fun") and to discuss how these words shape our understanding of time.

Student Alert: The issue of "balance" is introduced here. Many freshmen will challenge you to tell them "one right way" to manage time, and then come up with lots of reasons why *that* particular way will not work for them. Emphasize that effective time management is based on identifying priorities and making appropriate choices.

Time log
A record of how one spends one's time

Try It!
1

Create a Time Log

Keep track of your days on a log like this one. Be sure to make plenty of copies of this sheet before you fill it in.

Day of the week and date: _____

	hygiene	food	classes	studies	work	recreation	personal	sleep	other
12:00 A.M. (MIDNIGHT) to 1:00 A.M.									
1:00 A.M. to 2:00 A.M.									
2:00 A.M. to 3:00 A.M.									
3:00 A.M. to 4:00 A.M.									
4:00 A.M. to 5:00 A.M.									
5:00 A.M. to 6:00 A.M.									
6:00 A.M. to 7:00 A.M.									
7:00 A.M. to 8:00 A.M.									
8:00 A.M. to 9:00 A.M.									
9:00 A.M. to 10:00 A.M.									
10:00 A.M. to 11:00 A.M.									
11:00 A.M. to 12:00 P.M. (NOON)									
12:00 P.M. (NOON) to 1:00 P.M.									
1:00 P.M. to 2:00 P.M.									
2:00 P.M. to 3:00 P.M.									
3:00 P.M. to 4:00 P.M.									
4:00 P.M. to 5:00 P.M.									
5:00 P.M. to 6:00 P.M.									
6:00 P.M. to 7:00 P.M.									
7:00 P.M. to 8:00 P.M.									
8:00 P.M. to 9:00 P.M.									
9:00 P.M. to 10:00 P.M.									
10:00 P.M. to 11:00 P.M.									
11:00 P.M. to 12:00 A.M. (MIDNIGHT)									
Total Hours									

Analyze your log:

After you complete your log for a week, analyze how you spend your time according to the major categories on the log. Add up the amount of time you spend on (1) hygiene (showering, brushing teeth, etc.), (2) food (cooking, eating, shopping), (3) taking classes, (4) studying, (5) work, (6) recreation and leisure (sports, TV, concerts, exercise), (7) personal (writing, religious activities, family activities), (8) sleep, and (9) anything else that comes up. You can also create other broad categories that eat up significant amounts of time.

What do you spend most of your time on? Are you satisfied with the way that you are using your time? Are there any areas that seem to use up excessive amounts of time? Do you see some simple "fix" that will allow you to use time more effectively? **Working in a group:** Compare *your* use of time during an average week with that of your classmates. What are the major differences and similarities in the use of time?

A time log is simply a record of how you actually have spent your time—including interruptions. It doesn't have to be a second-by-second record of every waking moment. But it should account for blocks of time in increments as short as 15 minutes.

Look at the blank time log in Try It 1. As you fill out the log, be specific, indicating not only what you were doing at a given time (for example, "reading history assignment") but also the interruptions that occurred (such as "answered phone twice" or "switched to Internet for 10 minutes").

Keep your time log for at least seven days, using a "typical" week. Obviously, no week will be completely typical, but if it's near normal, it will provide you with enough information to give you a good sense of where your time goes.

By looking at how much time you spend doing various activities, you now know where your time goes. How does it match with your perceptions of how you spend your time? Be prepared to be surprised, because most people find that they're spending time on a lot of activities that just don't matter very much.

Identify the "Black Holes" That Eat Up Your Time Do you feel like your time often is sucked into a black hole, disappearing without a trace?

We all waste time, spending it on unimportant activities that keep us from doing the things that we should be doing or really want to do. For example, suppose when you're studying you get a phone call from a friend, and you end up speaking with her for an hour. You could have (a) let the phone ring and not answered it; (b) answered, but told your friend you were studying and promised to call her back; or (c) spoken to her, but only for a short while. If you had done any of these things, you would have taken control of the interruption, and kept time from sinking into a black hole.

To get a sense of how your time is sucked into black holes, complete Try It 2.

Try It! 2

Working in a Group: Identify the Black Holes of Time Management

The first 19 items on this list are common problems that prevent us from getting things done.[1] Check off the ones that are problems for you, and indicate whether you have personal control over them (controllable problems) or they are out of your control (uncontrollable problems).

	Big Problem for Me	Often a Problem	Seldom a Problem	Controllable (C) or Uncontrollable (U)?
1. Telephone interruptions				
2. Drop-in visitors				
3. E-mail interruptions				
4. Hobbies				
5. Mistakes				
6. Inability to say "no"				
7. Socializing				
8. Snacking				
9. Errands and shopping				
10. Meals				
11. Children's interruptions				
12. Perfectionism				
13. Family appointments				
14. Looking for lost items				
15. Redoing mistakes				
16. Jumping from task to task				
17. Surfing the World Wide Web				
18. Reading newspapers, magazines, recreational books				
19. Car trouble				
20. Other				
21. Other				
22. Other				
23. Other				
24. Other				
25. Other				

Working in a group: Examine the problems that affect each group member, and then discuss these questions: Do time management problems fall into any patterns? What strategies for dealing with such problems have you used in the past? Are there problems that at first seem uncontrollable that can actually be controlled? How have you dealt with time management challenges in the past?

Figure 2.1

List of Priorities

Priority	Priority Index
Study for each class at least 30 minutes/day	1
Start each major paper 1 week in advance of due date	2
Hand in each paper on time	1
Review for test starting a week before test date	2
Be on time for job	2
Check in with Mom once a week	3
Work out 3 x/week	3

IM Link: "Teaching the Text," Chapter 2—Sections IV and VIII; use the "168 Hours a Week" activity.

Set Your Priorities   By this point you should have a good idea of what's taking up your time. But you may not know what you should be doing instead.

To figure out the best use of your time, you need to determine your priorities. **Priorities** are the tasks and activities you need and want to do, rank-ordered from most important to least important. There are no right or wrong priorities; you have to decide for yourself what you wish to accomplish. Maybe spending time on your studies is most important to you, or maybe your top priority is spending time with your family. Only you can decide. Furthermore, what's important to you at this moment may be less of a priority to you next month, next year, or five years from now.

For the purpose of effective time management in college, the best procedure is to start off by identifying priorities for an entire term. What do you need to accomplish? Don't just choose obvious, general goals, such as "passing all my classes." Instead, think about your priorities in terms of specific, measurable activities, such as "studying 10 hours before each chemistry exam." (Look at the example of a priority list in Figure 2.1.)

Write your priorities on the chart in Try It 3 on page 32. After you've filled out the chart, organize it by giving each priority a "priority index" number from 1 to 3. A "1" represents a priority that absolutely must be done; without it you'll suffer a major setback. For instance, a paper with a fixed due date should receive a "1" for a priority ranking; carving out time to take those guitar lessons you always wanted to take might be ranked a "3" in terms of priority. The important point is to rank order your priorities to reveal what is and is not important to accomplish during the term.

Setting priorities will help you to determine how to make best use of your time. No one has enough time to complete everything; prioritizing will help you make informed decisions about what you can do to maximize your success.

Identify Your Prime Time

Take a look inward. Do you enthusiastically bound out of bed in the morning, ready to start the day and take on the world? Or is the alarm clock a hated and unwelcome sound that jars you out of

Priorities

The tasks and activities that one needs and wants to do, rank-ordered from most important to least important

Student Alert: Sometimes students (and teachers) are so busy handling the *urgent* priorities that making time for *important* priorities is difficult.

Each of us has an internal body clock that helps govern when we feel most alert. Becoming aware of your own body clock can help you to schedule study sessions at times when you're able to work at peak efficiency.

Try It!
3

Set Priorities

Set your priorities for the term. They may include getting to class on time, finishing papers and assignments by their due dates, finding a part-time job that fits your schedule, and reading every assignment before the class for which it is due. Include only items that are important, not everything that you may want to do. (For example, if you've always had a yearning to take a martial arts class but never got around to it before, it's reasonable to leave it off your list of priorities.)

To get started, list priorities in any order. Be sure to consider priorities relating to your schoolwork, other work, family, social obligations, and health. After you list them, assign a number to each one indicating its level—giving a "1" to the highest-priority items, a "2" to medium-priority items, and a "3" to the items with the lowest priority.

List of Priorities

Priority	Priority Index

Now redo your list, putting your number 1s first, followed by as many of your number 2s and 3s to which you feel you can reasonably commit.

Final List of Priorities

Priority
1.
2.
3.
4.
5.
6.
7.
8.
9.
10.
11.
12.

What does this list tell you about your greatest priorities? Are they centered around school, friends and family, jobs, or some other aspect of your life? Do you have so many "1" priorities that they will be difficult or impossible to accomplish successfully? How could you go back to your list and trim it down even more? What does this listing of priorities suggest about how successful you'll be during the upcoming term?

pleasant slumber? Are you the kind of person who is zombie-like by ten at night, or a person who is just beginning to rev up at midnight?

Each of us has our own style based on some inborn body clock. Some of us are at our best in the morning, while others do considerably better at night. Being aware of the time or times of day when you can accomplish your best work will help you plan and schedule your time most effectively. If you're at your worst in the morning, try to schedule easier, less-involving activities for those earlier hours. On the other hand, if morning is the best time for you, schedule activities that require the greatest concentration at that time.

> "Time moves slowly, but passes quickly."
>
> Alice Walker, *The Color Purple.*

But don't be a slave to your internal time clock. Even night people can function effectively in the morning, just as morning people can accomplish quite a bit in the evening. Don't let your concerns become a self-fulfilling prophecy.

rganize: Mastering the Moment

Your time management preparation has brought you to a point where you now know where you've lost time in the past, and your priority list is telling you where you need to be headed in the future.

Now for the present. You've reached the point where you can organize yourself to take control of your time. Here's what you'll need:

- A **master calendar** that shows all the weeks of the term on one page. You don't need to buy one; you can make it easily enough yourself. It need not be Great Art; a rough version will do. The important point is that it must include every week of the term and seven days per week. (See the example of a master calendar on page 34.)

- A **weekly timetable.** The weekly timetable is a master grid with the days of the week across the top and the hours, from 6:00 A.M. to midnight, along the side. This will permit you to write in all your regularly scheduled activities, as well as one-time appointments when they arise.

- A **daily to-do list.** Finally, you'll need a daily to-do list. The to-do list can be written on a small, portable calendar that includes a separate page for each day of the week. Or it can simply be a small notebook, with a separate sheet of paper for every day of the week. Whatever form your daily to-do list takes, you'll need to keep it with you all the time, so make sure it's not too cumbersome.

The basic organizational task you face is filling in these three schedules. You'll need at least an hour to do this, so set the time aside. In addition, there will be some repetition across the three schedules, and the task may seem a bit tedious. But *every minute you invest now in organizing your time will pay off in hours that you will save in the future.*

Follow these steps in completing your schedule:

- **Start with the *master calendar,* which shows all the weeks of the term on one page.** In most classes, you'll receive a syllabus, a course outline that explains what the course is all about. Traditionally, a syllabus includes course assignments and their due dates, and the schedule for tests that will be given during the term. Write on the master calendar *every* assignment you have, noting it on the date that it is due. If the instructor

Master calendar

A schedule showing the weeks of a longer time period, such as a college term, with all assignments and important activities noted on it

Weekly timetable

A schedule showing all regular, prescheduled activities due to occur in the week, together with one-time events and commitments

Daily to-do list

A schedule showing the tasks, activities, and appointments due to occur during the day

Teaching Tip: To teach time management effectively, be sure to have students bring calendars regularly to class, and take time to have students write in them.

Student Alert: Students need assistance moving between daily calendars and a semester plan. Help them make the connection between small steps and major accomplishments.

M	T	W	TH	F	SA	S
Sept. 7	8	9 classes start	10	11	12 camping →	13
14	Add/drop 15 ends	16	English 17 short paper due	18	19	20
21	22	23	English 24 short paper due	Russian 25 quiz	26	27
28	29	30 Psych exam	OCT 1 Music quiz English short paper due	1st Psych 2 paper due	3	4
5	Music 6 paper due	7	English 8 short paper due	Russian 9 quiz	10	11
12	13	14	Music quiz 15 English short paper due	16	17	18
First-yr 19 seminar journal due	20	Psych 21 exam	English 22 short paper due Dad's bd call	Theater 23 midterm	Bartending 24 job	25
Russian 26 midterm exam	English 27 midterm exam	28	Eng short 29 paper due Music quiz	30	31	NOV 1
2	3	4	English 5 short paper due	Russian 6 short paper due	7	8 Darcey's Wedding!
9	10	11 Holiday Veteran's Day	Eng short 12 paper due Music quiz	Russian 13 quiz Psych exam	14	15
First-yr 16 seminar group project due	17	18 Preregistration for next semester	English 19 short paper due	20	21	22
23	24	25	26 Thanksgiving	27 No Classes!	28	29
30	DEC 1 Music paper due	2	English 3 short paper due	Russian 4 quiz	5	6
First-yr 7 seminar final journal due	8	9	Music 10 quiz	Theater 11 project due Psych exam Last day of class!	12	13
English 14 final exam	Theater 15 final exam Russian final exam	16	Psych 17 final exam	Music exam 18 MY birthday!	19	20
21	22	23	24	25 Xmas	26	27

hasn't included due dates, ask; he or she probably already knows, or at least has a general idea, of the week that various assignments will be due. Pencil in tentative assignments on the appropriate date.

Don't only put assignments on the master calendar. Also include important activities from your personal life, drawn from your list of priorities. For instance, if you're involved in a club that is bringing a guest speaker to campus, mark down the date of the event. Finally, schedule some free time—time when you promise yourself you will do something that is just plain fun. Consider these days to be written in stone—promise yourself that you won't use them for anything else except for something enjoyable.

You now have a good idea of what the term has in store for you. In most cases, the first few weeks have few assignments or tests. But as the term rolls on—particularly around the middle and end of the term—

things will get more demanding. The message you should take from this: *Use the off-peak periods to get a head start on future assignments.*

Completing a master schedule also may help you head off disaster before it occurs. Suppose, for instance, you find that six weeks in the future you have two papers due and three tests—all in the same week!

After cursing your bad luck, it's time to take action. Begin to think of strategies for managing the situation, such as working on the papers, or studying in advance. You might also try to change some due dates. Instructors are far more receptive to requests for extensions on papers if the requests are made well in advance. Similarly, it might be possible to take a test later—or earlier—if you make prior arrangements.

- **Now move to the *weekly timetable* provided in Figure 2.2.** Fill in the times of all your fixed, prescheduled activities—the times that your classes meet, when you have to be at work, the times you have to pick up your child at day care, and any other recurring appointments.

IM Connection: "Teaching the Text" Chapter 2—Sections IV and VIII; the "Planning Backwards" activity can be used here.

Weekly Timetable

Week of: _____   Week # _____

	Mon	Tues	Wed	Thurs	Fri	Sat	Sun
6–7 AM							
7–8 AM							
8–9 AM							
9–10 AM							
10–11 AM							
11–12 AM							
12 (noon)–1 PM							
1–2 PM							
2–3 PM							
3–4 PM							
4–5 PM							
5–6 PM							
6–7 PM							
7–8 PM							
8–9 PM							
9–10 PM							
10–11 PM							
11 PM–12 (midnight)							

Figure 2.2

A Weekly Timetable

Make a single copy of the blank timetable on the left. Then fill in your *regular, predictable* time commitments. Next, make as many copies as you need to cover each week of the term. Then, for each week, fill in the date on the left and the number of the week in the term on the right, and add in your *irregular* commitments.

Once you've filled in the weekly timetable, as in the one below, you get a bare-bones picture of the average week. You will still need to take into account the specific activities that are required to complete the assignments on the master calendar.

Weekly Timetable

Week of: 9/28   Week # 3

	Mon	Tues	Wed	Thurs	Fri	Sat	Sun
6–7 AM							
7–8 AM							
8–9 AM							
9–10 AM	9 05 Psych	9 05 Music	9 05 Psych	9 05 Music	9 05 Psych		
10–11 AM							
11–12 AM		11 15 English		11 15 English			
12 (noon)–1 PM	12 20 Theater		12 20 Theater		12 20 Theater		
1–2 PM							
2–3 PM							
3–4 PM	3:00 Russian		3:00 Russian		3:00 Russian		
4–5 PM	First-year seminar	Work		Work			
5–6 PM							
6–7 PM							
7–8 PM							
8–9 PM							
9–10 PM							
10–11 PM							
11 PM–12 (midnight)							

To move from your "average" week to specific weeks, make photocopies of the weekly timetable that now contains your fixed appointments. Make enough copies for every week of the term. On each copy write the week number of the term and the specific dates it covers.

Using your master calendar, add assignment due dates, tests, and any other activities on the appropriate days of the week. Then pencil in blocks of time necessary to prepare for those events.

How much time should you allocate for schoolwork? One very rough rule of thumb holds that every one hour that you spend in class requires, on average, two hours of study outside of class to earn a B and three hours of study outside of class to earn an A. Do the arithmetic: If you are taking 15 credits (with each credit equivalent to an hour of class per week), you'll need to plan for 30 hours of studying each week to earn a B average—an intimidating amount of time. Of course, the amount of time you must allocate to a specific class will vary from week to week, depending on what is happening in the class.

For example, if you estimate that you'll need five hours of study for a midterm exam in a certain class, pencil in those hours. Don't set up a single block of five hours. People remember best when their studying is spread out over shorter periods rather than attempted in one long block of time. Besides, it will probably be hard to find a block of five straight hours on your weekly calendar.

Similarly, if you need to write a paper that's due on a certain date, you can block out the different stages of the writing process that we'll describe in Chapter 8. You'll need to estimate how much time each stage will take, but you probably have a pretty good idea from previous papers you've written.

Some classes may need only a few hours of study in a given week. With good luck, heavy weeks in one class will be compensated for by lighter weeks in others.

Keep in mind that estimates are just that: estimates. Don't think of them as set in stone. Mark them on your weekly calendar in pencil, not pen, so you can adjust them if necessary.

But remember: It's also crucial not to over-schedule yourself. You'll still need time to eat, to talk with your friends, to spend time with your family, and to enjoy yourself in general. If you find that your life is completely filled with things that you feel you must do in order to survive and that there is no room for fun, then take a step back and cut out something to make some time for *yourself* in your daily schedule. Finding time for yourself is as important as carving out time for what others want you to do. Besides, if you are overworked, you're likely to "find" the time by guiltily goofing off without really setting aside the time and enjoying it.

Discussion Prompt: Ask students to bring in or share their favorite method for keeping daily to-do lists.

- **If you've taken each of the previous steps, you're now in a position to work on the final step of organization for successful time management: completing your *daily to-do list*.** Unlike the master calendar and weekly timetable—both of which you develop at the beginning of the term—you shouldn't work on your daily to-do list far in advance. In fact, the best approach is to complete it just one day ahead of time, preferably at the end of the day.

List all the things that you intend to do during the next day. Start with the things you know you must do that have fixed times, such as classes, work schedules, and appointments. Then add in the other things that you need to accomplish, such as an hour of study for an upcoming test; working on research for an upcoming paper; or finishing up a lab report. Finally, list things that are enjoyable—set aside time for a run or a walk, for example.

The idea is not to schedule every single minute of the day. That would be counterproductive, and you'd end up feeling like you'd failed if you deviated from your schedule. Instead, think of your daily to-do list as a path through a forest. If you were hiking, you would allow yourself to deviate from the path, occasionally venturing onto side tracks when they looked interesting. But you'd also be keeping tabs on your direction so you end up where you need to be at the end and not miles away from your car or home.

Like the sample daily to-do list that follows, include a column to check or cross off after you've completed an activity. There's something very satisfying in acknowledging what you have accomplished. As you look at your to-do list with its check marks you will also feel a surge of energy, knowing you can get things done.

To-Do List for 9/28 (date)	
Item	**✓**
Call Chris & get English notes	✓
Meet with Prof. Hernandez	✓
Do laundry	
Work on outline for psych paper	
Return books to library	✓
Call Nettie	
Set up meeting with music group	
Meet Deena	
Review Russian	✓

W ork: Controlling Time

You're in luck: There is no work to time management—or at least not much more than you've already done. Time management is largely about preparation and organization; the work itself involves completing the activities that you need and wish to complete. If you've prepared and organized carefully, you'll be ready to complete your work.

In short, the work of time management is to follow the schedules that you've put together. But that doesn't mean it will be easy. *Our lives are filled with surprises:* Things take longer than we've planned. A friend we haven't spoken to in a while calls to chat, and it seems rude to say that we don't have time to talk. A crisis occurs; buses are late; computers break down; kids get sick.

The difference between effective time management and time management that doesn't work lies in how well you deal with the inevitable surprises.

There are several ways to take control of your days and permit yourself to follow your intended schedule:

- **Just say no.** You don't have to agree to every request and every favor that others ask of you. You're not a bad person if you refuse to do something that will eat up your time and prevent you from accomplishing your goals.

  Suppose, for example, a friend sees you in the library and asks to borrow the notes from a class that he missed yesterday and that you attended. It's not an unreasonable request; in fact, you've asked to borrow his notes in the past, so really you'd just be reciprocating. Here's the problem, though: You don't have your notebook with you, and you'd have to stop by your house to pick it up. Well, you tell yourself, the

Try It! 4

Build a Daily To-Do List

Copy the following blank to-do list as many times as you want or make your own. Then fill in your daily plans and commitments. As you complete them, check them off in the column on the right.

To-Do List for _____ (date)	
Item	**✓**

house is only 10 minutes from campus, so it really wouldn't take too long.

But think through what the request really entails. *It may be only 10 minutes to your house, but it's another 10 minutes back. That's 20 minutes. And then there's the time that you'll spend meeting her to give her the notes. And then the time it takes to meet her again, once she's copied the notes. Or suppose you decide to wait while she copies them. Overall, you may end up losing an hour.*

The solution? You should probably say no to the immediate request. It's not unreasonable to tell your friend, politely, that you don't have the time today to get your notebook. In fact, it's quite reasonable. You don't have to refuse her completely; it should be possible to work out some other way for her to get the notes. She could stop by your house in the evening to pick up the notes, or you could bring them with you the next day. In short, there are ways to accomplish the goal of helping out your friend without wasting time and sabotaging your schedule.

- **Get away from it all.** Go to the library. Lock yourself into your bedroom. Find an out-of-the-way unused classroom.

Any of these places can serve to isolate you from everyday distractions and thereby permit you to work on the tasks that you wish to complete. Try to adopt a particular spot as your own, such as a corner desk in a secluded nook in the library. If you use it enough, your body and mind will automatically get into study mode as soon as you seat yourself at it.

Teaching Tip: Encourage your students to mark or check items off their lists. This is a visual reminder of "getting things done" and can create a sense of accomplishment when the list seems overwhelming.

Teaching Tip: Have students generate a list of ways that they allow others to misuse their time, and then brainstorm solutions to the problem.

- **Enjoy the sounds of silence.** Although many students insist they accomplish most while a television, radio, or CD is playing, scientific studies suggest otherwise: We are able to concentrate most when our environment is silent. So even if you're sure you work best with a soundtrack playing, experiment and work in silence for a few days. You may find that you get more done in less time than you would in a more distracting environment.

- **Take control of your communications.** The telephone, e-mail, regular mail. Who doesn't love to receive messages from others?

  We may not control when communications arrive, but we can make the message wait until we are ready to receive it. Telephone calls can be stored on answering machines or voice-mail systems; e-mail can be saved on a computer; and regular mail can sit in a mailbox. If you wait until you have the time to take a message, you'll be able to follow your time management plans far better.

- **Let your fingers do the walking.** As an old telephone company advertisement for the yellow pages says, Let your fingers do the walking. Many things can be done over the phone—or via e-mail or voice mail—rather than in person. It is much faster to call the bank to check on your bank balance than it is to walk over, stand in line, and get waited on.

- **Expect the unexpected.** Interruptions and crises, minor and major, can't be eliminated. However, they can be prepared for. By making sure your schedule has some slack in it, you'll have the opportunity to regain time lost to unexpected events.

  Even more important, try to anticipate the unanticipated. How is it possible to plan for surprises? Though it may still be too early in the term to get a clear picture of what sorts of unanticipated events you'll encounter, you should keep an eye out for patterns. Perhaps one instructor routinely makes surprise assignments that aren't listed on the syllabus. Maybe you're asked to work extra hours on the weekends because someone doesn't show up and you have to work overtime.

  You'll never be able to escape from unexpected interruptions and surprises that require your attention. But by trying to anticipate them in advance, and thinking about how you'll react to them, you'll be positioning yourself to react more effectively when they do occur.

"I had a friend who was concentrating in pre-med. He put off studying for his chem midterm until 10 P.M. the night before, spending his time instead at the movies and the campus hang-out. After bombing the exam, he told us he did not have enough time to study. Basically, he gave himself an excuse to fail."

Thom McDade, Pomona College.[3]

- **Don't procrastinate.** Procrastination is like a microscopic parasite on your day, invisible to the naked eye, but eating up your time nonetheless.

  It's 10:30 A.M. You've just come out of your German class. You know that there's going to be a test next week, and you've planned to go over the vocabulary flash cards you made up last night. It's right there in your schedule: "10:30 A.M.—study German vocabulary." But you're thirsty after sitting in class, so you decide to go and buy yourself something to drink.

  As you head into the snack bar, you pass by the campus store, and you think about how you need to buy a couple of pens. After finding the kind of pen you like, you go to the checkout line. You pass by a rack of magazines, and, after leafing through a few, decide to purchase one. You can read it while you have your drink. You make your way to the snack bar, buy your soda, and sip it as you read the magazine.

Suddenly, a half hour has gone by. Because so much time has passed, you decide that it won't be worth it to start studying your German vocabulary. So you spend a little more time reading the magazine and then head off to your next class, which is at 11:00 A.M.

You can't control interruptions and crises that are foisted upon you by others. But even when no one else is throwing interruptions at us, we make up our own. **Procrastination,** the habit of putting off and delaying tasks that are to be accomplished, is a problem that many of us face. To identify whether you are a procrastinator, find your "Procrastination Quotient" (see Try It 5, page 42).

If you use the time management techniques that we've been discussing, procrastination should be minimized. But if you find yourself procrastinating, several steps can help you:

Break large tasks into small ones. People often procrastinate because a task they're seeking to accomplish appears overwhelming. If writing a 15-page paper seems nearly impossible, think about writing a series of five 3-page papers. If reading a 750-page book seems impossible, think of it as reading several 250-page books.

Start with the easiest and simplest part of a task, and then do the harder parts. Succeeding initially on the easy parts can make the harder parts of a task less daunting—and make you less apt to procrastinate in completing the task.

Work with others. Working with others who must accomplish the same task as you can help prevent procrastination. Just being in the same physical location with others can motivate you sufficiently to accomplish tasks that you consider unpleasant and on which you might be tempted to procrastinate. For instance, studying vocabulary words can be made easier if you plan a study session with several of your classmates. Beware, though—if you spend too much time socializing, you lower the likelihood of success.

Keep the costs of procrastination in mind. Procrastination doesn't just result in delay; it may also make the task harder than it would have been if you hadn't procrastinated. Not only will you ultimately have less time to complete the task, but you may have to do it so quickly that its quality may be diminished. In the worst scenario, you won't even be able to finish it at all.

If you have children: Balancing school and family demands. If you are a full-time student and full-time caregiver for children, time management is especially challenging. Not only do children demand—and

Procrastination
The habit of putting off and delaying tasks that are to be accomplished

Teaching Tip and IM Link:
Students will admit that procrastination is a problem. Use the TRY IT! 5 activity in class. See "Teaching the Text", Chapter 2, for suggestions and activities on this topic.

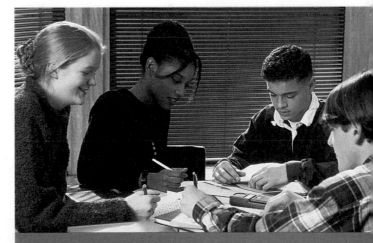

One antidote to procrastination is working in a study group. You'll be motivated by the presence of others who face the same challenges and assignments that you do.

Try It!
5

Find Your Procrastination Quotient

Do you procrastinate?[2] To find out, circle the number that best applies for each question.

1. I invent reasons and look for excuses for not acting on a problem.

   Strongly agree　　4　　3　　2　　1　　**Strongly disagree**

2. It takes pressure to get me to work on difficult assignments.

   Strongly agree　　4　　3　　2　　1　　**Strongly disagree**

3. I take half measures that will avoid or delay unpleasant or difficult tasks.

   Strongly agree　　4　　3　　2　　1　　**Strongly disagree**

4. I face too many interruptions and crises that interfere with accomplishing my major goals.

   Strongly agree　　4　　3　　2　　1　　**Strongly disagree**

5. I sometimes neglect to carry out important tasks.

   Strongly agree　　4　　3　　2　　1　　**Strongly disagree**

6. I schedule big assignments too late to get them done as well as I know I could.

   Strongly agree　　4　　3　　2　　1　　**Strongly disagree**

7. I'm sometimes too tired to do the work I need to do.

   Strongly agree　　4　　3　　2　　1　　**Strongly disagree**

8. I start new tasks before I finish old ones.

   Strongly agree　　4　　3　　2　　1　　**Strongly disagree**

9. When I work in groups, I try to get other people to finish what I don't.

   Strongly agree　　4　　3　　2　　1　　**Strongly disagree**

10. I put off tasks that I really don't want to do but know that I must do.

    Strongly agree　　4　　3　　2　　1　　**Strongly disagree**

Scoring: Total the numbers you have circled. If the score is below 20, you are not a chronic procrastinator and you probably have only an occasional problem. If your score is 21–30, you have a minor problem with procrastination. If your score is above 30, you procrastinate quite often and should work on breaking the habit.

If you do procrastinate often, why do you think you do it? Are there particular subjects or classes or kinds of assignments on which you are more likely to procrastinate? *Working in a Group:* Think about the last time you procrastinated. Describe it as completely as you can. What was the task? What did you do rather than doing what needed to be done? What could you have done to avoid procrastinating in this situation? Ask others what strategy they might suggest for avoiding procrastination.

deserve—substantial quantities of time, but juggling school and family obligations can prove to be more than a full-time job. There are some specific strategies that can help, however:

Provide activities for your children. Kids enjoy doing things on their own for part of the day. Plan activities that will keep them happily occupied while you're doing schoolwork.

Make spending time with your children a priority. Carve out "free play" time for your kids. Even 20 minutes of good time devoted to your children will give all of you—you and them—a lift. No matter how busy you are, you owe it to your children—and yourself—to spend time as a family.

Enlist your child's help. Children love to play adult and, if they're old enough, ask them to help you study. Maybe they can help you clear a space to study. Perhaps you can give them "assignments" that they can work on while you're working on your assignments.

Encourage your child to invite friends over to play. Some children can remain occupied for hours if they have a playmate.

Use television appropriately. Television viewing is not all bad, and some shows and videos can be not just engaging, but educational. The trick is to pick and choose what your children watch and not use TV as an all-purpose baby sitter. *The Magic Schoolbus, Sesame Street,* and videos of children's classics, for example, can, for an hour or so, be a worthwhile way for children to spend their time while you study.

Discussion Prompt: This section highlights the time pressures that non-traditional students face. It also provides an opportunity for traditional-age freshmen (18 years old) to look at life from someone else's perspective.

Find the best child care or baby sitters that you can. The better the care your children are getting, the better you'll be able to concentrate on your schoolwork. You may still feel guilty that you're not with your children as much as you'd like, but accept that guilt. Remember, your attendance in college builds a better future for your children.

Accept that studying will be harder with kids around. It may take you longer to study, and your concentration may suffer from the noise that kids make. But remind yourself what that noise represents: the growth and development of someone that you love. One day your children will be grown, and without a doubt there will be times that you'll miss their high level of energy and activity.

- **Balancing school and work demands.** Juggling school and a job can be exhausting. Not only must you manage your time to complete your schoolwork, but in many cases you'll also face time management demands while you are on the job. Here are some tips to help you keep everything in balance:

  Make to-do lists for work, just as you would for your schoolwork. In fact, all the time management strategies that we've discussed can be applied to on-the-job tasks.

  If you have slack time on the job, get some studying done. Of course, you should never do schoolwork without your employer's permission. If

Discussion Prompt: Ask your students how many have jobs outside of class. You might be surprised at how many hours they are working and how little time they believe they have free for studying.

Career Connections

Taking a Long-Term View of Time

In considering different careers, it is important to consider the length of time it takes to prepare for them. Every profession has a different set of educational and other preparatory requirements, and in order to have informed career goals, it is necessary to determine the kinds of things you need to do in order to prepare.

One of the most effective ways of comparing careers is to construct a career time line that compares the timetables involved in various careers. Use a time line like that shown in Figure 2.3 , marking off six-month periods initially and then years—extending the chart to "Ten years." Write in the preparatory steps for each career you wish to compare, including the kinds of courses you'll need to take, the educational and professional requirements that you'll need to fulfill, and any internships or residencies you will need.

Obviously your plan will change as time goes on and your interests become more firm. The idea is not to identify a rigid path for yourself but to begin the process of understanding what it takes to enter various professions. The more knowledge you have, the greater your ability to make wise choices.

you don't get permission, you may jeopardize your job.

Ask your employer about flextime. If your job allows it, you may be able to set your own hours, within reason, as long as the work gets done. If this is an option for you, use it. Although it may create more time management challenges for you than would a job with set hours, it also provides you with more flexibility.

Accept new responsibilities carefully. If you've barely been keeping up with the demands of work and school, don't automatically accept new job responsibilities without carefully evaluating how they fit with your long-term priorities. If your job is temporary and you're not planning to stay, you might want to respectfully decline substantial new duties or an increase in the number of hours you work. On the other hand, if you plan to continue in the job once you're done with school, then accepting new responsibilities may be more reasonable.

Always keep in mind why you're working. If you're working because it's your sole means of support, you're in a very different position from someone who is working to earn a bit of extra money for luxuries. Remember what your priorities are. In some cases, school should always come first; in others, your job may have to come first, at least some of the time. Whatever you decide, make sure it's a thoughtful decision, based on an evaluation of your long-term priorities.

E valuate: Checking Your Time

IM Link: "Teaching the Text" Chapter 2—Sections IV and VIII; "The Cost of a College Education" activity is relevant here.

Evaluating how you use your time is pretty straightforward: You either accomplished what you intended to do in a given period, or you didn't. Did you check off all the items on your daily to-do list? If you go over your list at the end of every day, not only will you know how successful your time management efforts have been, but you will be able to incorporate any activities you missed into the next day's to-do list.

Figure 2.3

Building A Career Time Line

	Possible Career	Possible Career	Possible Career	Possible Career	Possible Career
	Commercial Airline Pilot	*High School Guidance Counselor*			
Present–six months from now	Complete first term; take engineering course	Complete first term; take introductory education course			
Six months– one year	Complete first year; declare engineering major; take flying lessons	Complete first year; declare education major; volunteer in school			
Two years	Get flying license	Summer job at school			
Three years	Summer internship at airport				
Four years	Graduate with degree in engineering	Graduate with degree in education; take job as high school teacher			
Five years	Enroll in masters program in aeronautical engineering	High school teaching; take courses toward masters degree in counseling at night			
Six years	Graduate with masters degree in aeronautical engineering	Continue high school teaching and graduate training			
Seven years	Take job as co-pilot	Graduate with masters; move into counseling job			
Eight years		Full-time counselor in high school			
Nine years					
Ten years	Promotion to airline pilot				

The check-off is important because it provides an objective record of what you have accomplished on a given day. Just as important, it provides you with concrete reinforcement for completing the task. As we have noted, there are few things more satisfying than gazing at a to-do list with a significant number of check marks.

Of course, you won't always accomplish every item on your to-do list. That's not surprising, nor even particularly bad, especially if you've included some second- and third-level priorities that you don't absolutely have to accomplish and that you may not really have expected you'd have time for anyway.

IM Link: "Teaching the Text" Chapter 2—Section VII; "Making the Connection to the Individual Life."

Rethink: Reflecting on Your Personal Style of Time Management

At the end of the day, after you've evaluated how well you've followed your time management plan and how much you've accomplished, it's time to rethink where you are. Maybe you've accomplished everything you set out to do, and every task for the day is completed, and every item on your to-do list has a check mark next to it.

Or maybe you have the opposite result. Your day has been a shambles, and you feel as if nothing has been accomplished. Because of a constant series of interruptions and chance events, you've been unable to make headway on your list.

Or—most likely—you find yourself somewhere in between these two extremes. Some tasks got done, while others are still hanging over you. Now is the time to rethink in a broad sense how you manage your time by doing the following:

Reconsider Your Personal Style of Time Management We've outlined one method of time management (summarized in the P.O.W.E.R. Plan to the left). Although it works well for most people, it isn't for everyone. Some people just can't bring themselves to be so structured and scheduled. They feel hemmed in by to-do lists.

If you're one of the those people, fine. You don't need to follow the suggestions presented in this chapter exactly. In fact, if you go to any office supply store or even your college bookstore, you'll find lots of other aids to time management. Many publishing companies produce elaborate planners, such as Day-Timer. Similarly, software companies produce computerized time management software, such as Microsoft's Outlook and the Lotus Organizer, and some time management systems are on the World Wide Web (see the Resources section at the end of this chapter).

Whatever system you choose, the important thing is that you need to pay attention to how you use your time and follow *some* time management strategy. Perhaps it might consist of jotting down due dates, and then each day looking at them and figuring out what to do that day. Perhaps it might consist of visualizing yourself completing the tasks you need to and using that visualization to guide your behavior each day. Or perhaps it might mean working on assignments as soon as you get them. Rather than waiting until the last minute, you try to accomplish them as soon as you know they need to be done.

Whatever approach to time management you choose, it will work best if it is compatible with your own personal values and strengths. Keep experimenting until you find an approach that works for you.

Consider Doing Less If you keep falling behind, do less. Sometimes we just have so much to do that, even with the best time management skills in the world, we could never accomplish everything. There are only 24

PREPARE
Learn where time is going

ORGANIZE
Use a master calendar, weekly timetable, and daily to-do list

WORK
Follow the schedules you've put together

EVALUATE
Keep track of your short-term and long-term accomplishments

RETHINK
Reflect on your personal style of time management

P.O.W.E.R. Plan

Managing your time effectively will allow you to spend more of it doing the things that are important to you.

hours in the day, and we need to sleep for about a third of the time. In the remaining hours, it is simply impossible to carry a full load of classes *and* work full-time *and* care for a child *and* still have some time left to have a normal life.

Consequently, if you consistently fall behind in your work, it may be that you are just doing too much. Reassess your goals and your priorities, and make choices. Determine what is most important to you. It's better to accomplish less, if it is accomplished well, than to accomplish more, but poorly.

Do More If you consistently accomplish everything you want to do and still have time on your hands, do more. Although it is a problem that many of us would envy, some people have too much time on their hands. Their classes may not be too demanding, or work demands may suddenly slacken off. Or perhaps a child for whom they are caring begins to attend public school full-time. In such situations, they may suddenly feel like their life is proceeding at a more leisurely pace than before.

If this happens to you, there are several responses you might consider. One is to simply relax and enjoy your more unhurried existence. There is a good bit to be said for having time to let your thoughts wander. We need to take time out to enjoy our friends, admire the flowers in the park, exercise, consider the spiritual side of our lives, and the like.

On the other hand, if you consistently have more time than you know what to do with, rethink how to make use of your time. Reflect on what you want to accomplish with your life, and add some activities that help you reach your goals. For example, consider becoming involved in an extracurricular activity. Think about volunteering your time to needy individuals and organizations. Consider taking an extra course during the next term.

But whatever you decide to do, make it a decision. Don't let the time slip away. Once it's gone, it's gone forever. Think of time as a valuable natural resource that should be conserved.

> **"Our costliest expenditure is time."**
>
> Theophrastus, quoted in Diogenes Laertius, *Lives and Opinions of Eminent Philosophers.*

Speaking of Success

Name: *Jennifer Schulte*
Education: *Creighton University first-year student*
Home: *Omaha, Nebraska*

Jennifer Schulte knows first-hand the importance of being goal-oriented and managing time.

Jennifer, a first-year student at Creighton University in Omaha, Nebraska, is taking five courses. At the same time, she works as an office supervisor in the largest Sears department store in the state. Working 30 hours a week, she supervises an office that handles customer credit problems and paying store bills.

How does she manage to be a full-time student and carry out her job? "I actually enjoy the pace," comments Jennifer. "But I have to be really organized, or I couldn't do as many things as I do," she added.

She has help in the form of a daily planner, which Schulte says is her "lifeline."

"I carry my planner with me everywhere. My friends call it my Bible," she says. "Every scheduled activity of the day is written into my planner, even time with my friends." Schulte says she never says yes to an appointment unless she checks the planner first.

"I also make to-do lists that in-

CREIGHTON UNIVERSITY

clude my schoolwork, my work at Sears, and my community work. Each day, I prioritize the list to find out which things can be done today and which tomorrow. From there I decide what needs to be done in the morn-ing, afternoon, and evening, and when I can take a break. I'm always making mental lists as well," she added.

Jennifer's success at time management comes, in part, from the practice she received during high school. She not only achieved a 3.5 grade point average, but did so while also holding down an outside job, putting in as many as 35 hours a week. Fitting in school, work, extracurricular activities, and a social life was not easy, and she routinely got up at 6:00 A.M. and went to bed at midnight.

Jennifer knows most people don't aspire to fit so much into their days. But for her, juggling school, work, community activities, and a social life is worth it. "I have a specific set of goals that I want to achieve, and I love what I do."

How can I manage my time most effectively?

- Decide to take control of your time.

- Become aware of the way you use your time currently.

- Set clear priorities.

- Use such time management tools as a master calendar, weekly timetable, and a daily to-do list.

How can I deal better with surprises and distractions?

- Deal with surprises by saying no, getting away from it all, working in silence, taking control of communications, using the telephone to conduct transactions, and leaving slack in the schedule to accommodate the unexpected.

Teaching Tip: Ask students these same questions at mid-term.

- Avoid procrastination by breaking large tasks into smaller ones, starting with the easiest parts of a task first; working with other people; and calculating the true costs of procrastination.

How can I balance competing priorities?

- You *can* balance competing priorities if you begin to see how they coexist. Manage work time carefully, use slack time on the job to perform school assignments, use flextime, accept new responsibilities thoughtfully, and assign the proper priority to work.

Key Terms and Concepts

Daily to-do list (p. 33)
Master calendar (p. 33)
Priorities (p. 31)

Procrastination (p. 41)
Time log (p. 27)
Weekly timetable (p. 33)

Resources

On Campus

The college official that schedules classes on campus is known as the *registrar*. If you are having difficulty in scheduling your classes, the registrar's office may be helpful. In addition, your academic advisor can help you work out problems in enrolling in the classes you want.

    If you are having difficulty in managing your time, there are several places to turn to. The campus counseling center will help, as will campus learning centers. Your academic advisor can also be a source of aid.

In Print

Alan Axelrod and James Holtje offer a practical, hands-on guide to time management in *201 Ways to Manage Your Time Better* (McGraw-Hill, 1997).

The *10-Minute Guide to Microsoft Outlook 98* (Que, 1998), by Joseph W. Habraken, provides a quick, hands-on introduction to Microsoft's Outlook 98 software, a popular time management program that accompanies the word-processing program Word. (You can also find guides to other time management software programs.)

Veronique Vienne and Erica Lennard's *The Art of Doing Nothing: Simple Ways to Make Time for Yourself* (Clarkson Potter, 1998) is an antidote to the impulse to schedule every minute of our days. The book celebrates taking time out and devoting it to oneself, providing a practical guide to rest and relaxation.

On the Web

The following sites on the World Wide Web provide the opportunity to extend your learning about the material in this chapter. (Although the Web addresses were accurate at the time the book was printed, check the P.O.W.E.R. Learning Web site [http://mhhe.com/power] for any changes that may have occurred.)

http://www.coun.uvic.ca/learn/program/hndouts/slfman.html
   This site provides a handy self-management checklist that allows visitors to better achieve their goals with the time that they have. It also provides effective techniques for avoiding procrastination and digression, two major obstacles to effective time management.

http://www.mindtools.com/page5.html
   The focus of this site is how to get the most out of one's time. Topics covered include analyzing what time is really worth, prioritizing goals, and planning effective use of the time one actually has.

Taking It to the Net

1 Create a weekly organizer. Find a site on the Web that relates to time management (for example, **http://www.dayrunner.com/ideas_tips/index. asp**). Create a time management program for yourself based on information on this site. Be sure to consider all of your classes and any other regular obligations that you have.

2 Make a master calendar for the term. Go to Yahoo! (**www.yahoo.com**), click on "Reference," then again on "Calendars." Here you'll find many links to different calendar-related information such as when holidays occur. Use this information to create your own master calendar for the term. Be sure to indicate dates when important assignments are due and when exams occur.

The Case of . . .

The Time of His Life

Will Linz couldn't believe it. On the same day that he had completed his term paper and handed it in, his instructor announced a test for the following week. When the class protested that the test hadn't been listed in the syllabus, the instructor murmured that she'd made a mistake and was sorry about the short notice.

Will panicked when he remembered that next week he also had to complete two lab reports he had put off because he had been working on his term paper. Even worse, next weekend was lost. He had promised—promised!—his girlfriend, who was working full-time, that he would go with her to her annual company picnic. Although he dreaded the thought of being with a bunch of people he barely knew, he'd finally agreed to go just last week.

As he was driving home thinking about all this, his car started to sputter and then stalled. He was unable to get it started. That was it. He sat there on the side of the road, feeling like his life had completely fallen apart and wondering how he'd ever get it back together again.

1. What might you tell Will that could help solve his predicament?

2. Is there anything Will could have done to prevent the situation he now faces from occurring in the first place?

3. What specific time management techniques might Will have employed in the past to prevent these problems from arising?

4. What strategies might Will use now to take control over his limited time during the coming week?

5. What advice could you give Will for trying to prevent problems in time management during his next term?

Recognizing How You Learn, Who You Are, and What You Value

3

The transformation began when Shaniqua Turner got her first paper back from her English literature instructor. It wasn't the grade—which was good—that mattered so much, but what her instructor uttered, almost as an afterthought, as she handed the paper back to Shaniqua: "Nice job. Your insights were good, and you have great potential as a writer."

Shaniqua was thrilled. She had always thought of herself as having only modest talent in English, and, although at one point she had harbored the fantasy of being a newspaper reporter, she had never felt she was good enough to make it.

But now something clicked; her perspective on who she was started to change. Maybe she did have the ability to succeed in a career involving writing.

It would be a long and gradual transformation for Shaniqua, but the moment when her instructor praised her work was a turning point. From then on, Shaniqua's view of herself began to change forever.

Looking
Ahead

Through the experiences we have in life, we build up a sense of our strengths and weaknesses, what we like and dislike about ourselves. In the process, the sense of who we are also affects the choices we make and the things that we do. So it's not surprising that the accuracy of our understanding of ourselves has an important impact upon our success.

In this chapter you will be asked to consider various aspects of yourself. First you'll look at the ways in which you learn and how you can use your personal learning style to study more effectively.

You'll then explore who you are more broadly, considering the various aspects of your personality. You'll see how your self-esteem— the way you perceive your strengths and weaknesses—can lead to success or failure.

Finally, the chapter helps you investigate where you are headed. By creating your own personal mission statement, you'll begin to solidify the knowledge of who you are and where you would be happiest and most productive in the future.

After reading this chapter, you'll be able to answer these questions:

- **What are my learning styles, and how have they affected my academic success?**

- **What is self-concept and how does it affect me?**

- **How does my level of self-esteem affect my behavior?**

- **How can I determine my needs and make wise personal decisions throughout life?**

Teaching Tip and IM Link: Read this chapter and IM, "Teaching the Text" Chapter 3, "Chapter Summary" prior to teaching this chapter. It is the heart of the course.

Discovering Your Learning Styles

Consider what it would be like to be a member of the Trukese people, a small group of islanders in the South Pacific.

Trukese sailors often sail hundreds of miles on the open sea. They manage this feat with none of the navigational equipment used by Western sailors. No compass. No chronometer. No sextant. They don't even sail in a straight line. Instead, they zigzag back and forth, at the mercy of the winds and tides. Yet they make few mistakes. Almost always they are able to reach their destination with precision. How do they do it?

They can't really explain it. They say it has to do with following the rising and setting of the stars at night. During the day, they take in the appearance, sound, and feel of the waves against the side of the boat. But they don't really have any idea of where they are at any given moment, nor do they care. They just know that ultimately they'll reach their final destination.

It would be foolhardy to suggest that the Trukese don't have what it takes to be successful sailors. The fact that they don't use traditional Western navigational equipment when they're sailing does not mean that they are any less able than Western navigators. Certainly, if they took a test of Western navigational skills, they would do badly. But their ultimate success cannot be questioned.

What about academic success? Isn't it reasonable to assume that there are different ways to reach academic goals? Wouldn't it be surprising if everyone learned in exactly the same way, without any differences in what worked best for them?

It turns out that we don't all learn in the same way. Each of us has preferred ways of learning, approaches that work best for us. And our success is not just dependent on how *well* we learn, but on *how* we learn.

Trukese sailors, who live on a small group of islands in the South Pacific, are able to navigate with considerable accuracy across great expanses of open seas, and they do so without the use of any of the standard navigation tools used by sailors in Western cultures. The navigational achievements of the Trukese sailors illustrate that there are multiple ways to attain our goals and that there is no single route to success.

Learning styles reflect our preferred manner of acquiring, using, and thinking about knowledge. These styles are not abilities, but types of learning. They represent the ways we approach these tasks.

We don't have just one learning style, but a profile of styles. Even though our ability may be identical to someone else's, our learning styles might be quite different.

You probably already know quite a lot about your learning styles. Maybe you do particularly well in your biology classes while struggling with English. Or it may be the other way around. Because biology tends to be about natural processes, teachers present the subject as a series of related facts. English, however, requires you to think more abstractly, analyzing and synthesizing ideas presented in a variety of ways. Whichever subject you prefer, it is almost certain you prefer it because of your learning style.

Though we may have general preferences for fact-based learning or learning that requires more abstract thinking, we all use a variety of learning styles.

Learning style
One's preferred manner of acquiring, using, and thinking about knowledge

Student Alert: This chapter provides multiple ways to discuss the same information with your students; begin to agree on a common language for discussing learning issues. You will return to this topic repeatedly throughout the semester.

Some involve our preferences regarding the way information is presented to us, some relate to how we think and learn most readily, and some relate to how our personality traits affect our performance. Different approaches to learning overlap one another, and there are few distinct categories. We'll start by considering the preferences we have for how we initially perceive information.

Are You a Primarily Visual, Auditory, or Tactile Learner?

One of the most basic aspects of learning styles concerns the way in which we initially receive information from our sense organs—our **receptive learning style.** Some of us have primarily **visual learning styles,** recalling the spelling of a word, for example, or the structure of a chemical compound by reviewing a picture in our head. Or maybe you learn best when you have the opportunity to read about a concept rather than listening to a teacher explain it. Students with visual learning styles find it easier to see things in their "mind's eye"—to visualize a task or concept—than to be lectured about them.

Have you ever asked a friend to help you put something together by having her read the directions to you while you worked? If you did, you may have an **auditory learning style.** People with auditory learning styles prefer listening to explanations rather than reading about them. They love class lectures and discussions, because they can easily take in the information that is being talked about.

Students with a **tactile learning style** prefer to learn by doing—touching, manipulating objects, and doing things. For instance, some people enjoy the act of writing because of the feel of a pencil or a computer keyboard—the tactile equivalent of "thinking out loud" (which would be preferred by someone with an auditory learning style). Or they may find that it helps them to make a three-dimensional model to understand a new idea.

Having a particular receptive learning style simply means that it will be easier to learn material that is presented in that style. It does not mean you cannot learn any other way!

Receptive learning styles also have implications for effective studying. For instance, students with an auditory learning style may have greater success if they recite material out loud when studying. In contrast, a visual learner might do better producing time lines, charts, or other graphical study aids. Tactile learners may learn best by tracing or using other hands-on methods of studying.

Handling Information: Do You Focus on Pieces or the Whole?

When you are putting a jigsaw puzzle together, do you focus more on the individual pieces and how each one fits together with the one next to it, or is your strategy to concentrate on the whole picture, keeping the finished product in mind?

The way you approach a jigsaw puzzle provides a clue to the process by which you fit together bits of information. Specifically, the strategy you use suggests which of the following two learning styles you are more comfortable with:

- People with **analytic learning styles** learn most easily if first exposed to the individual components and principles behind a phenomenon or situation. Once they have identified the underlying components involved,

---

Receptive learning style
How the initial receipt of information relates to learning preferences

Visual learning style
A style that involves visualizing information in the mind's eye, favoring reading and watching over touching and hearing

Auditory learning style
A style that favors listening as the best approach to learning

Tactile learning style
A style that involves learning by touching, manipulating objects, and doing things

Analytic learning style
A style that starts with small pieces of information and uses them to build the big picture

Relational learning style
A style that starts with the big picture and breaks it down into its individual components

they find it easier to figure out and grasp the broad picture and determine whether particular cases exemplify the principle.

- Those with **relational learning styles** learn most readily if exposed to the full range of material that they are aiming to learn. Rather than focusing on the individual components of a problem, as those with analytic styles prefer to do, people with relational learning styles do best when they are first given the full picture. They can then take this broad view and break it down into its individual components.

For example, consider trying to understand the way that food is converted to energy in a cell. A more analytic learner would approach the task by learning each individual step in the process, first to last. In contrast, a more relational learner would consider the big picture, focusing on the general, overall process and its purpose.

Students who use an analytic style study most effectively by focusing on facts and specific principles, for they excel at organizing information. They often work best on their own, and science and math may come particularly easy to them. On the other hand, students with a relational style perceive concepts globally, thinking in terms of the "big picture." They may be drawn to subject areas that demand the ability to forge a broad overview of material, such as English and history. You probably already have a good idea of whether you have an analytic or relational learning style, but Try It 1 on page 58, "Assess Your Analytical and Relational Learning Styles," will help you understand your learning style further.

Personality Styles

Our learning styles are also influenced by our personality. Are you a person who is likely to try out for school productions? Or is the idea of getting on a stage something that is totally lacking in appeal (if not completely terrifying)? Do you relate to the world around you primarily through careful planning or by spontaneously reacting?

Journal Reflections

How I Learn

1. Suppose a friend is teaching you a new and complex procedure (such as a complicated card game or the way to use a piece of computer software). Do you prefer to get the "big picture" first, or the details?

2. Do you think you would ask your friend to slow down while you get the details, or are you impatient to get started? Would you rather try doing it while your friend talks you through it?

3. Do you tend to picture things while you're learning?

4. When you're in class, what do you do during lectures—try to write down the instructor's exact words, draw pictures, jot down a few big ideas, doodle, tune out?

5. When someone gives you directions to a new place, what do you do?

6. Would you rather read a newspaper, listen to the news on the radio, or watch it on TV? Why do you think you have this preference?

7. When you get a new piece of electronic equipment, do you like to read the instructions or just "play with it" until you get the hang of it?

Try It! 1

Assess Your Analytical and Relational Learning Styles

Consider the following pairs of statements. Place a check next to the statement in each pair that more closely describes your style.

_____ 1a. Before tackling a complex task that I'm unfamiliar with, I prefer to have detailed instructions on how to do it.

_____ 1b. I prefer to "dive into" a new task, trying things out to see what happens and finding my way as I go.

_____ 2a. I like watching movies a second time because then I know where they're going.

_____ 2b. I generally don't like watching movies a second time because I know their plots already.

_____ 3a. I prefer to solve math or science problems using formulas and directions.

_____ 3b. I prefer to figure out why formulas work.

_____ 4a. When I read mystery stories, I usually let the author tell the story and reveal the mystery.

_____ 4b. When I read mystery stories, I like to try figuring out the mystery before the author reveals it.

_____ 5a. I usually read the instruction booklet before trying out a new piece of software.

_____ 5b. I never read the instruction booklet before trying out a new piece of software.

_____ 6a. I prefer to have someone who knows about a subject explain it to me before I try my hand at it.

_____ 6b. I'm impatient when others try to explain things to me, preferring to get involved in them myself without much explanation.

_____ 7a. Whenever I see a really amazing special effect in a movie, I like to sit back and enjoy it.

_____ 7b. Whenever I see a really amazing special effect in a movie, I try to figure out how they did it.

If you tended to prefer the "A" statements in most pairs, you probably have a relational style. If you preferred the "B" statements, you probably have a more analytic style. Remember that no one is purely analytical or purely relational.

According to the rationale of the *Myers-Briggs Type Indicator,* a questionnaire frequently used in business and other organizations, our personality type plays a key role in determining how we react to different kinds of situations. Specifically, the idea is that we work best in situations in which others—both students and instructors—share our preferences and in which our personality preferences are most suited to the particular task on which we are working.

According to studies done on personality, four major dimensions are critical. Although we'll describe the extremes of each dimension, keep in mind that most of us fall somewhere in between each of the endpoints of each dimension.

- **Introverts versus extroverts.** A key difference between introverts and extroverts is whether they enjoy working with others. Independence is a key characteristic of introverted learners. They enjoy working alone and they are less affected by how others think and behave. In contrast, extroverts are outgoing and more affected by the behavior and thinking of others. They enjoy working with others, and they are energized by having other people around.

> "To be fond of learning is to be near to knowledge."
>
> Tze-Sze.

- **Intuitors versus sensors.** Intuitors enjoy solving problems and being creative. They get impatient with details, preferring to make leaps of judgment, and they enjoy the challenge of solving problems and taking a "big-picture" approach. People categorized as sensors, on the other hand, prefer a concrete, logical approach in which they can carefully analyze the facts of the situation. Although they are good with details, they sometimes miss the big picture.

- **Thinkers versus feelers.** Thinkers prefer logic over emotion. They reach decisions and solve problems by systematically analyzing a situation. In contrast, feeling types rely more on their emotional responses. They are aware of others and their feelings, and they are influenced by their personal values and attachments to others.

- **Perceivers and judgers.** Before drawing a conclusion, perceivers attempt to gather as much information as they can. Because they are open to multiple perspectives and appreciate all sides of an issue, they sometimes have difficulty completing a task. Judgers, in comparison, are quick and decisive. They like to set goals, accomplish them, and then move on to the next task.

Each personality type has specific likes and dislikes when it comes to learning preferences. For example, introverts enjoy working alone, while extroverts enjoy cooperative learning and projects involving many people. Intuitors most enjoy creative problem solving, while sensors flourish with assignments that are concrete and logical. Thinkers prefer to systematically use logic to analyze a problem, and feelers enjoy assignments that involve others and their emotional reactions. Finally, perceivers favor work on which there are multiple sides to an issue, while judgers' preferences are to be decisive, determining goals and sticking to them.

The Origins of Our Learning Styles

For many of us, our learning style preferences result from the kind of processing our brain "specializes" in. **Left-brain processing** concentrates more on tasks requiring verbal competence, such as speaking, reading, thinking, and reasoning. Information is processed sequentially, one bit at a time. For instance, people who are naturally inclined to use left-brain processing might be more likely to prefer analytic learning styles, because they first like to look at individual bits of information and *then* put them together.

On the other hand, **right-brain processing** tends to concentrate more on the processing of information in nonverbal domains, such as the understanding of

Left-brain processing
Information processing primarily performed by the left hemisphere of the brain, focusing on tasks requiring verbal competence

Right-brain processing
Information processing primarily performed by the right hemisphere of the brain, focusing on information in nonverbal domains

spatial relationships, recognition of patterns and drawings, music, and emotional expression. Furthermore, the right hemisphere tends to process information globally, considering it as a whole. Consequently, people who naturally tend toward right-brain processing might prefer relational learning styles.

Facts to remember about learning, personality, and processing styles

- **You have a variety of styles.** As you can see in the summary of different categories of styles in Table 3.1, there are several types of styles. For any given task or challenge, some types of styles may be more relevant than

Table 3.1

Learning, Personality, and Processing Styles. All of us have particular learning, personality, and processing styles that we tend to rely on. At the same time, we also have capabilities in less-preferred styles. So, for example, although you may be primarily a visual learner, you have the capacity to use auditory and tactile approaches. Note in particular that the four categories under "Personality Styles" are considered independent of each other. For example, you may be an extrovert and at the same time a sensor, a feeler, and a judger.

Category	Description
Receptive Learning Styles	
Visual	A style that involves visualizing information in the mind, favoring reading and watching over touching and listening
Auditory	A style in which the learner favors listening as the best approach
Tactile	A style that involves learning by touching, manipulating objects, and doing things
Information Processing Styles	
Analytic	A style in which the learner starts with small pieces of information and uses them to build the big picture
Relational	A style in which the learner starts with the big picture and breaks it down into its individual components
Personality Styles	
Introvert versus Extrovert	Independence is a key characteristic of introverted learners, who enjoy working alone and are less affected by how others think and behave. In contrast, extroverts are outgoing and more affected by the behavior and thinking of others. They enjoy working with others.
Intuitor versus Sensor	Intuitors enjoy solving problems and being creative, often taking a "big-picture" approach to solving problems. Sensors, on the other hand, prefer a concrete, logical approach in which they can carefully analyze the facts of the situation.
Thinker versus Feeler	Thinkers prefer logic over emotion, reaching decisions and solving problems by systematically analyzing a situation. In contrast, feelers rely more on their emotional responses and are influenced by their personal values and attachments to others.
Perceiver versus Judger	Before drawing a conclusion, perceivers attempt to gather as much information as they can and are open to multiple perspectives. Judgers, in comparison, are quick and decisive; they enjoy setting goals and accomplishing them.
Brain Processing Styles	
Left-Brain Processing	Information processing that focuses on tasks requiring verbal competence, such as speaking, reading, thinking, and reasoning; information is processed sequentially, one bit at a time.
Right-Brain Processing	Information processing focusing on information in nonverbal domains, such as the understanding of spatial relationships, recognition of patterns and drawings, music, and emotional expression. Information is processed globally.

others. Furthermore, success is possible even when there is a mismatch between what you need to accomplish and your own pattern of preferred styles. It may take more work, but learning to deal with situations that require you to use less-preferred styles is important practice for life after college.

- **Your style reflects your preferences regarding which abilities you like to use—*not* the abilities themselves.** Styles are related to our preferences and the mental approaches we like to use. You may prefer to learn tactilely, but that in itself doesn't guarantee that the products that you create tactilely will be good—you still have to work!

- **Your style will change over the course of your life.** You can learn new styles and expand the range of learning experiences in which you feel perfectly comfortable. In fact, you can conceive of this book as one long lesson in learning styles because it provides you with strategies for learning more effectively in a variety of ways.

- **You should work on improving your less-preferred styles.** Although it may be tempting, don't always make choices that increase your exposure to preferred styles and decrease your practice with less preferred styles. The more you use approaches for which you have less of a preference, the better you'll be at developing the skills associated with those styles.

- **Work cooperatively with others who have different styles.** If your instructor asks you to work cooperatively in groups, seek out classmates who have styles that are different from yours. Not only will your classmates' differing styles help you to achieve collective success, but you can learn from observing others' approaches to tackling the assignment.

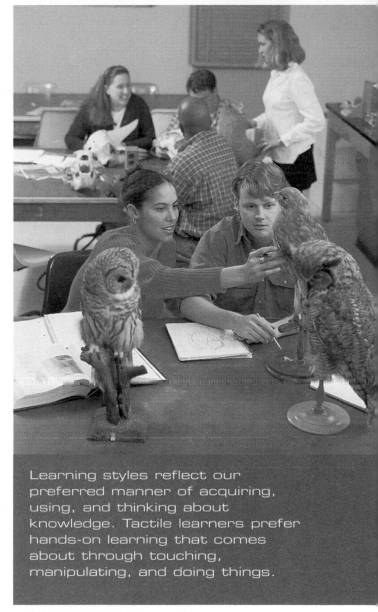

Learning styles reflect our preferred manner of acquiring, using, and thinking about knowledge. Tactile learners prefer hands-on learning that comes about through touching, manipulating, and doing things.

Using Your Instructors' Teaching Styles

In the same way that each of us has preferred learning styles, instructors have their own styles of teaching. They may not even be aware of them, but their learning styles have an important impact on the way they teach—and that, in turn, will help determine how well you do in their classes.

Instructors who make frequent requests to "list," "label," "diagram," "outline," or "define," may favor a more analytic learning style. In contrast, if their tendency is to ask you to "compare," "analyze," "discuss," "criticize," or "evaluate," they may be more in tune with relational learning.

Similarly, instructors who assign frequent projects that involve oral presentations and demonstrations might be indicating that their learning style is somewhat auditory. On the other hand, instructors whose assignments consist

Discussion Prompt: Encourage students to use the TRY IT! 2 model with other courses, without referring to instructors by name.

Try It! 2

🏂 Working in a Group: Instructor Styles

Working as a group with your classmates, try to determine your course instructor's learning style by answering the following questions:

1. What clues does the language your instructor uses give you about his or her learning style? _____
_____
_____
_____
_____

2. What assignments has the instructor scheduled, and what do they tell you about the instructor's learning style? _____
_____
_____
_____
_____

3. Are there constraints (such as class size, scheduling factors, school traditions) that also influence the instructor's teaching style, apart from his or her underlying learning style?
_____
_____
_____
_____
_____

of frequent written work may have a more visual style. Work on "Instructor Styles" (Try It 2) to get a sense of your instructor's learning style.

What if your learning styles are mismatched with those of your instructor? Several approaches might improve the situation:

Student Alert: Remind your students to make a direct connection between what faculty members value and what students chose to focus on when studying.

- **Consider the instructor's learning styles when studying.** If your natural tendency is to stick to the facts, and your instructor appears to prefer broad, conceptual views of the material, then be sure to consider the material from the instructor's broader view. In contrast, if your instructor's learning preferences lean toward factual views of material, pay special attention to the details that your instructor will likely be more interested in. For example, an instructor who focuses on the broad view is not likely to ask you to repeat a detailed series of dates of particular events during the French Revolution. Yet this may be exactly what another instructor, more focused on the details, is interested in.

  In short, if your instructor doesn't seem to share your learning preferences, pay particular attention to approaches that *don't* come naturally to you. They are the ones that may prove the most successful in the course.

- **Seek out alternative assignments.** A second approach to a mismatch between your learning styles and those of your instructor is to seek out alternative assignments. Occasionally instructors are willing to provide substitute assignments that tap into your preferences and strengths.

  What if your instructor is unwilling to accommodate your learning preferences? Instructors have many students, and it would be nearly impossible to come up with independent assignments for each one. Furthermore, many instructors feel that it is part of their job to maximize student exposure to various learning approaches—which leads to the final point about mismatches between student and instructor styles: *Understand that there are benefits to discomfort.*

- **Accept discomfort as a necessary evil.** Real learning is often difficult and uncomfortable. To become an accomplished student, you'll have to use a variety of strategies and approaches. Although you'll always have certain learning preferences, it is important to develop flexibility in the form of strategies that we'll be considering in future chapters.

"Know Thyself."

© The New Yorker Collection 1991 William Steig from cartoonbank.com. All Rights Reserved.

Learning styles are just one example of how your personal characteristics affect your academic success. We now turn to a broader consideration of who you are as we examine how your understanding of yourself influences your success in college.

Student Alert: Real learning and personal growth require hard work. It is not in our nature to seek out discomfort but it is in moments of struggle that life-altering reflection occurs.

Self-Concept: "Who Am I?"

Of course you know who you are. You know your first and last name. You know where and when you were born, and you have no trouble identifying your ethnic background. You can probably recite your social security number with ease.

But if this is all that comes to mind when you think about who you are, you're missing a lot of the picture. There's a lot more to you than name, rank, and serial number.

> "When I discover who I am, I'll be free."
>
> Ralph Ellison.

What makes you unique and special are your thoughts, your beliefs, your dreams. You have a unique past history, and this set of experiences together with your genetic makeup—the combination of genes you inherited from your parents—is unlike anyone else's.

Our view of ourselves—our **self-concept**—has three parts:

1. Our *physical self* is both who we are physically—the color of our eyes or the curliness of our hair—and how we feel about our physical form. We all have our blemishes, protruding stomachs, long noses, or other physical quirks, but we don't all feel the same way about them.

2. Our *social self* is made up of the roles we play in our social interactions with others. As you're reading these words, you're not only a student; you're also a son or daughter, a friend, a citizen, and possibly an employee, a spouse, a lover, and/or a parent. Each of these roles plays an important part in defining your self-concept. Each also helps to determine how you behave while acting in that particular role.

Self-concept
One's view of oneself that forms over time, comprising three components: the physical self, the social self, and the personal self

3. Finally, our self-concept also contains a *personal self*—our inner core, which is that private part of ourselves that no one knows about except us. It consists of the innermost thoughts and experiences that we may or may not choose to share with others.

Self-Concept and Self-Fulfilling Prophecies

The way we view ourselves determines how we interact with others, what challenges we feel ready to take on, and our expectations for future success. If you see yourself as a successful student, you are likely to expect that you'll continue to be a successful student. On the other hand, if you see yourself as an incapable, inept student, your chances for future success are diminished.

In short, our self-concept can act as a self-fulfilling prophecy. A **self-fulfilling prophecy** is the tendency to act in accordance with our expectations and beliefs, thereby increasing the likelihood that events or behaviors consistent with those expectations and beliefs will occur. In other words, believing that something will happen can lead to actions that make it more likely that it actually will happen.

For instance, a person who views herself as a poor student may find herself thinking: "Why bother working hard? I'm no good as a student; that's just the way I am." It's easy to see how such a view could lead to a self-fulfilling prophecy: By not working hard, the student guarantees that the prophecy of poor performance comes true.

On the other hand, self-fulfilling prophecies can have positive effects. A person who sees herself as a good student will probably be motivated to study and complete assignments enthusiastically. Her view of herself can therefore bring about the expected behavior—in this case, success.

To get a clearer picture of your own self-concept:

- **Examine the roles you play.** To understand who we are, we need to understand the different roles that we play in life. Consider which of these roles are central to who you are—and who you want to be. Think about the time you spend each day, and how much of it is devoted to each of these roles. Consider how an outsider might look at your actions, beliefs, and interests. How would that person characterize you?

- **Identify your strengths and weaknesses.** Look at yourself with a clear and objective eye, and consider what you do particularly well and what you don't do particularly well. If you're honest, you'll come up with several areas in which you need work—and many other areas in which you're already quite strong. (Use Table 3.2 to help you organize your thoughts and build an initial inventory of your strengths and weaknesses.)

    As you consider your strengths and weaknesses, don't place a value on them. The fact that you procrastinate and put off tasks doesn't make you a bad person, just as the fact that you're a good student doesn't necessarily make you a good person. The point in seeking to identify who you are is to determine your self-concept with accuracy, not to determine how good (or bad) a human being you are.

    Furthermore, be sure you construct your own definition of who you are. Don't let what you think others think about you determine what *you* think you're good at and bad at. See yourself through your own eyes, not somebody else's.

Self-fulfilling prophecy
The tendency to act in accordance with our expectations and beliefs, thereby increasing the likelihood that events or behaviors consistent with those expectations and beliefs will occur

IM Link: "Teaching the Text" Chapter 3—Section VII. Goal 1—To connect the information to the individual student's life.

Table 3.2

Inventory Your
Strengths and
Weaknesses

Aspects of Self	Strengths	Weaknesses
Physical Self		
Health and fitness		
Sports		
Nutrition and diet		
Appearance		
Other		
Social Self		
Friend		
Son/daughter		
Lover/spouse		
Citizen/community member		
Employee		
Student		
Roommate		
Classmate		
Team or group member (e.g., sports, band, club)		
Other		
Personal Self		
Personal experiences		
Unique traits		
Personality		
Spiritual self		
Habits		
Attitudes/opinions		
Ideas/thoughts		
Other		

Student Alert: Are your students able to answer these questions objectively? Do they appear to be either only negative or only positive?

- **Pull your selves together.** Try to form a coherent view of your self-concept. Seek to understand how the various parts of your self-concept—physical, social, and personal—fit together.

    If you consider your self-concept this way, you'll find that the whole is greater than the sum of the parts. We're not just a pile of the bodies we inhabit, the roles we play, and the experiences we have had, but something bigger and better.

- **Accept your entire self-concept.** If you're being honest with yourself, you'll find that there are parts of yourself that you like more than others. That's OK. Don't disown the parts you don't like; they're also part of who you are. Instead, accept that some parts of yourself need work, while others are the source of justifiable pride.

On the other hand, not everything we do belongs in our self-concept. If you once shoplifted when you were a child, that doesn't mean you were a juvenile delinquent then or are a criminal now. Failing a course in high school doesn't make you a failing student.

Make Sure Your Self-Concept Is Yours

Our own perceptions are not the only source of self-fulfilling prophecies. We sometimes permit *others'* views of who we are and their expectations about us to determine our behavior.

For example, if we think an instructor views us as a particularly hard worker, we may not want to disappoint him by slacking off. If we believe that our boss admires our persistence, we may be motivated to show her persistence when we're working on a difficult problem on the job.

> "Respect yourself if you would have others respect you."
>
> Baltasar Gracián.

Responding to others' positive perceptions can be fine, for the results are good. But what happens if someone holds a negative view of who we are? What if we're constantly told that we're not working hard enough . . . or that we're not as smart as our older brother . . . or that we are the hard worker, but not the creative one?

The results can be devastating. If we consistently hear such messages about who we are, we can come to believe them. Even worse, our behavior can begin to reflect the negative messages. If we're constantly told that we don't work hard enough, we may in fact *not* work very hard. If we're told we're not as smart as someone else, we may begin to think of ourselves as not very bright. Or if someone tells us we're not creative, we may not try very hard to be creative.

In short, the negative messages that we hear from others can come to act as a prison, placing us in bondage to others' negative beliefs about who we are and what our capabilities are. It's crucial, then, not to buy into others' negative views of who we are. Instead, we need to forge our own self-concept, independent of what we believe others think about us. Our biggest help, and sometimes handicap, in this effort is self-esteem.

Self-Esteem: Building a Positive View of Yourself

Discussion Prompt: Expect your students to take over the class with their need to spend time talking about self-concept and self-esteem issues. Let them! It will be time well spent.

Self-esteem

The overall evaluation we give ourselves as individuals

When you think about yourself as a student, you probably don't stop there. Instead, you likely see yourself as a "good" student, a "bad" student, or maybe a "just OK" student. Similarly, when you consider yourself in the role of friend, you may view yourself as a "loyal-to-the-end" friend or maybe, in the opposite case, a "fair-weather" friend. In short, when we look inward at who we are, we don't just stop with a characterization of the different roles that we play in the world. Instead, we place a value on them. We see the various facets of our self-concept not in neutral terms, but as either positive or negative.

Self-esteem is the overall evaluation we give ourselves as individuals. It reflects the degree to which we see ourselves as individuals of worth and determines our general acceptance of ourselves. If we have high self-esteem, we generally feel respect for and acceptance of ourselves. On the other hand, if we

Try It! 3

Measure Your Self-Esteem

To get an informal estimate of your self-esteem, complete the following scale by placing a check mark in the appropriate box after each statement.

Statement	Strongly Agree	Agree	Disagree	Strongly Disagree
1. On the whole, I am satisfied with myself.				
2. At times I think I am no good at all.				
3. I feel that I have a number of good qualities.				
4. I am able to do things as well as most other people.				
5. I feel I do not have much to be proud of.				
6. I certainly feel useless at times.				
7. I feel that I'm a person of worth, at least on an equal plane with others.				
8. I wish I could have more respect for myself.				
9. All in all, I am inclined to feel that I am a failure.				
10. I take a positive attitude toward myself.				

Scoring: For statements 1, 3, 4, 7, and 10, score as follows:

Strongly Agree	4 points
Agree	3 points
Disagree	2 points
Strongly Disagree	1 point

IM Link: "Teaching the Text," Chapter 3—Section IV. See information about using TRY IT! 3.

For statements 2, 5, 6, 8, and 9, score as follows:

Strongly Agree	1 point
Agree	2 points
Disagree	3 points
Strongly Disagree	4 point

The highest possible score (i.e., an apparently very high level of self-esteem) is 40 points, and the minimum score (i.e., an apparently very low level of self-esteem) is 10. Most people score in the 30- to 40-point range. A much smaller number of people score in the 20s. A score of 10 to 20 is often found in people who suffer from severe depression. Keep in mind that this is a very rough gauge of self-esteem, and that scores will vary depending on a number of factors, including your mood when you complete the questionnaire.[1]

Do the results of the questionnaire match your own gut feelings about yourself? Do you think your self-esteem has changed? Do you have any ideas as to why?

have low self-esteem, we generally lack respect for ourselves, reject parts of who we are, and judge ourselves negatively.

To get a sense of your own general level of self-esteem, complete the self-assessment in Try It 3.

Why Self-Esteem Matters

People with high self-esteem are generally happier and better able to cope with adversity. High self-esteem provides a sense of security, because people with high self-esteem feel they are able to deal with problems that may arise. They also have a sense of **self-efficacy,** the expectation that they are capable of achieving their goals in many different kinds of situations. High self-esteem can also give people a sense of purpose and the belief that they are productive members of society.

In contrast, individuals lacking in self-esteem are more insecure, and their belief in their ability to reach their goals is weak. They feel less tied to others, and their sense of purpose is not firm. And when others are successful, people with low self-esteem may feel jealousy and envy.

Discussion Prompt: Ask students to think about how this information is relevant to their own lives. Have they experienced a *cycle of failure* with activities or courses? How did they break the cycle?

Low self-esteem can produce a *cycle of failure* in which low self-esteem leads to low expectations, reduced effort, elevated anxiety, poor performance, and, finally, an affirmation of the low self-esteem that began the cycle in the first place. Such a cycle can be difficult to break (see Figure 3.1).

If a student with low self-esteem begins studying for a test believing that he is likely to do badly, he may put forth relatively little effort. After all, why should he bother, when he sees himself as an incompetent, inept student of little worth? Moreover, because he is virtually sure he is going to do poorly on the test, he may experience extremes of anxiety, feeling that (another) failure is lurking just ahead.

Figure 3.1

The Cycle of Failure.

Low self-esteem can lead to low performance expectations. In turn, low performance expectations can produce reduced effort and high anxiety, both of which can lead to failure—and ultimately reinforce the low self-esteem that started the cycle.

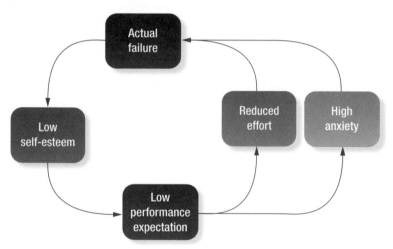

Calvin and Hobbes   by Bill Watterson

     Chapter 3   Recognizing How You Learn, Who You Are, and What You Value

Ultimately, the combination of lack of effort and anxiety produced by his low self-esteem do him in, and he actually does do poorly on the test. But the cycle of failure is not yet complete: Rather than telling himself that low effort and elevated anxiety caused his poor test performance, he views it as an affirmation of his inferior ability. In turn, this misperception serves to reinforce his low self-esteem.

Breaking the Self-Esteem Cycle of Failure

"OK," you may be saying to yourself, "I understand that self-esteem is important. But how am I supposed to ignore a lifetime of learning and improve my self-esteem? Especially when I have low self-esteem to begin with!"

It's not a simple matter to shed a less-than-ideal view of ourselves and adopt a more positive one. And you certainly won't be able to change your basic conception of yourself in the course of a few days.

But there are steps you can take to bring yourself closer to an ideal level of self-esteem. They include the following:

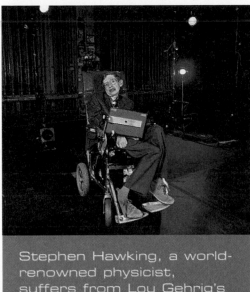

Stephen Hawking, a world-renowned physicist, suffers from Lou Gehrig's disease, a disorder that eliminates voluntary muscle control. However, despite significant physical limitations, Hawking continues to make important contributions to society.

- **Accept yourself, warts and all.** No one is perfect, and becoming a perfect person should not be your goal in life. If it were, you'd be doomed to failure, because you'd never measure up.

  Accept the fact that there are certain aspects of yourself and your life that you're not pleased with. In fact, embrace your awareness of your displeasure: If you didn't realize that there were some things about yourself that needed improvement, you'd be out of touch with who you are.

- **Understand that everyone has value and self-worth.** Every individual has value and self-worth, some unique spark that sets him or her apart from everyone else. Examine yourself and your life, and get a picture of the particulars that make you *you*.

- **Distinguish the different parts of who you are.** No one is all bad, just as no one is all good. Maybe a person who never reached the level of success she wanted to in school turns out to be an excellent employee, the person who always seems to be asked to solve problems or take on challenges no one else can deal with. Another person may not be the kind of husband he wants to be, but turns out to be a terrific parent.

  Understanding that you have failings in one arena of life doesn't mean that you can't be successful in others. It makes no sense to base your self-esteem on what you do worst in life, so don't make the mistake of focusing solely on your failings and minimizing your successes.

- **Don't just rely on—or wait for—others' praise.** Your self-esteem should not be solely dependent on the praise you get from others. Use your own judgment to evaluate the level of success you've achieved on a given task.

  For instance, you know when you've done your best in writing a paper. If you feel proud of it, celebrate your accomplishment and take pride in it. Instead of waiting for your instructor's feedback, permit yourself to feel good about what you've done. Your self-esteem should be based on your own assessment of your accomplishments, not only on others' assessments.

Teaching Tip: Look for opportunities to extend this discussion beyond the classroom—guest speakers, campus counseling services, films.

- **Understand that building self-esteem is a lifelong undertaking.** It's taken a lifetime to develop whatever level of self-esteem you currently have. Your self-esteem is not going to change overnight.

  Rebuilding self-esteem isn't easy. It's particularly hard to do at a time when you face a major life transition, such as the beginning of your college experience; your oldest friends and family may not be nearby, and the level of academic work you encounter presents new challenges. In fact, starting college presents a special opportunity to grow and develop. It's a new environment, giving you the opportunity to unlearn old patterns of behavior that have held you back and master new ones that will permit you to have a more positive view of yourself. Don't let low self-esteem keep you from becoming what you can be.

Preparing a Personal Mission Statement

The life which is unexamined is not worth living.

Twenty-five hundred years later, Plato's words are still true. If you never consider what you want out of life, what your dreams and aspirations are, and where you're heading, you're in danger of missing out on the most fundamental and meaningful parts of life. The day-to-day details of life will use up all your time, and you won't know exactly where it has gone.

One way to get a clearer picture of our life is to create a formal statement of what we actually hope to achieve during our lifetime. The P.O.W.E.R. framework provides a systematic series of steps that can help us look inward and determine the way we wish to carry out our lives.

P repare: Identifying Your Values

The first step toward understanding ourselves is to assess our underlying values systematically. To do this, work through the following steps:

Teaching Tip: The P.O.W.E.R. Process in this chapter culminates in "TRY IT! 5" (p. 75), which will be a personal reference point for each student that you should refer back to throughout the semester.

1. Choose the five values that you hold most dear. Here are some examples, but don't necessarily restrict yourself to these: a comfortable life, an exciting life, a sense of accomplishment, world peace, beauty, equality, security, freedom, happiness, inner harmony, love, national security, pleasure, religion, self-respect, fame, friendship, wisdom, work, financial security, risk taking, being challenged.

2. For each value, answer each of these questions: *why* is it important to you, *who* taught it to you, *how* has it affected your behavior in the past, and *in what ways* can you affirm it through your future behavior?

   Value #1 _____

   Why is it important:

   Who taught it to you:

   How has it affected your past behavior:

   In what ways can you affirm it through future behavior:

Value #2 _____

   Why is it important:

   Who taught it to you:

   How has it affected your past behavior:

   In what ways can you affirm it through future behavior:

Value #3 _____

   Why is it important:

   Who taught it to you:

   How has it affected your past behavior:

   In what ways can you affirm it through future behavior:

Value #4 _____

   Why is it important:

   Who taught it to you:

   How has it affected your past behavior:

   In what ways can you affirm it through future behavior:

Value #5 _____

   Why is it important:

   Who taught it to you:

   How has it affected your past behavior:

   In what ways can you affirm it through future behavior:

Organize: Placing Order on What Motivates You

Abraham Lincoln. Albert Einstein. Eleanor Roosevelt.

What is the common link among these three people? According to psychologist Abraham Maslow, each of them achieved **self-actualization,** a state of self-fulfillment in which people realize their highest potential in their own unique way.[2]

According to Maslow, self-actualization is the highest of the various needs that motivate our behavior. As you can see in the illustration in Figure 3.2, our underlying needs form a pyramid. At the bottom of the pyramid are our most basic needs, such as the biological needs that drive our behavior, including food, water, sleep, and sex. The basic needs are not much different from those that drive the behavior of nonhuman animals. The needs on the next higher level of the pyramid are safety needs; we need a safe, secure environment in order to function effectively.

But as humans are able to meet their more-basic survival needs, they have a chance to become acquainted with levels of need that relate to more-advanced qualities, such as the need for love. As the pyramid indicates, our love and belongingness needs come next: our need to form relationships with others and to look outside ourselves. We seek to give affection and to be contributing members of groups within society.

Self-actualization

A state of self-fulfillment in which people realize their highest potential in their own unique way

Figure 3.2
Pyramid of Motivational
Needs

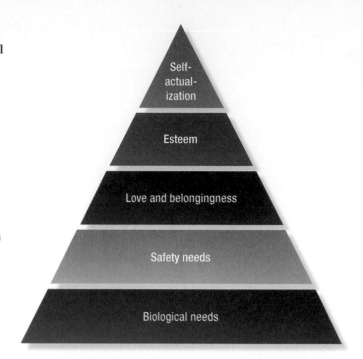

Discussion Prompt: Connect a
discussion on motivation to the
goals students set for
themselves in Chapter 1; i.e.,
"Why am I going to college?"

After these needs are fulfilled, we strive for the esteem of others. Esteem relates to the desire to develop a sense of self-worth. We want others to be aware of our competence and worth and to acknowledge our value in the world.

Only after we meet these physiological, safety, love and belongingness, and esteem needs can we strive for self-actualization. Although early views of self-actualization restricted this quality to a few well-known individuals, self-actualization is now generally regarded as a concept that can apply to any of us. For instance, a parent with excellent nurturing skills who raises a family, a teacher who year after year creates an environment that maximizes students' opportunities for success, and an artist who realizes her creative potential might all be self-actualized individuals.

> "Authentic values are those by which a life can be lived."
>
> Allan Bloom.

Teaching Tip: Don't forget to
constantly link the information
about values, motivation, self-
concept, etc., to learning
preferences and the goal of
academic success.

The crucial characteristic of self-actualization is that we feel at ease with ourselves and satisfied that we are using our talents to the fullest. Achieving self-actualization produces a relaxation of the striving and yearning for greater fulfillment that mark many people's lives. People who are self-actualized can find satisfaction in their current state of affairs.

The pyramid shown in Figure 3.2 can help you to understand yourself more accurately. Organize your needs in Try It 4 to discover the structure of your own motivational needs.

W ork: Creating a Personal Mission Statement

- *To make, distribute and sell the finest quality all natural ice cream and related products in a wide variety of innovative flavors made from Vermont dairy products.*
- *To operate the Company on a sound financial basis of profitable growth, increasing value for our shareholders, and creating career opportunities and financial rewards for our employees.*

Try It! 4

Organize Your Needs

Consider the motivational needs illustrated by the pyramid in Figure 3.2 (biological needs, safety needs, love and belongingness, esteem, and self-actualization). Using the blank pyramid below, fill in your own particular needs in the order that best illustrates your personal hierarchy of needs. Don't feel constrained by the ordering in Figure 3.2; each of us has a unique pattern of needs that defines who we are. For example, you might feel that love and belongingness are more-fundamental needs and therefore should be closer to the bottom of the pyramid. Remember, there are no right or wrong answers.

Answer the following questions about your personal hierarchy of needs:

1. What similarities are there between your order and that suggested by the pyramid in Figure 3.2?

2. What differences are there in your ordering and those suggested by the pyramid in Figure 3.2? What accounts for the differences?

3. How do the values you pinpointed earlier (see pages 70–71) relate to the needs you've described in the pyramid? Can you relate your key values to your motivational needs?

- *To operate the company in a way that actively recognizes the central role that business plays in the structure of society by initiating innovative ways to improve the quality of life of a broad community—local, national, and international.*[3]

You may have already guessed the name of the company that would make the statements reproduced above: Ben & Jerry's Ice Cream Corporation. Like almost every other major organization, Ben & Jerry's has a *mission statement,* a series of statements about what the organization does and the principles that guide its corporate life.

What's good for Ben & Jerry's is good for you. Each of us should set out a *personal mission statement*, a description encompassing our own personal objectives, long-term goals, and guiding philosophy. It's a kind of personal constitution that sets out broad principles of how we wish to conduct our lives. It is a guideline that allows us to adapt our behavior to the changing conditions of life without straying from our overall direction and purpose.

If we don't have a mission statement, or at least think about the components of one, we risk drifting aimlessly through life. Constructing a mission statement permits us to make the choices we need to make based on our own personal philosophy. It helps us to move from our abstract values and motivational needs to something concrete.

For example, consider the following mission statement created by one student:

> My mission is to use my personal abilities fully to become an engineer who will work on projects that will help others improve the quality of their lives. In addition, I hope to form meaningful relationships with others and to marry and raise children who will make their own contributions to society. Finally, I wish to participate in bettering the world by volunteering in organizations that will enhance the quality of my own community.

This mission statement reflects several underlying values and needs: the desire to use work to improve others' lives, the wish to form relationships with others, and the desire to make the world a better place. In some respects it is fairly specific (such as the desire to become an engineer and to marry and have children), while in others it is fairly vague (such as the wish to participate in organizations that can improve community life). The key point is that it provides a general framework, a way of evaluating whether any particular choice fits into this individual's overall personal mission.

To create your own personal mission statement, follow these three preliminary steps:

IM Link: "Teaching the Text" Chapter 3—Section VII. Goal 1, To connect the information to the individual student's life; connect the mission statement to the letter.

- **Summarize your most important values and motivational needs.** You've already assessed your values and motivational needs. Try to distill them into several key principles that will guide your life.

- **Consider what you want your major product to be.** Ben & Jerry's makes ice cream. What do you want to be known and remembered for? Your work? Your family? Your good deeds? Your relationships with others? Something you've created—art, photos, writings?

- **Reflect on the kind of person you want to be.** Do you wish to be kind, friendly, helpful, assertive, powerful, wealthy, altruistic?

Once you've completed these three steps, you're in a position to create your own mission statement. Write it in Try It 5.

Evaluate: Assessing Your Personal Mission Statement

After you've written a personal mission statement, consider whether it accurately captures what you are looking for out of life. Would a friend who knows you well see it as a valid reflection of who you are? Does the mission statement take a long-term view, reflecting not just where you are now, but where you wish to be in the future? Is it general enough to fit the many different circumstances in which you will find yourself?

Write a Mission Statement

1. What are your most important values (e.g., comfort, environmental awareness, kindness to others, inner harmony, challenge)?

2. What are your motivational needs (e.g., love and belonging, esteem, self-actualization)?

3. In what general area or career do you wish to work?

4. What will be your most important "product," for which you want to be known and remembered (e.g., good deeds, wealth, power, prestige, artistic creations, business acumen)?

5. What kind of person do you want to be (e.g., helpful, kind, solitary, powerful, wealthy)?

6. In what sort of community do you want to live (e.g., large city, small city, small town, suburbs, country, woods, farm)?

7. With whom do you want to live (e.g., spouse, friends, children)?

8. What words describe your ideal lifestyle (e.g., sophisticated, woodsy, agricultural, down-home, laid-back, ambitious)?

Now write a one-paragraph mission statement below. You might, for example, state how you plan to achieve your motivational needs and realize your values through your chosen career. Next you might describe the sort of person you want to be and the "product" you plan to contribute to the world. Finally, you might describe your intended lifestyle, including the type of community you would like to live in and the nature of your ideal family.

Personal Mission Statement:

Teaching Tip: Assign TRY IT! 5 as a formal writing assignment which will include composition, editing, conferencing, and rewriting.

Career Connections

Identifying Your Interests

Creating a personal mission statement can help you think more productively about one of the most important decisions of your college career: identifying your profession. One way to jump-start this process is to systematically identify your current interests, a critical step in determining what kind of work will be most fulfilling and satisfying for you. Career advisor Richard Bolles[4] suggests answering the following questions in order to identify the scope of your interests:

What are your favorite subjects and hobbies? What do you like to talk about most? When you go to a newsstand, what are the subjects of magazines that you are attracted to? When you read a newspaper, what section do you read first? If you're wandering around a bookstore, what kinds of books do you spend the most time looking at? When you surf the World Wide Web, what sites do you find yourself returning to regularly? When you watch TV game shows, what categories would you choose?

After answering these questions, prioritize them, rank ordering them from most interesting to least interesting. You can then use this rank-ordered list to investigate careers involving interests similar to your own. For example, if you have strong interests in the visual arts, you might explore careers involving graphic design, computer-assisted graphics, or architecture. If you avidly keep up with the news of the day, you might consider journalism or television news production. The critical point is to try to match what you like to do (as well as your learning- and personality-style strengths) with what you'll be doing when you're on the job. The closer the match, the happier and more successful you'll be.

Only you can determine the ability of your personal mission statement to capture what is important to you. If you feel it doesn't, rewrite it. Eventually you'll come up with a statement that illustrates what you feel makes you special.

R ethink: Reconsidering Your Options

Personal mission statements are not set in stone like the Ten Commandments. Instead, they should be considered living documents that you can change as you become clearer about what you want for yourself.

That's why it's important to periodically revisit your personal mission state-

PREPARE
Identify your values

ORGANIZE
Place order on what motivates you

WORK
Create a personal mission statement

EVALUATE
Assess your personal mission statement

RETHINK
Reconsider your options

P.O.W.E.R. Plan

ment. When you do, ask yourself if it's still representative of your values and motivational needs. Consider whether it should be amended to reflect changes that have occurred in your life.

Even if you don't modify it, periodically reading your personal mission statement is important. It will remind you of who you are and what you are trying to get out of the one life you have. (For a summary of the steps involved in creating a personal mission statement, see the P.O.W.E.R. Plan).

To Thine Own Self Be True: No One Is Responsible for Your Life but You

"Don't take too many English courses; they're a waste of time because they won't help you get a decent job." "How about doing pre-med? You'd make a great doctor." "You owe it to your family to be a business major so you can join the family business when you graduate."

Sound familiar? Many of us have heard suggestions like these proposed by parents or others close to us. Such comments are almost always well-intentioned, and often they sound quite reasonable.

Why, then, should suggestions like these be taken with great caution? The reason is they relate to decisions that you, and only you, should make. You are the one who must live with their consequences. You are the one who must live with yourself.

One of the worst reasons to follow a particular path in life is that other people want you to. Decisions that affect your life should be your decisions—decisions you make after you've considered various alternatives and chosen the path that suits you best.

Making your own decisions does not mean that you should ignore the suggestions of others. For instance, your parents do have their own unique experiences that may make their advice helpful, and they sometimes may know you better, in certain respects, than you know yourself: Having participated in a great deal of your personal history, they may have a clear view of your strengths and weaknesses. Still, their views are not necessarily accurate. They may still see you as a child, in need of care and protection. Or they may see only your strengths. Or, in some unfortunate cases, they may focus on only your flaws and shortcomings.

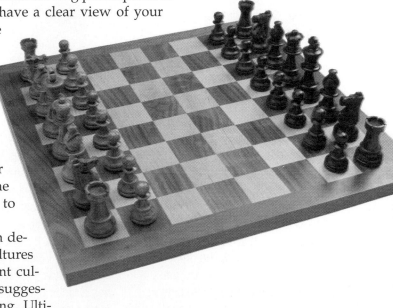

The bottom line is that you need to make your own decisions. People will always be giving you advice. It's up to you, though, to decide whether or not to heed the advice. You need to determine the course of your life and the way you want it to unfold.

It's important to realize that making your own decisions may have costs. For instance, in some cultures loyalty to family and family wishes is a dominant cultural value. If you don't follow your family's suggestions, you may be seen as rebellious and uncaring. Ultimately, though, you have to make your own judgments about what's right for you, following your head—and your heart.

Discussion Prompt: Recreate a childhood moment. Have students share a dream for the future. Ask them to respond to "If I could be anything I want to be" or a speech they might give in 10–20 years as the graduation speaker.

Speaking of Success

Name: *Bill Cosby*
Education: *Undergraduate, Temple University; Ph.D., University of Massachusetts*
Home: *Shelburne Falls, Massachusetts*

When comedian Bill Cosby received his Doctor of Education degree at the age of 40, he recounts that his mother was the happiest person at the graduation ceremony. According to Cosby, "She said to me, 'You finally got something that you can fall back on.'"[5]

Whether or not Cosby's mother actually believed what she said, it is clear that Cosby thinks that educational success has been a key part of his life. "I feel that school, achieving education and going higher, is something that I wanted to do for myself," he says.

He didn't start out in life as an educational success story. Attending school in the Philadelphia ghetto with friends Fat Albert, Old Weird Harold, Dumb Donald, and others who were later immortalized in his comedy routines, Cosby performed so poorly in the classroom that he was forced to repeat the 10th grade. He dropped out of high school and joined the Navy. Eventually, he finished high school through a correspondence course, realizing that he had to "use the intelligence I was born with."[6]

Cosby became determined to further his education. After completing his stint in the Navy, he enrolled at Temple University, supported by a football scholarship. His goal was to become a physical education teacher.

At Temple, Cosby's schedule was hectic; not only was he a member of several sports teams, but he also held down a number of part-time jobs. His most serious commitment, however, was to academics, and he maintained a B average. He commented, "If I didn't make good at Temple, I knew what waited for me was a lifetime as a busboy or factory hand. I was so afraid that I made myself do well. On an evening when all I wanted was to go out with the boys,

the specter of what might happen to me reared up, and boom, I was right back in my room studying."[7]

Cosby's life took another turn when, while in college, he began to work as a part-time bartender. Customers found him hilarious, and they encouraged him to take his brand of comedy on the road. The rest is legend: After graduating from Temple, he became one of the most successful comedians of our era.

Cosby has remained committed to education even after achieving fame and riches as an entertainer. Years after completing his undergraduate degree, he enrolled in a graduate program at the University of Massachusetts, where he received both a masters and a doctoral degree in education.

Cosby's advocacy of education has been substantial. He has supported various educational institutions with huge gifts, including $20 million to Spelman College in Atlanta. He sees education as a noble enterprise, saying, "Things are not all that hard as long as someone is there to explain it to you, and we should not be afraid of those things."

What are my learning styles, and how have they affected my academic success?

- People have patterns of diverse learning styles—characteristic ways of acquiring and using knowledge.

- Learning styles include visual, auditory, and tactile styles (the receptive learning styles), and analytic and relational styles (information processing styles).

- Personality styles that influence learning are classified along dimensions of introversion/extroversion, intuition/sensing, thinking/feeling, and perceiving/judging.

What is self-concept and how does it affect me?

- Self-concept is the understanding of the self that a person forms over time. Its major components are the physical, social, and personal self.

- Self-concept is important because of the effects it has on people's attitudes and behavior. Self-concept can act as a self-fulfilling prophecy, in that people act in accordance with their self-concepts.

How does my level of self-esteem affect my behavior?

- Self-esteem is the overall evaluation we give ourselves as individuals.

- High self-esteem can lead to greater happiness, an enhanced ability to cope with adversity, a sense of security and confidence, and a sense of self-efficacy.

- Low self-esteem can lead to insecurity, low self-efficacy, and a cycle of failure.

How can I determine my needs and make wise personal decisions throughout life?

- A personal mission statement can be used to determine important values and to state the principles by which we intend to lead our lives.

- People's needs can be organized into a hierarchy in which the most-basic and fundamental needs form the base of a pyramid and higher orders of needs sit atop the basic needs.

- Although we should take into account the ideas and opinions of others, we need to realize that we must make our own decisions and choose our own path.

Key Terms and Concepts

Analytic learning style (p. 56)
Auditory learning style (p. 56)
Learning style (p. 55)
Left-brain processing (p. 59)

Receptive learning style (p. 56)
Relational learning style (p. 56)
Right-brain processing (p. 59)
Self-actualization (p. 71)

Resources

On Campus

If you are interested in learning more about your pattern of learning styles, visit your campus counseling center or career center where you may be able to take special assessment tests that can pinpoint your learning preferences and offer study strategies based on those preferences.

When dealing with the uncertainties of life and establishing your own sense of direction, it may help to speak to someone who has perspective and experience with college students. Here, too, a good place to start on campus is either a general counseling center or one that is designed to help students choose career paths. Mental health offices can also be helpful in putting you in touch with a therapist with whom you can explore issues revolving around your self-concept and self-esteem. Don't hesitate to get help. You are doing it for yourself.

In Print

Gail Wood's 1998 book *How to Study: Use Your Personal Learning Style to Help You Succeed When It Counts* (published by the Learning Express Press) provides an introduction to learning styles that provides tips and suggestions for making use of the way that you learn.

Don't Sweat the Small Stuff . . . and It's All Small Stuff (Hyperion, 1997), written by Richard Carlson, is a down-to-earth guide that is meant to help you sort out what is—and is not—important in your life.

On the Web

The following sites on the World Wide Web provide the opportunity to extend your learning about the material in this chapter. (Although the Web addresses were accurate at the time the book was printed, check the P.O.W.E.R. Learning Web site [http://mhhe.com/power] for any changes that may have occurred.)

http://webster.commnet.edu/HP/pages/lac/styles/styles.htm
A site devoted to learning styles and their consequences for learning.

http://www.cmhc.com/psyhelp/chap3/
This site describes some recent research on human values and some of the difficulties involved in dealing with values. You may find this site helpful in sorting out your values as part of writing a personal mission statement.

http://barksdale.org/Evaluation/eval69.html
This site contains a detailed, on-line self-esteem evaluation. Simply click which response best describes how you feel about each statement. When you're done, click the submit button and your score will be automatically calculated.

Taking It to the Net

1 This exercise can help you write your own mission statement. Go to the Web page entitled "Values and Morals: Guidelines for Living" (**http://www.cmhc.com/psyhelp/chap3**) and click on "Selecting Your Guiding Principles." Scroll down the page until you find the tables listing "Ways of Living," "Values or Purposes," and "Values or Traits." Look over these items and see which of the ways of living you agree with and which of the values, purposes, and traits you think are important. Write down the most important.

2 Building Self-esteem. Go to the Web site entitled "Changing Your Self-Concept and Building Self-Esteem" (**http://www.cmhc.com/psyhelp/chap14/chap14c.htm**) and write down the seven suggested steps for changing your self-concept and building self-esteem. How do these suggestions compare to the suggestions offered in this book? Now use a search engine to locate other sources of information about raising self-esteem. A possible strategy is to go to the AltaVista home page, enter "raising self-esteem," and examine the search results. Did you locate any other suggestions for raising self-esteem? How do they compare to the suggestions in this book?

The Case of . . .

The Instructor Who Spoke Too Much

Lana Carlson, a 26-year-old woman living in Carlsbad, Missouri, was at her wits' end. The instructor in her introductory psychology class spent each 50-minute lecture talking nonstop. He barely paused to acknowledge students' questions, and his only goal seemed to be to present as much material as possible. He even gave assignments in the same fast, nasal tone that he used throughout class.

If it weren't for her friend Darren Rubbell, who was in the same class and patiently explained material after class was over, Lana would never have managed to figure out how to complete the homework assignments. The strange thing was that Darren didn't seem to have much trouble with the professor's endless talking. In fact, he claimed to enjoy the class a lot. He had no trouble following the lectures and understanding the assignments, seeming to absorb like a sponge the information the instructor was spouting.

1. Based on what you know about learning styles, what might be the source of Lana's difficulties?

2. What learning style does the instructor apparently assume all students have? Do you think this is one of Lana's learning styles? Why or why not?

3. How might the instructor change his presentation to accommodate diverse learning styles?

4. Why does Lana's friend Darren have so little trouble with the instructor's lectures?

5. Why do you think Lana has less trouble understanding Darren after class than she has understanding her instructor?

6. If you were Lana, what might you do to improve your situation?

Finding and Using Information

4

Kevin Sullivan had lost track of his friend Dan Gagnon. They had grown up in Houston, and as kids they had been inseparable. But when Dan was 12 years old, his family had moved to Tulsa, and Kevin hadn't seen him since. Although they stayed in touch for several years after Dan moved, at some point the letters began to dwindle, and they eventually lost touch. Now eight years had gone by.

As he began his first year of college, and faced the task of making a whole new set of friends, Kevin found himself thinking back on his friendship with Dan. That period of life now seemed so problem-free compared with the challenges that Kevin was facing as he adjusted to college life.

As Kevin thought about Dan, he wondered what had become of him. He realized that Dan, too, might well be starting college.

One day when he was in the college library working on a paper that required using the World Wide Web to locate some potential sources, Kevin entered the name "Daniel Gagnon" as a key term into the "Search for People" locator on the Web page he was logged onto.

To his surprise, several sites with "Daniel Gagnon" emerged. He looked at each site and found that one included some biographical information referring to a childhood in Houston. It had to be Dan! Excited, Kevin sent an e-mail, describing who he was, to the address included on the Web Site. A few hours later, Dan replied! It was like a miracle; after all those years, he and Dan were back in touch. And it had been so easy.

Looking
Ahead

Each day, tens of thousands of books and scientific articles are published. We're exposed to more information in a year than our grandparents were exposed to in their entire lifetime. Scientific knowledge doubles every seven years. Although the result doesn't always affect our personal lives the way Kevin Sullivan's Web search affected his, the increased availability of information does make finding and gathering information both easier and harder: The information you will need to complete course assignments is often easier to find, but there is more to sift through, so you need to become a good judge of information.

In this chapter we discuss information management—the ability to find, harness, and use knowledge. We'll consider information found in traditional libraries and in the virtual world of cyberspace. We'll examine how to find what we need in books and magazines and through the Internet and World Wide Web. And we'll consider how to use critical thinking skills to organize, use, and evaluate what we locate.

In short, after reading this chapter, you'll be able to answer these questions:

- **Why is knowing how to find information important?**

- **What are the basic sources for finding and gathering information?**

- **What are the most effective ways to use information sources?**

- **What do I need to keep in mind as I use information from reference resources?**

Finding Information

P repare: Becoming Acquainted with Information Sources

Before you set out to hunt for, gather, and sort through information (the steps of which are summarized in the P.O.W.E.R. Plan), you need to do several things to ready yourself—consider them survival skills for the trip ahead. As with an ascent of Mount Everest, the better prepared you are, the more likely you are to succeed.

In general, you'll find information stored in two distinct kinds of places, and you need to familiarize yourself with both of them. One you can walk or drive to—the library. The other—computer information networks—doesn't have a physical location. Both are indispensable in your quest for information.

Libraries No matter how humble or imposing its physical appearance, whether it contains only a few volumes or hundreds of thousands, the library is one good place to focus your efforts as you seek out and gather information. The library is an institution with a long and distinguished history that began literally thousands of years ago when people realized that information was so valuable that it must outlive the people who created it. Thus was born the idea of a physical place where people could store—and find—the great ideas of their time.

From the earliest stone and clay tablets, librarians eventually moved to papyrus, vellum, and finally paper for storage purposes. Now paper, long the primary medium for information storage, is giving way to new forms of storage—microfilm, microfiche, computer disks, and the World Wide Web.

Although every library is different, all share two key elements: the material they hold—their basic collections—and tools to help you *locate* the material you need.

What Can Be Found in a Library's Basic Collections? Libraries obviously contain books, but they typically have a lot more than that. In addition to the fiction and nonfiction books on their shelves, libraries usually have some or all of the following:

- **Periodicals.** *Periodicals* are magazines published for general audiences, specialized journals for professionals in a field, and newspapers. Magazines and journals are often bound and stored by year; newspapers are usually kept in **microform,** in which documents that have been photographed and greatly reduced in size are stored on either microfilm (reels of film) or microfiche (plastic sheets), which can be read with special microform readers.

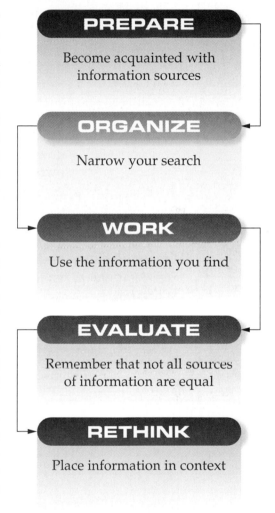

PREPARE

Become acquainted with information sources

ORGANIZE

Narrow your search

WORK

Use the information you find

EVALUATE

Remember that not all sources of information are equal

RETHINK

Place information in context

P.O.W.E.R. Plan

Teaching Tip: Go to the library. Spend time with a librarian.

Microform
A means of storing greatly reduced photographs of printed pages, which can be read using special microform readers; the two main types of microform are microfiche and microfilm

Abstract
A short summary of the contents of a journal article

IM Link: "Teaching the Text," Chapter 4—Section VII—Each of the goals suggests activities for this topic.

- **Indexes to Periodicals and Other Information Sources.** How can you learn what articles have been published in magazines, newspapers, and journals? Indexes provide the information.

  An index provides a listing of journal articles by subject area and author. Some indexes also provide a short summary, or **abstract,** of the contents of each article.

  Many kinds of indexes can be found. Some are general, such as the *Reader's Guide to Periodical Literature,* and cover a variety of general circulation magazines of the type you'd find at a decent newsstand, such as *Newsweek, Ebony,* and *Rolling Stone.* Others are more specialized and concentrate on a particular field. For instance, the *Music Index* is an index of articles about music, and the *Business Periodicals Index* provides information on articles about business.

  Indexes come in both book and computerized form. Although some people prefer to use indexes in book form, computerized indexes are considerably easier and quicker to use. Furthermore, you can often download the results of computerized searches at a library onto your own floppy disks, which you can later load into your computer.

- **Encyclopedias.** Encyclopedias provide a broad overview of knowledge. Some encyclopedias, such as the *Encyclopaedia Britannica* or *World Book Encyclopedia,* attempt to cover the entire range of knowledge, and they may take up several volumes. Others are more specialized, covering only a particular field, such as the *Encyclopedia of Human Behavior* or the *Encyclopedia of Religion.* Most are printed as multivolume sets of books, although an increasing number come in CD-ROM computerized versions. Although encyclopedias can provide a broad overview of a topic, they lack depth. Still, they provide a good general view of a topic, raising key issues that can lead you to more-specific and current sources. For this reason, they are often a good resource at the earliest stage of your hunt for information.

> "Knowledge is of two kinds: we know a subject ourselves, or we know where we can find information upon it."
>
> Samuel Johnson.

- **Rare books.** These are ordinarily stored in separate rooms and can be used only with special permission.

- **Government documents.**

- **Musical scores.**

- **Reserve collections.** Reserve collections hold heavily used items that instructors assign for a class. Sometimes reserve material can be checked out for only an hour or two and used in the same room; in other cases the material can be used overnight or for a few days.

  Most libraries offer information sheets describing all the different kinds of materials they have available and how you can find them. Find one of these sheets (often they are at the main desk closest to the entrance) and you have the key to the library.

Teaching Tip: Primary sources are much easier to identify and reference in the library than on the Web. Take time to explain this.

Using Catalogs Catalogs contain a listing of all materials that are held in the library. Because they list where the information is physically stored, they also help you find what you're looking for.

Traditionally, catalogs consisted of paper cards that were filed in trays. In large libraries, the card catalog sometimes extended across several huge rooms. Today, however, the catalogs of an increasing number of libraries are computerized. Rather than physically sorting through cards, users conduct a catalog search on a computer. In fact, you may be able to access your school's catalog from home as well as from computers housed in the library itself.

Other libraries use microform media (microfiche or microfilm), for their catalogs. And many libraries are in transition, using a combination of forms.

Although traditional card catalogs (consisting of records of information on actual cards) and computer catalogs (consisting of electronic records) are physically very different, the basic information each contains is the same. Information is usually sorted by title, author name, and subject, which means that each book (or other library holding) actually can be found in three different ways: searching for its author (*author listing*), its title (*title listing*), or its subject (*subject listing*). Individual entries generally include additional information, such as the publisher, date of publication, and similar information pertaining to the item.

Say, for example, you're writing a paper on Ernest Hemingway. To find his books in an electronic catalog, you enter his name, searching the catalog for author entries. You may be presented with the following listing:

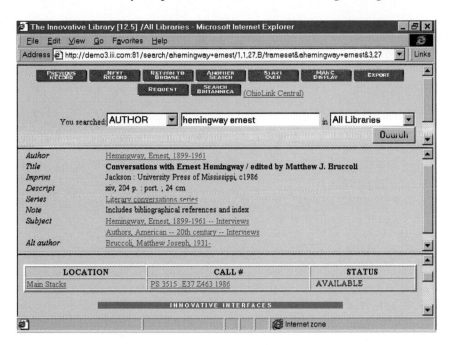

The key piece of information is the book's call number. The **call number** is a classification unique to a book that tells you exactly where to find it. Most college libraries use the Library of Congress classification system for call numbers, a combination of letters and numbers. The first letter indicates a general topical area, and the numbers provide further classification information. But you don't need to know the system; all that's really important is that it pinpoints the book's location in the library.

Because the record illustrated above is from an electronic search, it contains further helpful information. The word "AVAILABLE" under "STATUS" tells you that the book has not been checked out by another patron and should be sitting on the shelf. You'll need to familiarize yourself with your library's particular system in order to know what specific commands are available to you. Chances are there's a handout or posted set of instructions nearby. Try "Test Drive the Library Catalog" (Try It 1 on page 80) to get the hang of your school or community library's system.

Call number

A unique classification number assigned to every book (or other resource) in a library, which provides a key to locating it

Try It! 1

Test Drive the Library Catalog

Go to your college library catalog (card or electronic) and practice your research skills by looking up information on five of the following topics:

Gandhi's tactics of nonviolent demonstration

the end of the Cold War between the United States and the Soviet Union

the origins of rock-and-roll

George Balanchine's influence on ballet

the importance of the Lewis and Clark expedition

Huckleberry Finn

the Amistad revolt

cold fusion

Buckminsterfullerene

cricket versus baseball

women's basketball teams

Some topics are easier to find information about than others. Which topics among those you selected were the most difficult ones? Why do you think that the topics differ in terms of the ease of finding information? If some of the topics produced an overwhelming amount of information, how did you decide where to go first? (Later in the chapter you'll learn some tricks for choosing where to go first for information.)

Stacks
The shelves on which books and other materials are stored in a library

---

Teaching Tip: A scavenger hunt, done in teams, is an enjoyable way to introduce students to the physical space of the library.

Recall
A way to request library materials from another user who has them

---

Interlibrary loan
A system by which libraries share resources, making them available to patrons of different libraries

---

Locating Information Once you have identified the information you're seeking by using the card catalog, you need to actually locate it. In all but the biggest libraries, you can simply go into the **stacks,** the place containing shelves where the books and other materials are kept, and—using the call number—find what you're looking for. In some cases, however, you won't be permitted to enter the stacks. In libraries with closed stacks, you must fill out a form with the call numbers of the books you want. A library aide will find and deliver the material to a central location.

What if you go to the location in the stacks where the material is supposed to be and you can't find it? The most likely explanation is that the material is checked out or is in use by someone else at that time. It may also be incorrectly shelved or simply lost. Whatever the reason, don't give up. If the material is checked out to another user, ask a librarian if you can **recall** the material, a process by which the library contacts whoever has the book and asks him or her to return it because someone else needs to use it.

If the librarian informs you that the material is not checked out to someone else, wait a few days and see if it appears on the shelf. Someone may have been using it while you were looking for it, and then left it to be reshelved. If it was misshelved, the librarian may be able to find it. If the material is truly lost, you may be able to get it from another library through **interlibrary loan,** a system by which libraries share resources, making them available to patrons of different libraries. Ask the librarian for help; an interlibrary loan will take some time—between a few days and several weeks—but eventually you'll be able to get the material.

Finally, even if you do find exactly what you were looking for, take a moment to scan the shelves for related material. Because books and other materials are generally grouped by topic on library shelves, you may find other useful titles in the same place. One of the pleasures of libraries is the possibility of finding on the shelves an unexpected treasure—material that your catalog search did not initially identify, but that may provide you with exactly the kind of information you need even without your knowing it.

Life on the Internet   Be prepared: If you haven't already become acquainted with the Internet, your first encounter with it may permanently alter the way in which you keep in touch with others.

The **Internet** is a network connecting millions of computers together. Its immense "interconnectedness" permits a user to share information with virtually anyone else who has a computer. The resources available to users are vast; from your home desktop you can have access to information stored nearly anywhere around the globe. In fact, that's an understatement: Live images from as far away as the planet Mars have been transmitted to users via the Internet.

Because the Internet is constantly evolving, the best place to learn about it is on the Internet itself. Here are a few of the features that you are most likely to find useful:

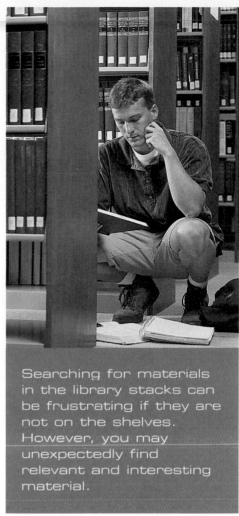

Searching for materials in the library stacks can be frustrating if they are not on the shelves. However, you may unexpectedly find relevant and interesting material.

- **E-mail.** The most widely used feature of the Internet is **e-mail,** short for "electronic mail." E-mail offers a way for people to send messages to one another instantly, and to receive replies rapidly. On some college campuses, e-mail is one of the most common forms of communication among students and faculty.

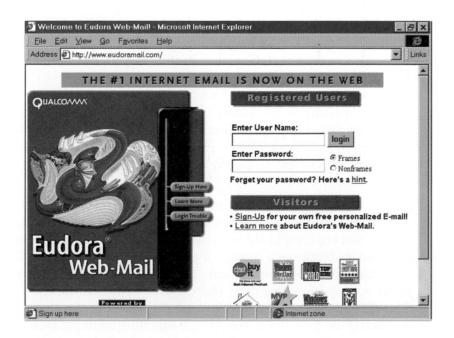

Internet
A vast network of interconnected computers that share information

IM Link: "Teaching the Text," Chapter 4, Section I. Find out what your students know before you proceed with teaching this part of the chapter. They may be able to teach it for you. Also see, Section V, PREPARE.

E-mail
Electronic mail, a system of communication that permits users to send and receive messages via the Internet

"First, they do an on-line search."

Telnet

A communication system that permits users to access computer databases and other resources

Newsgroup

An electronic Internet area in which users may post and read messages relevant to a particular topic

Listserv

A subscription service through which members post and receive messages via e-mail on topics of shared interest

World Wide Web

A graphical interface that permits users to transmit and receive text, pictorial, video, and audio information

Browser

A program that provides a way of navigating around the information on the World Wide Web

- **Telnet.** Using telnet, a dial-up communication system that permits users at remote locations to use computer databases and other resources housed on distant computers, a computer in one location can act as if it were present in another. For example, you may be able to access the catalog of your college or university's library across the campus from your dorm room. You'll still have to go over there to get the books, but you will arrive with a list of information sources in hand and won't have to risk having to wait for a terminal in the library itself.

- **Newsgroups.** The Internet contains thousands of electronic "areas," known as **newsgroups,** where people can read and post messages and news relevant to a particular topic. For example, there are newsgroups devoted to the stock market, snowmobiles, *Ally McBeal,* the Boston Celtics, the Spice Girls, and Shakespeare's sonnets.

- **Listserv Groups.** A **listserv** is a subscription service through which members can post and receive messages via e-mail on general topics of shared interest. A listserv automatically distributes messages via e-mail to people who have added their names to the listserv's mailing list. Individuals can respond to messages by replying to the listserv, and their responses will be distributed automatically to everyone on the mailing list. Among the thousands of listservs are those relating to jazz, tourism, privacy issues, and libertarianism.

- **World Wide Web.** The **World Wide Web** is a highly graphical—even multimedia—means of locating and browsing through information on the Internet. The Web is rapidly becoming the standard way to find and use material on the Internet, and many experts believe it will become the central storehouse for information in the twenty-first century. As we'll consider next, the Web provides a way to transmit not just typewritten text but pictorial information—such as graphs, photos, and video clips—and audio information as well.

The World Wide Web   Want to know how to order flowers for your girlfriend in Dubuque? Find a long-lost friend? The opening theme of Schubert's unfinished symphony? The latest health bulletin from the Centers for Disease Control?

There is one place where you can look for all this information—and stand a good chance of finding it: the World Wide Web. The Web is a computer resource that links a vast array of information to the user's computer terminal. The information may be text, photos, graphs, or video or audio clips.

Like a library, the Web involves several essential components. They include a browser, Web pages, links, and search engines.

- **Browsers.** In order to use the World Wide Web, your computer has to have a browser. A **browser,** as its name implies, is a program that provides a way of moving around the information on the Web. Among the major browsers are Netscape's Navigator and Microsoft's Internet Explorer.

    To use a browser, you indicate the location of the information that you're seeking by typing in an address. Web addresses are odd combinations of letters and symbols. They typically start off with "http://www" and then go on from there. The address identifies a unique location on the

Web page
A location (or site) on the World Wide Web housing information from a single source, and (typically) links to other pages

Link
A means of "jumping" automatically from one Web page to another

Search engine
A computerized index to information on the World Wide Web

Web, known as a *Web page* (or sometimes *Web site*), that you are directing your browser to find.

- **Web pages.** Also known as Web sites, Web pages are the heart of the World Wide Web. A **Web page** is a location on the World Wide Web that presents you with information. The information may appear as text on the screen, to be read like a book (or more accurately, like an ancient scroll). Or it might be a video clip, an audio clip, a photo, a portrait, a graph, or a figure. It may be a news service photo of the President of the United States or a backyard snapshot of someone's family reunion.

- **Links.** Web sites typically provide you with **links**—a means of automatically "jumping"—to other Web pages or to other places on that Web site. Just as an encyclopedia article on forests might say at the end, "See also *Trees*," Web pages often provide a means of reaching other sites on the Web—only it's easier than with a book, you just have to click on the link with your mouse and—*poof!*—you are there.

- **Search engines.** A **search engine** is simply a computerized index to information on the Web. Among the most popular are Yahoo!, Hotbot, AltaVista, and Excite!

  Search engines themselves are located on the Web, so you have to know their addresses. After you reach the specific Web address of a search engine, you enter the topic of the search. The search engine then provides a list of Web sites that may contain information relevant to your search.

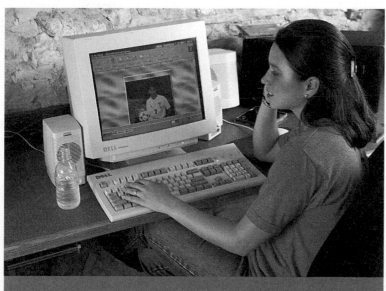

It is becoming increasingly easy for anyone to put material on the World Wide Web, and many students are creating their own personal Web page containing information and photos about their lives.

Try It! 2

Information, Please!

Try to find the answers to the following questions, using at least three of the search engines described in the text.

1. What was the French Revolution and when did it occur?

2. What are the titles of some recent biographies of Abraham Lincoln?

3. What are the words of Dr. Martin Luther King, Jr.'s "I Have a Dream" speech?

4. Is the birthrate in the United States higher or lower than that in Brazil?

5. What is the ecu?

Were some questions particularly easy or hard to answer? Why? Were there differences in ease of use of the different search engines? Which did you prefer, and why?

Some search engines, such as Yahoo!, specialize in identifying general directories of information, such as sites from which to search for information on different dog breeds, the Islamic religion, and car repair. Using this type of search engine is analogous to searching for reference books devoted to general topics in a library, rather than searching for the specific facts contained in the reference books.

Teaching Tip: Try to schedule this class in a computer lab. It makes teaching and learning this material more powerful.

Other search engines, such as Hotbot or AltaVista, are more useful when you are looking for specific pieces of information, such as who signed the Declaration of Independence, what is Viagra, and who is Keyser Soze. This category of search engine identifies pages containing specific keywords, drawn from millions of individual Web pages.

Finally, a third type of search engine is exemplified by Ask Jeeves and Dogpile. Known as *metasearch tools*, these sites send your search commands to other search engines, compiling the results into a single, unified list.

Table 4.1

Guide to Web Search
Engines

Yahoo! www.yahoo.com	An excellent, large directory of Web sites, Yahoo! is good for searching broad general topics.
AltaVista www.altavista.com	AltaVista is a very good tool for comprehensive and exact searches. Once mastered, it's easy and fast.
Infoseek www.infoseek.com	Despite its smaller index of Web pages, Infoseek's results are on the mark and suitable when searching news stories and Usenet posts.
Hotbot www.hotbot.com	Hotbot's interface requires some work to learn, but is easy to use when preparing exact search queries. Good for finding specific information.
Northern Light www.nlsearch.com	Northern Light searches pay-per-view periodical and book articles and sorts the findings into topic headings.
Lycos www.lycos.com	If you need to locate specific media types, e.g. JPEG files, Java scripts, etc., Lycos may be the engine for you. It also has advanced search abilities.
Ask Jeeves! www.askjeeves.com	A good place to start for beginners and for general queries. It also uses six other search sites simultaneously as well as guiding you through the search.
iSleuth.com www.isleuth.com	This is a specialized collection of more than 3,000 online databases. Like Ask Jeeves, it also searches six other search sites at the same time. Very good for highly specialized searches.
Excite www.excite.com	Another good engine for broad searches, Excite also finds news headlines, company information and sports scores.
Metacrawler www.metacrawler	A quick way to find out what's out there, Metacrawler uses Yahoo!, Excite, and five other search engines and then combines the results.
Dogpile www.dogpile.com	Similar to Metacrawler, Dogpile sifts through 13 search engines and scores of on-line news services. Findings are sorted by the search engine that found them. Good way to find out which search tool works best for you.

Student Alert: How have your students used this medium? Has it been for fun only or for academic purposes? They may want to share their experiences. What are the similarities and differences between using technology for entertainment and for educational purposes?

There's no single search engine that works best. In fact, most people develop their own preferences. The best advice: Try out several of them (whose pros and cons are summarized in Table 4.1) and see which works best for you. To get started, try, "Information, Please!" (Try It 2).

The Far Reaches of the Web As its name implies, the Web is vast—sometimes frustratingly so.

Although search engines permit you to locate specific information, they do not provide a complete record of everything that it is housed in cyberspace. In fact, no one knows how much material exists. Not only is more information added to the Web every day, but the information resides on thousands of individual computers. Anyone with a computer can set up a personal Web site.

The fact that anyone can put information on the Web is both the biggest asset and greatest disadvantage of using the Web as an information source. Because computer skill is the only expertise a person needs to set up a Web page,

> "Don't let that little glowing screen become an adversary. If you plan correctly, the computer can become your most useful tool at college—next to your brain."
>
> Greg Gottesman[1]

there may be as much *mis*information on the Web as there is information. Consequently, keep the usual consumer rule in mind: Buyer beware. Unless the Web site has been established and is maintained by a reliable organization, the information it contains may not be accurate. (We'll talk more about how to determine the trustworthiness of information on the Web when we discuss evaluating information sources later in the chapter.)

The various parts of the Web are similar to the components of traditional libraries as illustrated below. A Web browser is equivalent to a library; it "houses" the material. Web pages represent the books of a library; they contain the content of the information. Links are analogous to portions of books that suggest related information. And search engines are like a library's card catalog, directing you to specific locations.

Discussion Prompt: How comfortable and confident are we, and our students, with this "age of information?" What are the advantages and disadvantages of the information age? How do you and your students determine what information is important, credible, and useful?

Searching the World Wide Web   Using the World Wide Web to find information couldn't be easier—or more difficult. The ease of navigation around the Web makes finding information quite simple. At the same time, though, the mass of information that is tied into the Web can make finding *appropriate* information very tricky.

Consider the search illustrated on the next page. It is the result of entering "How do I use the World Wide Web?" into the home page of AltaVista, which is one of the major search engines that help locate material on the Web. The search identified almost ten million documents related to the topic.

Using the list of sites generated by the search is simple. With a computer

Try It! 3

Work the Web

Use the World Wide Web to locate information about the women's suffrage movement of the mid-nineteenth and early twentieth centuries. If you're doing it right, you should come across information about Susan B. Anthony, Elizabeth Cady Stanton, Lucretia Mott, the Seneca Falls Convention of 1848, the Declaration of Sentiments, the law case of *Minor* v. *Happersett,* and the 19th Amendment to the U.S. Constitution. Try to find (and print, if possible) the complete text of the Declaration of Sentiments, the 19th Amendment, and a chronology of the women's suffrage movement.

Print out or write down what you found, including source documents, bibliographies, interesting links, and dead ends (you are sure to find some strange things out there!).

Evaluate your overall satisfaction with using the World Wide Web for research on this topic. What are the advantages and disadvantages of using the Web to traditional, non-computerized research methods?

mouse, click on the site address of the relevant document, and the home page of the site will (eventually) appear on your computer screen. You can then take notes on the material, in the same way you'd take notes on material in a book.

The simplicity by which you can navigate great "distances" through the Web also can make it difficult to find exactly the material that will be most helpful. Most of what you will come across may well be of little use. In fact, it's easy to end up in a virtual dead end, in which the information you have found is only minimally related to the topic you're researching. In that case, use the "Back" command on the browser, which will allow you to retrace the route that led to the site in which you currently find yourself.

The other danger with Web searches is that you may come across information that is so fascinating that you stray off track and lose sight of what you should be doing. It's important, then, to keep in mind what you're supposed to be doing and resist the temptations that the Web offers.

Career Connections

Exploring Careers on the Web

The Web is one of the newest ways to explore careers that may interest you. You can begin to gather information by going to a Web site devoted to jobs, such as "The Catapult on Job Web" (**http://www.jobweb.org/catapult/catapult.htm**). The "Catapult" site presents a variety of career-related sites. You can also find other sites using the various search engines we've been discussing.

In addition, you can find help wanted advertisements for many jobs on the Web. In fact, it is possible to apply directly for jobs using the Web. Some firms advertise their job needs on their company sites, and you can send—directly to their site—a cover "letter" and a résumé listing your education and experience. An increasing number of jobs are obtained in this way.

Keep this in mind, too: The computer expertise you develop during college will later help you in your professional life. Already, more and more jobs require at least minimal computer skills, and every projection of the future suggests that computers will become a central facet of the workplace.

IM Link: "Teaching the Text," Section V. The P.O.W.E.R. process in the IM has several good activities for applying this information.

You and Computers: A Word to the Cyber-wary To make use of the Internet and the World Wide Web, you'll need to be familiar with computers—a device about which most of us have strong reactions. (To explore your feelings about computers, complete the *Journal Reflections* on page 97.)

If you are not yet at ease with computers, relax. With sufficient practice, using a computer will become second nature. No one is born with computer skills. Those computer wizards we're all familiar with, fearlessly sitting at a keyboard and tapping away—they, too, at some point knew nothing about computers. But they learned, and so can you. In fact, it's as much a necessity to learn to use a computer as it was for you to learn to use a calculator earlier in your schooling. No one facing the job market in the twenty-first century will want to leave college without basic computer skills.

Using Computers to Present as Well as Gather Information

What can computers do for you, aside from providing the gateway to library catalogs, e-mail, and the World Wide Web? Probably the most frequent use of computers by students is for writing. *Word-processing programs* turn a computer into a smart typewriter—a *very* smart typewriter. With a word-processing program, you can check the spelling of the words you type, automatically keep track of your footnotes, and "cut and paste" material with incredible ease. Most important, word processors take the sting out of revision. With no pain or sweat, you can quickly delete words and sentences that you don't want, substitute new material in place of what you deleted, and rearrange words, sentences, and entire paragraphs.

Other types of programs are also helpful. *Spreadsheet programs* help you with budgeting and financial projections and are necessary for accounting and engineering courses. *Presentation programs* can help you create slide shows and other visual materials that include words, charts, maps, and other graphical elements.

If you aren't yet at ease with computers, consider taking a workshop or class on the topic, offered by almost every college. In just a few hours, you'll be able to learn word processing and other basic computing skills. It doesn't take long to become proficient, and your mastery of basic computer skills is a prerequisite for achieving college—and, ultimately, occupational—success.

Organize: Narrowing Your Search

The biggest information management task most of us face is not the task of finding information. After taking advantage of the library and Web, we typically have just the opposite problem: too much information.

How you select and organize what you've found often makes the difference between success and failure. Keep in mind these tips for organizing information effectively:

- **Determine what you're looking for.** Suppose you have to write a paper for your biology class, and, because you have a good friend with AIDS, you decide to write about the disease. You go to the library card catalog and find that your college has dozens of books about AIDS. You take a look at the World Wide Web and the situation is even worse, with literally thousands of references to AIDS. What do you do next?

  You need to refine your topic, transforming it from a broad, open-ended domain to something more restricted and manageable. Look at a few of the sources you've found and consider the major issues surrounding AIDS. Perhaps some of the books have chapters on particular subtopics, such as potential cures for the disease or its effects on ethnic minorities. Because these topics are narrower, they make a more manageable topic for a paper. Try the exercise "Narrow Your Topics" (see Try It 4 on page 98) to learn more about ways to refine topics so that gathering information is easier.

- **Identify the key sources of information.** Every field has experts, and you need to make sure that you consider what they have said about your topic. How do you identify the experts? One way is to read through several books and see whose names keep popping up. Another way is to

Journal Reflections

How I Feel about Computers

1. If you had to characterize your general reactions when you hear the word "computer," what would you say?

2. How would you characterize your level of computer use in the past?

3. Do you anticipate that your level of computer use will change? Why or why not?

4. How satisfied do you feel with your level of expertise in using computers?

5. Do you enjoy learning new information about computers?

6. How do you feel about classmates who are experts in the use of computers? Do you think of them as "computer geeks"? Why do you think this stereotype about computer experts exists?

7. Do you think it is necessary to know how computers work in order to be able to use them effectively?

8. Do you think it is harder for older adults to learn about computers? Why or why not?

9. How comfortable are you asking for help if you have problems using a computer?

Try It!
4

Narrow Your Topics

Here are some broad topics for research that desperately need refining. After each, write down how you might go about generating a narrower question or topic that would be more suitable—and easier to research—for a paper that you might write. A few samples are given for the first broad topic to give you an idea of how to approach the others.

> French impressionist painters
>
> *I could narrow this topic first by focusing on one or another of the painters themselves such as Monet or Renoir and then go on to focusing on a painting or two of theirs or on some period of their lives. Or I could choose one aspect of the impressionist movement—its use of light, way of viewing nature, or how the idea of painting one's inner impressions came about.*

Now do the same thing for four of the topics below:

rap music

gender differences in education and work

ancient Greek philosophy

religion in the United States

the stock market crash of 1929

Milton versus Shakespeare

the big bang theory

human space travel

the Civil Rights movement

professional sports in the United States

Which of these topics was the most difficult to narrow? Is there a danger in narrowing a topic too much? In a group, compare your responses with those of your classmates. Which of your responses were most similar to those of your classmates? What was it about the original broad topic that led to the similarity?

use an encyclopedia to get an overview of your topic. Encyclopedia articles often end with suggested readings; these can guide you to the appropriate sources of information.

- **Keep in mind what you're going to do with the information.** As you begin to do your research, keep your goal in mind. Are you writing a short, two-page paper giving your opinion? A longer term paper? A speech? A worksheet? Knowing what you need to do with the information will help you to organize your information search appropriately.

- **Learn the key issues and controversies.** Every field has key issues and certain controversies that remain unresolved. For example, in psychology, one key issue is whether human nature is the product of biology in the form of genes and biochemical processes or the result of the influence of environment—the culture, religion, and historical events of a particu-

IM Link: "Teaching the Text," Chapter 4—Section V. The P.O.W.E.R. process has a good activity for dealing with controversial material.

lar time and place. Identifying these sorts of issues and controversies from the earliest stages of your research will ensure that you cover what is most important. They can also make the assignment you're seeking to complete—whether it's a paper, a speech, or a report—far more interesting than a mere recitation of facts. For instance, a paper on the treatment of cancer could focus on the use of herbal remedies and other nontraditional treatments that arouse great disagreement among physicians.

- **Use librarians effectively.** The stereotype of a librarian as someone whose main job is to stop people from talking in the library is dead. Librarians today are masters at information management—people who can help you find your way through a huge range of data sources and steer you to the right material.

    Make use of librarians—but do it properly. Start by looking for the information yourself. Then, if you're having trouble sorting through what you've found (or can't find material in the first place), ask for help.

    The better the question, the better the answer. Don't ask vague, unfocused questions (e.g., "Where are the books about nuclear power?"). Instead, sharpen your question, being as precise as possible ("I'm writing a paper on the environmental effects of using nuclear power to generate electricity. I've found two books, but they're not quite right. I wonder if you have any ideas about where I might find additional material?").

    Don't be afraid to ask. Think of librarians as highly trained guides who can save you hours of aimless wandering in an increasingly dense forest of information.

Using Information

W ork: Using the Information You Find

You've found the information that you've been seeking, and you've selected and organized it, focusing on the topic of your research. Now what?

Although we'll be concentrating in future chapters on how to prepare written and oral reports using the sources you have located, it's important to begin the process of putting the information you've gathered into a form that you can use in the future. One time-honored technique that works best is using file folders and note cards.

Assembling Information Folders After you have gathered information, break it down into subtopics by placing the raw information you've located (photocopies, computer printouts, and computer disks) into different multicolored file folders, one folder for each subtopic. Label each folder with a stick-on "Post-it" type label, which will permit you to easily modify the topic of the folder if necessary in the future. This initial sorting will permit you to take the next step in information management: creating note cards.

Note Cards: The Researcher's Basic Tool Taking notes on three-by-five-inch index cards is the best way of transforming information into a form that can easily be used. They may be low-tech, but they are

Try It!
5

Take Note

Read this passage:

> Selecting a target market is a matter of identifying the group of potential customers who are most likely to respond to your marketing efforts. This leads to an obvious question: Why not try to market your products to everyone and anyone? In some cases, this is in fact the best approach. If you market gasoline, potatoes, electricity, or some other product that most people need, it makes sense to market far and wide. Arco, for instance, would be happy if everyone bought the company's gasoline. However, in many situations, it doesn't make sense to market a particular product to every person on the planet. If someone isn't a likely customer, you'll waste both time and money trying to convince him or her to buy.[3]

Use the following note cards to take notes on this passage. Take the notes as if you were preparing to use this passage to support points you will make in a research paper on persuading consumers to use a common product.

Do any cards contain more than one major idea? How difficult was it to place ideas on the cards in your own words? Did you quote anything directly from the passage, and, if so, did you place quotation marks around it? Did you remember to identify the source on each note card?

Be careful when you put ideas into your own words. It's not just a matter of rearranging the words and choosing synonyms for them. For instance, consider the following passage from the book *Nation of Nations:*[4]

> In the 1860s they had come in a trickle; in the 1870s they became a torrent. They were farmers from the East and Midwest, black freedmen from the rural South, and peasant-born immigrants from Europe. What bound them together was a craving for land.

Here's one way of rephrasing the passage, but one that is so close to the original that it amounts to plagiarism:

> In the 1860s they had come in a drizzle; in the 1870s, they became a deluge. There were crop-growers from the East and Midwest; former black slaves from the rural South, and common people from Europe. Holding them together was a hunger for land.

A more appropriate rewording of the original passage would be the following, which more clearly rephrases the authors' ideas:

> There was a great deal of growth in the number of settlers from 1860 to 1879. The settlers represented several groups, including farmers from the eastern and midwestern United States, former Southern slaves, and poor Europeans who had come to the United States to better their lives. They all shared a dream of obtaining land.

We think you may be suffering from information underload.

Even in this case, it is still necessary to cite the source of the facts or ideas that you are rephrasing by adding a footnote reference to the original work. The keys to avoiding plagiarism are to use your own words and, if you use the words, ideas, or thoughts of others, to be sure to cite the source. On the other hand, it is not necessary to have a citation after every sentence. Some facts are so basic ("Japan and Germany were the enemies of the United States in World War II") that no source is necessary.

Keep in mind, too, that you must cite material that you find on the World Wide Web. Just because the material may appear on your home computer screen, it still was produced by someone else, and the author must be given credit. Although the rules for how to cite material found on the Web are still developing, it is still necessary to provide the source of anything you come across on the Web. At the very least include the site name, Web address, and author. (Try the exercise "Summarize, Don't Plagiarize," Try It 6, on page 104, to get some practice in the art of gathering information and ideas without stealing them.)

Student Alert: Many college campuses use student judicial boards to handle issues involving academic integrity. Invite one of the students to speak to your class.

Evaluate: Remembering Not All Sources of Information Are Equal

Having gathered and organized a great deal of information as you begin to work it into your final product, you must use your critical thinking skills to evaluate the information you have found. Some of the important critical thinking questions you must address before you can feel confident about what you've found include the following:

Try It!

6

 Working in a Group: Summarize, Don't Plagiarize

First, try to capture in your own words the overall meaning of at least two of the following quoted passages, without copying or plagiarizing them in any way. Assume that you intend to reflect the main points of each author in a paper of your own. Decide whether you would cite the work in a footnote or other reference within your paper.

1. From *No Ordinary Time* by Doris Kearns Goodwin (New York: Simon & Schuster, 1995), pp. 628–629, on the political relationship between President Franklin D. Roosevelt and his wife, Eleanor.

   > It was said jokingly in Washington during the war years that Roosevelt had a nightly prayer: "Dear God, please make Eleanor a little tired." But in the end, he often came around to her way of thinking. Labor advisor Anna Rosenberg had been one of those who criticized Eleanor's unceasing pressure on the president, but years later she changed her mind. "I remember him saying, 'We're not going to do that now. Tell Eleanor to keep away; I don't want to hear about that anymore.' And then 2–3 weeks later he would say, 'Do you remember that thing Eleanor brought up? Better look into it, maybe there's something to it—I heard something to indicate that maybe she's right.' I'm not sure she would have had the opportunity to bring things to his attention unless she pressured him—I mean he was so involved and in retrospect it was never anything for herself. . . . He would never have become the kind of President he was without her."

2. From "The Streak of Streaks" in *Bully for Brontosaurus* by Stephen Jay Gould (New York: W.W. Norton & Company, 1991), pp. 466–467, on baseball player Joe DiMaggio's 56-game hitting streak in 1941:

   > Ed Purcell, Nobel laureate in physics but, for purposes of this subject, just another baseball fan, has done a comprehensive study of all baseball streak and slump records. His firm conclusion is easily and swiftly summarized. Nothing ever happened in baseball above and beyond the frequency predicted by coin-tossing models. The longest runs of wins or losses are as long as they should be, and occur about as often as they ought to. . . .

Discussion Prompt: Should the World Wide Web be regulated? Has the lack of regulation caused more harm than good?

- **How authoritative is the information?** It is absolutely essential to consider the source of the material. Approach every piece of information with a critical eye, trying to determine what the author's biases might be. The best approach is to use multiple sources of information. If one source is divergent from the others, you may reasonably question the reliability of that source.

  Another approach is to consider the publisher of the material. For instance, books published by well-established publishers are carefully reviewed before publication to ensure their accuracy.

  Be especially critical of information you find on the World Wide Web. It's important to keep in mind that the Web is completely unregulated and that *anyone* can put *anything* on the Web.

But "treasure your exceptions," as the old motto goes. Purcell's rule has but one major exception, one sequence so many standard deviations above the expected distribution that it should never have occurred at all: Joe DiMaggio's 56-game hitting streak in 1941. . . . Purcell calculated that to make it likely (probability greater than 50 percent) that a run of even 50 games will occur once in the history of baseball up to now (and 56 is a lot more than 50 in this kind of league), baseball's rosters would have to include either four lifetime .400 batters or 52 lifetime .350 batters over careers of 1,000 games. In actuality, only three men have lifetime batting averages in excess of .350, and no one is anywhere near .400 (Ty Cobb at .367, Roger Hornsby at .358, and Shoeless Joe Jackson at .356). DiMaggio's streak is the most extraordinary thing that ever happened in American sports.

3. From "General Relativity" in *Who's Afraid of Schrodinger's Cat?* by Ian Marshall and Danah Zohar (New York: William Morrow and Company, 1997), pp. 170–171.

In 1916, Albert Einstein proposed an interaction between mass-energy and the structure of space-time. Mass-energy produces "curvature" in space-time—i.e., it deviates from flat, Euclidean space. Curved space-time in turn changes the paths of mass-energy through it. . .
.

One test of the worth of any new scientific theory is whether it offers us additional predictions. How do the predictions of General Relativity differ from those of Newtonian gravity? One obvious one is that curved space will deflect not only matter but also light rays passing through it. Thus, light from a distant star should be deflected if it passes near the sun. Newtonian gravitation predicts a similar effect, but only half as much. During an eclipse of the sun in 1919, the measured deflection of light from a distant star won international acclaim for Einstein's theory. Given the technology of the time, one other experimental verification was possible, an explanation for an anomaly in the orbit of Mercury, and this, too, was achieved successfully.

After you summarize the passages on your own, compare your answers with those of other classmates in a group. What are the different approaches taken by others in your group in attempting to restate the main points in their own words? Were any of the passages particularly difficult? Why? Is there one best way to capture the main points of the author of each passage? Discuss whether certain topics might present more difficulties in summarizing than others and ways that you might overcome those difficulties.

One way of evaluating Web information is to consider a site's sponsor. Commercial Web pages (whose address includes the letters *.com,* short for commercial) often tend to include the least objective material. On the other hand, addresses including the letters *.gov* (government), *.org* (nonprofit organization), *.mil* (military), and *.edu* (educational and research institutions) generally include more objective information. Still, each site must be evaluated on its merits.

- **How current is the information?** No matter what the discipline, information is changing at a rapid rate. Even a field like Chaucerian English, which concentrates on poetry written in the fourteenth century, advances significantly year by year as scholars make new discoveries, come to new insights, and reach new conclusions.

Teaching Tip: The group work suggested in TRY IT! 6 is a good opportunity to check and see if your students are understanding what you are teaching.

Consequently, don't assume that, because you're researching a historically old topic, old sources will suffice. Consider whether what you've found is the most recent and up-to-date approach. Compare older sources to newer ones to identify changes in the ways in which the topic is considered.

- **Is anything missing?** One of the hardest questions to answer is whether your research is complete. Have you found all the relevant sources? Have you missed anything that is important?

  Although there is no way to answer these questions definitively, you can do a couple of things. The best way to ensure that you haven't missed anything important is to check out the sources that you have found. Many will have bibliographies and lists of suggested additional readings. By carefully considering this information, you'll be able to get a good sense of the important work in your topic area and to verify that you haven't overlooked some critical source.

  You can also talk to your course instructor, describing generally what you've found. Librarians can also be helpful; they may be acquainted with the general topic and know the most definitive sources in the field.

R ethink: Placing Information in Context

The Information Age presents us with great promise and opportunity. Through the use of media such as e-mail and the World Wide Web, we have at our fingertips the ability to communicate with others around the world. We can break the bounds of our physical location and reach across geography to learn about others. The computer keyboard truly can be said to contain "keys"—to the entire earth and its peoples.

At the same time, the world of information can be overwhelming. It's important, then, to revisit our information-seeking strategies by taking the following points into account:

- **Consider alternative types of information.** Information comes in many forms, and you should make sure that you have exhausted every potential source on your topic. For example, libraries sometimes house graphics and audiovisual material, such as videotapes, audiotapes, compact disks, and CD-ROMs. Television, which includes both daily news programs and newsmagazines such as *60 Minutes* and *20-20*, can provide a useful source of information. Finally, once you identify experts in a field, you might try to contact them via letter, phone, or e-mail if you have a specific question that you wish answered. They won't always have the time to respond in a detailed fashion, but it's worth a try.

"Knowledge, in truth, is the great sun in the firmament. Life and power are scattered with all its beams."

Daniel Webster.

- **Gather information from more than one point of view.** Don't settle for one viewpoint. Even if there is consensus on an issue, some dissenters from the predominant view are sure to exist. Seek them out and try to figure out why they hold the views they do. This can help you to better understand the dominant view and may even spur you to reconsider your own opinion or to express it in a new way.

Speaking of Success

Name: *LeAlan Jones*
Education: *Florida State University*
Home: *Tallahassee, Florida*

When LeAlan Jones, a student at Florida State University, goes to his college library, he knows that it contains an achievement that few college students can claim: a book of which he is co-author.

Jones, who grew up in an impoverished inner-city neighborhood, co-authored *Our America: Life and Death on the South Side of Chicago,* a book about his life while he was still in his teens. The book grew out of a public radio series on life in a Chicago housing project in which Jones was featured. Ultimately, the series resulted in the book, a revealing look at the despair and tragedy that are all too common among those who live in poverty. But Jones is also proof that, with determination, discipline, and firm commitment, people cannot only overcome despair, but also realize their hopes.

Jones chose to attend Florida State University because of the reputation of its curriculum in criminology and because it allowed him to escape the diversions of urban living.

"I came all the way to Florida because I didn't want to deal with city life any more," Jones says. "I wanted an environment where I wouldn't be distracted. You have to study a lot more in college than you do in high school, so I had to find a place to study that wouldn't affect my concentration."

Enrolling in college challenged Jones to identify the things that were most important for him to achieve academically.

"When you first start college you'd better prioritize. Otherwise, you can try to do too much too soon and you mess everything up. It's important to step back and see where everything is at—and where you're at.

"I put in at least one to two hours every day studying. If you constantly stay with your studies you shouldn't have a heavy week, where you have to put in more hours. I make an effort to study every day.

"Studying is basically easy if you approach it with a plan," he adds. "The whole idea is that you have to put time and effort into it. I try to study as often as I can when I have the time. You have to keep up good study habits, and you have to discipline yourself to study. You have to let it flow.

"In high school I was a pretty average student with the potential to be a better student if I just worked a little harder. In college I began to realize that I could be a great student if I would put just a little more effort into studying. I find I can do that if I just make sure I'm not distracted by other things."

- **Identify your own biases and assumptions about a topic.** We are not empty-headed vessels into which information simply flows, like coffee into a cup. Instead, we consider information in terms of the considerable amount of knowledge we already have. Ask yourself whether your prior knowledge is affecting the way you view the new information to which you're exposed. Have you looked at it as objectively as possible? Do you know what your own biases are? Are you open to new information that might contradict your existing beliefs and feelings?

- **Use information to improve your own life.** Finally, don't get so caught up in gathering material for course assignments that you neglect thinking about how you can use information on a personal level. Wander around the stacks of the library and find a book you want to read. Surf the Web and see what you come across. Taking a break from the serious business of college will help you to concentrate more when you do go back to work.

Looking Back

Why is knowing how to find information important?

- The availability of information has increased so dramatically and continues to increase so rapidly that information management—the ability to find, focus, and use information—has become an essential survival skill.

What are the basic sources for finding and gathering information?

- Information in libraries is available in paper form and in several electronic forms, including microfilm, microfiche, computer disks, and the World Wide Web.

- The Internet is a network of linked computers throughout the world that permits users to share information which is physically located at numerous locations. Internet applications include e-mail, telnet, bulletin boards and newsgroups, listserv groups, and the World Wide Web.

- The World Wide Web is a computer resource that links a vast array of electronic information to users' computer terminals. Web users access Web "pages" (or sites) by using a browser, and may move from site to site by following links on each Web page.

What are the most effective ways to use information sources?

- After gathering information, users need to break it down into subtopics. One way to do this is to put the raw information—photocopies, computer printouts, and computer disks—on each subtopic into a separate file folder.

- The easiest procedure for translating raw information into a usable form is to take notes on three-by-five-inch index cards. Computers may also be used as a replacement for actual cards.

What do I need to keep in mind as I use information from reference resources?

- It is crucial to avoid plagiarism—passing off someone else's words or ideas as one's own.

- An important step in using information for research is evaluating the worth of the information that has been gathered by considering how authoritative the source is, whether the author has any potential biases, how recent the information is, and whether anything important is missing from the research.

- As you gather new information, think how it fits with your prior knowledge, and try to identify personal preconceptions or biases that may interfere with your ability to take in the new ideas.

Key Terms and Concepts

Abstract (p. 86)
Browser (p. 90)
Call number (p. 87)
E-mail (p. 89)
Interlibrary loan (p. 88)
Internet (p. 89)
Link (p. 91)
Listserv (p. 90)
Microform (p. 85)

Newsgroup (p. 90)
Plagiarism (p. 100)
Recall (p. 88)
Search engine (p. 91)
Stacks (p. 88)
Telnet (p. 90)
Web page (p. 91)
World Wide Web (p. 90)

Resources

On Campus

The librarians at your college library are the people to whom you should turn first if you need help in locating information. In recent years, librarians—most of whom hold advanced degrees—have undergone a significant change in what they do, and most are now equally at home using traditional print material and searching electronic information storehouses.

If you are having difficulty in gaining access to the World Wide Web, you may also find help at the college computer center. Most campuses have consultants who can help you with the technical aspects of computer usage.

In Print

The fourth edition of *Find It Fast: How to Uncover Expert Information on Any Subject* (HarperCollins, 1997), by Robert Berkman, provides a step-by-step guide to locating information of all sorts. A more specific how-to-do-it guide is Iris Blanc and Kathy Berkemeyer's *Learning Microsoft Word 97* (DDC Publishing, 1998), which introduces the basics of the most popular word processor, Microsoft's Word. Finally, Danny Goodman's *Living at Light Speed: Your Survival Guide to Life on the Information Superhighway* (Random House, 1995)

provides clear instruction and explanations for using the information super-highway.

On the Web

The following sites on the World Wide Web provide the opportunity to extend your learning about the material in this chapter. (Although the Web addresses were accurate at the time the book was printed, check the P.O.W.E.R. Learning Web site [http://mhhe.com/power] for any changes that may have occurred.)

http://wombat.doc.ic.ac.uk/foldoc/index.html
Free on-line dictionary of computing. If you're having a hard time trying to figure out some computer jargon, this site—a dictionary of computer termi-nology—might help. Topics are listed alphabetically, and a search engine helps locate specific information.

http://www.mjrb.org/islas/islas_05.htm#areas
Windows—An Overview. This site offers a brief overview of the Windows operating systems, with helpful descriptions of the workings of many Win-dows features. Especially helpful are the illustrations of different features and functions.

http://www.ipl.org
The Internet Public Library. This is the first public library on the Internet. Its mission is to discover and organize high-quality information resources. It offers an online text collection of over 7,000 titles, with a search engine to help you find what you're looking for, plus guides to periodicals and newspapers.

http://www.yahoo.com
This is a very popular Internet search engine, arranged for searching by specific topics or for browsing through prearranged categories (e.g., educa-tion, health, social science, and more). It also offers easy access to the latest news headlines and weather forecasts.

Taking It to the Net

1 Go to the University of California, Berkeley, library site (**www.lib. berkeley.edu/TeachingLib/Guides?Internet**). When you get there, click on "Teaching Library WWW Tutorial." Try the tutorial, which will help you understand many of the basic skills needed to use the Internet effectively.

2 To see for yourself how the Web can be a great resource for locating in-formation on important issues, try to find the answer to this question: "What are the effects of media violence on children?" Go to a search engine (try **www.northernlight.com**) and type in: "media violence and children" (be-ing sure to include the quotation marks). Look over the first page of docu-ments that the search engine turns up. Are they in fact about the effects of me-dia violence on children? Do they answer the question you are asking? What *is* the answer to the question?

The Case of . . .

Finding the Cure?

There it was. Not just in black and white, but in full color, and right before Trisha's eyes: a description of a drug that cured the kind of cancer that her Aunt Sally had.

Trisha had been randomly surfing the Web, not even thinking too much about where she was heading, when she found herself at a Web site featuring a discussion of different forms of cancer. When she followed a link to cancer of the uterus—her aunt's disease—she found a description of a research study that reported a reduction in uterine cancer for 16 people after they had taken a particular drug. The drug was not available in the United States, but it could be bought in Mexico.

Trisha was excited, but cautious, because she knew that her aunt's physicians had said no drug was effective for her. But then Trisha followed more links relating to the drug, and she found other research that seemed to support the effectiveness of the drug, as well as several people's accounts of how the drug had helped them. She was becoming convinced that she'd found something important and that perhaps the information would help prolong her aunt's life.

1. No one is ever completely objective, but why might Trisha be even less objective than the average person?

2. How might Trisha verify the validity of the information about the drug reported on the Web? Would it best to seek out more information on the Web, ask physicians she knows, or go to some other sources? What might such alternative sources be?

3. If the description of the drug study had appeared in a respected medical journal, such as *The Journal of the American Medical Association,* would Trisha be justified in being less skeptical in believing it? Why or why not?

4. If Trisha finds other Web sites that seem to support the value of the drug, will this be proof of the drug's efficacy? Why or why not?

For Hill Taylor, the realization that something fundamental had changed came when he went to his first class in the second term of college. Instead of taking a seat in the back row of class—as he had done in high school and at the start of his first college term—he sat down in the first row.

The change had come as a result of a workshop on notetaking he had participated in last semester after getting C's on three midterms. He had done every assignment and even reviewed extensively, but it turned out that what he reviewed—his notes—was the problem. In the workshop, he'd learned ways of making sure you got the important information down as you listened to lectures or read assignments. He tried them out, and—a bit to his surprise—found they helped. By the end of the semester, he'd pulled his grades up.

At the same time, Hill's improved notetaking skills led him to pay more attention in class, something he found easier to do sitting closer to the front. As a result, he had become considerably more engaged and interested in what his instructors were saying and ended up with some of the best grades of his scholastic career so far.

Looking
Ahead

Hill Taylor's move from the back to the front of the classroom was both a source and a symbol of his academic success. Hill's ability to take good notes was also likely to pay future dividends, because notetaking skills not only help produce academic success in college, but also contribute to career success.

In this chapter we discuss effective strategies for taking notes during class lectures, during other kinds of oral presentations, and from written sources such as textbooks. There's a lot more to good notetaking than you probably think—and a lot less if you view notetaking as essentially "getting everything down on paper." As we consider notetaking, we'll pause along the way to discuss the tools of the notetaking trade, how to think your way to good notes, and how to deal with disorganized instructors.

After reading this chapter, you'll be able to answer these questions:

- **What is effective notetaking?**

- **How can I take good notes in class?**

- **What techniques apply to taking notes from written materials?**

Student Alert: Students will tell you they need to learn new study skills but they will not easily change familiar habits such as how they take notes. Encourage them to systematically adopt the strategies in this chapter for a month before they decide to return to their old ways.

Taking Notes in Class

You know the type: the student who desperately tries to write down everything the instructor says. No spoken word goes unwritten. And you know what you think to yourself: "If only I could be so industrious, so painstaking in the notes I take, I'd do much better in my classes."

Teaching Tip: Ask students to bring the syllabus to class every time. Suggest that students ask if their faculty members update their syllabus on a web page or through some other format.

Contrary to what many students think, good notetaking does not mean writing down every word that an instructor utters. With notetaking, less is often more. We'll see why as we consider the basic steps in P.O.W.E.R. notetaking (summarized in the P.O.W.E.R. Plan).

Prepare: Considering Your Goals

As with other academic activities, preparation is a critical component of notetaking. The following steps will prepare you for action:

- **Identify the instructor's—and your—goals for the course.** On the first day of class, most instructors discuss what they'll be covering over the course of the term. They talk about their objectives, what they hope you'll get out of the class, and what you'll know when it's over. Most restate the information on the class syllabus, the written document that explains the assignments for the semester. For example, they may say that they want you to "develop an appreciation for the ways that statistics are used in everyday life."

    The information you get during that first session and through the syllabus is critical, because it allows you to calculate the basic direction the instructor plans to take during the course. And even if the instructor's goals aren't stated explicitly, you should attempt to figure them out. But don't just stop with the instructor's goals for the course. In addition to those "external" goals, you should have your own goals. What is it you wish to learn from the course? What is it you hope to accomplish? How will the information from the course help you to enhance your knowledge, achieve your dreams, improve yourself as a person?

- **Complete assignments before coming to class.** Your instructor enthusiastically describes the structure of the neuron, recounting excitedly how neurons don't physically touch one another and how electrons flow across neurons, changing their electrical charge. One problem: You have only the vaguest idea what a neuron is. And the reason you don't know is that you haven't read the assignment.

    Chances are you have found yourself in this situation at least a few times, so you know firsthand that sinking feeling as you become more and more confused. Because you can't follow the discussion, you can't

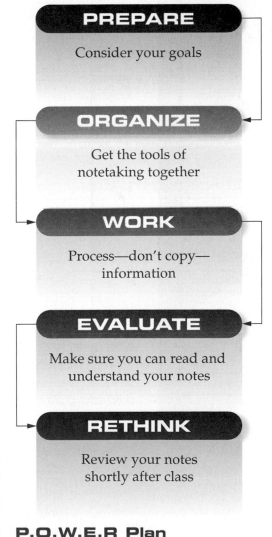

PREPARE

Consider your goals

ORGANIZE

Get the tools of notetaking together

WORK

Process—don't copy— information

EVALUATE

Make sure you can read and understand your notes

RETHINK

Review your notes shortly after class

P.O.W.E.R Plan

Try It! 1

Identify Course Goals

What are your goals for each of your courses? What seem to be your instructors' goals for these courses? Use the form below to jot down both your own and your instructors' goals for your courses this term.

	Course	My Goals	Instructor's Goals
1.			
2.			
3.			
4.			
5.			
6.			

What are the major differences among your instructors' goals for your various courses this term? Are there common threads among the instructors' course goals? How about your own goals—are they specific to various courses, or are there some common themes? Are you satisfied that your short-term goals for the courses you are taking are consistent with your long-term goals?

Student Alert: Freshmen do not realize that faculty members often do not announce textbook reading assignments; faculty assume that students will do this without being told. The text material needs to be read prior to the discussion about that topic in class—not afterwards!

get interested either, so the class seems boring. But really it is you who are lost. Not only have you begun to fall behind in your course work, you have now wasted an entire class session, simply because you didn't complete the reading you were supposed to before class.

Always go to class prepared: Do all of your assignments beforehand. Instructors assume that their students have done what they've assigned, and their lectures are based upon that assumption. It's virtually impossible to catch on to the gist of a lecture if you haven't completed the assignments.

An engaging lecturer can make even the most complex material come alive in the classroom, whereas an instructor who is unorganized or dull can make coming to class sheer drudgery. No matter what the lecturer's style, however, you need to be prepared to take effective notes.

- **Accept the instructor, warts and all.** Not every instructor is a brilliant lecturer. Accept the fact that, just as there are differences in skills among students, some instructors are more adept at lecturing than others.

  Don't let a lousy lecture style—or the fact that the instructor has a bad haircut or a mouth that droops to one side or badly wrinkled clothing—get in the way of your education. You're going to notice these things, but don't let them interfere with your goals. Good notetaking requires being prepared to listen to the material.

- **Perform a pre-class warm-up.** No, this doesn't mean doing jumping jacks just before each class. As you head to class or settle into your seat, review your notes from the previous lecture, looking over what the instructor said and where that lecture left off. You should also briefly review any reading you've been assigned.

  Just read the main headings or summary section. The warm-up doesn't have to be long. The goal is simply to refresh yourself, to get yourself into the right frame of mind for the class. In the same way that a five-minute warm-up before a run can prevent muscle spasms in your legs, a five-minute mental warm-up can prevent cramped and strained brain muscles.

Discussion Prompt: Ask students to create a list of "distracting behaviors of faculty." Then, you share a list of "distracting behaviors of students." Use this as a way to illustrate that despite our biases, we still have to find a way to accomplish the goal of classroom time—learning.

> "The highest result of education is tolerance."
>
> Helen Keller

rganize: Getting the Tools of Notetaking Together

Student Alert: Remind students that they need to be rested and alert when they come to class.

Do you have a favorite pen? A preferred type of notebook?

By the time we reach college, most of us have developed distinct tastes when it comes to the materials we use in class. Although taking your favorite kind of notebook and pen to class will not make you a better notetaker, not having them certainly will interfere with your getting the most out of class. Yes, you probably will be able to borrow pen and paper from another student, but having to do so sends a message to both your instructor and yourself. To your instructor, who quite likely will notice your scrambling, it says that you're unorganized and unprepared. The message to yourself is that, as a student, you're neither serious nor particularly concerned with success.

What kind of writing utensil and paper will work best? There are several considerations. First, using a pen is generally better than using a pencil. Compared with pencil, ink is less likely to smudge, it generally requires less effort to complete the physical act of writing, and what you produce with ink is usually brighter and clearer—and therefore easier to use when studying. On the other hand, for math and science classes, where you may be copying down formulas in class, a pencil might be better, because it's easier to erase if you make a mistake when copying detailed, complex information.

Sometimes you may want to use a combination of pen and pencil. And in some cases you might use several different colors. One color—such as red—might signify important information that the instructor mentions will be on the test. Another color might be reserved for definitions or material that is copied from the board. And a third might be used for notes on what your instructor says.

Figure 5.1

In this example of a student's notes on a lecture about memory, she has written the material in the larger right-hand column during class. Later, when reviewing her notes, she wrote down key pieces of information in the left-hand column.

	3 ways to store information
	sensory memory everything sensed
aka working memory (like	short term memory 15-25 sec.
computer RAM)	stored as meaning
	5-9 chunks
(like hard disk)	long-term memory inlimited
Rehearsal: STM to LTM	rehearsal
	visualization
Chunking	Organize information into chunks:
	birds, instruments, body parts, etc.
	Mnemonics
Roy G. Biv	acronyms
Every good boy deserves fun	acrostics
30 days hath September	rhyming
Unfinished Symphony	jingles
pato, caballo	keyword technique
room and furniture	loci technique
sun, zoo, me, store . . .	peg method
	Using senses
	moving
	draw, diagram
	visualize
	Overlearning

Keep in mind that your notes will probably be easier to read if you write with something other than a ballpoint pen. Although ballpoint pens are convenient, they also force you to apply more pressure than other kinds of writing utensils and can lead to illegibility. Using a fountain pen or a higher-quality "easy-rolling" pen requires less pressure.

You also have a choice of many different kinds of notebooks. Loose-leaf notebooks are particularly good because they permit you to go back later and change the order of the pages or add additional material in the appropriate spot. But whatever kind of notebook you use, *only use one side of the page for writing; keep one side free of notes.* There may be times when you're studying that you'll want to spread out your notes in front of you, and it's much easier if no material is written on the back of the pages.

You should configure notebook pages spatially to optimize later review. According to educator Walter Pauk,[1] the best way to do this is to draw a line down the left side of your notebook page, about 2¼ inches from the left-hand margin (illustrated in Figure 5.1). Keep the notes you write in class to the right of the line. Indent major supporting details beneath each main idea, trying to use no more than one line for each item, and leave space between topics to add information. When it comes time to review your notes later, you'll be able to jot down a key word, phrase, or major idea on the left side of the page.

Should You Take Your Text? You may or may not need to take your textbook to class. Sometimes instructors will refer to information contained in it, and sometimes it's useful to have it handy in order to clarify information that is being discussed. You can also use it to look up key terms that may momentarily escape you. But don't, under any circumstances, use class time as an opportunity to read the textbook!

Finally, if you're quite comfortable with computers and have a laptop, you might want to consider using it to take notes. There are several advantages: Legibility problems are avoided, and it's easy to go back and revise after you've taken the notes. It's also simple to add material later.

Journal Reflections

How Do I Take Notes?

1. Describe your typical notetaking techniques in a few sentences. Do you try to write down as much of what the instructor says as possible? Do you tend to take only a few notes? Do you often find you need more time to get things down?

2. Overall, how effective are your notetaking techniques?

3. In which classes do your techniques work best? Worst? Why?

4. Do your notes ever have "holes" in them—due to lapses of attention or times when you couldn't get down everything you wanted to? When do you usually discover them? What do you do about them?

5. Do you ever ask to borrow someone else's notes, even when you've been to class and taken your own notes?

6. Does anyone ever ask to borrow your notes? Would others want to use your notes?

7. How often—and when—do you consult your notes (after each class, before the next class, while doing homework assignments, when writing papers, when preparing for exams, etc.)?

Despite their pluses, laptops also have minuses. For one thing, you may be tempted to take down everything that the instructor says—far more than is optimal, as we'll see next when we discuss the actual process of taking notes. In addition, it's hard to make notes in the margins, copy graphical material that the instructor may present in class, reproduce formulas, or circle key ideas. Furthermore, the clattering of the keyboard may be annoying to your fellow students.

Work: Processing—Not Copying—Information

With pen poised, you're ready to begin the work of notetaking. The instructor begins to speak, and you start to write as quickly as you can, taking down as many of the instructor's words as possible.

Stop! You've made your first mistake. The central act in taking notes is not writing. Notetaking involves *listening* and *thinking* far more than writing. The key to effective notetaking is to write down the right amount of information—not too much, and not too little. To see how this is true, consider the following recommendations for taking notes:

> "I had tons of notes—I copied *every word* the professor said. Actually, I was so busy writing that I didn't understand a thing."
>
> Junior, Saint Joseph's University.[2]

- **Listen for the key ideas.** Not every sentence in a lecture is equally important, and one of the most useful skills you can develop is separating the key ideas from supporting information. Good lecturers strive to make just a few main points. The rest of what they say consists of explanation, examples, and other supportive material that expands upon the key ideas.

  Your job, then, is to distinguish the key ideas from those that are of less importance. To do this, you need to be alert and always searching for the meta-message of your instructor's words. The **meta-message** consists of the underlying main ideas that a speaker is seeking to convey—the meaning behind the overt message you hear.

  How can you discern the meta-message? One way is to *listen for key words.* Instructors know what's important in their lecture; your job is to figure it out, not from what they say, but from how they say it.

  For instance, listen for clues about the importance of material. All phrases like "don't forget . . . ," "be sure to remember that . . . ," "you need to know . . . ," "the most important thing that must be considered . . . ," "there are four problems with this approach . . . ," and—a big one— "this will be on the test . . . " should cause you to sit up and take notice. Another good sign of importance is repetition. If an instructor says the same thing in several ways, it's a clear sign that the material being discussed is important.

  Be on the lookout for nonverbal signals too. When instructors pause, raise their eyes, glance at their notes, or otherwise change their demeanor, these behaviors are a signal that what they're about to say is important.

- **Use short, abbreviated phrases—not full sentences.** Forget everything you've ever heard about always writing in full sentences. If you try to write notes in complete sentences, you'll soon become bogged down, paying more attention to your notes than to your instructor. In fact, if you use full sentences, you'll be tempted to try transcribing every word the instructor utters, which, as you now know, is not a good idea at all.

Instead, write in phrases, using only key words or terms. Save full sentences for definitions or quotes that your instructor clearly wants you to know word for word. For example, consider the following excerpt from a lecture:

> There are two kinds of job analyses: job- or task-oriented analyses, and worker- or employee-oriented analyses. Job analyses just describe the tasks that need to be accomplished by a worker. Employee-oriented job descriptions need to describe knowledge, skills, and abilities the employee must have in order to get the job done. Most job analyses include elements of both job-oriented and employee-oriented types.

If you were taking notes, you might produce the following:

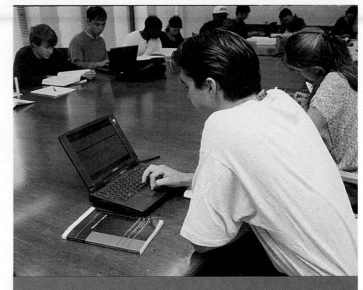

Using a laptop computer to take class notes ensures that they will be legible, and that it will be easy to revise them after class. On the other hand, it's difficult to input graphical material, such as complex formulas, and there's also a danger that you'll be tempted to take too many notes.

2 kinds job analyses:
(1) job-oriented (= task-oriented): what worker must do to get job done
(2) worker-oriented (= employee-oriented): describe knowledge, skills, abilities needed
most analyses include both

Note how the lecturer used 67 words, while the notes used only 29 words—fewer than half.

- **Use abbreviations.** One way to speed up the notetaking process is through the use of abbreviations. Among the most common:

and *& or +*	with *w/*	without *w/o*
care of *c/o*	leads to; resulting in *↗*	as a result of *∠*
percent *%*	change *∠*	number *#*
that is *i.e.*	for example *e.g.*	and so forth *etc.*
no good *n.g.*	question *?*	compared with *c/w*
page *p.*	important! *!!*	less than *<*
more than *>*	equals, same as *=*	versus *vs.*

- **Take notes in outline form.** It's often useful to take notes in the form of an outline. An *outline* summarizes ideas in short phrases and indicates the relationship among concepts through the use of indentations.

When outlining, it's best to be formal about it, using roman numerals, regular numbers, and capital and small letters (see the example in Figure 5.2 on page 122). Or, if you prefer, you can also simply use outlining indentations without assigning numbers and letters.

Outlining serves a number of functions. It forces you to try constantly to determine the structure of the lecture to which you're listening. Organizing the key points and noting the connections among them helps you

Teaching Tip and Discussion Prompt: Remind students to keep their abbreviations consistent in all of their notes. Can your students suggest other abbreviations to use?

Student Alert: The outline form works best with instructors who use it to create their lectures. It is generally not a useful format for discussion classes.

Figure 5.2

A Sample Outline

I. Difficulties faced by college students seeking affordable housing
   A. Students are subjected to high rents for housing close to campus
      1. Forced to share apartments
      2. Sometimes must live far from campus
   B. Made to sign leases with strict provisions
II. Possible solutions
   A. College offers subsidized housing
      1. Advantage is that housing costs can be lowered
      2. Potential problems
         a. College becomes students' landlord
         b. College uses funds for housing that could be otherwise invested in education
   B. Rent control
      1. Advantage: Rent control can provide fixed, reasonably priced rents
      2. Disadvantages
         a. Creates a permanent, expensive rent-control bureaucracy
         b. Landlords may neglect rent-control property
         c. The present shortage of apartments would worsen, because little incentive for owners to increase the number of rental units
         d. Competition for rent-fixed units would dramatically increase
III. Summary
   A. There are advantages and disadvantages to both solutions
   B. May need new, creative solutions

remember the material better because you have processed it more. Outlining also keeps your mind from drifting away from the lecture. The effort involved in seeking out the structure of the lecture will help keep you focused on the material being discussed. Use Try It 2, "Outline a Lecture," to practice your outlining skills.

- **Copy information written on the board or projected from overheads.** If your instructor takes the time to write something out to be displayed in class, you should take the time to copy it. Definitions, quotes, phrases, and formulas—if you see them in writing, they're quite likely important enough to include in your notes. In fact, material displayed prominently has "test item" written all over it. You might want to highlight such material in some way in your notes.

- **Use different note-taking techniques for class discussions.** Not every course is structured as a lecture. Classes that are based less on lectures and more on class discussion pose greater challenges for notetaking.

  For example, a discussion of the use of tax support of private schools in a sociology class may raise a variety of issues. As students in the class provide their ideas about the meaning of the work, how much—and what—should you place in your notes?

  In such situations, the best approach is to take your cue from the course instructor. Often the instructor will pose some questions to get the discussion rolling. Note those questions—they're an important indicator of what the instructor is interested in. The instructor's reaction to particular comments is another clue. Listen to his or her responses. If he or she responds enthusiastically to a particular point, you'll want to highlight it in your notes.

Try It! 2

Working in a Group: Outline a Lecture

Working with others in a group, take turns slowly reading several paragraphs of the following lecture to each other.[3] As the paragraphs are being read, outline the main arguments in the space that follows the passage.

Today most of us think that the Civil War was about slavery. We think: The Southern states seceded because they wanted to preserve the system of slavery, and the Northern states entered the war bound and determined to free the slaves. This is at best an oversimplification. In fact, only the fairly extremist Abolitionist wing of Lincoln's Republican Party ever saw the war this clearly and simply.

Not even Abe Lincoln, the Great Emancipator himself, ever saw the war as solely about slavery. And the Emancipation Proclamation, which he did eventually sign in late 1862, was never a simple matter of clear conscience and moral decision. Lincoln saw slavery as one of many ills that afflicted and divided the nation, and the decision to issue the Emancipation Proclamation was to him a deeply political one.

Personally, Lincoln's feelings about slavery were complex. At times he spoke of slavery as "the greatest wrong inflicted on any people" and condemned it on essentially moral grounds. At other times, he observed that emancipation of the slaves should be seen as a *means* to victory, not as an *end* in itself. The slaves, once freed, would be available to serve the needs of the Union Army—not necessarily as soldiers, but as laborers, cooks, hospital attendants, helpers. At still other times, Lincoln mirrored the prevailing prejudice of the time, advocating emigration and colonization of freed slaves in Central America, rather than their integration into U.S. culture.

Write your outline here:

After you have outlined the passage, compare your outline with that of others who took notes on the same passage. What were the main ideas of each passage? How do your notes differ from others', and what are the similarities? How might you improve your notes to better capture the main points? Would a different topic produce greater or fewer difficulties? Collectively, produce what you believe is the ideal outline, and compare it with those produced by other groups.

Take Notes during Discussions

Take notes on the following class discussion about Virgil's *Aeneid.* Use cues from the instructor about the importance and accuracy of each point, and record in your notes only the key points that shed light on the topic.

Instructor: Why was the *Aeneid* so important to the Romans, especially the Romans of the first century B.C.? What messages did a Roman take from Aeneas?

Alicia: Um, well, I think Aeneas displayed strength and adventurousness, with all his wanderings and the shipwreck and all.

Instructor: O.K. He was certainly strong. But this is more than an adventure story, right? Anyone else? Bart?

Bart: Yeah, his sense of duty. The way nothing could get him to quit his mission of finding a new place to live.

Instructor: Good, good. Yes, he was very determined that he would find a suitable place to found his new settlement and put down solid roots for a powerful civilization. What else?

Catherine: Well, the nature of the civilization—it turned out to be Rome, right? And to the Romans, that meant that their civilization went back hundreds or thousands of years to the time of the Trojan War. That was a lot of, you know, legitimacy for the Roman Empire, saying it was really the ancient Trojans who were the ancestors of the Romans.

Instructor: Exactly! Legitimacy is a good way to put it. With one stroke . . . David?

David: Yeah, I was just going to say, with one stroke Aeneas—I mean, Virgil—ties the Romans, including the emperor . . . what's his name . . . Augustus, to the ancient Trojans, great enemies of the Greeks who were around as long as the Greeks were. If you're Rome and you find yourself in charge of the world, it helps if you've got ancestors who are every bit as noble and, you know, the sons of divinities, gods, as the Greeks were always claiming to be.

Emily: Right. It's a pedigree. It's like Americans who suddenly discover that their pedigree goes back to the Mayflower or something. The Romans must have been pretty tired of the Greeks and their superiority—cultural superiority—when the Romans knew very well that *they* were the ones who had conquered the world and that they were better than the Greeks. Militarily, I mean. The *Aeneid* must have given them some real status.

- **Pay particular attention to the points raised by instructors at the end of discussion and lecture classes.** Instructors often provide a summary of the discussion, which is worthy of inclusion in your notes.

Use Special Techniques for "Problem Instructors"

Student Alert: It is a good policy to encourage students to discuss the behaviors without using specific names of faculty members.

As all of us know from painful experience, some instructors' lectures are impossible to outline. How do you take notes when the instructor starts talking about one topic and then rambles off onto another one without warning and never seems to get back to the original point? Or if he or she speaks very quickly and covers too much material too fast for you to follow?

The fact is that all you can do is make the best of a bad situation and adapt your notetaking strategy to it. If there is no clear message or logical sequence to the lecture material, you may be unable to take notes in outline form. In

Instructor:	You've really hit it now. Virgil is writing this for Augustus and Rome of the first century B.C. What did Augustus want for Rome at this time? Not just power, but honor and respectability. Exactly!
Frances:	Well, if you ask me he was, Aeneas was, not really much of a hero. I mean, he meets Dido, makes love to her, lives with her for a while, and then dumps her to sail off with his buddies. Sounds familiar.
Instructor:	OK. What of that? Any other thoughts on Aeneas the cad? Gina?
Gina:	Yeah, OK, he was a jerk with Dido, but I'll bet the Romans only saw his actions as what would be expected of a hero. I mean, a hero with a fate, with a destiny, to found Rome has to go on and finish the job, right? He can't stay with Dido and dally away his time. He's got a city to found. Know what I mean?
Instructor:	Very well put, Gina. You're exactly right. The Roman concept of duty would have demanded that Aeneas remember his mission. Dido was a distraction, and to stay with her would have seemed to the Romans as much a public betrayal as to our modern eyes his "dumping" her—is that the word, Frances?—appears a private, personal betrayal. And in Augustan Rome, public duty always comes before personal feelings and desires. Excellent discussion, folks.

Write your notes here:

Were you able to identify the information that was most important? How would actually seeing the instructor's nonverbal reactions to the students' comments be helpful? **Working in a group,** compare your notes on the discussion with those of your classmates. As a group, try to create an optimal set of notes, reflecting the most important points.

such cases, focus more on creating a summary of what is being said, rather than trying to tease out its underlying structure. Write short "paragraphs" that focus on the major ideas being presented. Although the paragraphs certainly shouldn't consist of full sentences, they should provide a reasonable condensation of what the instructor said.

When you're writing in paragraph form, be sure to leave space after each paragraph. By leaving space, you'll make it easier to go back later and restructure the material at a point when its underlying meaning is clearer.

You might be able to get a better sense of what the instructor is trying to convey by using your textbook to clarify obscure points. It also may be helpful to pool your notes with those of other students in the class. When the instructor's train of thought is all over the place, two—or more—heads are better than one!

Teaching Tip: Encourage students to leave room in their notes to add information, to revise the language, or to ask questions.

Figure 5.3

Notes on a Lecture

Here is an instructor's introductory lecture on Toni Morrison's *Beloved*. At the bottom of the page are two students' notes. Which student—A or B—did a better job of capturing the important points in the lecture?

Teaching Tip: Point out that *thinking* results from questioning the relevance of a fact or idea.

Instructor: In today's class, we'll discuss Toni Morrison's *Beloved*. As I'm sure you all know, Morrison is both a popular and an acclaimed author—and it's not easy to be both. Born Chloe Anthony Wofford in 1931, Morrison has written some of the most affecting and intelligent works on the African-American experience ever written by anyone, and yet to call her an "African-American writer" doesn't seem to do her justice. In many ways, she is simply an American writer—and certainly one of our best.

Beloved is a truly remarkable work. It was nominated for nearly every major literary prize, including the National Book Award and the National Book Critics Circle Award, and it in fact won the Pulitzer Prize for fiction in 1988. Morrison herself is distinguished for having won the Nobel Prize for literature in 1993.

What makes *Beloved* unique is the skillful, sure way in which Morrison blends intensely personal storytelling and American history, racial themes and gender themes, the experience of Blacks with the experience of all people everywhere, the gritty down-to-earth reality of slavery with a sense of mystical spirituality.

We will be paying special attention to these themes as we discuss this work. I am particularly interested in your views on the relative importance of race and gender in this book. Is it more important that Sethe, the main character, is black or that she's a woman? Which contributes more to her being? How does Morrison use both race and gender to drive her plot? What does she tell us about both?

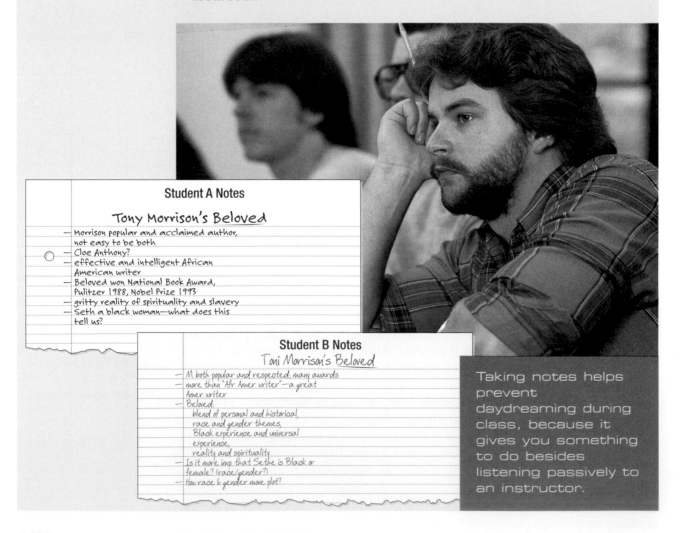

Student A Notes

Tony Morrison's Be*lov*ed

— Morrison popular and acclaimed author, not easy to be both
○ — Cloe Anthony?
— effective and intelligent African American writer
— Beloved won National Book Award, Pulitzer 1988, Nobel Prize 1993
— gritty reality of spirituality and slavery
— Seth a black woman—what does this tell us?

Student B Notes

Toni Morrison's *Beloved*

— M both popular and respected; many awards
— more than "Afr. Amer. writer"—a great Amer. writer
— Beloved:
    blend of personal and historical,
    race and gender themes,
    Black experience and universal experience,
    reality and spirituality
— Is it more imp that Sethe is Black or female? (race/gender?)
— How race & gender move plot?

Taking notes helps prevent daydreaming during class, because it gives you something to do besides listening passively to an instructor.

Finally, don't hesitate to ask instructors to clarify what they are saying. In some cases, they simply may not realize how far off track they have gotten. You'll be doing them—and certainly your fellow classmates—a favor by asking for clarification.

Keep a Balance between Too Many Notes and Too Few Notes The key to effective notetaking is to keep a balance between too many and too few notes.

The best way to achieve this balance is by paying close attention in class. By being alert, engaged, and involved in class, you'll be able to make the most of the techniques we've discussed. The result: notes that capture the most important points raised in class and that will optimize your recall and mastery of the course subject matter (see a sample of two students' notes in Figure 5.3).

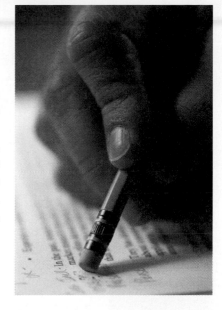

E valuate: Thinking Critically about Your Notes

IM Link: "Teaching the Text," Chapter 5—Section VII, Goal 1, Activity 1.

Toward the end of class, look over your notes. Now's the time—before the class has ended—to evaluate what you've written.

After being sure you can answer "yes" to the most basic question—can I read what I've written?—ask yourself these questions:

- Do my notes do a good job of representing what was covered in class?
- Do they reflect the emphases of the instructor?
- Are there any key points that are not entirely clear?
- Do I need help clarifying any of the points my instructor made?

Evaluating your notes is a critical part of the notetaking process. You can get a sense of how effective your notetaking has been while you still have a chance to ask your instructor to clarify anything that is still not clear.

Perhaps, for example, you've left out a key word in a definition. Maybe you don't understand a concept fully, even though you've written about it in your notes. Possibly you've left out the third step in a list of six steps necessary to accomplish something.

If you look over your notes while you're still in class, you have time to ask your instructor for clarification. Or you can wait till the end of class and then go up and raise your question. Most instructors will be happy to answer questions from students who have obviously been actively listening. Just make sure that you add what they tell you to your notes so you'll be able to refer to them later. (To practice evaluating your notes, complete Try It 4 on page 128.)

R ethink: Activating Your Memory

The lecture has ended and class is over. You put the top on your pen, close your notebook, stash everything in your backpack, and head out for a cup of coffee before your next class.

Wait! Before you close up your notebook, finish the P.O.W.E.R. process. Rethink what you've heard. Spending 5 or 10 minutes reconsidering what you've written right now can save you *hours* of work later. The reason:

Try It! 4

Evaluate Your Class Notes

Take a set of notes you made recently during one of your classes and evaluate it on the following criteria.

Statement	Not Even Slightly	Slightly	Moder-ately	Pretty Well	Very Well
1. I can read my notes (i.e., they are legible).					
2. Someone else can read my notes.					
3. My notes are complete; I missed nothing important.					
4. My notes represent the key points that were covered in class.					
5. My notes reflect the instructor's emphases.					
6. The instructor's key points are clear and understandable.					
7. The notes contain only important points, with no extraneous material.					
8. I understand not only the notes but the class content they reflect.					
9. Using only the notes, I will be able to reconstruct the essential content of the class in three months.					

What do your answers tell you about the effectiveness of your notetaking skills? What might you do differently the next time you take notes? In a group, evaluate and compare the notes you took during the previous 20 minutes of the class you are in now. How do your notes compare to those of the other members of your group?

Rethinking promotes the transfer of information into long-term memory (something discussed more in Chapter 9). As you link the new information you've taken down to what you already know and then integrate it, you essentially plug this information into your memory in a much more meaningful way, which means you can remember it better and more easily.

If you looked over your notes to clarify and evaluate the information in them in class, you've already begun the process. But once class is over, you need to review the material more formally. Here's how to do it:

- **Rethink as soon as possible.** Time is of the essence! The rethinking phase of notetaking doesn't have to take long; 5 to 10 minutes is usually sufficient. The more critical issue is *when* you do it. The longer you wait before reviewing your notes, the less effective the process will be.

  There's no doubt that the best approach is to review the material just after the class has ended. As everyone else is leaving, just stay seated and go over your notes. This works fine for classes late in the day, when no other class is scheduled in the room. But what if you must vacate the room immediately after class? The next best thing is to find a quiet space somewhere nearby and do your rethinking there.

Even if you have another class immediately afterwards, you can do your rethinking before that class if you get there early enough. However you do it, the same rule holds: Sooner is better.

> "I'd think to myself 'I don't need to write that down, I'll remember it.' A few days later, it was like, 'What did he say . . . ?' "
>
> Junior, Duke University.[4]

In any case, don't let the day end without examining your notes. In fact, reconsidering material just before sleep is sometimes thought to be particularly effective.

- **Make rethinking an active process.** Some people feel the notes they take in class are akin to historical documents in a museum, with Do Not Touch! signs hanging on them. On the contrary, think of your notes as a construction project and yourself as the person in charge of the project.

  When you review your notes, do so with an eye to improving them. If any information is not entirely clear, change the wording in your notes, adding to or amending what's there. If certain words are hard to read, fix them; it won't be any easier to read them the night before a test—in fact, chances are you'll have even more trouble.

  If, on rethinking the material, you just don't understand something, ask your instructor or a friend to clarify it. And when you receive an explanation, add it to your notes so you won't forget it. (You might want to use a different-colored pen for additions to your notes, so you'll know they came later.)

- **Take the broad view.** When you rethink your notes, don't think of them only in terms of a single lecture or a single class. Instead, take a longer view. Ask yourself how they fit into the broader themes of the class and the goals that you and the instructor have for the semester. How will the information be useful to you? Why did the instructor emphasize a particular point?

  If you've configured your notes by leaving a 2½-inch column on the left-hand side of the page, now is the time to make use of that blank column. Write down key words, significant points, major concepts, controversies, and questions. The process of adding this information will not only help you to rethink the material now, it will also provide guideposts when you study before a test.

- **Create concept maps. Concept mapping** is a method of structuring written material by graphically grouping and connecting key ideas and themes. In contrast to an outline, a concept map visually illustrates how related ideas fit together. The pictorial summary gives you another handle to store the information in memory, and it focuses your thinking on the key ideas from the lecture.

  In a concept map, each key idea is placed in a different part of the map, and related ideas are placed near it—above, below, or beside it. What emerges does not have the rigid structure of an outline. Instead, a "finished" concept map looks something like a map of the solar system, with the largest and most central idea in the center (the "sun" position), and related ideas surrounding it at various distances. It has also been

Student Alert and Teaching Tip: Many students believe that reading their notes is "actively" studying them. Demonstrate the processes of rewriting notes, creating questions from notes, summarizing notes, and discussing notes as more active ways to study and "rethink" one's notes.

Student Alert: Note taking is like time management. There are daily notes that support the overall course goals just like daily to-do lists support the semester (and lifetime) plan. Help students to make the connection between daily habits and "the bigger picture."

Concept mapping
A method of structuring written material by graphically grouping and connecting key ideas and themes

IM Link: "Teaching the Text," Chapter 5—Sections IV and VIII. See the film activity.

compared to a large tree, with numerous branches and sub-branches radiating out from a central trunk. (Figure 5.4 presents a sample concept map.)

Building a concept map has several advantages. It forces you to rethink the material in your notes in a new style—particularly important if you used traditional outlining while taking the notes. In addition, it helps you to tie together the material for a given class session. Finally, it will help you to build a master concept map later, when you're studying the material for a final exam. (To practice in the techniques we've been discussing, see Try It 5, "Practice Your Notetaking Skills.")

Figure 5.4

A Concept Map of Toni Morrison's *Beloved*

Try It! 5

Practice Your Notetaking Skills

Practice your notetaking skills, using any techniques you find helpful, in one of the classes in which you are enrolled this term. Bring your notes to the class in which you are using this book, and answer these questions:

1. Which specific techniques did I use in taking notes?

   _____

   _____

2. Which of the notetaking techniques detailed in this chapter was I unable to use, and why?

   _____

   _____

   _____

3. Could I take the notes I made in class and re-do them, using one of the techniques in this chapter such as a concept map? _____

After you have taken notes, use the techniques discussed in this chapter to evaluate and rethink them. Creating a concept map on a separate sheet of paper may be particularly helpful.

Taking in a Talk: When the Speaker Isn't Your Teacher

You're thrilled to find that Laura Esquivel, an author whose most recent book, Like Water for Chocolate, *you loved, is giving a talk on your campus in two weeks. You buy a ticket and eagerly anticipate her presentation.*

Finally, the night of the talk arrives and you head off to hear her. She begins to speak, and she communicates one interesting and provocative idea after another. You're entranced throughout the one-hour talk.

After it's over, and you're walking to the bus stop, a friend comes by. She asks you where you've been, and you tell her. She then asks what Esquivel talked about. You start to answer, and suddenly you realize that you've already forgotten most of what you just heard. If only you had taken some notes!

IM Link: "Teaching the Text," Chapter 5—Section VII, Goal 2, Activity 1.

Do you feel that the only appropriate place to take notes is in class? If so, you may have had experiences like the one described above. Even the most active listening will not permit you to remember many details a speaker provides—unless you take written notes.

Every suggestion for taking class notes that we've discussed in this chapter holds as well for nonclassroom speakers. *It's not bad manners to bring a notebook to a nonclass talk.* In fact, almost all speakers welcome the practice because it shows that their audience is really interested in their message. Of course, you don't want to spend the entire talk with your head hunched down over your notebook! Speakers feed off the energy of their audiences, and if it seems as if listeners lack enthusiasm, the speakers' performances will suffer.

Taking Notes As You Study

Weighing as much as five pounds, bulky and awkward, and filled with more information than you think anyone could ever need to know, it's the meat-and-potatoes of college life: your course textbook. You might feel intimidated by its size; you might be annoyed at its cost; you might think you'll never be able to read it, let alone understand, learn, and recall the material in it. How will you manage?

The answer involves taking **study notes,** notes taken for the purpose of reviewing material. They are the kind of notes that you take now to study from later. (We'll consider *research notes,* notes that you take to write a paper or prepare a report, in Chapter 8 when we discuss writing papers.)

Several strategies are useful for taking study notes from written material such as magazines, books, journals, and web pages. Which approach works best depends on whether you're able to write on the material you wish to take notes on.

Taking Notes on Material You Can Write On

Here are some suggestions for creating study notes for material you own, on which you're free to annotate the text directly by underlining, highlighting, or writing in the margins:

- **Integrate your text notes into your study notes.** If you wish to create study notes from written material on which you can write, start by annotating the pages as you normally would. Use the techniques that work best for you: highlighting, underlining, circling, making marginal notes—whatever you generally use. These techniques are discussed in detail in Chapter 7; you may want to look ahead to that discussion.

  After you've finished reading and annotating the material, it's time to create study notes. While it's still fresh in your mind, go back over the material and your text annotations, and create your study notes.

  The study notes should provide a summary of the key points. They might be in outline form or in the form of concept maps. Whatever their form, they should supplement and summarize the annotations you've made on the printed page.

  Furthermore, any notes you take should stand on their own. For instance, they should include enough information to be useful whether or not you have the book or article on hand.

- **Use flash cards.** If you feel confident that the annotations you've written in the book are sufficiently comprehensive, you might consider taking notes on flash cards. **Flash cards** are simply index cards that contain key pieces of information that you need to remember.

  Flash cards are particularly useful in subjects that present many small bits of information to remember, such as foreign language vocabulary words or scientific formulas. When you need to learn a list of foreign words, for instance, you can write a foreign word on one side of a card and its English meaning on the other side.

Study notes
Notes taken for the purpose of reviewing material

Teaching Tip: Encourage students to "argue" with the author, create questions, circle new or important words, and/or write their own ideas as they read. Point out that it is important to own the book.

Flash cards
Note cards that contain key pieces of information to be remembered

Speaking of Success

Name: Rebecca Lobo
Education: B.A. from University of Connecticut
Home: Hartford, Connecticut

When basketball star Rebecca Lobo enrolled in an 8:00 AM English literature class during college, she was a bit concerned about the wisdom of her choice. But her enthusiasm overcame her doubts. "That class was so enjoyable," says Lobo. "It showed me how easy something can be if you like it, even at that hour."[5]

Lobo, an All-American who was voted Female Athlete of the Year and is a star player on the New York Liberty women's basketball team, attended the University of Connecticut as an undergraduate. Academics and sports were both a central part of her first-year college experience.

"Like any freshman, I was nervous when I first entered college. I didn't know what to expect from basketball, from classes, or anything else,"[6] she says.

However, her participation on the basketball team gave her something that lowered her anxiety level. "It was my first time away from home, but I was better off than most because I had teammates who looked out for me and who took care of me,"[7] she says.

Because practice and games reduced the time left for studying

during basketball season, Lobo developed strategies for making the most of the off-season.

"During the summers I usually took classes and lived at school so I could get ahead of my courses and take fewer credit hours during the basketball season," she says. "Since there were not many people on campus then, I headed over to Gampel [arena] in the morning to shoot hoops. The emptiness of the court on these mornings provided me with a comfort zone I have not been able to find anywhere else in my life."[8]

During the school year there was always the need to juggle basketball and studies, but hard work and planning allowed Lobo to succeed in both endeavors.

"Come exam time, I stressed out and studied as much as I could. I was the sort who read every book on the syllabus and attended every class," she recalled. "I was known among the other athletes at school for being a nerd. "Where were you last night, Lobo? At the *library?'* " She adds, "I could always be counted on to have the notes from every lecture."[9]

Her strategies must have worked: As a political science major, she was on the dean's list every semester and graduated with an A– average.

Career Connections

Taking Notes on the Job: Meetings of the Minds

For many people, meetings take up a good part of their professional workdays, and being able to take effective notes can provide a significant career advantage.

Meetings are similar to class discussions. During a meeting you will want to look for key topics and make note of the ideas that receive the most emphasis or enthusiastic response. Note these areas and keep them in mind as likely priorities.

During meetings, tasks are often assigned. Not only do you want to clearly note what you are to do and when you are supposed to do it, but keeping track of what others are doing will also be helpful, because you may need to get information from them or remind them to do what they have to do. For instance, if you are assigned the task of coordinating the development of your company's Web site, you'll want to clarify in your notes who has agreed to do what portion of the task.

Taking notes when others are speaking also shows that you are paying attention to what the speaker is saying. It's a kind of compliment that suggests you find what the speaker is saying to be so important that you will want to refer to it later.

Finally, notetaking plays another role: It can make seemingly interminable meetings appear to proceed faster by providing something for you to do that's more active than simply listening. In short, not only can notetaking provide you with a clear record of what occurred in a meeting, it can keep you engaged in what is going on.

One of the greatest virtues of flash cards is their portability. Because they are small, they can fit into your pocket or handbag, and you can look at them at odd times when you have a spare moment.

Taking Study Notes on Material You Can't Write On

Taking notes on material that can't be written on is a different story. Library books, magazines, journal articles, and materials on library reserve that are shared with others require a different approach.

- **Approach the written material as you would a class lecture.** The techniques we discussed earlier for taking notes in class can all be adapted for taking notes from written material. In fact, the task is often easier, because, as is not the case with the spoken word, you'll be able to refer back to what was said earlier—it's in black and white in front of you.

- **Laptop computers can be especially helpful in creating study notes.** Because it's often easier and quicker to take notes using a word-processing program (if you're a good typist), computers can help you take more-detailed notes from written material on which you can't write.

- **Use all the tricks of the trade we discussed earlier for taking notes from a class lecture.** Look for the key ideas, definitions, quotes, and formulas and include them in your notes. Use the headings that are included in the text, such as chapter and section titles. Bold or italic type is also a clue that an important point is being made. Graphs and charts often provide critical information.

- **Use the same form of notetaking that you use in class lectures.** If you take notes in class using the two-column method (in which you reserve a 2½-inch column on the left side of your paper for adding comments during later review of the notes), use that technique here as well. If you write your notes in outline form, create an outline based on the written material. If you often create graphics such as concept maps, create them now. The point is to produce notes that are consistent with those you take during class lectures.

Looking
Back

What is effective notetaking?

- The central feature of good notetaking is listening and distilling important information—not writing down everything that is said.

How can I take good notes in class?

- Prepare for taking notes by identifying the instructor's and your own goals for the course, completing all assignments before arriving in class, and "warming up" for class by reviewing the notes and assignments from the previous class.

- Before writing notes, listen and think, processing the information that the instructor is attempting to deliver.

- Notes should be brief phrases rather than full sentences and, if possible, in outline form to reveal the structure of the lecture. Material written on the board should usually be copied word for word.

- Before leaving class, evaluate your notes, verifying that they are complete and understandable while there is still time to correct them. As soon as possible after class, actively rethink your notes.

What techniques apply to taking notes from written materials?

- Taking good study notes from written materials involves many of the principles that apply to taking good notes from oral presentations, although the source material can be consulted repeatedly, making it easier to get the information down accurately.
- Concept maps and flash cards can be helpful tools for notetaking from textbooks.

IM Link: "Teaching the Text," Chapter 5—Section V; EVALUATE. Make a direct connection between your students' evaluation of their note taking style and the grades they receive. If students are not satisfied with their grades, they might consider changing their note taking style.

Key Terms and Concepts

Concept mapping (p. 129)
Flash cards (p. 132)

Meta-message (p. 120)
Study notes (p. 132)

Resources

On Campus

If you are having difficulty taking class notes effectively, talk with your course instructor. Bring your notes with you soon after a class has ended, and let the instructor assess what you are doing correctly and what could stand improvement.

If your problems persist, and you have great difficulty translating the spoken word into notes, then there's a small possibility that you suffer from an auditory learning disability. Be tested by your college learning disabilities office or counseling office to address this or rule it out.

In Print

Take Notes (Career Press, 1994), by Ron Fry, provides an overall view of how to take good notes in classes. Another approach can be found in James Roberts's *Bud's Easy Note Taking System* (Lawrence House, 1995), which offers many useful suggestions. Finally, *Noteworthy: Listening and Notetaking Skills* (2nd ed.), by Phyllis Lim and William Smalzer (William S. Hein & Co., 1995) provides a fine overview of strategies for increasing your listening and notetaking expertise.

On the Web

The following sites on the World Wide Web provide the opportunity to extend your learning about the material in this chapter. (Although the Web addresses were accurate at the time the book was printed, check the P.O.W.E.R. Learning Web site [http://mhhe.com/power] for any changes that may have occurred.)

http://www.econ.ilstu.edu/Mark_Walbert/ECO101/Other/CornellNTS.html
Notetaking Formats. This notetaking system can help you improve the organization of your notes. One advantage of this system is that it allows you to make use of your existing strengths as a notetaker.

http://www.coun.uvic.ca/learn/program/hndouts/class1.html
Organization Practice: Mapping. Another effective method for organizing complicated information is through concept mapping. This site is a tutorial that presents information in passage form and then asks you to create a concept map. The concept map created by the authors is only a click away.

http://137.132.225.6/UFM/effect/Es4_1_1.html
Effective Learning: Different Learning Modes—Lectures. This page offers guidance in learning material that is presented in lectures. After describing the purpose of a lecture, the authors offer several helpful hints for figuring out which lecture information is most important.

Teaching Tip: Ask students to review (and take notes on) the sites indicated, and to share their opinion of the usefulness of each one with the class. Ask them to bring in their notes.

Taking It to the Net

1 The best way to improve notetaking skills is to practice. Locate a current news story of interest on the Internet and take notes while reading it. Remember to leave the left margin large enough to add key points and summary information. One possible strategy is to go to the "Today's News" section of the Yahoo! home page (**www.yahoo.com/**). Click on one of the news categories (i.e., Sports, Politics, Business, etc.) and look for a story that sounds interesting.

2 Taking notes during lectures is an important part of classroom learning, but keeping up with a speaker for an entire hour can be difficult. You can improve your notetaking skills for lectures by taking notes while listening to recorded speeches on the Internet. For example, go to an Internet site containing audio recordings of speeches (e.g., **www.pbs.org/newshour/convention96/realaudio/**) and take notes while listening to a speech. Afterwards, go back and indicate the key points and terms in the left margin of your notes.

The Case of . . .

The Human Dictation Machine

Everyone wanted to borrow Zena Bauman's notes.

If they missed a class, or even if they had been in attendance but had just spaced out, other students in Zena's classes knew that they could find out what had happened in class by borrowing her notes. It was all there in black and white. The woman was virtually a human dictation machine. She spent class in a whirlwind of notetaking, writing down seemingly every word her instructor uttered in a clear, meticulous script. By the end of a term, her notebooks were so lengthy that they approached the size of telephone books from a small city.

The strange thing, though, was that—despite her copious notes—Zena was only a mediocre student. Before tests she studied her notes thoroughly, but it never seemed that she could get grades much higher than a C+. She didn't know why, especially in light of what she saw as her notetaking expertise.

1. How do you think Zena defines "good notetaking"?

2. Why does Zena's method of notetaking produce such poor results? What is she missing?

3. If you asked Zena to summarize the instructor's main ideas after a class lecture, how successful do you think she would be? Why?

4. Do you think it would be easy or hard to study for a final exam using Zena's notes? Why?

5. Do you think Zena *evaluates* her notes during or after class? Do you think she ever *rethinks* them? What questions would you ask to help her perform these steps?

6. In general, what advice would you give Zena on notetaking?

Taking Tests

6

So it all comes down to a test.

That was the thought that ran through Imani Brown's mind as he got ready to start the test of a lifetime. Yes, he had taken tests all through his school career, and yes, he had suffered through the S.A.T. standardized exam in order to get into college. But now, on the verge of starting his career as a high school teacher, there was one more hurdle to jump over: The state legislature had recently decided that all new graduates of teacher training programs had to take and pass a competency test prior to starting to teach. Imani, who had wanted to be a teacher as long as he could remember, knew he had to pass in order to start the teaching job he had landed for the fall.

So here he was, facing what he hoped would be the last test of his life. Although he was confident he could pass—he had studied hard—there was always a degree of uncertainty. Nothing had stopped him so far, and he wasn't going to let one test thwart him now. But still . . .

Although most tests don't hold as much significance as Imani Brown's teacher competency exam, tests do play a significant role in everyone's academic life. For many students, tests represent the most anxiety-producing events in their college careers.

They needn't be *so* bad. There are strategies and techniques you can learn to reduce the fearsomeness of tests. In fact, in some ways learning *how* to take tests is as important as learning the content that they cover. Taking tests effectively is an acquired skill. It does not just involve mastering a body of information; it also requires mastering specific test-taking skills.

It is those skills we consider in this chapter. One of the first steps is to demystify tests. You will learn about the different types of tests and strategies that you can apply before you even take a test. You will become familiar with various types of test questions and learn a strategy that matches each type of question.

We will also explore two aspects of test taking that may affect your performance: test anxiety and cramming for a test. You will learn ways to deal with anxiety, keep your cramming to a minimum, and make the most of cramming if you *do* have to resort to it.

The chapter ends with suggestions for evaluating your performance toward the end of a test session and for using your test results to improve your performance the next time you take a test.

After reading this chapter, you'll be able to answer these questions:

- **What kinds of tests will I encounter in college?**

- **What are the best ways to prepare for and take various kinds of tests?**

- **What are the best strategies for answering specific kinds of test questions?**

Getting Ready

Although tests are a fact of academic life, there are aspects of them that those who give tests—as well as those who take them—don't like very much.

Students hate tests because they produce fear, anxiety, apprehension about being evaluated, and a focus on grades instead of learning for learning's sake. Instructors hate tests because they produce fear, anxiety, apprehension about being evaluated, and a focus on grades instead of learning for learning's sake. That's right: Students and instructors dislike tests for the very same reasons.

On the other hand, tests are also valuable. A well-constructed test identifies what you know (and don't know), and where there are gaps in your knowledge. They help you see how your performance compares to that of others. And knowing that you'll be tested on a body of material is certainly likely to motivate you to learn material more thoroughly.

But there's another reason why you may dislike tests: You may assume that tests have the power to define your worth as a person. However, *tests are not a measure of your value as an individual—just how well (and how much) you studied and how well you learned the material.*

If you do badly on a test, you may be tempted to believe that you've received some fundamental information about yourself from the professor and the college, information that says you're a failure in some significant way.

This is a dangerous—and wrong-headed—assumption. If you do badly on a test, it doesn't mean you're a bad person. Or stupid. Or that you'll never do better again, and that your life is ruined. If you don't do well on a test, you're the same person you were before you took the test—no better, no worse. You just did badly on a test. Period.

Tests are tools; they are indirect and imperfect measures of what we know. Someone with a great deal of knowledge can do poorly on a test; perhaps her nerves made her blank out or she went too slowly early on and was unable to complete the test. Another person may know considerably less and still do better on the test simply because he may have learned some test-taking skills along the way.

How much we reap the benefits of a test depends on a number of considerations: the kind of test it is, the subject matter involved, and above all how well we prepare for it. Let's turn, then, to the first step in test taking: preparation. (The five steps are summarized in the P.O.W.E.R. Plan below.)

P repare: Readying Your Test-Taking Strategies

Preparation for tests requires a number of strategies. Among the most important are the following:

Remember Everything You Do in a Course Is Preparation for a Test Completing a reading assignment. Writing a paper. Filling out a worksheet.

Everything you do during a course helps to prepare you for a test. There is no surer way to get good grades on tests than to attend class faithfully and to complete all class assignments seriously and on time.

Preparing for tests is a long-term proposition. It's not a matter of "giving your all" the night before the test. Instead, it's a matter of giving your all to every aspect of the course.

Know What You Are Preparing For Determine as much as you can about the test before you begin to prepare for it. The more you know about a test, the better you'll be able to get ready.

To find out about an upcoming test, ask these questions:

- Is the test called a "test," "exam," "quiz," or something else? As you can see in Table 6.1, the names imply different things. For simplicity's sake, we'll use the term *test* throughout this chapter, but know that these distinctions exist and they should affect the way you prepare.

- What material will the test cover?

- How many questions will be on it?

- How much time is it expected to take? A full class period? Only part of a period?

- What kinds of questions will be on the test?

- How will it be graded?

- Will sample questions be provided?

- Are tests from previous terms available?

Form a Study Group **Study groups** are small, informal groups of students who work together to learn the course material and study for a test. Forming such a group can be an excellent way to prepare. Some study groups are

PREPARE

Review your work on a regular basis

ORGANIZE

Bring the right tools to the test; follow directions carefully

WORK

Tackle the test

EVALUATE

Save time to check your work; know when to stop

RETHINK

Reflect on what you've learned when you get a test back

P.O.W.E.R. Plan

Table 6.1

Quizzes, Tests, Exams . . .
What's in a Name?

Although they may vary from one instructor to another, the following definitions are the ones most frequently used:

Quizzes. A **quiz** is a brief assessment, usually covering a relatively small amount of material. Some quizzes cover as little as one class's worth of reading. Although a single quiz usually doesn't count very much, instructors often add quiz scores together, and collectively they can become a significant part of your final course grade.

Tests. A **test** is a more extensive, more heavily weighted assessment than a quiz, covering more material. A test may come every few weeks of the term, often after each third or quarter of the term has passed, but this varies with the instructor and the course.

Exams. An **exam** is the most substantial kind of assessment. In many classes, just one exam is given—a *final exam* at the end of the term. Sometimes there are two exams, one at the midpoint of the term (called, of course, a midterm) and the other at the end. Exams are usually weighted quite heavily because they are meant to assess your knowledge of all the course material up to that point.

Teaching Tip: A student's ability to focus and work productively in a study group has a lot to do with his or her learning style (see Chap. 3). Encourage students who want to become part of a study group to complete the TRY IT! 1 activity.

Study groups

Small, informal groups of students whose purpose is to help members work together and study for a test

formed for particular tests, while others meet consistently throughout the term.

The typical study group meets a week or two before a test and plans a strategy for studying. Members share their understanding of what will be on the test, based on their own perceptions of what an instructor has said in class about the upcoming test. Together, they develop a list of review questions to guide their individual study. The group breaks up, and the members study on their own.

A few days before the test, members of the study group meet again. They discuss answers to the review questions, go over the material, and share any new information they may have about the upcoming test. They may also quiz one another about the material to identify any weaknesses or gaps in their knowledge.

Study groups can be extremely powerful tools because they help accomplish several things:

- They help members to organize and structure the material, which forces members to approach the material in a systematic and logical way.

- They aid in the sharing of different perspectives on the material.

- They help prevent students from overlooking any potentially important information.

- They force their members to rethink the course material, explaining it in words that they and the other group members will understand. As we will discuss in Chapter 9, this helps both understanding and recall of the information when it is needed on the test.

- They also help motivate members to do their best. When you're part of a study group, you're no longer working just for yourself; your studying also benefits the

Study groups, made up of a few students who study together for a test, can help organize material, provide new perspectives, and motivate members to do their best.

Try It! 1

Working in a Group

Form a Study Group

The next time you have to prepare for a test, form a study group with about three to five classmates. They may have a variety of study habits and skills, but all must be willing to take the group seriously.

The first time you meet, plan your activities and divide up responsibilities. Then compare notes about what is likely to be on the test and brainstorm ideas for questions. If the instructor hasn't given you detailed information about the test (i.e., number and types of questions, weighting, etc.), one of you should ask for it.

After you've taken the test and gotten your results, meet again. Find out if members felt the group was effective. Did the members feel more confident about the test? Do they think they did better than they would have without the group? What worked? What didn't? What could you do differently next time?

other study-group members. Not wanting to let down your classmates in a study group may sometimes give more of a push to your study habits than you get from working only for yourself.

There are some some potential drawbacks to keep in mind. Study groups don't always work well for students with certain kinds of learning styles in which they prefer to work independently. In addition, "problem" members, who don't pull their weight, may result in difficulties for the group. In general, though, the advantages of study groups usually far outweigh their possible disadvantages.

Match Test Preparation to Question Types Test questions come in different types (see Table 6.2), and each requires a somewhat different style of preparation.

- **Essay questions.** Essay questions are meant to see if you have a broad knowledge of the material being tested. You'll need to know not just a series of facts, but also the connections between them, and you will have to be able to discuss these ideas in an organized and logical way. Essay exams focus on the ways in which the various pieces of information on a topic fit together.

    The best approach to studying for an essay exam involves four steps:

    1. Carefully read your class notes and any notes you've made on assigned readings that will be covered on the upcoming exam. Also go through the readings themselves, reviewing underlined or highlighted material and marginal notes.

    2. Play professor: Think of likely exam questions. To do this, you can use the key words, phrases, concepts, and questions you've earlier

Student Alert: Some high schools do not use essay questions as a way of evaluating students. Find out how familiar your students are with writing essays on exams.

Table 6.2

Types of Test Questions

Essay

Requires a fairly extensive, on-the-spot composition about some topic. An essay question may call on you to describe some person, process, or event, or it may ask you to compare or contrast two separate sets of material.

Multiple-choice

Usually contains a question or statement, followed by a number of (usually four or five) response choices. You are supposed to choose the most correct response from the possible response choices that are offered.

True–false

Presents statements about a topic that are either accurate or inaccurate. You are to indicate whether each statement is accurate (true) or inaccurate (false).

Matching

Presents two lists of related information, arranged in column form. Typically you are asked to pair terms, concepts, and definitions with one another.

Short-answer

Requires brief responses (at most a few sentences) in a kind of mini-essay.

Fill-in

Requires you to add one or more missing words to a sentence or series of sentences.

Teaching Tip: Earlier in the term, students should have noted in their planners when all their tests, projects, etc., are scheduled for the entire semester. Extend that activity to include a notation of what type of test will be given next to each date that a test is scheduled.

created in your notes. In addition, your class instructor may have given you a list of possible essay topics.

3. Without looking at your notes or your readings, answer each potential essay question—aloud. Don't feel embarrassed about doing this. Talking aloud is often more useful than answering the question silently in your head.

   You can also write down the main points that any answer should cover. But you probably shouldn't write out complete and full answers to the questions, because your time is probably better spent learning the material you'll be tested on. The one exception: if your instructor tells you exactly what essay question is going to be on the exam. In that case, it pays to write out the answer.

4. After you've answered the questions, check yourself by looking at the notes and readings once again. If you feel confident that you've answered particular questions adequately, check them off. You can go back later for a quick review.

   But if there are questions that you had trouble with, review that material immediately. Then repeat the third step above, answering the questions again.

- **Multiple-choice, true–false,** and **matching questions.** While the focus of review for essay questions should be on major issues and controversies, and on integration of the material—more of a "big picture" focus—studying for multiple-choice, true–false, and matching questions requires more attention to the details.

   Almost anything is fair game for multiple-choice, true–false, and matching questions, and so you can't afford to overlook anything when studying. This means that your studying needs to be detail-oriented. And it means that you must put your memory into high gear and master a great many facts.

It's a particularly good idea to write down important facts on index cards like those below. Remember the advantages of these cards: They're portable and available all the time, and the act of creating them helps drive the material into your memory. Furthermore, you can shuffle them and test yourself repeatedly until you know you've mastered the material.

Political reforms of progressive age:

-direct primaries: people vote for whom they want to run; not appointed

-initiative: people propose laws on their own

-referendum: gov. proposes; people say yes or no

-recall: people can remove politicians from office before they finish term

Endoplasmic reticulum (ER):

Smooth ER—makes fats (lipids)

Rough ER—has ribosomes which make proteins

Together, they make membranes for whole cell (for plasma membrane, mitochondrion, etc.) Also make more of themselves.

- **Short-answer** and **fill-in questions.** Short-answer and fill-in questions are similar to essays in that they require you to recall key pieces of information; that is, you have to dredge the information up from your memory rather than, as is the case with multiple-choice, true–false, and matching questions, finding it on the page in front of you. However, short-answer and fill-in questions—unlike essay questions—typically don't demand that you integrate or compare different types of information. Consequently, the focus of your study should be on the recall of specific, detailed information.

Test Yourself   Once you feel you've mastered the material, test yourself on it. There are several ways to do this. One is to create a complete test for yourself, in writing, making its form as close as possible to what you expect the actual test to be. For instance, if your instructor has told you the classroom test will be primarily made up of short-answer questions, your test should be too. One bonus: Constructing a test is actually an excellent way of studying the material and cementing it into memory.

You might also construct a test and administer it to a classmate or a member of your study group. In turn, you could take a test that someone else has constructed. The combined experience of making and taking a test on the same general subject matter is among the very best ways to prepare for the real thing.

Test anxiety
A temporary condition characterized by fears and concerns about test taking

Deal with Test Anxiety   What does the anticipation of a test do to you? Do you feel shaky? Frantic, like there's not enough time to get it all done? Do you feel as if there's a knot in your stomach? Do you grit your teeth?

Fortunately, **test anxiety** is a temporary condition characterized by fears and concerns about test taking. Almost everyone experiences it to some degree; but if it is too great, it can make it harder for you to study and do your best on a test. (To assess your own test anxiety, see Try It 3 on page 148.)

Try It! 2

Complete a Test-Preparation Checklist

Before taking your next test, complete the following test-preparation checklist.

Test-Preparation Checklist

- ☐ I checked whether it's a quiz, test, or exam.
- ☐ I began preparation long before the test (e.g., by taking notes in class).
- ☐ I understand what material will be covered.
- ☐ I know how many questions will be on the test.
- ☐ I know how long it will take.
- ☐ I know what kinds of questions will be on the test.
- ☐ I know how it will be graded.
- ☐ I obtained sample questions and/or previous tests, if available.
- ☐ I formed or participated in a study group.
- ☐ I studied with my study group more than once.
- ☐ I used different and appropriate preparation strategies for each type of question.
- ☐ I read class notes.
- ☐ I composed some essay questions.
- ☐ I answered essay questions aloud.
- ☐ I actively memorized facts and details.
- ☐ I made and used note cards.
- ☐ I created and used a test like the real test.

You'll never eliminate test anxiety completely, nor do you want to. A little bit of nervousness can energize us, making us more attentive and vigilant. Like any competitive event, testing can motivate us to do our best. So think of test anxiety as a desire to perform at your peak—an ally at test time.

On the other hand, for many, anxiety can spiral into the kind of paralyzing fear that makes your mind go blank. So you definitely want to keep it in its place. There are several ways to do this:

1. *Prepare thoroughly.* The more you prepare, the less test anxiety you'll feel. Good preparation can give you a sense of control and mastery, and it will prevent test anxiety from overwhelming you.

2. *Take a realistic view of the test.* Remember that no single test determines how you'll do for the rest of your life. Your future success does not hinge on your performance on any single exam.

3. *Learn relaxation techniques.* You can learn to reduce or even eliminate the jittery physical symptoms of test anxiety by using relaxation techniques. These techniques are covered in Chapter 14, but the basic process is straightforward: You want to breathe evenly, gently inhaling

IM Link: "Teaching the Text," Chapter 6, Sections IV and VIII; consider using the pretest activity. Elaborate on the last item on this list.

Teaching Tip: Test anxiety is a good topic for a guest speaker to address. Many campuses have experts in this area and since you test and evaluate your students, someone "outside" that relationship provides a valuable, and possibly different, perspective.

Try It! 3

Measure Your Test Anxiety

Check off every statement below that applies to you.

☐ 1. The closer a test date approaches, the more nervous I get.

☐ 2. I am sometimes unable to sleep on the night before a test.

☐ 3. I have "frozen up" during a test, unable to think or respond.

☐ 4. I can feel my hands shaking as I pick up my pencil to begin a test.

☐ 5. The minute I read a tough test question, all the facts I ever knew about the subject abandon me and I can't get them back no matter how hard I try.

☐ 6. I have become physically ill before or during a test.

☐ 7. Nervousness prevents me from studying immediately before a test.

☐ 8. I often dream about an upcoming test.

☐ 9. Even if I successfully answer a number of questions, my anxiety stays with me all through the test.

☐ 10. I'm reluctant to turn in my test paper for fear that I can do better if I continue to work on it.

If you checked off more than four statements, you have experienced fairly serious test anxiety. If you checked off more than 6 statements, you should deal with your anxiety because it is probably interfering with your test performance. In particular, statements 3, 5, 6, 7, and 10 may indicate serious test anxiety.

If, based on your responses to this questionnaire and your previous experience, your level of test anxiety is high, follow some of the steps described for dealing with the issue.

---

and exhaling. Focus your mind on a pleasant, relaxing scene such as a beautiful forest or a peaceful spread of farmland, or on a sound such as ocean waves.

Teaching Tip: Visualization is being used more and more in such varied areas as athletics and wellness. Model this activity with your class.

4. *Visualize success.* Think of an image of your instructor handing back your test, on which you've received an A. Or imagine your instructor congratulating you on your fine performance the moment you walk into your classroom on the day after the test. Positive visualizations such as these, which highlight your potential success, can help replace negative images of failure that may be fueling your test anxiety.

Cramming: You Shouldn't, But . . . You know, of course, that **cramming,** hurried, last-minute studying, is not the way to go. You know that you're likely to forget the material the moment the test is over because long-term retention is nearly impossible without thoughtful study. But . . .

Cramming
Hurried, last-minute studying

. . . it's been one of those weeks where everything went wrong.

. . . the instructor sprang the test on you at the last minute.

. . . you forgot about the test until the night before it was scheduled.

Whatever the reason, there may be times when you can't study properly. What do you do if you have to cram for an exam?

The first thing to do is choose what you really need to study. You won't be able to learn everything, so you have to make choices. Figure out the main fo-

Have you ever crammed for a test? If so, you know how exhausting it can be, and how easy it is to overlook crucial material. On the other hand, time pressures sometimes make cramming your only option. When that happens, there are strategies you can use to help you make the best use of limited time.

cus of the course, and concentrate on it. Don't spend a lot of time on what you're unable to do. Beating yourself up about your failings as a student will only hinder your efforts.

Instead, admit you're human and fallible like everyone else. Then spend a few minutes developing a plan about what you can accomplish in the limited time you've got.

Once you have a strategy, prepare a one-page summary sheet with hard-to-remember information. Just writing the material down will help you remember it, and you can refer to the summary sheet frequently over the limited time you do have to study.

Next, read through your class notes, concentrating on the material you've underlined and the key concepts and ideas that you've already noted. Forget about reading all the material in the books and articles you're being tested on. Instead, only read the passages that you've underlined and the notes you've taken on the readings. Finally, maximize your study time. Using your notes, note cards, and concept maps, go over the information. Read it. Say it aloud. Say it aloud again. Think about it and the way it relates to other information. In short, use all the techniques we've talked about for learning and recalling information.

Just remember: When the exam is over, material that you have crammed into your head is destined to leave your mind as quickly as it entered. If you've crammed for a midterm, don't assume that the information will still be there when you study for the final. In the end, cramming often ends up taking more time for worse results than does studying with more-appropriate techniques.

Organize: Facing the Day of the Test

You've studied a lot, and you're happy with your level of mastery. Or perhaps you have the nagging feeling that there's something you haven't quite gotten to. Or maybe you know you haven't had enough time to study as much as you'd like, and you're expecting a disaster.

Whatever your frame of mind, it will help to organize your plan of attack on the day of the test. What's included on the test is out of your hands, but what you bring to it you can control.

For starters, bring the right tools to the test. Have at least two pens and two pencils with you. It's usually best to write in pen because, in general, writing tends to be easier to read in pen than pencil. But you also might want to have pencils at the ready. Sometimes instructors will use machine-scorable tests,

Teaching Tip: This is a good time to mention the physical aspects of test preparation, from sleep and nutrition to techniques for dealing with sweaty palms and fluttering stomachs, to the actual location where the test is given and how your students may need to adapt to that setting to be successful.

which require the use of pencil. Or there may be test questions that involve computations, and solving them may entail frequent reworking of calculations.

You should also be sure to bring a watch to the test, even if there will be a clock on the wall of the classroom. You will want to be able to pace yourself properly during the test. Just having your own watch—even if there is a clock in the classroom—will help you feel more in control of your time during the test.

Sometimes instructors permit you to use notes and books during the test. If you haven't brought them with you, they're not going to be of much help. So make sure you bring them if you can. Even for closed-book tests, having such material available before the test actually starts may allow you a few minutes of review after you arrive in the classroom.

On the day of a test, avoid the temptation to compare notes with your friends about how much they've studied. Yes, you might end up feeling good because many of your fellow classmates studied less than you. But chances are you'll find others who sound like they have spent significantly *more* time studying than you, and this will do little to encourage you.

> ## "High school is memorization and regurgitation. Here you have to think."
>
> Junior, Engineering, Notre Dame.[1]

Student Alert: Do your students agree with this quote or do they believe their high school provided more rigorous preparation for college?

Plan on panicking. Although it sounds like the worst possible approach, permitting yourself the option of spending a minute feeling panicky will help you to recover from your initial fears.

Finally, listen carefully to what an instructor says before the test is handed out. The instructor may tell you about a question that is optional or worth more points or inform you of a typographical error on the test. Whatever the instructor says just before the test, you can be sure it's information that you don't want to ignore.

Taking the Test

 Work: Tackling the Test

Student Alert: Students often miss the importance of this information. Emphasize the importance of skimming the entire exam with the main purpose of balancing time and point totals for each section of the test.

Take a deep breath—literally.

There's no better way to start work on a test than by taking a deep breath, followed by several others. The deep breaths will help you to overcome any initial panic and anxiety you may be experiencing. It's OK to give yourself over for a moment to panic and anxiety, but, to work at your best, use the relaxation techniques that we spoke about earlier to displace those initial feelings. Tell yourself, "It's OK. I am going to do my best on this." Don't let your mind get sidetracked by panicky thoughts.

Read the test instructions and *then skim through the entire exam.* Look at the kinds of questions that are asked and pay attention to the way they will be scored. If the point weighting of the various parts of the exam is not clear, ask the instructor to clarify it. Your goal is to know how to allocate your time. You don't want to spend 90 percent of your time on an essay that's worth only 10 percent of the points, and you want to be sure to leave time at the end of the test to check your answers. An initial read-through also helps you verify that you have every page of the exam and that there is no other physical problem with it, such as badly copied pages or ink marks that partially obscure some of the questions.

If there are any lists, formulas, or other key facts that you're concerned you may forget, jot them down now on the back of a test page or on a piece of scrap paper. You may want to refer to this material later during the test.

Once this background work is out of the way, you'll be ready to proceed to actually answering the questions. These principles will help you to do your best on the test:

Discussion Prompt: Ask students to share their experiences here. What testing principles have worked for them?

- **Answer the easiest questions first.** By initially getting the questions out of the way that are easiest for you, you accomplish several important things. First, you'll be leaving yourself more time to think about the tougher questions later. In addition, moving through a series of questions without a struggle will build your confidence. Finally, working through a number of questions will build up a base of points that may be enough to earn you at least a minimally acceptable grade.

- **Write legibly on one side of the paper.** If an instructor can't read what you've written, you're not going to get credit for it, no matter how brilliant your answer. So be sure to keep your handwriting legible.

  It's also a good idea to write your answers to essay questions on only one side of a page. This will allow you to go back later and add or revise information.

- **Master machine-scored tests.** Tests will sometimes be scored, in part, by computer. In such cases, you'll usually have to indicate your answers by filling in—with a pencil—circles or squares on a computer answer sheet.

  Be careful! A stray mark or smudge can cause the computer scanner to misread your answer sheet, producing errors in grading. Be sure to bring a good eraser in addition to a pencil; the biggest source of mistakes in machine grading is incomplete erasing on a test.

  It's best to write your answers not only on the answer sheet but also on the test itself (if the test is not intended for future re-use). That way you can go back and check your answers easily—a step you should take frequently.

> "Computerized test-scoring isn't perfect. Smudges can kill you. If your grade seems incorrect, ask to see the answer sheet."
>
> Graduate, Physiology, Michigan State University.[2]

Use Strategies Targeted to Answering Specific Types of Test Items Every type of item requires a particular approach. Use these strategies to tailor your approach to specific kinds of questions:

- **Essay Questions.** Essay questions, with their emphasis on description and analysis, often present challenges because they are relatively unstructured. Unless you're careful, it's easy to wander off and begin to answer questions that were never asked. To prevent that problem, the first thing to do is read the question carefully, noting what specifically is being asked. If your essay will be lengthy, you might even want to write a short outline.

  Pay attention to key words that indicate what, specifically, the instructor is looking for in an answer. Certain action words are commonly used in essays, and you should understand them fully. For instance, knowing the distinction between "compare" and "contrast" can spell the

Table 6.3

Action Words for Essays

These words are commonly used in essay questions. Learning the distinctions among them will help you during tests.

Analyze: Examine and break into component parts.

Clarify: Explain with significant detail.

Compare: Describe similarities and differences.

Compare and contrast: Describe and distinguish similarities and differences.

Contrast: Explain and distinguish differences.

Critique: Judge and analyze, explaining what is wrong—and right—about a concept.

Define: Provide the meaning.

Discuss: Explain, review, and consider.

Enumerate: Provide a listing of ideas, concepts, reasons, items, etc.

Evaluate: Provide pros and cons of something; provide an opinion, and justify it.

Explain: Give reasons why or how; clarify, justify, and illustrate.

Illustrate: Provide examples; show instances.

Interpret: Explain the meaning of something.

Justify: Explain why a concept can be supported, typically by using examples and other types of support.

Outline: Provide a framework or explanation—usually in narrative form—of a concept, idea, event, or phenomenon.

Prove: Using evidence and arguments, convince the reader of a particular point.

Relate: Show how things fit together; provide analogies.

Review: Describe or summarize, often with an evaluation.

State: Assert or explain.

Summarize: Provide a condensed, precise list or narrative.

Trace: Track or sketch out how events or circumstances have evolved; provide a history or time line.

difference between success and failure. Table 6.3 defines common action words.

Use the right language in essays. Be brief and to the point in your essay. Avoid flowery introductory language. Compare the two sentences that follow:

"In our study of world literature, it may be useful to ponder how *The Canterbury Tales* came to represent such an important milestone in the field, and it will be seen that there are several critical reasons why it did have such an impact."

"*The Canterbury Tales* were groundbreaking for several reasons."

This second sentence says the same thing much more effectively and economically.

Essays are improved when they include examples and point out differences. Your response should follow a logical sequence, moving from major points to minor ones, or following a time sequence. Above all, your answer should address every aspect of the question posed on the test. Because essays often contain several different, embedded questions, you have to be certain that you have answered every part, in order to receive full credit.

- **Multiple-Choice Questions.** If you've ever looked at a multiple-choice question and said to yourself, "But every choice seems right," you understand what can be tricky about this type of question. However, there are some simple strategies that can help you deal with multiple-choice questions.

First, read the instructions carefully to determine whether only one response choice will be correct, or whether more than one of the choices may be correct. Almost always only one choice is right, but in some cases instructors may permit you to check off more than one answer.

Turn to the first question and read the question part—the part before the response choices. *Before you look at the choices, try to answer the question in your head.* This can help you avoid being confused by inappropriate choices.

Next, *carefully read through every choice.* Even if you come to one that you think is right, keep reading—there may be a subsequent answer that is better.

Look for absolutes like "every," "always," "only," "none," and "never." Choices that contain such absolute words are rarely correct. On the other hand, less-absolute words, such as "generally," "usually," "often," "rarely," "seldom," and "typically" may indicate a correct response.

Be especially on guard for the word "not," which negates the sentence ("The one key concept that is not embodied in the U.S. Constitution is . . . "). It's easy to gloss over "not," and if you have the misfortune of doing so, it will be nearly impossible to answer the item correctly.

If you're having trouble understanding a question, underline key words or phrases, or try to break the question into different short sections. Sometimes it is helpful to work backwards, *Jeopardy* style, and look at the response choices first to see if you can find one that is clearly accurate or clearly inaccurate.

*Use an **educated guessing** strategy*—which is very different from wild or random guessing. Unless you are penalized for wrong answers (a scoring rule by which wrong answers are deducted from the points you have earned on other questions, rather than merely not counting at all toward your score), it always pays to guess.

The first step in educated guessing is to eliminate any obviously false answers. The next step is to examine the remaining choices closely. Does one response choice include a qualifier that makes it unlikely ("the probability of war always increases when a U.S. president is facing political difficulties")? Does one choice include a subtle factual error ("when Columbus began his journey to the New World in 1492, he went with the support of the French monarchy")? In such cases, you may be able to figure out the correct response by eliminating the others.

Discussion Prompt: The cartoon poses an interesting premise. Do your students agree or disagree? Encourage your students to place the specific techniques presented in the context of the bigger picture; namely, what is higher education all about?

Educated guessing

The practice of eliminating obviously false multiple-choice answers and selecting the most likely answer from the remaining choices

Understand Action Verbs in Essay Questions

Answer the following questions about the First Amendment to the United States Constitution by outlining your responses to them, paying attention to the various action verbs that introduce the questions.

The First Amendment states:

Congress shall make no law respecting an establishment of religion, or prohibiting the free exercise thereof; or abridging the freedom of speech or of the press; or the right of the people peaceably to assemble, and to petition the government for a redress of grievances.

1. Summarize the First Amendment of the Constitution.

2. Interpret the First Amendment of the Constitution.

- **True–False Questions.** Although most of the principles we've already discussed apply equally well to true–false questions, a few additional tricks of the trade may help you with this question type.

  Begin a set of true–false questions by marking the items you're sure you know the answer to. But don't rush; it's important to read every part of a true–false question, because key words such as "never," "always," and "sometimes" often determine the appropriate response.

  If you don't have a clue about whether a statement is true or false, here's another last-resort principle: Choose "true." In general, more statements on a true–false test are likely to be true than false.

- **Matching Questions.** Matching questions typically present you with two columns of related information, which you must link using a process of elimination. For example, a list of terms or concepts may be presented in one column, along with a list of corresponding definitions

3. Evaluate the First Amendment of the Constitution.

4. Discuss the First Amendment of the Constitution.

5. Analyze the First Amendment of the Constitution.

How do your answers differ for the each of the questions? Which of the questions provoked the lengthiest response? Which of the questions could you answer best?

or explanations in the second column. The best strategy is to reduce the size of both columns by matching the items you're most confident about first; this will leave a short list in each column, and the final matching may become apparent.

- **Short-Answer and Fill-In Questions.** Short-answer and fill-in questions basically require you to *generate and supply* specific information in your own words. Unlike essays, which are more free-form and may have several possible answers, short-answer and fill-in questions are quite specific. There is usually only one answer, which you must come up with on your own. Responding to them, then, requires that you pay special attention to what, in particular, you are being asked.

    Use both the instructions for the questions and the questions themselves to determine the level of specificity that is needed in an answer. Try not to provide too much or too little information. Usually, brevity is best.

Career Connections

Doing Well on Standardized Professional Tests

MCAT. LSAT. GMAT.

If you are thinking about a career in medicine, law, or business, you may already have heard these abbreviations. They stand for the names of some of the national, standardized tests that you will need to take in order to enroll in a post-undergraduate course of study. Many states also require that students who wish to enter particular professions pass a specialized standardized test, such as the teaching exam described at the beginning of the chapter, before they begin work.

Here are some general tips that can help you perform well on them:

- Learn as much as you can about the test before you take it. Know what sections will be on the test and how much each section is worth.

- Practice. Try as many practice tests as you can find. The more practice you have, the easier it will be when you actually take the test.

- If the test is administered on a computer, as many increasingly are, take practice tests on a computer. The more familiar you are with computers, the more at ease you will feel when you sit down to actually take the test.

- Time yourself carefully. Don't spend too much time on early items at the expense of later ones.

- Be aware of the scoring policy. If you are not penalized for wrong answers, guess. If there are penalties, be more conservative in terms of guessing.

- Complete the answer sheet accurately. Check, and check again.

About Academic Honesty

Perhaps it's a tempting thought: A glance at a classmate's test may provide the one piece of information that you just can't remember.

You owe it to yourself not to do it. **Academic honesty**—completing and turning in only your own work under your own name—is the foundation of college life—and of your personal life. Copying from a classmate's paper is no different from reaching over and stealing that classmate's calculator or watch.

Cheating can take several forms. It may involve copying another's work, using a calculator when it's not allowed, discussing the answer to a question, copying a computer file when it's unauthorized, taking an exam for another person, or stealing an exam. Whatever the form, academic dishonesty is wrong. It diminishes the academic community, it makes the grading system unfair, and it ultimately reduces the meaning of your grade. It certainly damages academic and personal growth. It can't help but reduce one's self-esteem, and it robs the cheater of self-respect. Finally, getting caught leads to a number of unpleasant scenarios: failing the exam on which the cheating has taken place, failing the entire course, being brought before an academic honesty board, having a note placed in one's academic file, being placed on academic probation, or even being thrown out of school. Cheating is simply not worth it.

E valuate: Taking Your Own Final Examination

The last few minutes of a test may feel like the final moments of a marathon. You need to focus your energy and push forward harder. It can be make-or-break time.

Save some time at the end of a test so you can check your work. You should have been keeping track of your time all along, so plan on stopping a few minutes before the end of the test period to review what you've done. It's a critical step, and it can make the difference between a terrific grade and a mediocre one. It's a rare person who can work for an uninterrupted period of time on a test and commit absolutely no errors—even if he or she knows the material backwards and forwards. Consequently, checking what you've done is crucial.

Start evaluating your test by looking for obvious mistakes. Make sure you've answered every question and haven't skipped any parts of questions. If there is a separate answer sheet, check to see that all your answers have been recorded on the answer sheet and in the right spot.

If the test has included essay and short-answer questions, proofread your responses. Check for obvious errors—misspellings, missing words, and repetitions. Make sure you've responded to every part of each question and that each essay, as a whole, makes sense.

Check over your responses to multiple-choice, true–false, and matching questions. If there are some items that you haven't yet answered because you couldn't remember the necessary information, now is the time to take a stab at them. As we discussed earlier, it usually pays to guess, even randomly if you must. On most tests, no answer and a wrong answer are worth the same amount—nothing! Only occasionally will instructors deduct points for wrong answers, and you will know in advance if that is their policy.

What about items that you initially were genuinely unsure about, and you guessed at the answer? Unless you have a good reason to change your original answer—such as a new insight or a sudden recollection of some key information—your first guess is likely your best guess.

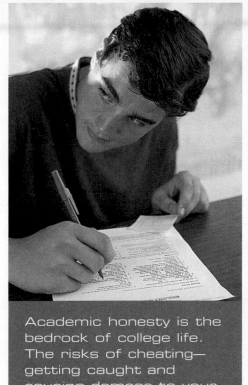

Academic honesty is the bedrock of college life. The risks of cheating—getting caught and causing damage to your sense of self-worth—far outweigh any momentary benefits.

Know When to Stop   After evaluating and checking your answers, you may reach a point when there is still some time left. What to do? If you're satisfied with your responses, it's simply time to tell yourself, *Let it go.*

Permit yourself the luxury of knowing that you've done your best and it's time to hand the test to your instructor. Just because there is time remaining in the class period and some of your classmates are still working on their tests, you don't have to continue reviewing your work over and over. In fact, such behavior is often counterproductive, because it may lead you to start overinterpreting test items and reading things into questions that really aren't there.

Disaster! I've run out of time! It's a nightmarish feeling: The clock is ticking relentlessly, and it's clear that you don't have enough time to finish the test. What should you do?

Stop work! Although this advice may sound foolish, in fact the most important thing you can do is to take a minute to calm yourself. Take some deep breaths to replace the feelings of panic that are likely welling up inside you. Collect your thoughts, and plan a strategy for the last moments of the test.

If there are essays that remain undone, consider how you'd answer them if you had more time. Then write an outline of each answer. If you don't have time even for that, write a few keywords. Writing anything is better than handing in a blank page, and you may get at least some credit for your response. The key principle here: Something is better than nothing, and even one point is worth more than zero points.

The same principle holds for other types of questions. Even wild guesses are almost always better than not responding at all to an item. So rather than telling yourself you've certainly failed and giving up, do as much as you can in the remaining moments of the exam.

Academic honesty
Completing and turning in only one's own work under one's own name

Try It! 5

Take a Test-Taking Test

Take the following test on test-taking skills, which illustrates every question type discussed in this chapter. Answers to all questions except short-answer and essay questions are provided at the end of the test.

Before taking the test, think of the test-taking strategies we've discussed in the chapter, and try to employ as many of them as possible.

Multiple-choice section

1. Tests are useful tools for which of the following purposes?
   a. determining people's likely level of future career success
   b. indicating strengths and gaps in people's knowledge
   c. defining people's fundamental abilities and potentials
   d. evaluating people's individual worth and contributions

2. One of the main advantages of study groups is that
   a. every individual must contribute equally to the group.
   b. group members can help each other during the test.
   c. each member has to memorize only a fraction of the material.
   d. groups motivate their members to do good work.

3. Which of the following is a good way to deal with test anxiety?
   a. visualizing success on the test
   b. drinking coffee or other stimulants
   c. telling yourself to stop worrying
   d. focusing on the importance of the test

4. Which of the following is likely to be the most effective cramming technique?
   a. preparing a one-page summary of the most important information
   b. quickly reading all articles and textbook chapters covered on the test
   c. neatly recopying all class notes and note cards while reading them aloud
   d. underlining or highlighting key information in the textbook and other resources

Matching section

___ 1. Essay question	A.	A question in which the student supplies brief missing information to complete a statement
___ 2. Quiz	B.	Hurried, last-minute studying
___ 3. Multiple-choice question	C.	An informed attempt to select an answer by eliminating clearly incorrect answers
___ 4. Matching question	D.	A question in which the student must link information in two columns
___ 5. True–false question	E.	A brief test
___ 6. Fill-in question	F.	A question requiring a lengthy response in the student's own words

___ 7.	Short-answer question	G. Deduction of points for incorrect responses
___ 8.	Guessing penalty	H. Representing another's work as one's own
___ 9.	Test anxiety	I. A question requiring a brief response in the student's own words
___ 10.	Cramming	J. A question that requires selection from several response options
___ 11.	Academic dishonesty	K. A feeling of fear induced by testing
___ 12.	Educated guess	L. A question requiring students to distinguish accurate and inaccurate statements

Fill-in section

1. Fear of testing that can interfere with test performance is called _____.

2. Last-minute studying is called _____.

3. The primary source of error on machine-scored tests is incomplete _____.

4. After inspecting the test and identifying areas that will be easy and those that will be hard, a reasonable test-taking strategy is to answer the _____ questions first.

True–false section

1. The best way to prepare for an essay test is to review detailed factual information about the topic. T _____ F _____

2. True–false questions require examinees to determine whether given statements are accurate or inaccurate. T _____ F _____

3. You should never permit yourself to feel panicky during a test. T _____ F _____

4. A good evaluation strategy toward the end of a test is to redo as many questions as time permits. T _____ F _____

5. For short-answer questions, examinees must select brief responses from response choices listed on the test form. T _____ F _____

6. In responding to essay questions, you should answer briefly and use plain language. T _____ F _____

7. In a multiple-choice question, the words "always" and "never" usually signal the correct response. T _____ F _____

8. It is usually unwise to guess on a multiple-choice test. T _____ F _____

9. If you run out of time at the end of a test, it is best to write brief notes and ideas down in response to essay questions, rather than leave them completely blank. T _____ F _____

(continued on next page)

Try It! 5

Take a Test-Taking Test— Continued

10. Students' comments on the amount of studying they have done before a test are generally accurate. T _____ F _____

Short-answer section

1. What are five things you should find out about a test before you take it?

2. What is academic honesty?

Essay section (write your answers on a separate sheet of paper)

1. Explain how tests can be useful to students and teachers.

2. Discuss the advantages of using a study group to prepare for an examination.

3. Why is academic honesty important?

Answers. Multiple-choice: 1B, 2D, 3A, 4A; Matching: 1F, 2E, 3J, 4D, 5L, 6A, 7I, 8G, 9K, 10B, 11H, 12C; Fill-in: test anxiety, cramming, erasing, easy; True–False: 1F, 2T, 3F, 4F, 5F, 6T, 7F, 8F, 9T, 10F.

After you have completed the test, consider these questions: Did you learn anything from taking the test that you might not have learned if you hadn't been tested on the material? How effective were the test-taking strategies you employed? Were any types of strategies easier for you to employ than others, and were any types of questions easier for you to use them on than others? Exchange your essay responses with a classmate, and critique the essays. How do the responses of your partner compare to those of your own?

R ethink: Reflecting on the Real Test of Learning

Your instructor is about to hand the graded exams back. All sorts of thoughts run through your head: How did I do? Did I perform as well as my class-mates? Will I be pleased with my results? Will the results reflect the amount of effort I put into studying? Will I be embarrassed by my grade?

Most of us focus on the evaluative aspects of tests. We look at the grade we've received on a test and take it to be a measure of something important. It's a natural reaction.

But there's another way to look at test results: They can help guide us toward future success. By looking at what we've learned (and haven't learned) about a given subject, we'll be in a better position to know what to focus on when we take future exams. Furthermore, by examining the kinds of mistakes we make, it's more likely that we can do better in the future.

When you get your test back, you have the opportunity to reflect on what you've learned and to consider your performance. Begin by looking at your mistakes. Chances are they'll jump out at you since they will be marked incorrect. Did you misunderstand or misapply some principle? Was there a certain aspect of the material covered on the test that you missed? Were there particular kinds of information that you didn't realize you needed to know? Or did you lose some points because of your test-taking skills? Did you make careless errors, such as forgetting to fill in a question or misreading the directions? Was your handwriting so sloppy that your instructor had trouble reading it?

Once you have a good idea of what material you didn't fully understand or remember, get the correct answers to the items you missed—from your instructor, fellow classmates, or your book. If it's a math exam, rework problems you've missed. Finally, summarize—in writing—the material you had trouble with. This will help you study for future exams that cover the same material.

> "The test of any man lies in action."
>
> Pindar, *Odes.*

Finally, if you're dissatisfied with your performance, talk to your instructor—not to complain, but to seek help. Instructors don't like to give bad grades, and they may be able to point out problems in your test that you can address readily so you can do better in the future. Demonstrate to your instructor that you want to do better and are willing to put in the work to get there. The worst thing to do is crumple up the test and quickly leave the class in embarrassment. Remember, you're not the first person to get a bad grade, and the power to improve your test-taking performance lies within you.

IM Link/Teaching Tip: Post-exam surveys or rethinking the test are activities we often overlook in the testing process. Make them a part of your course throughout the semester. See "Teaching the Text," Chapter 6—Section V: "Using the P.O.W.E.R. Learning process in your instruction," and Section VIII.

Looking Back

What kinds of tests will I encounter in college?

- Although tests are an unpopular fact of college life, they can provide useful evaluative information about one's level of knowledge and understanding about a subject.

- There are several types of tests, including brief, informal quizzes; more substantial tests; and even more weighty exams, which tend to be administered at the midpoint and end of a course.

What are the best ways to prepare for and take various kinds of tests?

- Good test preparation begins with completing the course assignments, attending class regularly, and paying attention in class. It also helps to find out as much as possible about a test beforehand and to form a study group to review material.

- If cramming becomes necessary, focus on summarizing factual information broadly, identifying key concepts and ideas, and rehearsing information orally.

- When you first receive the test, skim it to see what kinds of questions will be asked; figure out how the different questions and sections will be weighted; and jot down complex factual information that is likely to be needed for the test.

- Answer the easiest questions first, write legibly, use only one side of each sheet of paper, mark answer sheets carefully, and record answers in the test book as well as the answer sheet.

What are the best strategies for answering specific kinds of test questions?

- For essay questions, be sure to understand each question and each of its parts, interpret action words correctly, write concisely, organize the essay logically, and include examples.

- For multiple-choice questions, read the question very carefully and then read all response choices. Educated guessing based on eliminating incorrect response choices is usually a reasonable strategy.

- For true–false and matching questions, quickly answer all the items that you are sure of and then go back to the remaining items.

- The best strategy for short-answer and fill-in questions is to be very sure what is being asked. Keep answers complete but brief.

Key Terms and Concepts

Academic honesty (p. 157)   Study groups (p. 143)
Cramming (p. 148)   Test anxiety (p. 146)
Educated guessing (p. 153)

Resources

On Campus

Colleges often provide a variety of resources for students having difficulties with test taking. Some offer general workshops for students, reviewing test taking strategies. Furthermore, if you are planning to take a specific standardized test, such as the tests required for admission to business, law, or medical school, you may be able to sign up for a course offered through your college (or through such commercial organizations as *Princeton Review* or *Kaplan*).

If you find that you are experiencing significant test anxiety when taking a test or in the days leading up to it, talk to someone at your campus counseling center or health center. They can help you learn relaxation techniques and can provide psychological counseling to help make your anxiety manageable.

In Print

In *'Ace' Any Test* (3rd ed., Career Press, 1996), Ron Fry provides a variety of techniques designed to improve your performance on any kind of test. *Taking the Anxiety Out of Taking Tests* (New Harbinger Publications, 1997), by Susan Johnson, is a step-by-step guide to dealing with test anxiety, providing a variety of concrete suggestions dealing with the problem.

Speaking of Success

Name: *Theresa Winebrenner*
Education: *A.A., Austin Community College*
Home: *Austin, Texas*

There's nothing like a test to create anxiety in students. We have all felt it. Theresa Winebrenner, a student at Austin Community College, is no different, except that her techniques for coping with test anxiety are a bit specialized. Both blind and hearing-impaired, Winebrenner combines human and technological solutions with her own ingenuity to cope with the task of preparing for the approximately 16 exams she has to take each semester.

Winebrenner's preparation begins with careful notetaking.

"In class, I have a notetaker, called a Type and Speak, which is like a laptop computer. When I get home, I can download the lecture into my other computer, which has a synthesized voice capability," she notes. "Then, as the computer speaks the lecture for me, I take notes in Braille.

"I also have a machine called a Reading Edge that reads to me. If I place a book face down on its screen, it reads the page while I take Braille notes.

"Because of my hearing impairment, I have to take notes in Braille because the audible signal doesn't

always stick in my memory. Reading my notes in Braille is very helpful; it forces me to have a clear understanding of what I'm saying," Winebrenner says.

As for taking tests, that's more a matter of motivation and human help than technological assistance, Winebrenner says.

"I usually start about a week early to study for a test," Winebrenner explains. "I prepare a schedule for myself so I have a set of clear deadlines that I need to meet. Then I collect my notes, take them home, and review them.

"For the actual tests, the college's Special Services Department provides students who read the tests for me and write down my answers," she says. "One of the problems I run into is that some students are not familiar

with the academic background of the course I'm taking and don't read the test well or write the answers appropriately.

"If that's the case, I have to find another student who does have a background in the specific course, or else I ask the instructor to record the test on tape. If this is the way I go, I then dictate my answers to another student, who writes them down."

While she prefers multiple-choice tests, Winebrenner has been successful on many different kinds of tests, using different techniques to study for each type.

"If it's a test with multiple-choice questions, I focus more on the end-of-chapter reviews. I go through those and make notes on the questions in the text. If it's an essay test, I look more at the examples in the book or in my notes and use the essay-type questions and solutions at the end of the chapter as a guideline.

"Finally," she adds, "it gets to the point where you have to stop memorizing the material and start understanding it. There's no substitute for understanding the content of what you learn and its applications."

On the Web

The following sites on the World Wide Web provide the opportunity to extend your learning about the material in this chapter. (Although the Web addresses were accurate at the time the book was printed, check the P.O.W.E.R. Learning Web site [http://mhhe.com/power] for any changes that may have occurred.)

http://www.coun.uvic.ca/learn/program/hndouts/multicho.html
The Multiple Choice Exam. This page offers some valuable suggestions on how to approach multiple-choice exams. Several types of multiple-choice questions are described and strategies for answering them are explained. There are helpful hints about what to look for in the wording of both the questions and the answer choices in a multiple-choice exam.

http://www.coun.uvic.ca/learn/program/hndouts/simple.html
Simplified Plans of Action for Common Types of Question Words. This page gives examples of question words that are often found in essay assignments or in essay questions on exams. Possible "plans of action" for each of the question types are outlined. These outlines can be useful as a starting point for understanding how to approach essay questions.

http://www.coun.uvic.ca/personal/stress.html
Tactics for Managing Stress and Anxiety. This site offers several suggestions that you might find helpful in managing and reducing your level of stress and anxiety. The techniques may help you deal with test-related anxiety as well as academic anxiety in general. Not all of the techniques work for everyone. Try them and use the ones that work best for you.

Taking It to the Net

1 Seeing exams from other classes can help you get an idea of the kinds of questions that are often asked on exams. Use an Internet search engine to locate examples of exams from other colleges and universities. Look at several exams. How many of the questions on these exams were true–false? How many were multiple-choice? How many were essays? A possible strategy would be to use the AltaVista search engine (**www.altavista.digital.com/**) and type "examples of exams" at the search prompt.

2 Practice answering essay questions by comparing and contrasting the information different Web pages offer about the same topic. For example, go to AltaVista (**www.altavista.digital.com/**) and enter the keywords "essay + exams." Read the strategies for essay exams offered in the first two Web sites. Then write a paragraph describing the information both sites had in common and another paragraph describing the information that was unique to each site.

The Case of . . .

Too Many Questions, Too Little Time

There was no reason to panic, said Mia Varela to herself at the start of the test. The exam, a midterm in her Greek civilization class, contained 50 multiple-choice questions (each worth 1 point) and two short-answer essays (worth a total of 50 points). And she did have 75 minutes to complete the test.

"Let's see," she said to herself. "At 1½ minutes per multiple-choice question, that would take 75 minutes. Hmm . . . that's no good. How about a minute for each one? Fifty minutes for the multiple-choice questions, leaving 25 minutes for the essays. That ought to work. I'll get the multiple-choice questions out of the way first."

But things didn't work out the way she planned. After an hour she had completed only 40 of the multiple-choice questions and hadn't even started on the essay questions. With only 15 minutes left, panic began to set in. She had trouble thinking. She began to be certain that she'd fail the test. She thought about how she hadn't studied enough. If only she'd worked harder. How could she explain this failure to her friends . . . to her parents . . . to herself. The thoughts kept coming, and time kept ticking away.

1. Is there evidence that Mia didn't study effectively for this type of test?

2. What was right about Mia's initial approach to the test?

3. What should Mia have done differently in calculating the amount of time to devote to each portion of the test? Why?

4. What should Mia have done to be aware of and address her timing problem sooner?

5. How should Mia have dealt with her panic? Were her thoughts productive or counterproductive? Why?

6. If you were in Mia's shoes, what would you do now, with only 15 minutes left in the test?

Building Your Reading and Listening Skills

7

"Read the first two chapters in the text by next Thursday." "I've put three articles on reserve in the library, and you'll need to have them read by our next class." "Take a look at the first three Shakespeare sonnets in your book, and see if you can derive the major themes."

For Chris O'Hara, these reading assignments—handed down by different instructors on the same day in early October—felt like nails in his coffin. How was he supposed to finish all this reading in the next two days, in addition to studying for a Spanish test, writing a paper for history, and putting in eight hours at his part-time job?

Although the papers and tests were hard enough to deal with, it was the constant reading that was proving the most difficult challenge for Chris during his first term of college. He was a conscientious student who attempted to get everything done, but no matter how hard he tried, he just couldn't get everything read on time. When he pushed himself to read quicker and absorb more, he actually read and retained *less*. Thoughts about how he needed to read more quickly crowded out the meaning of whatever he was reading, and he had to go back over the material all over again, slowing him down even more as the reading assignments just kept piling up.

For many students like Chris, reading assignments are the biggest challenge in college. The amount of required reading is often enormous. Even skilled readers are likely find themselves wishing for a way to read more quickly and effectively.

Fortunately, there is a way to improve your reading skills. In this chapter, we'll go over a number of strategies that will help you to read more effectively. You can assess your attention span, consider what you should do before you even start reading an assignment, and discover some ways of getting the most out of your reading.

Then we shift gears, moving from the written word to the spoken word. We'll look at ways of listening effectively and actively. We'll consider how you should listen and what you should be listening *for*. We'll also talk about "problem" instructors, whose lectures . . . well, let's just say they leave something to be desired.

In short, after reading this chapter, you'll be able to answer the following questions:

- **How do my reading styles and attention span affect my reading?**

- **How can I improve my concentration and read more effectively?**

- **What is active listening, and what is the difference between hearing and listening?**

- **How can I improve my listening skills?**

Sharpen Your Reading Skills

What kind of reader are you? Do you plod through reading assignments, novels, and magazines and, like Chris, end up feeling that you're taking far too long? Or maybe you whip through chapters, devour books, and fly through the daily newspaper but then find you can't recall the information as precisely as you'd like or remember where you saw the data on television violence that you need for your sociology paper?

Before going any further, think about your own *reading style*—your characteristic way of approaching reading tasks—by completing the Journal Reflections.

Read for Retention, Not Speed

You may have seen advertisements promoting reading "systems" that promise to teach you to read so quickly that you'll be reading entire books in an hour or so and whizzing through assigned readings in a few moments.

Forget it: It's not going to happen. For one thing, certain biological aspects relating to the eye movements involved in reading simply prevent people from reading (and ultimately comprehending) so rapidly. Claims of speed reading, then, are simply groundless, and it is unlikely that any system will overcome the built-in limitations of the human eye.

But even if it were physically possible to read a book in an hour, ultimately it probably doesn't matter very much. Reading is not a race, and faster readers are not necessarily better readers.

The act of reading is designed to increase our knowledge and open up new ways of thinking. It can help us achieve new levels of understanding and get us to think more broadly about the world and its peoples. In the end, then, it ultimately doesn't matter how fast we can read.

Journal Reflections

How I Read

Think about how you read by answering these questions.

1. When you open a textbook you have never seen before, what do you tend to look at first? Do you read any of the materials in the front or back of the book? Do you check out the table of contents?

2. When you start a new textbook chapter, what do you do first?

3. Are your reading habits the same or different for "pleasure reading" versus "assignment reading"?

4. What is the most difficult book you are reading this semester? Why is it difficult?

5. What is the easiest book you are reading this semester? Why is it easy?

6. How do college reading assignments differ from high school reading assignments?

7. What do you do when something you're reading makes absolutely no sense to you?

8. Do your reading habits differ depending on the subject area you're reading about?

Speed matters far less than what we take away from what we've read. The key to good reading is understanding—not speed.

In describing how the principles of P.O.W.E.R. Learning can be used to become a better reader, we'll focus on the type of reading that is typically called for in academic pursuits—text chapters, original texts, worksheets, and the like. However, the same principles will help you get more benefit and enjoyment out of your recreational reading as well.

P repare: Approaching the Written Word

Preparation to begin reading isn't hard, and it won't take very long, but it's a crucial first step in applying P.O.W.E.R. Learning (summarized in the P.O.W.E.R. Plan below). Your aim in preparation is to become familiar with any advance organizers provided in your text or other reading material or to create a set of advance organizers regarding the material you're planning to read. **Advance organizers** are broad, general ideas related to new material. Advance organizers pave the way for subsequent learning, and ultimately they can help us recall material better after we've read it. (To prove the value of advance organizers, take a look at Try It 1, "Discover How Advance Organizers Help.")

PREPARE

Approach the written word

ORGANIZE

Gather the tools of the trade

WORK

Get the most out of your reading

EVALUATE

Consider what it means and what you know

RETHINK

Get it the second time

P.O.W.E.R. Plan

What's the Point of the Reading Assignment? Before you begin an assignment, think about what your goal is. Will you be reading a basic textbook, on which you'll be thoroughly tested? Is your reading supposed to provide background information that will serve as a context for future learning but that isn't essential to your success in the course? Is the material going to be useful to you personally? Realistically, how much time can you devote to the reading assignment?

The way you answer questions about your goal for reading will help you determine the reading strategy to adopt. You aren't expected to read everything with the same degree of intensity. Some material you may feel comfortable skimming; for other material you'll want to put in the maximum effort.

Understand the Point of View of the Material Itself Is what you are reading a textbook or an essay or article? If it is an essay or article, why was it written? To prove a point? To give information? To express the author's personal feelings? Knowing the basic purpose behind what you are reading (even if its specific point and message aren't yet clear) can really help you as you read because it gives you a sense of why the writer is writing what you are to read.

Start with the Frontmatter If you'll be using a text or other book extensively throughout the term, start by reading the preface and/or introduction and scanning the table of contents—what publishers call the **frontmatter.** Instructors often don't formally assign the frontmatter, but reading it can be a big help because it is there that the author

Try It! 1

Discover How Advance Organizers Help

Read this passage. What do you think it means?

The procedure is actually quite simple. First you arrange items into different groups. Of course, one pile may be sufficient, depending on how much there is to do. If you have to go somewhere else due to lack of facilities, that is the next step; otherwise, you are pretty well set. It is important not to overdo things. That is, it is better to do too few things at once than too many. In the short run this may not seem important but complications can easily arise. A mistake can be expensive as well. At first, the whole procedure will seem complicated. Soon, however, it will become just another facet of life. It is difficult to foresee any end to the necessity for this task in the immediate future, but then one can never tell. After the procedure is completed, one arranges the materials into different groups again. Then they can be put into their appropriate places. Eventually, they will be used once more and the whole cycle will then have to be repeated. However, this is a part of life.[1]

If you're like most people, you don't have a clue about what this all means. But suppose you had been given some context in advance and you knew before reading it that the description had to do with washing laundry. Now does it all fall into place? Read the passage once more, and see how having an advance organizer helps out.

---

has a chance to step forward and explain, often more personally than elsewhere in a scholarly book, what he or she considers important. Knowing this will give you a sense of what to expect as you read.

By reading the frontmatter, you can get inside the author's head, obtaining insight into the author's goals, values, and strategies in writing the book. You also might find information about the author's background, and perhaps even a photo. Use this material to "personalize" the author, to gain some insight into the kind of person he or she is. The information you obtain from the frontmatter will provide a mental "hook" on which you can hang the new ideas to which you'll be exposed. (For practice with frontmatter, do Try It 2, page 172.)

Create Advance Organizers To create advance organizers, skim through the table of contents, which provides the main headings of what you will be reading. Textbooks often have chapter outlines, listing the key topics to be covered, and these also can provide a way of previewing the chapter content. As you read over the outline, thoughts about what you already know about the topic are likely to come to mind, and you can begin to consider how the new material in the book may relate both to what you know as well as to your goals for the reading assignment itself and your more long-term goals.

Texts also often have end-of-chapter summaries, and many articles include a final section in which the author states his or her conclusions. Take a look at these ending sections as well. Even though you haven't read the material yet and the summary probably won't make complete sense to you, by reading the summary, you'll get an idea of what the author covers and what he or she considers important in the chapter.

You can also get a sense of advance organizers from what your course instructor says about the chapter or its topic. Sometimes instructors will mention things to pay particular attention to or to look for, such as "When you read Tom Payne's *Commonsense*, notice how he lays out his argument and

Advance organizers
Broad, general ideas related to material that is to be read or heard, which pave the way for subsequent learning

Frontmatter
The preface, introduction, and table of contents of a book

Student Alert: Some students in your class will be excellent readers, some weak. Let the strong readers share their methods and model them in small group settings or in pairs.

Try It! 2

Read the Frontmatter

Have you read the frontmatter of *this* book? Go there now. If you've already read it, review it. If you haven't, read it now. Then answer the following questions:

What are the goals of this book? _____

_____

_____

_____

Who is the author, and what qualifies him to write this book? _____

_____

_____

Do you think the author has an understanding of students? _____

Do you think the author has an understanding of what students should do to become successful in their studies? _____

Is there anything in the frontmatter that made you curious? Does anything seem particularly interesting? _____

_____

_____

After reading the frontmatter, do you feel confident that you can learn what the author wants to teach? Do you feel that you *want* to learn it? _____

what his key points are." Sometimes they will say why they assigned a reading. Such information provides clues that can help develop a mental list of the key ideas relating to the chapter.

Whatever you use to construct them, the crucial feature of advance organizers is to provide a framework and context for what you'll be reading. And having a framework and context can spell the difference between fully comprehending what you read and misunderstanding it.

Now it's time to put all this practice to good use. Create an advance organizer for this chapter in Try It 3.

Organize: Gathering the Tools of the Trade

Discussion Prompt: With this chapter, you are half way through this text. Use the TRY IT! 2 as a mid-term evaluation. Are your students learning what the author (and you) want to teach? Are they learning what they want to learn?

It's obvious that the primary item you'll need to complete a reading assignment is the material that you're reading. But there are other essential tools you should gather to organize yourself, potentially including the following:

- A pencil or pen to write notes in the margin.

- A highlighter to indicate key passages in the text.

Create an Advance Organizer

Use any information you have available to create an advance organizer for this chapter. Feel free to return to the frontmatter, skim the section headings, read the "Looking Back" chapter summary, or recall anything your instructor may have said about the chapter. (If you come across words, phrases, or ideas that seem unfamiliar or incomprehensible, it may be helpful to think of several questions you would ask if you had the opportunity.)

Complete the following statements to prepare your organizer:

The key topics that will be covered in the rest of this chapter are . . .

_____   _____

_____   _____

_____   _____

_____   _____

I think I will be most interested in . . .

_____

_____

_____

_____

I think I will be least interested in . . .

_____

_____

_____

_____

I hope the chapter covers this topic: _____

Words, phrases, and ideas that are unfamiliar to me include . . .

_____

_____

_____

If the author were here, I would ask . . .

_____

_____

_____

Note: You may want to use this Try It as a starting point for advance organizers for each chapter in this book.

IM Link: "Teaching the Text," Chapter 7—Section V; Consider using the activities in this P.O.W.E.R. process to assist in practicing these skills.

PEANUTS reprinted by permission of United Feature Syndicate, Inc.

Student Alert:
Place/environment is so important when considering reading assignments and attention span. Making the transition from private spaces at home to public space such as libraries and dorm rooms can be difficult for students.

- A copy of the assignment, so you'll be sure to read the right material.

- A pad of paper and/or index cards for notetaking if the material is particularly complex. If you routinely use a word processor to take notes, get it ready.

- A dictionary. You never know what new words you'll encounter while you're reading, and a dictionary is the reference tool of choice. If a dictionary is not handy, you'll be tempted to skip over unfamiliar words—a decision that may come back to haunt you. Avoid the temptation to say "I'll do it later" by keeping a dictionary close by.

Give Yourself Time There's one more thing you need in order to prepare successfully for a reading assignment: enough time to complete it. The length of reading assignments is almost never ambiguous. You will typically be given a specific page range, so you will know just how much material you will need to cover.

Now get a watch and time yourself as you read the first three pages of your assignment, being sure to pay attention to the material, not the time! Timing how long it takes to read a representative chunk of material provides you with a rough measure of your reading speed for the material—although it will vary even within a single reading assignment depending on the complexity of the material.

Attention span
The length of time that attention is typically sustained

You'll also need to consider your current reading **attention span**—the length of time that you usually sustain attention. You can get a general sense of this by using Try It 4, "Discover Your Attention Span."

Use the three pieces of information you now have—the length of the assignment, your per-page reading speed at full attention, and your typical attention span—to estimate roughly how long it will take you to complete the reading assignment. In addition to distractions, you may need to interrupt your reading to look up words in the dictionary, get a drink, stretch, answer the phone, or do a number of other things. You may also decide to break your reading into several sessions, in which case your total reading time may be greater since you will have to get reacquainted with the reading assignment each time you sit down again. Finally, as you begin to use the techniques in this chapter regularly, your reading attention span should increase, which will change your calculation.

Work: Getting the Most Out of Your Reading

Finally, it's time to get down to work and start reading.

Obviously—because it's what you're doing at this very moment—you know how to read. But what's important is what you do *while* you're reading.

Try It!
4

Discover Your Attention Span

To get an idea of the length of your current attention span for reading, perform this exercise over the next few days.

1. Choose one of the textbooks that you've been assigned to read this semester.

2. Start reading a chapter, without any preparation, noting in the chart below the time that you start reading.

3. As soon as your mind begins to wander and think about other subjects, stop reading and note the time on the chart below.

4. Using the same textbook, repeat this process four more times over the course of a few days, entering the data on the chart below.

5. To find your reading attention span, find the average number of minutes across the five trials.

Trial #1:   Starting time: _____   Ending time: _____
            Number of minutes between start and end times: _____

Trial #2:   Starting time: _____   Ending time: _____
            Number of minutes between start and end times: _____

Trial #3:   Starting time: _____   Ending time: _____
            Number of minutes between start and end times: _____

Trial #4:   Starting time: _____   Ending time: _____
            Number of minutes between start and end times: _____

Trial #5:   Starting time: _____   Ending time: _____
            Number of minutes between start and end times: _____

Reading attention span (the average of the number of minutes in the last column, found by adding up the five numbers and dividing by 5) = _____ minutes

---

Ask yourself these questions about your reading attention span.

1. Are you surprised by the length of your reading attention span? In what way?

2. Does any number in the set of trials stand out from the other numbers? For instance, is any number much higher or lower than the average? If so, can you account for this? For example, what time of day was it?

3. Do the numbers in your trials in either reading show any trend? For instance, did your attention span tend to increase slightly over the course of the trials, did it decrease, or did it stay about the same? Can you explain any trend you may have noted?

4. Do you think your attention span figures would be very different if you had chosen a different textbook? Why?

Despite the throngs of students walking by on the campus of the University of Texas in Austin, the student seated on the bench seems to have no trouble concentrating on what she's reading. On the other hand, if you are easily distracted, choosing an isolated location to read is a wise strategy.

Here are several things that will help you get the most out of the process of reading:

Stay focused The TV show you watched last night . . . your boyfriend forgetting to meet you at the bus stop . . . your father's heart attack . . . your grumbling stomach. There are a million and one possible distractions that can invade your thoughts as you read. Your job is to keep distracting thoughts at bay and focus on the material you are supposed to be reading. It's not easy, but there are things you can do to help yourself stay focused:

- **Read in small bites.** If you think it is going to take you four hours to read an entire chapter, break up the four hours into more manageable time periods. Promise yourself that you'll read for one hour in the afternoon, another hour in the evening, and the next two hours spaced out during the following day. One hour of reading is far more manageable than a four-hour block.

- **Take a break.** Actually, plan to take several breaks to reward yourself while you're reading. During your break, do something enjoyable—eat a snack, watch a bit of a ball game on television, play a video game, or the like. Just try not to get drawn into your break activity to the point that it takes over your reading time.

- **Deal with distractions.** Sometimes problems have a way of popping into our minds and repeatedly distracting us. If a particular problem keeps interrupting your concentration—such as a difficulty you're having on the job—try to think of an action-oriented strategy to deal with it. You might even write your proposed solution down on a piece of paper. That can move the problem out of the mental realm of your head and put it into concrete form on paper, potentially making it less intrusive.

Write While You Read Writing is one of the most important aspects of reading. If you haven't underlined, jotted notes to yourself, placed check marks on the page, drawn arrows, constructed diagrams, and otherwise defaced and disfigured your book while you're reading, you're not doing your job as a P.O.W.E.R. reader.

The idea of writing on a book page may go against everything you've been taught in the past. (And of course you should never write on a library book or one that you've borrowed from a friend.) If your practice has been to "save" your textbooks, either because you want to keep them untarnished for your old age or because they will fetch a higher price if you sell them back to the bookstore, rethink your strategy. The

Discussion Prompt: For a humorous aside, allow a few minutes for the class to share some of their favorite excuses for *not* reading. What is *your* best example of being distracted?

"What is reading but silent conversation?"

Walter Savage Landor, *Imaginary Conversations.*

greater success you'll experience by writing extensively in your book while you're reading is a far better tactic in the long run.

What should you be writing while you are reading? There are several things you should write down:

- **Rephrase key points.** Make notes to yourself, in your own words, about what the author is trying to get across. Don't just copy what's been said. Think about the material, and rewrite it in words that are your own.

  Writing notes to yourself in your own words has several consequences, all good. First, you make the material yours; it becomes something you now understand and part of your own personal knowledge base.

  Second, trying to summarize a key point in your own words will make it very clear whether you truly understand it. It's easy to be fooled into thinking we understand something as we're reading along. But the true test is whether we can explain it to ourselves (or someone else) on our own, without referring to the book or article.

  Third, the very act of writing engages an additional type of perception—involving the tactile sense of moving a pen or pressing a keyboard. Engagement of an additional perceptual system will help you learn the material in a more active way.

  Finally, writing notes and phrases will help you study the material later. Not only will the key points be highlighted, but your notes will quickly bring you up to speed regarding what you were thinking about initially.

- **Highlight or underline key points.** Very often the first or last sentence in a paragraph, or the first or last paragraph in a section, will present a key point. (Remember those lessons about "topic sentences" you had in high school English classes? Writers really use them.)

  Before you highlight anything, though, read the whole paragraph through. Then you'll be sure that what you highlight is, in fact, the key information. Topic sentences do not always fall at the beginning of a paragraph.

  Be selective in your highlighting and underlining. A page covered in yellow highlighter may be artistically appealing, but it won't help you understand the material any better. Highlight only the key information. It may be that only one or two sentences or phrases are highlighted on a page. That's fine. What is important is that when you go back to study the material, your memory will be jogged. *In highlighting and underlining, less is more.* One rule of thumb: No more than 10 percent of the material should be highlighted or underlined.

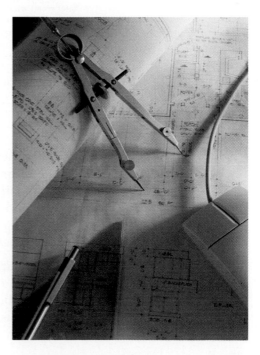

- **Use arrows, diagrams, outlines, tables, time lines, charts, and other visuals to help you understand and later recall what you are reading.** If there are three examples given for an assertion, number them. If a paragraph discusses a situation in which an earlier point does not hold, link the original point to the exception by an arrow. If a sequence of steps is presented, number each step.

  For example, after you have annotated *this* page, it might look something like what is shown on page 178:

strategy. The greater success you'll experience by writing extensively in your book while you're reading is a far better tactic in the long run.

What should you be writing while you are reading? There are several things you should write down:

(handwritten note: Put key points into my own words.) ①

- **Rephrase key points.** Make notes to yourself, in your own words, about what the author is trying to get across. Don't just copy what's been said. Think about the material, and rewrite it in words that are your own.

  Writing notes to yourself in your own words has several consequences, all good. First, you make the material yours; it becomes something you now understand and part of your own personal knowledge base. *(handwritten: ✓✓)*

  Second, trying to summarize a key point in your own words will make it very clear whether you truly understand it. It's easy to be fooled into thinking we understand something as we're reading along. But the true test is whether we can explain it to ourselves (or someone else) on our own, without referring to the book or article.

  Third, the very act of writing engages an additional type of perception—involving the tactile sense of moving a pen or pressing a keyboard. Engagement of an additional perceptual system will help you learn the material in a more active way.

  Finally, writing notes and phrases will help you study the material later. Not only will the key points be highlighted, but your notes will quickly bring you up to speed regarding what you were thinking about initially.

(handwritten note: Use highlighter but less is more. Not more than 10% highlighted.) ②

- **Highlight or underline key points.** Very often the first or last sentence in a paragraph, or the first or last paragraph in a section, will present a key point. (Remember those lessons about "topic sentences" you had in high school English classes? Writers really use them.) *(handwritten: ← topic sentence)*

  Before you highlight anything, though, read the whole paragraph through. Then you'll be sure that what you highlight is, in fact, the key information. Topic sentences do not always fall at the beginning of a paragraph.

  Be selective in your highlighting and underlining. A page covered in yellow highlighter may be artistically appealing, but it won't help you understand the material any better. Highlight only the key information. It may be that only one or two sentences or phrases are highlighted on a page. That's fine. What is important is that when you go back to study the material, your memory will be jogged. *(handwritten: ✓)* *In highlighting and underlining, less is more.* One rule of thumb: No more than 10 percent of the material should be highlighted or underlined.

(handwritten note: use visuals →) ③

- **Use arrows, diagrams, outlines, tables, time lines, charts, and other visuals to help you understand and later recall what you are reading.** If there are three examples given for an assertion, number them. If a paragraph discusses a situation in which an earlier point does not hold, link the original point to the exception by an arrow. If a sequence of steps is presented, number each step.

  For example, after you have annotated *this* page, it might look something like what is shown on page 178:

Particularly if your learning style is a visual one, representing the material graphically will get you thinking about it—and the connections and points in it—in new and different ways. Rather than considering the material solely in verbal terms, you now add visual images. The act of creating visual annotations will not only help you to understand the material better, but it will ease its later recall as well.

Teaching Tip: Preferences play a big role in reading styles (see Chap. 3).

- **Look up unfamiliar words in a dictionary.** Even though you may be able to figure out the meaning of an unfamiliar word from its context, use a dictionary anyway. This way you can be sure that what you think it means is correct. A dictionary will also tell you what the word sounds like which may be important if your instructor uses the word in class.

Try It! 5

Working in a Group:
Mark Up a Book Page

First, working alone, read the following excerpt and use the techniques we've discussed for marking up a page to highlight its key points.

The more parents speak to their children, the better their children's language skills.

Understanding Language Acquisition: Identifying the Roots of Language

Anyone who spends even a little time with children will notice the enormous strides that they make in language development throughout childhood. However, the reasons for this rapid growth are far from obvious. Two major explanations have been offered: one based on learning theory and the other on innate processes.

The **learning-theory approach** suggests that language acquisition follows the principles of reinforcement and conditioning discussed in Chapter 6. For example, a child who utters the word "mama" is hugged and praised by her mother, which reinforces the behavior and makes its repetition more likely. This view suggests that children first learn to speak by being rewarded for making sounds that approximate speech. Ultimately, through a process of shaping, language becomes more and more like adult speech (Skinner, 1957).

learning-theory approach: The theory suggesting that language acquisition follows the principles of reinforcement and conditioning

The learning theory approach is supported by research that shows that the more parents speak to their young children, the more proficient the children become in language usage (see Figure 8-11). In addition, higher levels of linguistic sophistication in parents' speech to their young children are related to a greater rate of vocabulary growth, vocabulary usage, and even general intellectual achievement by the time the children are 3 years of age (Hart & Risley, 1997).

On the other hand, the learning theory approach is less successful when it comes to explaining the acquisition of language rules. Children are reinforced not only when they use proper language, but also when they respond incorrectly. For example, parents answer the child's "Why the dog won't eat?" as readily as they do the correctly phrased question "Why won't the dog eat?" Both sentences are understood equally well. Learning theory, then, has difficulty in providing the full explanation for language acquisition.

Pointing to such problems with learning theory approaches to language acquisition, Noam Chomsky (1968, 1978, 1991), a linguist, provided a ground-breaking alternative. Chomsky argued that humans are born with an innate linguistic capability that emerges primarily as a function of maturation. According to his analysis, all the world's languages share a similar underlying structure called a **universal grammar.** Chomsky suggests that the human brain has a neural system, the **language-acquisition device,** that both permits the understanding of the structure of language and provides strategies and techniques for learning the unique characteristics of a given native language.

universal grammar: Noam Chomsky's theory that all the world's languages share a similar underlying structure
language-acquisition device: A neural system of the brain hypothesized to permit understanding of language

 Working in a group, compare and contrast your annotations with those of some classmates. How do their annotations differ from yours? Why did they use the annotations they did? Which annotation techniques worked best? Which were easiest to use? How might these annotations help you to remember what is important? If there were different sorts of material presented on the page, such as mathematical formulas, would you use different kinds of annotations?

Evaluate: Considering What It Means and What You Know

Evaluation is a crucial step in reading. You need to be able to answer the seemingly simple question: "What does all this mean?"

But there's another aspect to evaluation. You need to evaluate, truthfully and honestly, your own level of understanding. What do you know as a result of your reading? Evaluation, then, consists of the following steps:

Teaching Tip: Encourage students to think of evaluation in another way. How directly do their reading skills determine how they will be evaluated (graded) in their other classes?

- **Identify the main ideas and themes and their value *to you personally*.** Try to determine the take-home message of the material you've read. For example, the take-home message of a chapter of an American history text might be, "Although Abraham Lincoln eventually called for the end of slavery, initially he was hesitant because of political considerations."

  Sometimes the main ideas and themes are spelled out, and at other times you will have to deduce it for yourself. Evaluate the main ideas and themes in terms of their usefulness to your own understanding of the topic.

- **Prioritize the ideas.** Of all the information that is presented, which is the most crucial to the main message and which is the least crucial? Make a list of the main topics covered and try to rank them in order of importance.

- **Think critically about the arguments presented in the reading.** Do they seem to make sense? Are the author's assertions reasonable? Are there any flaws in the arguments? Would authors with a different point of view dispute what is being said? What other perspectives might the author have taken?

- **Pretend you are explaining the material (talking—out loud!—about the material) to a fellow classmate who missed the assignment.** This is one time when talking out loud when no one is around is not only normal, but beneficial. Summarize the material aloud, as if you were talking to another person.

  Talking out loud does two things. First, it helps you identify weak spots in your understanding. Talking to yourself will help you nail down concepts that are still not clear in your own mind. Second, and equally important, because you are transforming the written word into the spoken word, you are thinking about the information in an additional way, which will help you remember it better.

- **Be honest with yourself.** Most of us are able to read with our minds on cruise control. But the net result is not much different from not reading the passage at all. If you have drifted off while you've been reading, go back and reread the passage.

- **Pat yourself on the back.** Just as you've done during each of your reading breaks, reward yourself for completing the reading passage. But keep in mind there's one more step before you can really relax, and it's a crucial one: rethinking what you've read.

Rethink: Getting It the Second Time

You're human, so—like the rest of us—when you finish a reading assignment you'd probably like nothing more than to heave a sigh of relief and put the book and what you've read away.

By now you know that there's a crucial step you should take that will assist you in cementing what you've learned into memory: rethinking what you've read. If you do it within 24 hours of first reading the assignment, it can save you hours of work later.

The best way to rethink an assignment is to reread it, along with any notes you've taken. "Yeah, right," you're probably thinking. "Like I have time for that." The benefits of rereading can't be overstated. Rereading transfers material from your short-term memory to your long-term memory. It solidifies information so that it will be remembered far better over the long haul.

Rereading will take *far* less time than it did the first time. In fact, it isn't necessary to read word for word. You already know what's

> "Reading furnishes the mind only with materials of knowledge; it is thinking that makes what we read ours."
>
> John Locke, *Of the Conduct of the Understanding* (1706)

important and what's not important, so you can skim some of the less important material. But it is wise to reread the more difficult and important material carefully, making sure that you fully understand what is being discussed and why.

Rethinking should be the central activity as you reread the passage and your notes. You need to be sure that your understanding is complete and that you're able to answer any questions that you had earlier about the material.

The Concept Map As a Rethinking Tool As we saw in Chapter 5, **concept mapping** is a method of structuring written material by graphically grouping and connecting key ideas and themes. Each key idea is placed in a different part of the map, and related ideas are placed near it—above, below, or beside it. A concept map looks similar to a graphic of the solar system, with the central idea in the center, surrounded by related concepts.

Concept mapping
A method of structuring written material by graphically grouping and connecting key ideas and themes

Concept maps help you to rethink material you've read about, especially if you have used a more traditional outline earlier. Furthermore, once you have developed a concept map for a particular aspect of the material, you can create additional, expanded concept maps involving related information.

Concept maps are particularly useful for people with learning styles that have particular strengths involving spatial relationships. Furthermore, students with certain kinds of learning disabilities—a topic to which we turn in the next section—can also benefit from the use of concept maps.

An example of a concept map involving the material we've discussed so far is illustrated on the top of page 182. Note how it summarizes the material and shows how it is related to the central topic of "Reading with Understanding."

This concept map illustrates the key ideas of reading with understanding.

Teaching Tip: Spend a few minutes here connecting this information to Chapter 9 on Memory.

ORGANIZE
Tools
Time!

WORK
Focus:
  bites
  breaks
  deal with distractions
Write while reading
  rephrase
  highlight
  arrows, lines, etc.
  mark up the page!

PREPARE
Advance organizers
Strategy: goal intensity
Frontmatter

READ WITH UNDERSTANDING

EVALUATE
Personal value of ideas
Prioritize ideas
Think critically (Do I agree?)
Teach someone else
Talk out loud
Honesty!

Reading style
Speed
  unimportant
  understanding matters!
Attention span

RETHINK
Reread (skim)
Concept map

Dealing with Learning Disabilities

Learning disabilities

Difficulties in processing information when listening, speaking, reading, or writing, characterized by a discrepancy between learning potential and actual academic achievement

Millions of people in the United States have learning disabilities of one sort or another. **Learning disabilities** are characterized by difficulties in processing information when listening, speaking, reading, or writing, in which there is a discrepancy between learning potential and actual academic achievement.

One of the most common kinds of learning disabilities is dyslexia, a reading disability that produces the misperception of letters during reading and writing, unusual difficulty in sounding out letters, spelling difficulties, and confusion between right and left. Although its causes are not yet completely understood, one likely explanation is a problem in the part of the brain responsible for breaking words into the sound elements that make up language.

People with learning disabilities are sometimes viewed as unintelligent. Nothing could be further from the truth: There is no relationship between learning disabilities and I.Q. For instance, dozens of well-known and highly accomplished individuals suffered from dyslexia, including physicist Albert Einstein, U.S. General George Patton, poet William Butler Yeats, and—as we discuss in *Speaking of Success* later in this chapter—writer John Irving.

By the time they reach college, most people with learning disabilities have already been diagnosed. If you do have a diagnosed learning disability, it is important to disclose your situation to your instructors and other college officials if you need special services.

Discussion Prompt: Take a moment to discuss disabilities. Developing sensitivities to differences of all kinds should be a theme throughout this course.

In some cases, students with learning disabilities have not been appropriately evaluated prior to college. If you have difficulties such as mixing up and reversing letters frequently and suspect that you have a learning disability, there is a unit on campus that can provide you with guidance. One place to start: your college counseling or health center.

However, just because you are having trouble with reading assignments doesn't automatically mean that you have a learning disability. Not only is the kind of reading you do in college more difficult than what you did in high school, there's more of it. It's only when reading represents a persistent, long-term problem—one that won't go away no matter how much work you do—that a learning disability becomes a possible explanation.

Building Listening Skills

Consider these basic two facts: Most of us talk at a rate of around 125 words a minute. But the average listener can comprehend close to 700 words per minute.

Then why is it so hard to listen closely to what someone is saying? Why do our minds wander, and why do we often recall so little about a class when it is over?

The answer rests on the difference between *hearing* and *listening*. Although our sensory capabilities permit us to *hear* far more words than are produced in a given minute by the average speaker, that doesn't mean we actively *listen* to speech. **Hearing** is the involuntary act of sensing sounds. The annoying drip of a faucet or the grating sound of a roommate's voice speaking on the phone in the next room are two examples of how hearing is both involuntary and often meaningless.

Hearing
The involuntary act of sensing sounds

In contrast, **listening** is the voluntary act of focusing on what is being said, making sense of it, and thinking about it in a way that permits it to be recalled accurately. Listening involves concentration. And it requires shutting out competing thoughts, such as what we need to pick up at the grocery store or why our date last night was so terrific.

Listening
The voluntary act of focusing on sounds and making sense of them

Active listening is an essential component of success, not only in school but in the broader world. For animals, recognizing the warning cry of another member of one's species can literally mean the difference between life and death. For us people, effective listening permits us to know that even though our friend says its "OK" if we postpone our hiking trip, she is really disappointed; it enables us to hear the sound of a horn warning us not to walk into a car's path; allows us to respond emotionally to the lyrics of a song; and helps us decide whether a defendant in a trial is telling the truth.

> "I'm glad I understand that while language is a gift, listening is a responsibility."
> Nikki Giovanni, *Racism 101.*

When you are in class, it's essential that you listen and understand. Active listening will help you understand class presentations better. It will aid you in mastering material, permit you to participate more in class, and help you work with your classmates more effectively.

Career Connections

Listening between the Lines

Honing your listening skills now will pay big dividends when you enter the world of work. Much of what you need to know to do your job effectively will be communicated to you by the spoken word. The better you are at absorbing verbal information, the better you'll be at carrying out your job.

Because not all supervisors are effective communicators, you'll sometimes need to read between the lines and make inferences about what you need to do. Being able to clarify directions from your boss by assertively asking questions can spell the difference between being able to carry out a task correctly and failing at it.

Good listening skills are also important if *you* become a supervisor. Listening to what your staff has to say requires careful attention. Take notes on what you hear; writing things down not only will help you remember what you've been told, but it demonstrates that you think what you're hearing is important.

Finally, keep in mind that there are significant cultural differences in the kinds of things people say and the type of language they use. Individuals for whom English is a second language or who come from different cultures may say things that strike you as unusual. For instance, in some cultures asking virtually anyone his or her salary is the norm, while in U.S. culture such a question generally would be considered out-of-bounds. Being sensitive to the cultural background of colleagues will permit you to more accurately interpret and understand what you are hearing.

Tips for Active Listening: Listen Up!

You already know many of the techniques of effective listening from the chapter on note-taking. In fact, if you are taking good notes, chances are you are an active listener already. What follows is a list of the most important techniques of active listening and some tips for listening even when the speaker is making it difficult to stay interested.

- **Choose a seat that will promote active listening.** You should certainly choose a seat that will permit you to see and hear clearly, but there's more to your choice than that. Picking the right seat in a classroom can make a big difference.

  Where is the best place to sit? Usually it's near the front center of the classroom. Instructors make more eye contact with the people near them, and they sometimes believe that the best, most-engaged students sit closest. Conversely, they may assume that students who sit as far toward the back of the room as they can get are less involved. (There's a certain reality to that assumption: Research shows that more questions are asked by students sitting close to instructors than those farther back.)

  Furthermore, sitting in the back of the class may make you feel disengaged and out of touch with what is happening at the front of the room. In turn, this may make it easier for your mind to wander.

  But everyone needs to make a personal choice about what works best. If you feel as if you're on display in the front of the class and sitting there inhibits your asking questions, then choose a different seat.

- **Focus on what is being said.** Active listening involves listening not just to a speaker's individual sentences, but to the overall message. Ask yourself what the speaker's overall theme is. As you saw in the chapter on taking notes, compared with the written word, which provides thematic clues such as titles, headings, and paragraphs, the spoken word is less concrete. Consequently, you have to work to figure out the structure of the speaker's message. Good lecturers have a series of broad ideas that they wish to convey. It's your job, as an active listener, to unearth them, while still not losing track of the details of the message.

In essence, successful listening involves paying attention to two kinds of messages: the actual message and what's called the meta-message. The actual message consists of the verbatim transcript; it is what the speaker actually says, on a surface level. But all speakers also have a **meta-message,** the underlying main ideas that they seek to convey through the spoken message.

Sometimes a speaker will explicitly state the meta-message. For example, an instructor might say at the start of a class, "Today I'll be trying to give you a feel for the ways that social protest informed the national consciousness in the 1960s." In other cases, though, the meta-message may not be so obviously stated, and listeners will have to figure out the underlying themes. Some strategies for doing so are:

Meta-message
The underlying main ideas that a speaker seeks to convey through a spoken message

- **Pay attention to the nonverbal messages that accompany the verbal message.** Does an instructor get excited about a particular topic? Does he or she get agitated? Does the speaker seem unenthusiastic when talking about something? Use nonverbal cues to gauge the importance of a particular part of a message relative to other things being said. Being able to "hear" nonverbal messages can also help you pick up the unspoken messages people give. (See, also, *Career Connections,* for a discussion of the importance of listening in a professional context.)

- **Listen for what is *not* being said.** Sometimes silence is not just golden, but informative as well. By noting what topics are *not* being covered in class, or are presented only minimally, you can gauge the relative importance of ideas in comparison with one another.

  This is where preparation comes in. The only way to know what's not being discussed is to have done the assigned readings in advance. This information is important. It will help you get a good sense of an instructor's priorities and help you later when the time comes to study for exams.

- **Take notes.** As you no doubt know from experience, no one's memory is infallible. Unless you take careful and accurate notes, you're likely to end up with little or even no recollection of the details of a speaker's message, as we discussed in Chapter 5. Furthermore, taking notes will aid active listening by helping you to focus on the speaker's message.

- **Adopt a questioning attitude, in which your goal is not passive acceptance of the instructor's message but active evaluation.** Do you agree with the speaker? Do you understand the reasoning behind the speaker's arguments? Are the arguments logical? Is this information consistent with other material that's been presented earlier?

- **Ask questions.** One of the most important things you can do during a class is to ask questions. Raising questions will help you evaluate, clarify, and ultimately better understand what your instructor is saying. Even beyond these critical goals, questions serve several other purposes.

  For one thing, raising questions will help you to personalize the material being covered, permitting you to draw it more closely into your

Student Alert: Role playing is a wonderful way for students to see the importance of give and take in listening situations.

Asking questions in class does more than just provide you with the opportunity to clarify points you don't understand. It often will make you feel more a part of the class, and it will encourage other students to participate.

own framework and perspective. Furthermore, when you ask a question and it is answered satisfactorily, you become personally engaged in what the instructor is saying.

Questioning also increases your involvement in the class as a whole. If you sit back and never raise questions in class, you are much less likely to feel a real part of the class. Becoming an active questioner will rightly make you feel like you have contributed something to the class. Remember, if you are unclear about some point, it is likely that others share your lack of clarity.

Finally, by asking questions in class, you serve as a role model for other students. Your questions may help break the ice in a class, making it easier for others to raise issues that they have about the material. And ultimately the answers that the instructor provides to *others'* questions may help *you* to better understand and/or evaluate your understanding of the material.

Breaking the Ice: Tips for Getting Over Stage Fright and Asking Questions in Class

Raising your hand in class can be intimidating. You may be afraid that you'll say something dumb, making it clear to the whole class just how out of it you are; or that everyone will be staring at you; or that your instructor and fellow classmates will resent your wasting valuable class time with your own trivial questions.

Although it may not be possible to fully banish such self-defeating thoughts, there are several strategies that you can follow to make it easier to raise the questions you have.

Student Alert: Have students describe the questioning process in other courses. Which types of courses tend to encourage questions and which ones seem to make it more difficult?

1. **Sit in the front of the room.** Sitting close to the instructor will make it easier to ask questions. Moreover, if you sit in the back of the room and ask a question, the students in front of you will likely swivel around and look at you. In that case, if you already feel intimidated, your feelings of anxiety may rise off the charts.

2. **Write down your question.** If you anticipate that you'll stumble or forget what you want to say, write down your question before raising your hand. The idea is not to read it word for word, or even refer to it at all when you actually ask your question. But writing it will help you quickly organize your thoughts, and having it handy in written form will reduce your anxiety because you know you have a safety net.

Teaching Tip: An excellent way to use the TRY IT! 6 is to take your class to a campus event/common lecture. Have students create and bring their concept maps to class for comparisons.

3. **Be one of the first students to ask a question.** One reason people sometimes give for not having asked questions is that others have already asked so many questions that there's no time. Or that others have already addressed the issue. Or that others' questions were so good that they make yours look silly. To avoid this difficulty, be among the first to ask questions. Don't wait for others to break the ice; go for it.

Try It!
6
Make a Concept Map

Here's a chance to create a concept map. Using the space provided below, map out the "Building Listening Skills" section of this chapter. Place the main topic ("Tips for Active Listening . . .") in the center and group other related concepts together. Feel free to link concepts with lines or add any other marks that will help you structure the content and make sense of the section when you return to it for rethinking and review.

The Problem Instructor

He talks too fast . . . she mumbles . . . he puts down people when they ask a question . . . she rambles and goes off on boring tangents . . . she explains things in a way that doesn't make much sense.

In the real world of the college classroom, not every instructor comes to class with a finely honed lecture that is clear, compelling, and interesting and presents it beautifully. As we first discussed when we considered strategies for taking notes in Chapter 5, all of us have suffered through instruction that is deficient in one or more ways. What should you do when you find yourself in such a situation?

1. *Remember that this too shall pass.* First, keep in mind that this is a temporary condition; your experience usually won't last more than one

Discussion Prompt: Take this discussion's typical focus on identifying petty and "bad" habits to a consideration of which characteristics truly interfere with the learning process. What other strategies have your students employed to solve these problems?

term. Most instructors are conscientious and well prepared, and unless you have enormously bad luck, the unpleasant experience you're having now will not be routine.

2. *Ask questions about the material.* Even if you have no idea what is going on in class—or *especially* if you have no idea—ask questions. You are not the only one struggling with the instructor's shortcomings. You will be doing everyone in the class a favor if you admit you're not following what an instructor is saying and ask for clarification.

3. *Ask—privately—for the instructor to change his or her behavior.* It is not bad classroom etiquette to ask an instructor to speak a little slower. Instructors sometimes get carried away with enthusiasm and begin speaking faster and faster without even being aware of it. Very often a reality check from a student will be welcome. But don't couch your comment in way that makes the instructor feel inept ("Could you slow down; you're going too fast and losing me"). Instead, keep the comment neutral, without placing blame. For instance, you might simply say, "I'm having trouble keeping up with you; would it be possible for you to speak a little more slowly?"

4. *Pool your resources.* Get together with other students in the class and work out a strategy for dealing with the situation. If an instructor speaks too fast and you just can't keep up with the flow of information, meet with your fellow students and compare what you've gleaned from the class. They may have understood or noted material that you missed, and vice versa. Together, you may be able to put the pieces of the puzzle together and get a fuller understanding of the material.

5. *Listen to the lecture again.* You might bring a tape recorder to class (but request the instructor's permission first!). Then, after class, you can play back the tape at your leisure.

There's another option: Many instructors teach multiple sections of the same course. If this is the case, you might, schedule permitting, sit in on an additional section of the course. The second time around the information may become much clearer.

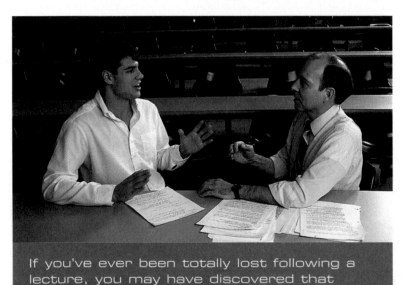

If you've ever been totally lost following a lecture, you may have discovered that speaking with your instructor immediately after class was helpful. Most instructors are very happy to go over and clarify key points that they've covered during class. They also appreciate your initiative and interest.

6. *Talk with the instructor after class.* If you feel totally lost after a lecture, or even if you've missed only a few points, speak with the instructor after class. Ask for clarification and get him or her to re-explain points that you missed. Such a dialogue will help you to understand the material better. But it will also do something more: help build your relationship with your instructor.

Speaking of Success

Name:	*John Irving*
Education:	*BA, University of New Hampshire*
Home:	*New Hampshire*

The author of such novels as *The World According to Garp* and *Ciderhouse Rules,* John Irving is one of America's foremost storytellers. But his road to success was not always smooth, particularly because he suffers from the learning disability of dyslexia, which makes both reading and writing difficult.

While attending Exeter Academy, his high school, Irving knew something was wrong. But in the 1950s, there was little known about learning disabilities.

"I was a mediocre student—as it turned out, I was dyslexic, but no one knew this at the time,"[2] Irving noted. "To say that Exeter was hard for me is an understatement. I was the only student in my genetics class who failed to control his fruit-fly experiment. The Red Eyes and the White Eyes were interbreeding so rapidly that I lost track of the generations."

While at Exeter, Irving developed a love of wrestling, which became an important arena of his life. As a member of the wrestling team, he learned from his coach how he could compensate for his shortcomings as

an athlete: by being dedicated. "Talent is overrated," said his coach. "That you're not very talented needn't be the end of it. . . . An underdog is in a position to take a healthy bite."

Irving continued, "This was a concept of myself that I'd been lacking. I was an underdog; therefore, I had to control the pace of everything. . . . The concept was applicable to my creative writing—to all my schoolwork, too.

"If my classmates could read our history assignments in an hour, I allowed myself two or three. If I couldn't learn to spell, I would keep a list of many most frequently misspelled words, and I kept the list with me; I had it handy even for unannounced quizzes," Irving said.

Irving's hard work and dedication permitted him to overcome his learning disability. Ultimately, he became one of the most prominent authors of our time. To what does he attribute his success? "Writing is one-eighth talent and seven-eighths discipline," he believes.

How do my reading styles and attention span affect my reading?

- The most important aspect of reading is understanding, not speed. People have different reading styles that can be modified to improve their ability to read with understanding.

- One problem people have with reading is a limited attention span. However, attention span can be increased with self-awareness and practice.

How can I improve my concentration and read more effectively?

- Reading should be approached with a clear sense of purpose and goals, which will vary from assignment to assignment. Examining the front-matter of a book and creating advance organizers is also useful.

- Maintain focus by breaking down the reading into small chunks, taking breaks as needed, dealing with distractions, and writing while reading. It is also helpful to identify the main ideas, prioritize them, think critically about the arguments, and explain the writer's ideas to someone else.

- Concept maps that structure and relate ideas can aid rethinking.

What is active listening, and what is the difference between hearing and listening?

- Listening is a voluntary act that involves focusing on what is being said, making sense of it, and thinking about it. In contrast, hearing is the involuntary act of sensing sounds.

- Active listening involves paying attention to what is being heard. It permits the mastery of material, facilitates class participation, and enables cooperation with other students.

How can I improve my listening skills?

- Active listening involves focusing on what is being said, including the speaker's meta-message; paying attention to nonverbal messages; listening for what is not being said; and taking notes.

- Asking questions in class clarifies ambiguous information, helps to personalize the material being covered, increases one's level of involvement in the class, and makes it easier for other students to ask questions.

- Active listening also involves carefully analyzing the speaker's message, presentation, arguments, and nonverbal behavior, and examining one's own listening behavior and reactions.

Key Terms and Concepts

Advance organizer (p. 171)
Attention span (p. 174)
Concept mapping (p. 181)
Frontmatter (p. 171)

Hearing (p. 183)
Learning disabilities (p. 182)
Listening (p. 183)
Meta-message (p. 185)

Resources

On Campus

If you are experiencing unusual difficulties in reading and the problem is one you encountered in high school, you may have a learning disability. If you suspect this is the case, take action. Many colleges have an office that deals specifically with learning disabilities. You can also talk to someone at your college's counseling center, they will arrange for you to be tested.

In Print

The third edition of Kathleen McWhorter's book *Academic Reading* (Addison Wesley, 1997) provides a complete set of guidelines for reading textbooks and other kinds of writing you will encounter during college. Another useful volume is *Breaking Through: College Reading* (Longman, 1998), by Brenda Smith.

You can get information on listening skills in Marc Helgesen and Steven Brown's *Active Listening: Building Skills for Understanding* (Cambridge, 1994).

On the Web

The following sites on the World Wide Web provide the opportunity to extend your learning about the material in this chapter. (Although the Web addresses were accurate at the time the book was printed, check the P.O.W.E.R. Learning Web site [http://mhhe.com/power] for any changes that may have occurred.)

http://www.basenet.net/~eagle/educate/1997/june97/list.html
   Check out this list of 163 of the most classic titles in literature, called the "Ultimate Reading List." You're sure to find something that looks appealing.

http://www.ucc.vt.edu/stdysk/sq3r.html
   This site introduces an approach to reading, and retaining, textual material.

http://www.cabsju.edu/academicadvising/help/eff-list/html
   This site presents a series of tips on effective listening.

Taking It to the Net

1 Read a historical document. Choose a document that interests you by going to the Netscape search site (**http://netscape.com**) and conducting a search by entering "historical documents." After finding a document, read it, and summarize it in a short essay.

2 Practice your listening skills. Visit the CNN video archives (**http://www.cnn.com/videoselect/**) and choose a speech to which you can listen. During the speech, take notes, and later write a summary of the speech.

The Case of . . .

War and Peace

One thousand four hundred eighty-four.

That's all Chenille Lawrence could think about when she got to the bookstore to purchase *War and Peace,* which her instructor said they'd be reading over the next four weeks. Sure, she thought to herself, it's Great Literature, as her instructor had said. It's undoubtedly a classic that every well-educated person should read some time in his or her life. Sure, maybe reading it would change her life in unimaginable ways, as her instructor had also argued (although she had strong doubts that its immediate effect would be anything but pain).

All she could think about, though, was its length—1,484 pages, not even counting the introduction. How would she ever get through such a giant volume?

1. How would you advise Chenille to prepare for her reading of *War and Peace*? What sort of advance organizers would you suggest she create?

2. What organizational strategies would you advise Chenille to apply to her reading of this novel? How would you suggest she organize her time?

3. How might Chenille stay focused on her reading? How might she most effectively use writing as a way to accomplish her task?

4. Why is evaluation important for reading a long book such as *War and Peace* with understanding? How might Chenille evaluate her understanding as she reads?

5. In what ways can Chenille use rethinking techniques to improve her understanding of the book?

Writing
and
Speaking

8

It was 3:23 A.M. Maria Ramos knew the exact time because that's what the numbers on her digital clock radio indicated at the precise moment she bolted awake in a cold sweat from a sound sleep. She had been dreaming about the upcoming moment in her English class, now only a few hours away, when she would have to give an oral presentation.

Maria was nothing less than terrified by the thought. A quiet and shy person by nature, she didn't like to be the center of attention in groups. The thought of everyone in the class observing her intently and listening to what she had to say filled her with fear.

A few hours later, after failing to get back to sleep, the moment she so dreaded arrived. She timidly made her way to the front of the classroom, well aware of her thumping heart and sweaty palms.

And then, as she began to speak, something happened. As she noticed the faces of her classmates and instructor showing interest in what she was saying, she calmed down. Suddenly she realized that not only would she manage to get through her talk, but she actually might be doing a decent job at it. "I can do this!" she said to herself.

Maria had found her voice, and her classmates were listening.

Looking
Ahead

Few activities raise so many concerns as writing and public speaking. Yet few are as important to your success, not only in college, but in the world outside the classroom. Writing and oral presentations are something that will be a major part of your college classes, and you shouldn't be surprised to find them a part of your professional life in the future. Learning how to write and speak well will not only increase your success in college and beyond, but it will improve your peace of mind!

This chapter focuses on writing and speaking. We begin by considering how to write college-level papers, as well as other kinds of writing. We'll talk about how to get started writing a paper, and how you can move from a rough first draft to a final draft of which you can be proud.

The second part of the chapter looks at oral presentations. We'll discuss ways of getting over stage fright and how to engage listeners from the very start of your talk. We consider the importance of practicing neither too little, nor too much.

After reading this material, you'll be able to answer these questions:

- **What are the best techniques for getting started and writing a first draft?**

- **How can I move from my first draft to my final draft?**

- **How can I lose my fears of public speaking and make effective oral presentations?**

The Writing Process

What happens when you sit down to write? Does the sight of a blank page or blank screen leave your mind similarly blank? Do your fingers, which move so quickly when you're playing your John Madden football video game on the computer, become sluggish when poised over a keyboard to write a paper?

Writing is not easy, and for many students, writing assignments raise more anxieties than any other academic task. There are many reasons for this anxiety. For one thing, papers often have a large impact on your final course grades, putting pressure on you to do well. Maybe you have done all your writing at the last minute, with a deadline looming, so you think of it as tension-filled. Perhaps you've never really been taught how to write well. Or maybe you believe that there's some sort of special writing gene that you just weren't born with.

Stop! Delete from your memory any negative preconceptions you may have about writing. There is no mystery to writing; it's a skill that can be taught, and a skill that, with practice, anybody can learn. *Writing is not a product you read; it is a thinking and reasoning process that is the means of producing that product,* a skill that can be learned like any other, not a talent one is born with or without.

Using strategies based on P.O.W.E.R. Learning (summarized in the P.O.W.E.R. Plan), you will be able to achieve the goal of writing clearly and competently. These strategies will help you to build upon your strengths and maximize your abilities. They will permit you to translate what's inside your head into words that communicate your experience or thoughts directly.

P repare: Confronting the Blank Page

There is nothing more intimidating than a blank piece of paper (or computer screen!). It is something that every writer faces, no matter how proficient. Shakespeare, Jane Austen, Mark Twain, Anna Akmatova, Ralph Ellison, and Sandra Cisneros all felt the challenge of having to fill that void with words.

Looked at another way, though, there is nothing more liberating than a blank page. It offers every possibility, and it gives you the freedom to say whatever you want to say. And therein lies the key to good writing: deciding what it is you want to say.

Preparation is a central aspect of successful writing. Writing is a process, and preparation for it encompasses the following steps:

Deciding What Your Goal Is To write successfully, you need to think about the end product. Is it a long research paper, based on information you must gather? An essay arguing a particular point of view? A fictional short story? A critique of someone else's work or argument? A book or movie review?

IM Link: "Teaching the Text," Chapter 8—Section IV activity on creating a list of beliefs and fears.

Teaching Tip: Assign the task of writing a paper that relates to this course, or allow students to bring in an assignment from another course, to practice the processes discussed in this chapter.

PREPARE
Approach writing as a process

ORGANIZE
Write a flexible outline and construct a thesis statement

WORK
Get it down in the first draft; Refine it in the second draft

EVALUATE
Be your own best critic: finetune your work

RETHINK
Reflect on the writing process: what worked, what didn't?

P.O.W.E.R. Plan

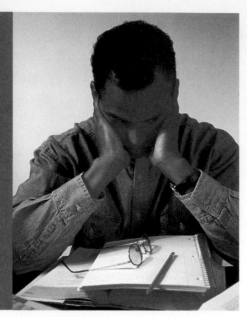

Nothing is more intimidating than a blank piece of paper—or a blank computer screen. On the other hand, it can also be liberating, offering you the freedom and opportunity to say what *you* want to say.

Most often, you'll be working to complete a class assignment that will explain what the goal is. But sometimes the assignment will provide you with several choices; it may even be vague or imprecise. If this is the case, your first step will have to be to decide just what you'll be doing through your writing.

If there is a choice among different types of writing, decide which will make you most comfortable. If one choice is to prepare an essay, and you are creative and enjoy expressing your opinions, choose that option. If you enjoy gathering information and drawing a conclusion from your findings, a research paper might well be the best choice.

Choosing Your Topic Once you've determined the specific type of writing you are going to do, the next step is to choose a topic. Although instructors usually assign a particular topic, in some cases the choice will be left to you. However, the freedom to choose a topic does not come without a price. In fact, many students find that choosing what to write about is harder than actually writing the paper itself. Here are some things you can do to help pick an appropriate topic:

"How do I know what I think 'til I see what I say?"

character in an E.M. Forster novel.

- **Use "freewriting."** According to Peter Elbow, a writing expert who has revolutionized the teaching of writing, one of the reasons we find writing so hard is that we have a set of censors inside our heads.[1] At a moment's notice, those censors are ready to spring up and whisper, "That's no good," when we set pen to paper.

  However, there is a way to keep these internal voices at bay. You can use a technique called "freewriting." In **freewriting,** you write continuously for a fixed period of time, such as 5 or 10 minutes. The only rule that governs freewriting is to write continuously, without stopping. It doesn't matter if the product is bad; it doesn't matter if it's good. The only principle you must follow in freewriting is to get something—anything—down on paper.

  Try it, and you'll see how liberating freewriting can be. Of course the product will not be perfect, but you'll most likely find that you've written something of value to you.

  Suppose, for example, you are stuck for a topic. Through freewriting you can explore your feelings about the course you are going to be writing for, what you like and don't like, and from there go on to get some rough ideas down on paper. What's more, you'll probably form an "attitude" toward one or more potential topics, which can be used to add a personal voice and authenticity to your writing.

  Once the freewriting session is completed, you may want to write a single sentence that captures the main point of what you have written—

Freewriting
A technique involving continuous, nonstop writing, without self-criticism, for a fixed period of time

Brainstorming
A technique for generating ideas by saying out loud as many ideas as can be thought of in a fixed period of time

the "center of gravity," Elbow calls it. You can then use this sentence as a springboard for further exploration of ideas the next time you write.

- **Use brainstorming.** The oral equivalent of freewriting is brainstorming. While freewriting is done alone, brainstorming is most often done with others. In **brainstorming,** you say out loud as many ideas as you can think of in a fixed period of time. Although brainstorming works best when you do it with a group of friends or classmates, you can do it by yourself. (This is one of those times when talking to yourself has its benefits.) Initially, the goal simply is to produce as many ideas as possible, no matter how implausible, silly, or irrelevant. Jot down the ideas that intrigue you as they come up, so you don't forget them.

  As with freewriting, the idea is to temporarily silence the censors that prevent us from saying whatever comes into our heads. In brainstorming, the initial goal is not to produce high-quality ideas, but a high quantity of ideas. You can revisit and evaluate the ideas you've come up with later.

Deciding Who Your Audience Is That's easy, you may be thinking; it's my instructor. *Not so fast.* Although the instructor is the most obvious reader for what you write, you should think of your audience in terms of the ultimate purpose of the writing assignment. For example, if you're writing a paper about the dangers of global warming, are you directing it to a layperson who knows little about the issue? Or are you writing it for someone with a good understanding of science, someone who already knows about atmospheric pressure, *El Niño,* and the ozone layer? Clearly, the answer to this question will make a difference in how and what you write.

In short, it's crucial to know—and to keep in mind—the persons to whom you are writing. What is their level of knowledge about the topic? Are they already

Journal Reflections

How I Feel about Writing

Reflect on the feelings you have about writing by answering the following questions:

1. When I receive a writing assignment, my initial reaction is . . .

2. Do you ever write for pleasure? When? Under what circumstances?

3. Which writing experiences are particularly pleasant for you? Which are unpleasant?

4. What tools do you need to gather when preparing for a lengthy writing assignment? Do you have special pencils or pens? A favorite chair? Do you prefer to use a computer?

5. Are you particularly good at finding ways to put off writing tasks? Do you do anything to prevent this?

6. When faced with a lengthy writing assignment, how do you decide what to write? How do you organize your thoughts?

7. When you take a test that involves writing, such as an essay test, how do you approach it? Do you outline your responses? Do you do anything to gather your ideas?

Try It! 1

Set Yourself Free: Freewriting

Use this space to practice freewriting for a five-minute period. Optional guidance is offered below, but if you want to go ahead and "just do it," simply start writing. Be sure to keep your hand moving; stop controlling yourself. Write only for yourself; forget about what others might think—be frank.

If you need a little more guidance, you are not alone; most people need help the first time they try it. There are actually two kinds of freewriting: plain vanilla freewriting (like that above) and *focused* freewriting. Focused freewriting gives you a starting point.

Here are some starting points for focused freewriting:

Today I feel . . .	I get sick when . . .
I remember . . .	I know . . .
I don't like . . .	I am . . .
I really like . . .	I am not . . .

Using one of these lead-in phrases as a starting point, return to the blank space and begin your freewriting.

What is the main point of what you wrote? Was freewriting effective in helping you get something down on paper? Was it easy or difficult for you? Can you think of how the process of freewriting might help you when it's time to write a paper?

predisposed to a particular position? What do you think they would like to take away with them after reading what you've written?

Keeping an audience in mind serves another purpose: It personalizes your writing. Rather than targeting your writing to a nondescript group of individuals ("all the people who might be worried about global warming"), you individualize your audience. Think of the reader as your sister, or a friend, or your next-door neighbor. Think of how that individual would feel after reading what you've written, and what you would say to convince him or her. Remember, your writing is a representation of you as an individual. It means something to you, and you want its impact to be felt just as personally by another individual.

Researching the Topic   In order to write most papers, you must do research. This can also help you further refine your topic. We discussed methods of doing research in Chapter 4, and you might wish to review the process.

Discussion Prompt: Ask students to generate a list of all of the "10-minute tasks" associated with writing a 10 page paper.

Breaking the Task Down into Pieces   If authors planning to write a book sat down at their word processor and thought about the 500 pages that they needed to write to complete the book, they probably would never finish the book. Such thoughts are at best mind-numbing and at worst totally unproductive and paralyzing. Instead, professional writers break their task down into smaller, more-manageable pieces. Maybe they decide that they'll write a certain number of pages in a given period of time, such as four or five pages a day. Or maybe they plan on writing a chapter each week.

You probably don't have as much time to devote to your writing as a professional writer, so the chunks you break your writing into should be shorter. For instance, if you have to write a 10-page paper, don't think of it as 10 pages. Instead, break it down into chunks of two pages a day, spread out over five days. Or think of it in terms of the major sections: an introduction, a description of the background of an issue, arguments in favor of a position, arguments against a position, and a conclusion. You could then schedule writing each of those five sections on a different day.

rganize: Constructing a Scaffold

When we read and listen to information, the organization phase is really pretty easy: The author or speaker has (hopefully!) already constructed a framework for presenting the information to us. Our job as readers and listeners is to figure out what that organization is, like detectives following a trail of clues.

When we're writing, however, we're creating something that hasn't existed before. Consequently, it's up to us to come up with the scaffolding on which to place our written product.

Construct an Outline (and Be Ready to Change It!)

The fundamental key to organizing an extended piece of writing is the outline. Outlines provide a roadmap to follow when we're writing, a set of sequential steps that show us where we are heading and how we are going to get there.

The secret of successful outlining is flexibility: It is essential to keep an open mind about sequencing and to avoid getting "locked in" too early to a pattern that might later prove unworkable. The best approach is to place possible outline topics, based on your research, on index cards. Then read through all the cards and try to place them in a logical order. Ask yourself how the information represented by the cards builds up into a complete and convincing presentation. Remember your audience and treat your readers

Try It! 2

Working In a Group: Get Your Brain Storming: Using Brainstorming to Generate Ideas

Your American History professor has asked you to come up with 10 ideas for a five-page paper on some aspect of the 1960s. Brainstorm in a group and come up with a list of possible topics, assigning one member of the group to record ideas below.

As you brainstorm, keep the length of the paper assigned and the sort of topic suited to American History generally in mind. Remember, the idea is to produce as many possibilities as you can, without evaluating how realistic or feasible they may be. Think quantity over quality.

After your group has concluded brainstorming, go back to your answers and circle each that you think is realistic for a paper topic. Did brainstorming work? Did you surprise yourself with the number of possibilities you generated?

courteously. Ask yourself what a reader would have to know already in order to understand a given fact or argument. Try out several sequences, and determine which order works best.

You can do the same sort of thing on a computer screen using a word-processing program. List all your topics and rearrange them to your heart's content. If you use the program's outlining feature, it will even renumber the outline as you make changes.

Develop the Paper's Structure. Although sometimes instructors provide a structure for a paper, you may have to construct one yourself. One way to do this is to follow the **ABBCC structure.** "ABBCC" stands for the five parts of a typical research paper: argument, background, body, counterarguments, and conclusion. Each of these parts plays a specific role in the overall paper:

- **Argument.** Just as we introduce ourselves when we meet someone for the first time, a writer needs to introduce a reader to the main argument being put forward in the paper. Every paper should have a main argument or **thesis,** a one- or two-sentence description of the main point or stand that is being taken in the paper. For instance, your thesis might make the argument that "Personal character does not matter in leaders; what matters is their effectiveness in accomplishing the goals for which they were elected."

  A thesis should be stated as a contention ("people are their own worst enemies") or in terms of some action verb ("the technological revolution requires that people receive more education"). An effective thesis statement takes a position on some issue and includes such key words as "should" or "ought." For instance, "Smoking should be banned from restaurants and bars" presents a thesis statement. On the other hand, "This paper will discuss smoking in restaurants and bars" is simply stating the topic.

  The argument need not be the first sentence of the paper. In fact, it is usually wise to start off with something that grabs readers' attention. Begin with a controversial quote, an illustrative story, or a personal encounter—anything that is likely to make a reader sit up and take notice.

  In addition to presenting the main thesis of the paper, the argument section should lay out the areas that you will cover and the general scope of the paper. You should use this section to present the paper's overall perspective and point of view. However, you shouldn't provide evidence yet for why your arguments are correct; save that for the body of the paper.

- **Background.** You'll need to provide readers with a context in which to place your paper's arguments, and the background section is the place to do it. Provide a brief history of the topic, talking about different approaches that have been taken and different schools of thought. Introduce any unusual terminology you might need to employ. If the topic is highly controversial, trace the controversy, and discuss why people have found the topic so controversial. For example, if you are arguing that the independent counsel law should be repealed, you could review why the law was created.

- **Body.** The body makes up the bulk of most papers. In the paper's body, you restate your thesis and provide evidence as to why the thesis is correct.

Teaching Tip: There are many organizational structures for preparing papers other than ABBCC. Ask your students which ones they have heard about already.

ABBCC structure
The structure of the typical research paper, consisting of argument, background, body, counterarguments, and conclusion

Thesis
The main point or position being argued in a paper, typically stating the writer's opinion about the paper's topic

IM Link: "Teaching the Text," Chapter 8, Section V; have students identify the thesis statement in the two papers referred to in this section.

Make Your Point: Write a Thesis Statement

Write a thesis statement for each of the topics below. Remember that the thesis should be a contention or should use an action verb.

global warming and modern technology

campaign finance reform

prayer in schools

bank charges for using an ATM

limits on the content of World Wide Web pages

the death penalty

homosexual marriages

Evaluate each of the thesis statements that you wrote. Do they all contain a contention or action verb? Is there a relationship between how controversial a topic is and how easy it is to write a thesis statement? **Working in a Group:** Each group member should generate three potential topics for a paper and compose a thesis statement for each. Then, as a group, evaluate each of the thesis statements.

This evidence should be presented in a logical order. Exactly what this means depends upon your topic. You may need to work chronologically if you are discussing a historical event. In other cases, you will want to start with the least controversial arguments and gradually move into the ones that are most debatable.

When deciding the order in which to present information, keep your audience firmly in mind. For instance, a paper on the dangers of electromagnetic radiation written for a community law class would be very different from one written for a physics class.

Student Alert: The ambiguity of this information is frustrating to first year students. They want to know the "one right way," and of course, there isn't just one.

- **Counterarguments.** You will also need to touch on information that runs counter to your own thesis. Acknowledge the counterarguments to your position, and then go on to systematically refute each one. This section need not be long, but it is crucial. By doing this you help reinforce your own position and strengthen your argument, showing that you have arrived at your point of view fully aware of—and unconvinced by—opposing views.

- **Conclusion.** A good ending to a paper is as important as a good beginning. It's where you pull everything together. And it is your last chance to drive home your thesis.

IM Link: "Teaching the Text," Chapter 8—Section V. Use these same papers to view a conclusion in the context of a thesis statement.

  The conclusion should summarize the thesis and the arguments that you have made regarding it. Do not introduce new information; all information should have been introduced earlier. The conclusion is a recap of the information and ideas in the paper. Close with a flourish. You might cite a quotation, present an anecdote that is linked to one you presented at the start of the paper, or pose a question ("If the government turns its back on welfare recipients, how can we claim to have a just society?"). However you choose to conclude the paper, make sure that it ties the various pieces together.

W ork: Writing the Work

Now comes the moment that so many dread: It's time to face that blank page or screen and actually start writing. However, if you've followed the steps above and carefully prepared and organized, this phase is likely to be easier than you expect. In fact, you should be so well prepared that you know just how to proceed: Your outline provides a clear roadmap of where you are headed, and your research note cards will permit you to flesh out the points of your outline. One way to look at your outline is that it provides you with the major headings of your paper. The job of writing the paper then becomes a matter of matching up the research to the appropriate outline heading, rather than starting with a blank sheet of paper.

Still, the work of writing is rarely problem-free. The best way to proceed is to divide the actual work of writing into two stages: writing the first draft and revising your draft.

Writing the First Draft Starting a first draft is like diving into a cold-water lake. You know the initial plunge will be painful because the water is icy cold, but you know that once you're in the lake it won't be so bad.

It's the same thing with writing a first draft. Getting started is often the hardest part. However, once you've put even a few words on paper, it gets easier.

When you set pen to paper or fingers to keyboard to begin writing, don't feel that you are carving your words in stone. Permit yourself to be less than perfect. Don't worry about word choice, grammar, sentence structure, spelling, or punctuation. That can come later. The first draft is meant to give you something to move on from. The important thing is to fill up that blank space with *something*.

What's the rationale for such an approach? It's considerably easier to work from an existing draft—even one that is far from perfect—than to work from nothing. In most ways, the first draft is the hardest work you'll have to do, and it's important to get the process underway. By liberating yourself from the constraints of getting things perfect the first time, you will make the process—that of translating what's in your head into a final form that others can see—far easier.

There are several strategies you can use to make writing the first draft less painful:

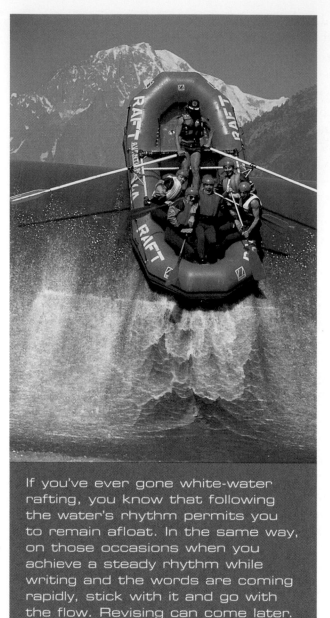

If you've ever gone white-water rafting, you know that following the water's rhythm permits you to remain afloat. In the same way, on those occasions when you achieve a steady rhythm while writing and the words are coming rapidly, stick with it and go with the flow. Revising can come later.

- **Start where you like.** You need not follow the order of the outline when you write. For example, some writers start a paper by writing the conclusion section first. By keeping the end in mind, they know just where they are headed, making the journey a little easier. Similarly, other writers save the beginning of the paper for last, reasoning that they'll be better able to tell their readers where the paper is going after it has actually gotten there.

  What's most important is that you start writing *something*. Write whatever part of the paper you feel most comfortable writing, because just having something on paper is a comforting feeling and will encourage you to write the rest.

- **Turn off your inner critic.** If you're anything like most people, with every word you write, there's probably a voice somewhere in your head that's whispering, "Terrible sentence. Dumb idea. Forget it, you idiot, you'll never finish this paper." That's the voice of your inner critic, and it's a voice that keeps many of us from reaching our potential as good writers.

  Your job is to turn that voice off, at least for now. (You'll want to use it later, when the nagging may come in handy as you revise your work.) While you're working on your first draft, you want to give yourself permission to let your creative processes put words on paper. As long as you write things down, you'll be able to go back, change things, and make your paper better. But you can't revise what isn't there.

- **Go with the flow.** When you're writing your first draft, try to write quickly. Writing often takes on a rhythm, and you should try to write in sync with the flow of that rhythm. If you're on a roll, go with it. Don't stop to edit your work; that will happen later.

On the other hand, if you're having trouble getting into a rhythm, and each word is like pulling teeth, take a break. Do something entirely different for a few minutes and then return with a fresh mind.

If you're really having trouble, try rearranging your note cards. You might even shuffle them (after you've first numbered them so you can go back to the original order). Placing them in a random order may provide a fresh way of looking at your topic, and this may in turn free you enough to get your writing started.

- **Don't be afraid to modify your outline.** When you start writing, it's easy to fall into the trap of viewing an outline as a rigid, unbending framework. But this is not what an outline is. Your outline is a living document, and you should feel free to rearrange headings and even to deviate from it as you're creating your first draft. You'll have the opportunity later to check that the writing still follows a logical course.

  Many writers find that their outlines need to be revised, and so might you. The outline you started with may be incomplete, or the topics may have to be presented in a different order. As you're writing your draft, you may uncover gaps in the outline. That's fine; that's why you're writing a first draft and not pretending to start with a final one.

- **Use your own voice.** Just as you have a distinctive speaking voice, each of us has a distinct *writing* voice. That voice represents our own unique style, a reflection of our outlook on life and of our past writing experiences.

  Novice writers sometimes get hung up trying to use a voice that isn't their own. For example, they may use words they would never normally use when speaking to someone else.

  Avoid the temptation to write as if you were someone else. Instead, use your own natural voice and vocabulary, and don't use big words in an effort to impress your audience. If you'd feel foolish saying "heretofore" in a conversation, you shouldn't use it when you're writing a paper. Don't scan the thesaurus in search of unusual words, and don't give in to the temptation that word-processor thesauruses offer of plugging in new and unusual words for simple ones. Just because you *can* do something doesn't mean you should.

> "I spend a great deal of my time thinking about the power of language—the way it can evoke an emotion, a visual image, a complex idea, or a simple truth."
>
> Amy Tan, author.

Teaching Tip: Ask students to bring in a favorite novel and to identify an actor whose voice would sound right reading it. Can they tell you why? Ask them to analyze the characteristics of "their own voices."

Voice
The unique style of a writer, expressing the writer's outlook on life and past writing experiences

- **Forget about it.** The last step in creating a first draft is the easiest: When you have finished your sketch of the entire paper, from introduction through conclusion, put it aside. To revise your draft effectively—the next step in writing—it's necessary to mentally remove yourself from the situation. Like waiting for tea to steep to reach its full potency, you need to let your mind idle in neutral for a while so that it will be at full strength when you move on to the next phase of writing: revision.

Revising Your Draft Remember that inner critic—that voice in your head—that you tuned out while you were writing the first draft? It's time to tune it back in.

The fact is that most of writing is *re*writing. That's why you should not torture yourself over your first draft too much. The difference between success and failure in writing rests in the revision process. Sure, it's possible to hand in a first draft, and sometimes you'll even get a passable grade. But if you want to reach your own potential as a writer, you *must* revise.

Don't feel that revising is something that only students have to do. Professional writers may go through dozens of drafts—and still not be completely satisfied. Virtually no one has the ability to write a first-draft paper that is so lucid and compelling that it stands on its own.

Following several basic rules can make the revision process work smoothly for you:

IM Link: "Teaching the Text," Chapter 8—Sections IV and VIII activity on "Reading a Paper Out Loud."

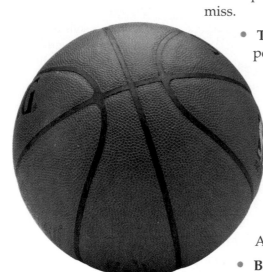

- **Read the first draft out loud.** Read your paper out loud—to yourself, a friend, or your computer. It doesn't matter who's listening.

  Reading out loud does several things. You'll more easily discover missing words, verbs that don't match the subject of the sentence, shifts in tense, missing transitions, and other things that you might have to fix. The combination of speaking and reading helps make problems more apparent than if you were simply reading the first draft to yourself silently.

  But reading aloud does something more: It slows you down. Speaking takes longer than silent reading, and the slowed pace of oral reading can help you identify things that need revising that you'd otherwise miss.

- **Take the long view.** Start off by taking the broadest perspective possible and asking yourself a series of questions:

  What is the purpose of my paper and has that purpose been fulfilled?

  Have I addressed every aspect of the assignment?

  Does the paper tell its audience everything they need to know?

  Will readers be able to follow its logic?

  Does the paper make its points clearly?

  Are the transitions between sections clear?

- **Be ruthless.** Remember, writing isn't etched in stone. The tendency is to feel that once we've put words on paper, they are something more than just words. They tend to take on a life of their own—a life that we have created and so are often reluctant to change or part with.

  It is natural to feel a bit parental towards our first draft, but it is important to fight this instinct. Now is the time to give full voice to your inner critic. You need to be merciless and unforgiving with passages, paragraphs, phrases, and words that don't sound right or that do not ultimately add to the arguments you're trying to make. Don't tear *yourself* down, but, like a coach demanding the best from his or her players, be demanding of your performance.

  Start pruning at the paragraph level. Assess each paragraph to make sure that it adds to the final message, that it flows from the previous paragraph logically, and that it is consistent with what you are trying to accomplish in the section of the paper in which it is located.

  Then move to the level of sentences and words. Evaluate each sentence, and then each word, to make sure that it adds to the clarity of your message.

By paring down your writing, you let your ideas stay closer to the surface, rather than being obscured by repetition and excess words. If you are extremely fond of a phrase or a group of words that seem to be unnecessary, start by cutting them out and setting them aside. You can ease the pain by saving what you've cut. Write

"Wrestling with words gave me my moments of greatest meaning."

Richard Wright, author.

down or print out the sections and phrases of which you're particularly proud, put them into an envelope, and toss the envelope into the top drawer of your dresser. You never know when you might need it. More important, knowing that you can save the cut material may make it easier to do the necessary cutting.

Teaching Tip: Ask students to read each others' papers and to provide feedback.

- **Check sequence and logic.** It's now time to reverse course. Whereas before the focus was on cutting extraneous material, you now need to check what's left with a view toward *adding* material.

  For example, because of earlier deletions, it may be necessary to add or modify transitions between sections and paragraphs. Ideas should flow logically, and the reader should be able to understand the structure in which they are set.

  If the logic or the structure of the paper has been lost, restore it by reordering the ideas you've presented. You can reorder sentences within paragraphs, and you can reorder paragraphs within sections.

- **Check punctuation and spelling.** Make sure you've fulfilled the basic requirements of punctuation that have been drummed into you since elementary school. Check for the obvious stuff: Sentences should start with capital letters and end with the appropriate punctuation; commas should set off dependent clauses; and the like. Use a style manual if you're unsure.

Discussion Prompt: Rather than spending time trying to convince students about the importance of good spelling, ask them to tell you why correct spelling matters.

  Check spelling carefully. This is one of the areas in which word processors earn their keep best, by checking the spelling of every word. The spell-check feature not only will identify every misspelled word (that is, every word not in its dictionary), but it will prompt you with alternatives for those words that are misspelled.

  Be careful not to rely completely on the spell-checker, however. Such programs can find only misspellings that do not happen to form actual words; if what you typed forms words, the spell-checker will leave it alone, even if the words you typed are not the ones you wanted to use. *Foe instants, know spelt-cheek pogrom wood fined eras inn thus settings.* And yet every word is spelled incorrectly in this context.

- **Make it pleasing to the eye.** Instructors are human. They can't help but react differently to a paper that is neatly typed compared with one that is handwritten in a difficult-to-read scrawl.

  A neat paper conveys a message: I'm proud of this paper. I've put time and effort into it. This is my best work.

  A sloppy paper says something different.

Teaching Tip: Bring in examples of appropriate "final" products.

  Take the time, then, to make sure your paper looks good. This doesn't mean that you need to invest in a fancy plastic cover, or worry about the alignment of the staples, or spend a lot of time deciding which font to use on your word processor. But it does mean that you should make sure the quality of the paper's appearance matches the quality of the writing.

Evaluate: Acting As Your Own Best Critic

IM Link: "Teaching the Text," Chapter 8—Section VII, Goal 2.

Because you've already put so much work into your paper, you might be tempted to rush through the final stages of the P.O.W.E.R. process. Avoid the temptation. If you've carefully revised your paper, the last stages will not be time-consuming, and they may have a significant impact on your paper's ultimate quality—and your success.

Take these steps to *evaluate* what you've written:

- **Ask yourself if your paper accomplishes what you set out to do.** The beginning of your paper contains a thesis statement and the argument that you intended to make. Does your paper support the thesis? Are the arguments upheld by the evidence you've reported? Would an impartial reader be convinced by what you've written?

Student Alert: Students may resist the idea that they can predict an instructor's evaluation. Help them see why it's important to make the effort to do so.

- **Put yourself in your instructor's shoes.** Does the paper precisely fit the assignment requirements? Does it meet the instructor's underlying goals in making the assignment?

- **Check the mechanical aspects of the paper.** Make certain the paper represents you the way you want to be represented. Not only should the grammar and spelling be correct, but the paper should look good. If your instructor requires that citations or references be reported in a certain style, make sure you've followed that style.

If you've revised the paper with care, it will likely pass muster. If it doesn't, though, go back and work on it once again. By this point, it should require only minor tinkering to get it into shape.

Rethink: Reflecting on Your Accomplishment

Rethinking is the homestretch of the writing process. It's a moment to savor, because it permits you take a long view of what you've accomplished. You've gone from a blank page to words on paper that tell a story, a story that you've put together. You've turned nothing into something—an achievement in and of itself.

Discussion Prompt: Pair up students and have them talk about rethinking the message and the mechanics.

Rethinking occurs on several levels: rethinking the message, mechanics, and method. But don't address them until a little time has passed since you completed the evaluation of the paper. Wait a day or so, and then reread the paper. Then, bringing your critical thinking skills to bear, reflect on the following:

- **Rethink the message.** Be sure that the overall message your paper conveys is appropriate. A paper is like an advertisement. In most papers, you are seeking to communicate information in order to convince someone of a particular opinion. Make sure that the message is what you wish to communicate, and that ultimately the paper is successful in making the case.

- **Rethink the mechanics.** A television commercial filled with fuzzy images and jerky camera shots would not be very compelling, no matter how good the underlying product. In the same way, a paper with mechanical errors will not impress your readers or persuade them that your arguments are correct. Take another look at your writing style, then, to make sure you are putting your best foot forward. Look at grammar, punctuation, and word usage to make sure the choices you've made are appropriate.

- **Rethink the method.** Every time you finish a paper, you learn something—something about the topic of your writing and something about yourself. Ask yourself what you have learned to help you become a better writer in the future. What might you have done to improve the writing process? What could have gone better? What will you do differently the next time you write? Keep in mind that the P.O.W.E.R. approach represents a general process and that you may choose to emphasize particular stages according to what works best for you.

Above all, remember what you've accomplished: You've transformed what's inside your head—your thoughts, your ideas, your values—into something that can reach and potentially influence other people. Through your writing, you have exercised the ability to move others and get them to think in new ways. You've made a difference. That's the real power of writing.

Teaching Tip: Ask students to attach a page to the end of every paper they turn in with responses to these questions.

Speaking Your Mind

Public speaking ranks right at the bottom of most first-year college students' rankings of their academic abilities.[2] In fact, surveys of the general population find that most people are more afraid of public speaking than dying! It's not surprising. How often are we so totally exposed to others' scrutiny? Not only do we have to worry about the message we're communicating—just as with our writing—but in addition, each of us has to be concerned about nonverbal behavior and the impression we are making. . . . *Is my hair sticking out? . . . This sweater was a big mistake. . . . Are they bored? . . . I wish my hands would stop shaking.*

Although you may always be a little nervous about public speaking, it's important to keep several points in mind:

- Audiences are generally sympathetic. They've all been where you are and probably share your fears about public speaking. They're on your side and are rooting for you to succeed.

- Once you start speaking, it will become easier. Anxiety tends to be highest *before* you start talking. Most people find that after they start a talk, their nervousness tends to decline.

- Practice helps. Practice and preparation for the talk will go a long way toward easing your tension.

Teaching Tip: Connect this information to the discussion of learning styles in Chapter 3.

Keep in mind, too, that in many fundamental ways, speaking is like writing. You need to consider who your audience is, muster your arguments, and decide how to sequence those arguments. Consequently, the P.O.W.E.R. writing framework that we presented earlier in the chapter applies to speaking as well:

- **Prepare** what you will say and how you will say it. Think about your audience and the occasion on which you will speak, and try to be sure your words match both audience and occasion.

Career Connections

Write Away

The first step in getting a job is putting pen to paper (or, probably more accurately, finger to keyboard). Whether you receive a lead for a job from a college career center, read an ad in the paper, or see a job listing on the Internet, you'll need to communicate in writing to the potential employer.

You are selling yourself in a letter of application. To be effective, keep these guidelines in mind:

- **Brief is better.** Employers are likely to get many letters, and long ones are least likely to be read.

- **State what you can do for the employer, not what the employer can do for you.** Don't tell a potential employer you really, really need a job to pay off your credit card bills. Instead, explain how your skills can help further an organization's goals.

- **Summarize your qualifications.** Respond specifically to the skills required for the job. List specific experiences you've had that are relevant to what the employer is looking for.

- **Enclose a résumé.** Your résumé should contain a detailed summary of your educational background and achievements, qualifications, and work experience.

- **Ask for an interview.** Close your letter with a request to get together and discuss the job. Provide your telephone number and e-mail address.

- **Proofread!** You must have zero tolerance for errors. Any mistake is likely to put you at the bottom of the pile of applications.

- **Organize** your thoughts, using notes to cue you to the main parts of your presentation and making logical connections for your audience to follow.

- **Work** carefully during your presentation by speaking clearly and calmly to your audience and avoiding distracting mannerisms or body language.

- **Evaluate** your performance after you finish your presentation and ask others to evaluate it, too. Take notes on the feedback you receive from yourself and others.

- **Rethink** your entire approach to preparing for and delivering presentations each time you make one. Make the changes you feel you should make to improve your performance over time.

Meeting the Challenge of Public Speaking

Although speaking and writing are both concerned with communicating your thoughts to others and they share many features, they are not exactly the same. In fact, speaking presents several unique challenges. Among the factors that you need to take into account when you are speaking are these:

- **The first minute counts—a lot.** If you can get your audience's attention, arouse their interest, and engage them in the first few minutes, you're on your way to a successful speech. On the other hand, let them drift off early on and you've lost them—potentially for good.

  How do you get them interested? There are several ways:

  Begin with an anecdote. *"It was a scientist's dream, experienced as he dozed off in front of a fire, that led to one of the most important biological discoveries of all time."*

  Start with a quotation. *" 'I have seen the enemy, and he is us.' But are we really the enemy? I believe . . . "*

Arouse their curiosity. *"I have a secret, one that I've kept hidden for many years—until now."*

Talk about the significance of the topic. *"If you think that global warming is not a problem, take a look at what's happening to the beachfront up and down the Atlantic coast this year."*

Ask a question. *"Have you ever wondered how you could save enough money to buy a new car?"*

Use humor. *"My introduction to gardening was not promising: Seeking to surprise my mother, I 'weeded' her garden so enthusiastically that I pulled up all her flower seedlings."*

- **Provide oral transition points.** When we're reading a textbook selection, we usually have the luxury of knowing exactly when a transition point occurs. It's marked by a title, section heading, or new paragraph. These markers help us construct a mental map that permits us to understand the overall structure of the piece we're reading.

  Listeners don't have the same advantage. Unless the speaker orally signals that he or she is moving to a new part of a talk, listeners will get lost. Not only will they be unable to understand the structure of the talk, they won't know where the talk is headed.

  However, there are several ways to erect verbal signposts throughout a speech. By using phrases such as the following, you can alert listeners that a twist in the journey lies ahead:

  "To understand the problem, we need to consider . . . "

  "The problems are clearly daunting. But there are solutions. Let's consider some of them. . . . "

  "Now that we've considered the solutions, we need to take a look at their costs. . . . "

Try It! 4

Let's Talk

Devise a one-minute opening to a talk about the thing you know most about in this world: you. The topic can be about one of your experiences or about anything that concerns you or reveals a little bit about your past, your feelings, or your opinions. Use any of the opening strategies that we've considered.

Which strategy are you going to employ? _____

Now write your opening:

_____

_____

_____

_____

_____

_____

_____

_____

_____

_____

Now try it out on a friend or classmate. Remember: Limit what you say to the one-minute opening.

When you're finished, ask yourself these questions: How well do you think your strategy worked? Why? Would another strategy have worked as well or better? What did your audience think of your opening? Why do you think it had the effect it did? Did your opening make your audience want to hear more? Did your opening make you want to write more?

"Let's go back for a moment to an earlier point I made. . . ."

"To sum up, the situation offers some unexpected advantages. . . ."

- **Make your notes work for you, not against you.** A speaker is giving a talk, and suddenly she loses her place in her notes. She fumbles around, desperately trying to find her place and figure out what comes next.

  It's a painful situation to watch—and even worse for the person experiencing the problem. How do you avoid finding yourself in such a predicament?

  One way is by thoroughly acquainting yourself both with what you are going to say *and* with your notes. Once again, practice is your best friend. But the type of notes you have also makes a big difference.

  There are as many forms of notes as there are speakers. Some speakers write out their entire talk in advance; others use no notes at all, counting on memorizing their talk. Avoid either extreme. If you write out your complete speech in advance, you'll experience an overwhelm-

Discussion Prompt: Ask students to discuss advantages and disadvantages of giving a presentation using a paper (8½ × 11 sheets), note cards (3 × 5), overhead transparencies, slides, computers, videos, etc.

ing urge to read it to your audience. Nothing could be more deadly. On the other hand, if you memorize your talk and have no notes at all, you'll be susceptible to a memory lapse that can make you feel completely foolish. Even if you can remember your talk successfully, you may end up sounding mechanical, like an amusement park guide who has given the same speech about the "jungle cruise" at least a thousand times.

The best approach is to choose a middle ground. Develop an outline that includes the major points you wish to cover, and have this outline in front of you when you speak. It might be written or typed on a sheet of paper, or you might use index cards (number them!). In addition, write out and memorize your opening and closing statements.

By memorizing the opening and closing statements, you'll have the opportunity to look your audience in the eye and engage them nonverbally at two of the most crucial junctures in your talk—the beginning and the end. Using an outline for most of your talk permits you to sound natural as you speak. You'll probably use slightly different words every time you give your talk, which is fine.

Audio-visual aids, such as pictures, are not only worth a thousand words, they will keep your audience more interested in what you are saying. They also take the focus away from you, making the enterprise of public speaking less nerve-wracking.

- **A picture can save you a thousand words.** Maps, charts, photos, drawings, figures, and other illustrations add another dimension to a presentation, helping to engage listeners. Computer programs, such as PowerPoint, permit you to create graphics relatively painlessly.

  IM Link: "Teaching the Text," Chapter 8—Section IV; activity regarding visual aids.

  You can even use props. For example, if you are talking about a series of Supreme Court rulings, you might incorporate a gavel into your talk. Visual aids make abstract concepts more concrete and immediate.

  Visual aids serve another function: They can reduce your anxiety. You can be assured that when an audience is focusing on an illustration or prop, their attention is drawn away from you, at least temporarily. Just knowing this may be enough to lower your anxiety level. (Just resist the temptation to play with your props as you talk!)

- **Use the right amount and kind of practice.** After you've written your opening and closing statements, constructed an outline, and decided what visual aids to use, it's time to practice. It's not just the amount of practice that is critical. *How* you practice is as important as *how much* you practice.

  Running through your speech mentally will help you to familiarize yourself with your presentation, but you really need to give the speech out loud. Only by hearing yourself speak can you actually get a sense of how the presentation works as an oral presentation.

  Practice in front of a friend or classmate. It is only by actually trying your talk out in front of a warm body that you'll be able to approximate the experience of actually speaking in public, and your audience can provide you with feedback regarding what is working and what is not.

Try It! 5

Prop Yourself Up

Think of at least three visual aids or props that could accompany the various presentation ideas listed below:

a speech on the dangers of biological warfare

a three-minute talk on the times when lying is acceptable

a talk about the significance of the Clinton–Lewinsky scandal

a review of the movie "Titanic"

IM Link: "Teaching the Text," Chapter 8—Sections IV and VIII, "Reading a Paper Out Loud" activity.

Audio- or video taping your talk can also be helpful, but if you tend to be your own worst critic, it is best to use someone else.

How much practice is enough practice? You've probably done enough when you do a good job giving a talk twice in a row. That's sufficient. You don't want to overpractice. If you practice your talk too many times, you'll become so bored with it that the actual talk will sound canned and unconvincing.

● **Fight stage fright.** As you know, for many people, the mere thought of speaking in front of others causes a knot of fear to form deep in their gut. Even those who routinely speak in front of others experience some degree of anxiety. (Ask one or two of your course instructors if they ever feel nervous when teaching a class. You may be surprised at the answer you get.)

Although you won't be able to alleviate your stage fright completely, several techniques can reduce the anxiety that public speaking produces. First, make sure you're wearing clothes that are comfortable and that make you feel pleased with your appearance on the day of a talk. If you feel good about your appearance, you'll be more relaxed.

Five minutes before you get up to speak, take three slow, deep breaths. Concentrate on the feeling of the air going in and out of your body. If a particular part of your body feels tense, tighten it up even more and then relax it. Do it several times. Finally, visualize yourself giving the speech successfully and the relief that you'll feel afterwards.

● **Monitor your nonverbal behavior.** Anxiety about public speaking can do strange things to people's bodies. Their hands may shake or feel icy cold. They may pace back and forth like a caged lion. They may sweat profusely. They may stand rigidly while speaking, looking like stiff toy soldiers. Or they may slump over a podium as if they wished they could dissolve into thin air.

To avoid appearing as if you were scared to death—even if you are—stand up straight and tall. Let your hands fall comfortably at your sides, using them smoothly—not jerkily—when you need to gesture to make a point. Look directly at different members of your audience, shifting your gaze from one person to the next. Eye contact engages audience members, making them feel that your words are directed straight toward them.

If the thought of eye contact scares you, try a trick that some speakers use. Look directly at the *hairline* of different audience members; to your listeners, this is generally indistinguishable from eye contact, and yet it can help you avoid becoming distracted by a facial expression that you may interpret—or misinterpret—negatively: *Is she bored? . . . Is he angry at what I'm saying?*

Teaching Tip: Videotape your students and allow them to take the video home to watch in private. Ask them to provide you with a written critique of their performance.

Speaking Off-the-Cuff:
Extemporaneous Speaking

What do you do when an instructor calls on you in class and asks, "What do you think the point of this poem is?" Just as anxiety-producing as giving a prepared talk (and probably a lot more common) is public speaking that is extemporaneous. **Extemporaneous talks** are unprepared presentations that require you to speak on a moment's notice.

Extemporaneous speaking happens far more frequently than you may like to think: your professor asks you to explain why historians have begun to consider reconstruction a failed enterprise; a co-worker or classmate asks you to explain how a particular software program works; you visit your landlord to complain about the water heater that keeps breaking, and the landlord asks you for details about the problem. The response you give in each of these situations (and many others) is very much an exercise in extemporaneous speaking.

Extemporaneous talk
An unprepared, off-the-cuff oral presentation

"PREPing" to Speak Extemporaneously Just because extemporaneous speaking is, by definition, unplanned, it does not have to be totally off the top of your head. There is a simple process that you can use when you're put on the spot. Known as the PREP formula,[3] it consists of breaking down an answer into four parts:

- **Point of view.** Initially provide your point of view, delineating a clear view of where you stand on the issue.

- **Reasons.** Provide the chief reasons why you believe your position is correct.

- **Evidence or examples.** Give specific evidence to support your point of view.

- **Point of view, restated.** Restate your point of view.

"I could have been a big celebrity but for my fear of public speaking."

Try It! 6

🌴 Working in a Group: Put Yourself on the Spot

Each member of a class group should write two questions on separate note cards. Some examples: "Are basketball players paid too much?" "What's the best way to wash dishes?" "How can you get people to exercise more?"

Place the cards, face down, on a table. Have the first group member choose one of the cards at random and immediately answer the question using the PREP system. Every person should take a turn answering a question.

After each person gives his or her extemporaneous speech, evaluate the responses by answering the following questions as a group: Generally, how effective was the person's response to the question? What were its greatest strengths? What could have been done better?

Here's an example:

Professor Fiske: Who can tell me if racism is a uniquely American problem? Stephanie, why don't you take a stab at the question.

Stephanie: I don't believe racism is uniquely American at all. **[point of view]** If we look at other times in history or other parts of the world today, we find all sorts of racial problems. **[reasons]** For example, consider Bosnia and the Middle East. Or look at the difficulties that South Africa had. Or look at Nazi Germany. **[evidence or examples]** So it's hard for me to understand how anyone could contend that racism is uniquely American. Racism, unfortunately, is a universal fact of life. **[point of view, restated]**

Although using the PREP system may seem awkward at first, you'll find it easy to learn. And with sufficient practice, it will become automatic, saving you lots of mental scrambling the next time you're called on in class.

Remember: You're Already an Accomplished Public Speaker

Discussion Prompt: Ask students to list several occasions when they have spoken in public. Why did they speak? What were the results?

Speaking in front of others is something you've done all your life. It may have been in moments of intimacy or friendship with just one other person present. It may have been with a group of friends deciding on what kind of pizza to order, with you arguing against anchovies and your friends arguing in favor. It may have been as a sports team member, with you shouting encouragement to your fellow athletes. The point is that you've already spoken in front of others—lots of times.

When you are faced with giving a formal presentation, then, give yourself credit for the times you've already spoken publicly. Let go of your fears and enjoy your moment in the spotlight. You may well find that the ability to impart what you know to others is a satisfying and rewarding experience.

Speaking of Success

Name: *ThaoMee Xiong*
Education: *Mt. Holyoke College, South Hadley, Massachusetts*
Home: *Appleton, Wisconsin*

It's a long way from the Southeast Asian country of Laos to Mt. Holyoke College, but for ThaoMee Xiong it's been a journey of success. The high point so far is being named to *USA Today*'s 1998 All-USA College First Academic Team. Xiong's success is all the more remarkable given that she immigrated with her family from Laos to Thailand, and then to Wisconsin in 1978. In Wisconsin she not only entered a totally different culture, but she also faced the challenge of learning to speak and write the language of that culture.

"I've always struggled with writing and have never been confident with it," she says. "Once I get an idea for a paper, I try to do some research on the subject to see if there's enough information on the topic before I start writing about it. Then I just start writing," she adds. "I feel better when I get something down on paper."

Although writing may be difficult

for Xiong, speaking before groups of people is more comfortable.

"I find speaking a lot easier and feel far more confident than when I write," she explains. "In high school I took up forensics and participated in mock trials. I found this helped me a lot with language and speaking. It taught me not to be fearful of speaking in public.

"In high school I was one of the few students of color. I always felt it was my responsibility to speak up and get my issues out there," Xiong notes. "I had some concerns about my community, and I was dealing with the feeling of always being put on the spot. Speaking up helped."

Xiong has continued to speak out, although this time in a different way: Her most recent accomplishment is co-authoring an article on Hmong refugee women that will be published in the book *Outside the Master Narratives: Women's Untold Stories*.

What are the best techniques for getting started and writing a first draft?

- Freewriting and brainstorming can help you choose a topic.

- Identifying the audience for writing is essential.

- Breaking down large writing tasks into smaller, more-manageable pieces helps pave the way to completing a writing assignment.

- Good organization, which is essential to both writer and reader, often follows the ABBCC structure: argument, background, body, counterarguments, and conclusion.

How can I move from my first draft to my final draft?

- Use your outline as your roadmap.

- The best way to begin writing the first draft is to plunge in, starting anywhere in the paper.

- Revision is an essential part of writing: Most of writing is rewriting.

How can I lose my fears of public speaking and make effective oral presentations?

- Although public speaking can be intimidating, audiences are generally sympathetic, speaking becomes easier once it is underway, and practice leads to success.

- The first minute of the presentation, oral transition points, visual aids, and having enough practice are important.

- Use the PREP system for giving extemporaneous (unrehearsed) talks.

Key Terms and Concepts

ABBCC structure (p. 201)
Brainstorming (p. 196)
Extemporaneous talk (p. 215)

Freewriting (p. 196)
Thesis (p. 201)
Voice (p. 205)

Resources

On Campus

If you are having difficulties with writing, the first place to turn to is a cooperative classmate. Ask someone to read a draft of a writing assignment. He or she may be able to make enough constructive comments to allow subsequent drafts to come more easily. In addition, some colleges have writing clinics where you can bring a draft of your paper and work with a counselor. Finally, your instructors may be willing to read preliminary drafts of your work.

In Print

The second edition of Peter Elbow's book *Writing with Power* (Oxford University Press, 1998) presents a fine introduction to the art and practice of writing, with specific suggestions for how to get started and for refining and polishing first drafts.

Another excellent guide to writing is William Zinsser's classic, *On Writing Well: The Classic Guide to Writing Nonfiction* (Harperreference, 1998). A widely used guide to writing, Zinsser's book is helpful both for beginners and for more-experienced writers.

Finally, Hamilton Gregory's book *Public Speaking for College and Career* (McGraw-Hill, 1999) provides an excellent introduction to public speaking. It is filled with tips for planning and delivering a talk.

On the Web

The following sites on the World Wide Web provide the opportunity to extend your learning about the material in this chapter. (Although the Web addresses were accurate at the time the book was printed, check the P.O.W.E.R. Learning Web site [http://mhhe.com/power] for any changes that may have occurred.)

http://andromeda.rutgers.edu/~jlunch/writing/
This site provides a list of grammatical rules and explanations, comments on style, and suggestions on usage. There are two types of entries: specific articles on usage and more general articles on style. An alphabetical search engine is provided to help locate information more quickly.

http://www.la.psu.edu/speech/100a/workbook/wrkbk.htm
This site is an online tutorial for preparing an effective speech. The tutorial takes you through the step-by-step process of preparing a speech, including selecting an appropriate topic, analyzing one's audience, and structuring a speech.

http://www.cc.columbia.edu/acis/bartleby/strunk/index.html
Based on the classic text recommended by writing instructors for many years—Strunk and White's *The Elements of Style*, this site is filled with helpful hints on word usage, punctuation, and common mistakes to avoid. This site is a must for writers serious about improving their writing.

Taking It to the Net

1 Write a brief essay. Go to Yahoo! (**www.yahoo.com**) and click on "Today's News." Select one of the available categories (for example, "Top Stories") and read the first story. Summarize the news story, including only the most important facts, in a brief essay.

2 Practice public speaking. Again, go to Yahoo! (**www.yahoo.com**) and click on "Today's News" and then on "Top Stories." Read the two top stories and write brief notes for each on an index card. Now find a willing classmate or friend and explain the details of each story using your index cards for reference. Did your listener follow the story? Did he or she find it of interest? Were you able to answer any questions that your listener had?

The Case of . . .

the Reluctant Speaker

"No one," thought Erik Phillips to himself, "could hate public speaking more than I do."

Erik, who already thought of himself as somewhat shy, was horrified at the thought of giving a presentation. Not only did he not like talking in front of others, exposing himself to their scrutiny, but he was embarrassed by his thick Louisiana accent, which his friends at the northern college he attended teased him about constantly.

He was sure he'd never be able to stand up in front of the class. Erik made up his mind to ask his instructor if he could write a paper instead of making the oral presentation. But before he could, one of his friends in the class told him that he had already asked for an alternative assignment for himself and that the instructor had flatly refused. The instructor hadn't even taken the request seriously, merely saying that it would be a "good experience" to give the talk.

Erik was stuck.

1. How would you advise Erik to prepare and organize for his talk?

2. Erik expressed a willingness to write a paper instead of giving a talk. Should he prepare the paper and read it for his presentation? Why or why not? How might he use the research for his paper to help with his talk?

3. Erik is especially nervous about speaking because he believes that his accent interferes with understanding. How might he deal with this particular anxiety? How could friends or classmates help him?

4. Do you think props would be helpful for Erik? What purpose might they serve?

5. What advice would you give Erik about what to do during his talk to reduce his anxiety?

Improving Your Memory

9

The stack of note cards kept getting higher and higher.

And as it grew, so did Carlita Lizzigara's sense of panic. Carlita had methodically written each new French vocabulary word she had encountered over the term onto an index card, just as her instructor had recommended. But as the term wore on, and the stack grew higher, Carlita felt she'd never be able to memorize all the words in time for the final exam. There were already hundreds of words, and there was still a few weeks left in the term. How could she ever manage to recall them all?

Carlita decided that desperate measures were called for. She began to take her stack of cards with her everywhere she went. Whenever she had a spare moment, she would shuffle through the cards, trying to memorize the words, one by one. She sometimes felt a little silly, sitting in the Laundromat, eating meals, and riding on the bus with her thick stack of cards, but as she spent more time going over the words, she became more confident, and she began to recall more of them each time she reviewed them.

It worked! By the time of the final exam, half of which consisted of translating words from French into English, she was thrilled to realize that she had succeeded in memorizing most of the words. The exam was easy for her, and she ended the semester with an A in the course.

Looking
Ahead

Most of us have experienced the challenge of memorizing a seemingly insurmountable amount of information, and we tend to focus on our memory failures far more than our successes. But the truth is that our memory capabilities are truly astounding. If you are like the average college student, your vocabulary contains some 50,000 words. You know hundreds of mathematical facts, and you can recall detailed images from scenes you saw years ago. In fact, simply cataloging the memories you already have might well take a lifetime.

In this chapter, you'll learn how you can improve the memory skills you already have. We'll examine what memory is, why it sometimes fails us, and how this can be prevented. Finally, you will become acquainted with specific ways you can learn information that will help you recall it when you need to.

In short, after reading this chapter, you'll be able to answer these questions:

- **What is memory and how does it function?**

- **Why might I have problems with memory, and how can I deal with those problems?**

- **What are some techniques I can use for memorizing information?**

The Secret of Memory

There's one well-kept secret about memory, and you should never forget it: You remember everything.

Sure, sometimes you have trouble recalling information that you know you've learned. Or maybe you don't recall that you learned it, even though in fact you did. But this is not because information has disappeared from your head. The problem is one of *retrieval*. **Retrieval** entails finding information stored in memory and returning it to consciousness for further use. Every piece of information that you've ever learned—if you really learned it at some point in the past—is buried somewhere in your brain. The problem is that you can't always find it.

The proof of this assertion comes from the biology of memory. Consider what happens when you're exposed to some new material. Say your geometry instructor spends a class talking about the Pythagorean formula in geometry, which maintains that the square of the length of the hypotenuse of a right triangle is equal to the sum of the squares of the two other sides. (You may recall this formula as $a^2 + b^2 = c^2$.)

When you first learn the formula, the wiring connecting a handful of the 70 trillion or so brain cells in your head is changed—forever. The information on the Pythagorean formula is etched into some tiny part of your brain, and unless that part of the brain is damaged in some way through injury or disease, it will stay there for the remainder of your life. This doesn't mean that you will easily find the information when you need it. But it does mean that that particular piece of information remains patiently in place, potentially retrievable the next time you encounter a geometry problem.

> "A retentive memory may be a good thing, but the ability to forget is the true token of greatness."
>
> Elbert Hubbard, *The Note Book.*

The practical outgrowth of this biological process is straightforward: You already remember everything you need to know, and a lot more. With some effort, you could remember the names of everyone in your third-grade class. You know what you ate when you went to the eighth-grade dance. You remember the name of the body of water that borders Iraq. And you even could have remembered where you left your keys the last time you misplaced them.

The key to successful recall is to learn the material initially in a way that will allow you to recall it easily later. If you have trouble remembering material that you've already learned, then the trick is figuring out a way to retrieve that material from memory. In short, we need to devise ways to free the memories that reside within our brains.

As important as memory is, however, forgetting is helpful at times, too.

The Value of Forgetting

Legend has it that the actress Ingrid Bergman once said, "Happiness lies in good health and a bad memory."[1]

Although it's tempting to think of forgetting as the enemy of memory, in fact it's just the opposite. If we never forgot anything, think how cluttered our minds would be. Forgetting permits us to disregard inconsequential details

Remember Details

Read the following story. Pay attention to the details, but don't take notes or make lists.

Demain entered the marketplace slowly, feeling his way. He had never seen such confusion.

Hundreds of wagons, caravans, booths, and carts were drawn up in a broad U, occupying three sides of the enormous town square, their awnings and curtains open and inviting. The colors and odors were a sensual assault; he perceived them not just through his eyes and nose, but as if they were pressing forcibly against his skin. And the sounds! He could scarcely keep himself from bolting back the way he had come, to the safety of the countryside.

A sense of wonder pushed him forward. He walked past gold merchants, with their gray cloaks and watchful eyes, and a potter, her shop filled three shelves high with vases, bottles, and jars of deep blues, reds, and yellows that Demain—accustomed to the brown clay that adorned his mother's kitchen—had never even imagined possible. Cloths were on sale in the booth next to the potter's—shamelessly long bolts of impossibly patterned prints, depicting herons, bulls, schools of fish, a field of wheat, great bowls of fruit, and men and women engaged in the pursuits he knew from stories: They danced in bold colors and graceful postures, harvested vast fields of bounty, fought battles of intricate strategy, and drank and courted in riotous taverns.

Past the dealers in rugs, chairs, hats, shoes, and wagons; past the blacksmith's huge muddy arms beating out rugged tools and fine weapons; past the fortune tellers and musicians, Demain at last came to the vendors of food and drink. Never had he felt so hungry. He was lifted off his feet—he swore he was floating—by the aroma of long lines of sausages, sides of beef, whole lambs, chickens on spits the length of spears, bacon and hams, fried potatoes, great vats of boiling vegetables, stewing tomatoes, and breads—all shapes and sizes of loaves, twisted into braids, curled into circles, flattened, puffed, elongated, pocketed, and glazed.

Demain felt the two coppers in his pocket—his holiday bounty—and hoped they would be enough.

Note: We'll return to the story of Demain later. For now, read on . . .

about people, experiences, and other sources of information that otherwise would burden us.

For example, would it really be useful to know that we dropped our fork in the middle of dinner six weeks ago? Would it be helpful to remember that a professor wore the same stained sweater six classes earlier? Would our lives be any richer if we knew that the subway car we took a day ago had a defaced advertisement for tanning lotion? One man—whose memory was so good that he could repeat passages that he'd read 15 years earlier (in a foreign language he didn't even speak!)—was dull and disorganized. He couldn't even read with ease, because virtually every word he came across evoked a tidal wave of memories from his past.

In short, think of forgetting as a friend that permits your memory to operate at peak efficiency. Of course, forgetting shouldn't be your *best* friend. The focus of this chapter will be to figure out how to hold onto memories that we want to keep, using the strategies summarized in the P.O.W.E.R. Plan on the next page.

Prepare: Determining What You Need to Remember

Memorize what you need to memorize. Forget about the rest.

The average textbook chapter has something like 20,000 words. If you had to recall every word of the chapter, it would be nearly impossible. Furthermore, it would be a waste of time. Being able to spew out paragraphs of material is quite different from the more important ability to recall and deeply understand academic material in meaningful ways.

It helps to approach learning the material in a chapter in a different way. You are not going to learn or memorize 20,000 words, but within those words there may be only 20 different concepts that you do need to learn. And perhaps there are only 10 keywords that are totally unfamiliar to you. *Those* are the pieces of information that should be the focus of your efforts to memorize.

In short, the first step in building a better memory is to determine just what it is that you wish to recall. By extracting what is important from what is less crucial, you'll be able to limit the amount and extent of the material that you need to recall and you'll be able to focus, laserlike, on what you need to remember.

To be able to determine what is important, look at the overall, big picture. Don't get lost in minute details. Instead, prepare yourself by taking a broad overview of the material you need to know and decide what your goal is going to be.

Organize: Relating New Material to What You Already Know

Don't think of memorization as pumping gasoline (new information) into an almost-empty gas tank (your brain). You're not filling something that is empty. On the contrary, you are filling a container that already has a lot of things in it, that is infinitely expandable, and that never empties out.

If you approach each new memorization task as something entirely new and unrelated to your previous knowledge, you'll have enormous difficulty recalling it. On the other hand, if you connect it to what you already know, you'll be able to learn it more easily and recall it far better than if you just dump it into your head. The way to get your brain to do this organizational work for you is by thinking about the associations the new material has with the old.

Say, for example, you need to remember information about the consequences of global warming, such as the fact that the level of the oceans is predicted to rise. One way to think about the new material you want to remember is to relate it to information that you already possess.

PREPARE
Determine what you need to remember

ORGANIZE
Relate new material to what you already know

WORK
Use proven strategies to memorize new material

EVALUATE
Test your recall of new information

RETHINK
Consolidate memories through repeated review

P.O.W.E.R. Plan

Student Alert: Often students have difficulty discriminating between what's important and what can be done. Spend time talking about how to make this distinction.

> "Human memory works its own wheel, and stops where it will."
>
> William Saroyan, *Chance Meetings* (1978).

What would help you remember a person's name after you were introduced to him for the first time?

For example, you might think about the rising level of the ocean as it relates to your personal memories of visits to the beach. You might think what a visit to the beach would be like with dramatically higher water levels, visualizing a severely reduced shoreline with no room for sunbathing. Then, whenever you think about global warming in the future, your mind is likely to associate this fairly abstract concept with its concrete consequences for beaches. The association you made while rehearsing the information makes it personal, long-lasting, and useful.

Memories can also be organized by place. *Where* you learn something makes a difference in how well you can recall it. Memory researchers have found that people actually remember things better in the place where they first studied and learned them. Consequently, one of the ways to jog your memory is to try to recreate the situation in which you first learned what you're trying to remember. If you memorized the colors that litmus paper turns when it is placed in acids and bases while you were lying in bed, it might be helpful during a test to recall the correct colors by imagining yourself lying on your bed thinking about the colors. By "recreating" your previous study session in bed, you can jog your memory.

Another effective place-related strategy is to introduce new data into your mind in the place that you know you're going to need to recall it at some future moment. For instance, suppose you know that you're going to be tested on certain material in the room in which your class is held. Try to do at least some of your studying in that same room. (The reviewing techniques we covered when discussing notetaking in Chapter 5 will be very helpful in this way as well.) Then, when you take the test, the associations you've formed between the material and the physical location of your studying may aid your recall.

Rehearsal
The process of practicing and learning material to transfer it into memory

Mnemonics
Formal techniques used to make material more readily remembered

Acronym
A word or phrase formed by the first letters of a series of terms

 ork: Using Proven Strategies to Memorize New Material

One of the good things about the work of memorization is that you have your choice of literally dozens of techniques. Depending on the kind of material you need to recall and how much you already know about the subject, you can turn to any number of methods.

As we sort through the various options, keep in mind that no one strategy works by itself. Choose a combination of strategies that works best for you, and feel free to devise your own strategies or add those that have worked for you in the past.

Rehearsal Think it again: rehearsal. Say it aloud: rehearsal. Think of it in terms of the three syllables that make up the word: re—hear—sal. OK, one more time—say the word "rehearsal."

If you're scratching your head over the last paragraph, it's to illustrate the point of **rehearsal:** to transfer material that you encounter into memory. If you don't rehearse information in some way, it will end up like most of the information to which we're exposed: on the garbage heap of lost memory.

To test if you've succeeded in transferring the word "rehearsal" into your memory, put down this book and go off for a few minutes. Do something entirely unrelated to reading this book. Have a snack, catch up on the latest sports scores on ESPN, or read the front page of the newspaper.

Are you back? If the word "rehearsal" popped into your head when you picked up this book again, you've passed your first memory test. You can be assured that the word "rehearsal" has been transferred into your memory.

Rehearsal is the key strategy in remembering information. If you don't rehearse material, it will never make it into memory. Repeating the information, summarizing it, associating it with other memories, and above all *thinking about it* when you first come across it will ensure that rehearsal will be effective in pushing the material into memory.

Mnemonics This odd word (pronounced in an equally odd fashion, with the "m" silent—"neh MON ix") describes formal organization techniques used to make material more readily remembered. **Mnemonics** are in fact the tricks-of-the-trade that professional memory experts use, and you too can use them to recall the sort of list items you will often need to recall for tests.

Among the most common mnemonics are the following:

- **Acronyms.**

    FACE

    Roy G. Biv

    P.O.W.E.R.

    You're already well acquainted with **acronyms,** words or phrases formed by the first letters of a series

What Sort of Memory Do I Have?

1. What kinds of information do you remember best: faces, shapes, colors, smells, names, dates, or facts? Why?

2. What kinds of information do you have the greatest difficulty remembering? Why do you think this type of information is hard for you to remember?

3. Is there any particular source of information about which you can remember exceptional amounts, such as baseball records or movie trivia? Why do you think you remember this information so readily?

4. Think about some of the information from your early school years that you can still easily recall. What factors contributed to this information becoming firmly embedded in your memory?

5. What kinds of memorization techniques do you now use? Have you ever tried any in the past that didn't work? What would you think you could do to improve your memory?

6. Do you ever find yourself recognizing someone's face but being unable to recall the name that goes with it? What do you do? When you're introduced to new people, do you do anything special to remember their names?

7. Do you ever feel that information is "on the tip of your tongue" but you just can't seem to retrieve it? Have you ever recalled the information you were seeking just a few minutes too late?

Try It! 2

Organize Your Memory

As critical thinking expert Diane Halpern points out, having an organized memory is like having a neat bedroom: Its value is that you know you'll be able to find something when you need it. To prove the point, try this exercise she devised.[2]

Read the following 15 words at a rate of approximately one per second:

girl

heart

robin

purple

finger

flute

blue

organ

man

hawk

green

lung

eagle

child

piano

Now, cover the list, and write down as many of the words as you can on a separate sheet of paper. How many words are on your list? _____

of terms. For instance, FACE spells out the names of the notes that appear in the spaces on the treble clef music staff ("F," "A," "C," and "E," starting at the bottom of the staff.) Roy G. Biv is a favorite of physics students who must remember the colors of the spectrum (**r**ed, **o**range, **y**ellow, **g**reen, **b**lue, **i**ndigo, and **v**iolet.) And P.O.W.E.R. stands for—well, by this point in the book, you probably remember.

The benefit of acronyms is that they help us to recall a complete list of steps or items. The drawback, though, is that the acronym itself has to be remembered, and sometimes we may not recall it when we need it. For instance, Roy G. Biv is not exactly the sort of name that readily comes to mind. And if we're unable to remember an acronym, it won't be of much use to us. Even if we do remember Roy G. Biv, we might get stuck trying to recall what a particular letter stands for. (For example, we'd probably prefer not to spend a lot of time during a test trying to remember if the "B" stands for brown, or beige, or blue.)

After you've done this, read the following list:

green

blue

purple

man

girl

child

piano

flute

organ

heart

lung

finger

eagle

hawk

robin

Now cover this second list and write down as many of the words as you can on the other side of the separate sheet of paper.

How many words did you remember this time? Did you notice that the words on both lists are identical? Did you remember more the second time? (Most people do.) Why do you think most people remember more when the words are arranged as they are in the second list? Does it seem plausible that the organization of the second list makes it easier to remember the words?

Working in a group: Discuss with your classmates ways in which you can organize material from one of your current classes to make it easier to remember.

- **Acrostics.** After learning to use the acronym "FACE" to remember the notes on the spaces of the music staff, many beginning musicians learn that the names of the *lines* on the staff form the acrostic, "**E**very **G**ood **B**oy **D**eserves **F**udge." **Acrostics** are sentences in which the first letters spell out something that needs to be recalled. The benefits—as well as the drawbacks—of acrostics are similar to those of acronyms.

- **Rhymes and jingles.** "Thirty days hath September, April, June, and November . . . " If you know the rest of the rhyme, you're familiar with one of the most commonly used mnemonic jingles in the English language. Similarly, some of us learned the main theme of Schubert's Unfinished Symphony by singing the words "This is the symphony that Schubert wrote and never finished" when the theme first appears. For those who learned to recognize the symphony by using this mnemonic, it is virtually impossible to hear the symphony without recalling the words.

Acrostic

A sentence in which the first letters of the words correspond to material that is to be remembered

Discussion Prompt: Start a well-known advertising jingle or slogan and ask your students to finish it. Can they? Does it surprise anyone that so many people can "know" the same thing? What implications does this have for society? for memory? for learning?

Try It! 3

Working in a Group: Do It Yourself Acronyms and Acrostics

In the first part of this Try It, work individually to create an acronym and an acrostic.

1. Figure out a Great Lakes acronym using the first letters of their names (which are Erie, Huron, Michigan, Ontario, and Superior).

2. Devise an acrostic to help remember the nine planets in order of their average distance from the sun. Their names, in order, are Mercury, Venus, Earth, Mars, Jupiter, Saturn, Uranus, Neptune, and Pluto.

After you've tried to create the acronym and acrostic, meet in a group and discuss these questions: How successful were you in devising effective acronyms and acrostics? Do some of the group member's creations seem to be more effective than others? Why? Is the act of creating them an important component of helping to remember what they represent, or would having them created by someone else be as helpful in recalling them? For your information, a common acronym for the Great Lakes is **HOMES** (**H**uron **O**ntario **M**ichigan **E**rie **S**uperior), and a popular acrostic for the order of the planets is **M**y **V**ery **E**ducated **M**other **J**ust **S**erved **U**s **N**ine **P**izzas.

Although mnemonics are helpful, keep in mind that they have a number of significant shortcomings. First, they don't focus on the meaning of the items being remembered. Instead, mnemonic devices use characteristics such as the letters that make up the words being memorized. Consequently, the information is learned by rote, rather than by considering what it means and thinking critically about its relationship to other material. Because information that is learned in terms of its surface characteristics—such as first letters that form a word—is less likely to be retained than information that is learned in terms of its meaning, mnemonic devices are an imperfect route to memorization.

There's another problem with mnemonics: Sometimes it takes as much effort to create a mnemonic device as it would to memorize the material in the first place. And because the mnemonic itself has no meaning, it can be forgotten.

Despite their drawbacks, mnemonics can be useful. They are particularly helpful when the material being memorized includes a list of items or a series of steps.

The Keyword Technique Learning the vocabulary of a foreign language is often one of the toughest tasks for beginning students. The **keyword technique** can help ease the pain. In the keyword technique, a foreign word is paired with a common English word that has a similar sound. The English word is known as the keyword.

Keyword technique
A memory technique by which a foreign word to be learned is linked by an image to an English word with a similar sound

For example, suppose you needed to learn the Spanish word for duck, which is *pato*, pronounced "pot-o." The first thing you'd do would be to think of an English word that sounds like "pot-o" and to picture it in your mind. One obvious choice would be a pot, simmering on a stove. This is your keyword.

The next step is to form an image in your mind that relates the meaning of the Spanish word to the image of the keyword. Because *pato* means duck, the desired image will relate a duck and a pot. The clear choice: a duck simmering in a pot on a stove.

Here's another example. The Spanish word for horse is *caballo*, pronounced "cob-eye-yo." In this case, you might link a horse with a corncob and an eye, both of which would be keywords, and come up with an image of a horse with huge, bulging eyes munching on a corncob. Or perhaps you could incorporate all three syllables of *caballo* and form an image of a horse with bulging eyes eating a corn cob and playing with a yo-yo (see Figure 9.1). It's fine that the result is an outlandish image. In fact, the more eccentric the image, the easier it will be to recall.

The Method of Loci and the Peg Method: Special Help for Recalling Sequences and Lists The ancient Greeks had a way with words. Their orators could deliver speeches that went on for hours, without notes. How did they remember what they wanted to say?

They used a procedure called the **method of loci.** *Loci* is the Latin word for "places," and it helps describe a procedure in which items in a sequence you wish to remember—such as the sections of a speech or a series of events—are thought of as "located" in a different place in a building.

Consider, for example, a speech that has three major sections: an introduction, a main body, and a conclusion. Imagine further that each of the three sections has various subcomponents that you need to recall.

To use the method of loci, you'd first visualize the living room, kitchen, and bedroom of a house with which you were familiar. Next, you'd mentally "place" the introduction of the speech into the living room of the house. You would mentally place each of the *parts* of the introduction on a different piece of furniture, following the way in which the furniture was laid out in the room (for example, you might proceed clockwise from the door). The easy chair might contain the first point of the introduction, the sofa the next point, and an end table the last point. Then you'd move into the kitchen and do the same thing with the body of the paper, laying out your arguments on different pieces of kitchen furniture or appliances. Finally, you'd end up in the bedroom, where you'd "place" the conclusion.

A close cousin of the method of loci is the peg method. The **peg method** uses a series of key words tied to numbers to help in the recall of numeric information. For instance, a set of "pegs" that you could use would link numbers with these words:

One is a sun,

Two is a zoo,

Three is me,

Four is a store,

Five is a dive,

Six are sticks,

Figure 9.1

In this example of the keyword technique, the Spanish word for horse, *caballo*, is recalled with this image of a horse with bulging eyes, munching on a corn cob, and playing with a yo-yo.

Method of loci

A memory technique by which the elements in a list are visualized as occupying the parts of a familiar place

Peg method

A memory technique by which a series of memorized words is linked by images to a list of items to be remembered

Teaching Tip: Encourage students to create stories or images that bring life to difficult ideas.

Seven is heaven,

Eight is a gate,

Nine is a pine,

Ten is a den.

By thinking of exotic images using the peg words tied to the numbers, you can recall specific numbers that you need to memorize. For instance, suppose you had trouble remembering the value of *pi*, used to calculate the circumference of a circle (3.14, in case you don't remember). Translate the number into the relevant peg words—me (three), sun (one), and store (four)—and imagine an image linking the three. One obvious possibility is an image of yourself wearing sunglasses, heading out to a store on a sunny day. A less obvious and more exotic possibility is an image of yourself bowling a large sun into the front of a store.

The peg system can also be used to memorize ordered lists of items, when the sequence in which they appear is important. In this use, the peg system is very similar to the method of loci. You simply link images of the ordered set of items to the 10 "numbers." The first item is linked with the sun, the second with a zoo, and so on.

Involve Multiple Senses   The more senses you can involve when you're trying to learn new material, the better you'll be able to remember. Here's why: Every time we encounter new information, all of our senses are potentially at work. For instance, if we witness a car crash, we receive sensory input from the sight of the two cars hitting each other, the sound of the impact, and perhaps the smell of burning rubber. Each piece of sensory information is stored in a separate location in the brain, and yet all the pieces are linked together in extraordinarily intricate ways.

What this means is that when we seek to remember the details of the crash, recalling a memory of one of the sensory experiences—such as what we heard—can trigger recall of the other types of memories. For example, thinking about the *sound* the two cars made when they hit can bring back memories of the way the scene *looked*.

You can make use of the fact that memories are stored in multiple ways by applying the following techniques:

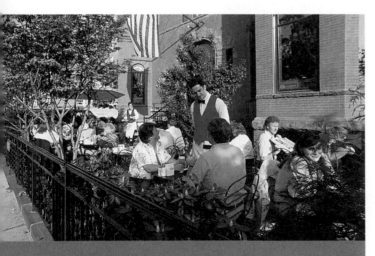

Have you ever wondered how some waiters can remember what their customers have ordered without writing anything down? They use the same simple memory strategies that you can use to recall information you'll need to remember for tests.

- **When you learn something, use your body.** Don't sit passively at your desk. Instead, move around. Stand up; sit down. Touch the page. Trace figures with your fingers. Talk to yourself. Think out loud. It may seem strange, but doing this increases the number of ways in which the information is stored. By involving every part of your body, you've increased the number of potential ways to trigger a relevant memory later, when you need to recall it. And when one memory is triggered, other related memories may come tumbling back.

- **Draw and diagram the material.** We've already considered (in Chapter 5) the power of concept

Try It! 4

Peg the Memory

After you've learned the "peg" poem, it can come in handy in a variety of areas. Try it. Use the peg system to memorize the sequence of events related to the Civil War era on the list below. For instance, for Lincoln being elected president, think of an image that links Lincoln with the sun (remember "one is the sun" from the poem). Do the same for the rest of the events.

1. Lincoln elected president

2. South leaves the Union

3. Confederacy established

4. Emancipation Proclamation issued

5. Congress passes 13th Amendment to Constitution

Now cover up the list. What is number two on the list? What is number four on the list?

How well did the peg method work for you? Do you see its value for other topical areas? If you are taking a foreign language class, can you apply the method? Could you apply it to other kinds of classes? Do you see any drawbacks to its use?

---

maps, the method of structuring written material by graphically grouping and connecting key ideas and themes. When we create a concept map, one of the things we're doing is expanding the modalities in which information can be stored in our minds.

Other types of drawing can be useful in aiding later recall. Creating drawings, sketches, and even cartoons can help us remember better. Your creations don't have to be Great Art, or detailed, involved illustrations. Even rough sketches are effective, because creating them gets both the visual and tactile senses involved.

- **Visualize. Visualization** is a technique by which images are formed to ensure that material is recalled. For instance, suppose you're told that memory requires three basic steps: the initial recording of information, the storage of that information, and, ultimately, the retrieval of the stored information. As you read the three steps, you probably see them as logical and straightforward processes. But how do you remember them?

You might visualize a computer, with its keyboard, disks, and monitor (as in Figure 9.2). The keyboard represents the initial recording of

Visualization
A memory technique by which images are formed

Recording of information

Storage of information in memory

Display of information retrieved from memory

Figure 9.2

information. The disk represents the storage of information. And the monitor represents the display of information that has been retrieved from memory. If you can put these images in your mind, it will help you to remember the three basic memory steps later.

Visualization serves several purposes: it helps make abstract ideas concrete; it engages multiple senses; it permits us to link different bits of information together; it provides us with a context for storing information.

What kind of visualization works best? There's a simple rule: Weird is good. The more extreme, outlandish, and eccentric the image you create, the more notable it will be and so the easier it will be to remember. And if you can remember the image, you'll probably remember the information that's attached to it.

Discussion Prompt: Can your students attach powerful emotions to information they can remember?

Think Positively   Emotions matter. If you're in a negative frame of mind when you try to memorize something, your negative feelings can become attached to the memory, making you less likely to recall it because you'll automatically tend to avoid those bad feelings. The opposite is also true: If you think positively about the process of memorization, those more-positive feelings will end up being etched into your memory.

Of course, feelings can't be turned off in the same way we're able to turn off a light. If you feel nervous and scared about memorizing all the formulas you need to for your chemistry midterm, you can't just tell yourself it's great fun. But if you recognize your feelings, they lose much of their power to influence you and to block memories.

Overlearning   Think back to when you were learning your basic multiplication facts ($1 \times 1 = 1$; $1 \times 2 = 2$; and so forth). Let's suppose you had put each multiplication problem on a flash card, and you decided to go through your entire set of cards, trying to get every problem right.

> "Don't let those few Einsteins who can ace a test by never attending class and by sleeping on the textbook the night before trick you into using their study methods. My roommate tried to convince me that studying by osmosis was a proven method. Trust me, it isn't."
>
> Keith Vernon, University of Puget Sound.[3]

The first time you went through the set of cards and answered all the problems correctly, would you stop there? Would you feel as if you'd actually learned and memorized them perfectly and that you'd never again make an error?

Probably not. The prudent assumption would be that you needed a few more instances of flawless performance before you'd be justified in concluding that you had adequately memorized the problems.

If this was your gut feeling—that you needed several instances of perfect performance to be sure you had learned the multiplication facts completely—you'd have stumbled upon the principle of overlearning. **Overlearning** consists of studying and rehearsing material past the point of initial mastery. Through overlearning, recall becomes automatic. Rather than searching for a fact, going through mental contortions until perhaps the information surfaces, overlearning permits us to recall the information without even thinking about it.

To put the principle of overlearning to work, don't stop studying at the point when you can say to yourself, "Well, I'll probably pass this test." You

Overlearning
Studying and rehearsing material past the point of initial mastery, to the point at which recall becomes automatic

Try It! 5

Visualize the Possibilities

You may have noticed how important visualization is to memory. In fact, many of the techniques we've discussed in this chapter rely in some measure on visualization, especially your visualization of extreme or absurd images.

Test the truth of this statement by drawing a concept map—itself a visual form of organizing material—of the concept of visualization. Using the space below, place the word "Visualization" in the center of the map and link as many other memory and mnemonic techniques to it as you can. You may be surprised at the richness of your map.

How well does the concept map reflect what you know about visualization? Is it a useful tool for you? Do you think that the act of creating a concept map itself is helpful in memorizing the material and that using someone else's concept map would be less helpful than creating your own? **Working in a group:** Compare your concept map with those of your classmates. What are the major similarities and differences, and why do you think they occurred? Are some of the particular concept maps likely to help recall information about visualization more easily than others?

Career Connections

Memory On the Job

Increasing your memory skills is not only something that will help you do better in college. Having a good memory also will prove to be an important component of your future job success.

Not all professionals need the same kind of memory skills, of course. A camera operator at a television network must remember lighting combinations; lawyers need to recall the details of witness testimony; elementary school teachers must remember what kinds of exercises work best for certain students; physicians need to keep track of a host of medical conditions and medicines. But in each of these professions, memory abilities are an important aspect of job performance.

One particularly important on-the-job memory task is remembering people's names. Being able to recall the names of those with whom you work, professional colleagues from other companies, and clients is an important skill. People are flattered when you remember their names. It says you think they are important and worth noticing.

One easy way to improve your memory for names: Whenever you are introduced to someone new, choose one distinctive physical characteristic relating to their appearance and transform it into a nickname. For instance, Hannah with the loud laugh could be Happy Hannah and Barry with the thinning hair could be Bald Barry. When you next see the person whom you've nicknamed, the physical cue you've used should help pop their name out of your memory vault and into consciousness.

may be right, but that's all you'll do—pass. Instead, spend extra time learning the material until it becomes as familiar as an old, comfortable shoe. At that point, overlearning has occurred, and you'll be able to recall the material with ease.

E valuate: Testing Your Recall of New Information

The memory strategies just described can bring you to a point where you probably feel comfortable in your ability to remember the material you've been learning. Once you've used one or more of them to help you process the material you are learning, it's time to test yourself—to evaluate whether you'll be able to recall the material when you need it. There are several ways to evaluate your memory:

- **Use in-text review questions and tests.** Many textbook chapters end with a quiz or a set of review questions about the material. Some have questions scattered throughout the chapter. Don't avoid them! Not only do such questions indicate what the writer of the book thought was important for you to learn and memorize, but they can provide an excellent opportunity for evaluating your memory.

  Even if you've answered the review questions earlier—while you were first reading the material (which is always a good idea), answer them again later as you study for the test and then the final.

- **Test yourself.** Temporarily transform yourself into your instructor, and prioritize what you're most likely to be tested on. Then create your own test, writing out some questions.

  Later, after as little as a few hours, take the test, and then grade it. How have you done? If you've achieved a "grade" that you're satisfied with, then fine. If, on the other hand, you've missed some key pieces of information, then you'll want to return to work and spend more time on memorization.

IM Link: "Teaching the Text," Chapter 9, Section I—Chapter Summary; read the information in the *Message to the Instructor*.

- **Team up with a friend.** When it comes to evaluating your memory, two heads are often better than one. Working with a classmate can help you test the limits of your memory and assess areas in which you need work.

  For instance, you and a friend can take turns testing yourselves, switching back and forth between asking and answering questions. Turn it into a contest: One of you can be Alex Trebek of *Jeopardy*, and the other, a contestant. You can even work in groups. The important thing is to switch who's asking and who's answering the questions. Even when you're directing questions to others—officially evaluating their memory—you're giving your own memory a workout.

Rethink: Consolidating Memories through Repeated Review

Like fine wines, memories need time to age. Psychologists talk about this as the process of **memory consolidation.** What this means is that the physical links between brain cells that represent memory in the brain need time to become fixed and stable. This process explains why information is not suddenly and permanently established in memory the first time we're exposed to it. In fact, the process of consolidation may continue for days and even—in some cases—for years.[4]

Memory consolidation

The process by which the physical links between brain cells that represent memory become fixed and stable over time

Obviously you don't have years to wait. But it does pay to try to memorize material in advance of the time that you'll really need to use it. Then, when you go back to reconsider it, it will become even more well-established in your mind.

The phenomenon of memory consolidation explains why cramming is not a great idea. As we discussed in the chapter on taking tests, cramming is the process of spending the preceding evening or even the hours just before a test trying to memorize as much as possible. The memories that come from cramming simply don't last, because they aren't rehearsed and processed sufficiently. It's far more effective to distribute studying over many shorter sessions, rather than squeezing it into a single, long session just before a test. Fatigue and anxiety prevent long, last-minute practice sessions from being as effective as practice that is spread out.

The best way to ensure good memory is to return to the material even after your personal evaluation tells you that you can recall it easily. Wait several days, if possible, and then review it again. You'll be able to identify the aspects of the material that you know well, as well as the things that just haven't jelled yet in memory. Rethinking the material, then, not only permits you to take another look at the stuff of your memory, but helps you identify where you need more work.

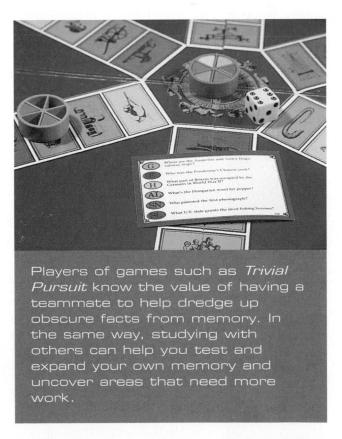

Players of games such as *Trivial Pursuit* know the value of having a teammate to help dredge up obscure facts from memory. In the same way, studying with others can help you test and expand your own memory and uncover areas that need more work.

Try It!

6

Remember Demain

Remember the passage earlier in this chapter (Try It 1) about Demain, who found himself in the midst of a colorful, aromatic bazaar of booths and shops? Without turning back to the passage, write down everything you can remember about what Demain experienced in the marketplace—the shops, sights, and foods.

_____

_____

_____

_____

_____

_____

_____

_____

_____

_____

_____

_____

Now re-read the passage, trying to remember its details by using one or more techniques from this chapter. You might use the method of loci, the peg method, the method of organizing ideas into chunks, or other techniques. Then answer these questions about the passage:

1. What scenes were depicted on the cloths? _____

_____

_____

2. What were the gold merchants wearing? _____

_____

3. After the cloth shop, what businesses did Demain pass to arrive at the vendors of food and drink? _____

_____

4. What foods did Demain see and smell at the fair? _____

_____

_____

How would you assess your performance on these questions? Do you think you would have remembered more initially if you had used some of the memory techniques in this chapter? Do you see how you could employ these techniques in your own studying? Did one seem to work better for you than others?

Speaking of Success

Name: *Lamar Heckstall*

Education: *Virginia Commonwealth University, Richmond, Virginia; major in art illustration and communication arts*

Home: *Richmond, Virginia*

For college sophomore Lamar Heckstall, an art major, developing memory skills has required proceeding along two fronts simultaneously. Not only has it been important for him to remember the written word, but also the many images and visuals that are the stock-in-trade of an art major.

"For me visual memorization is actually easier," says Heckstall. "When it comes to remembering verbal information, like artists' names or titles of paintings, I try to create associations with the images. If the name of the artist is hard to pronounce, I try to put it into a rhyme or think of something I like that I can associate with the name. When we're viewing slides of artwork, I sometimes redraw the figure and then write the title underneath, and that helps. Most of the time I get them all right, or maybe miss only one or two."

Heckstall says he started developing his memory skills toward the end of high school, but the larger intellectual demands of college forced him to intensify his approach.

"Basically what I do when I'm studying is to take a word or defini-tion and say it to myself five times," he explains. "I then write it down five times and actively try to recall it later on.

"I do have problems with memorizing long definitions or long descriptions of people. In the past I found myself trying to memorize too much and not learning anything, so what I've been doing is concentrating

VCU

Virginia Commonwealth University

on one or two main things about the definition or individual," he says.

In conjunction with memorization techniques, Heckstall says that his study habits have changed dramatically since high school, and now he finds that getting an early start on studying reaps rewards.

"In high school the work was easier, and while I took it seriously, I didn't put in as much time as I should have," he admits. "Now that I'm in college, I have to use my time wisely every day. As soon as I find out a test is scheduled, I start studying for it and generally put in about two or three hours a day until the day of the test."

He adds that he uses the same approach for writing papers.

"I enjoy creative writing much more, but if I have a paper due I try to get an early start on it. It may take me two or three days just to get the theme of the paper. I feel that if I have to write about something, it has to be something I enjoy."

Concentration is important as well for Heckstall, and he's learned that being focused goes a long way toward making things easier.

"My biggest difficulty with studying is distractions," he notes. "As a result, I have to set a fixed time for myself to study—and I have to stick to it. I focus on one project at a time.

"Once I start, if someone knocks on my door, I don't open it. If the phone rings, I don't answer it. I have so many things to do during the day that I find late nights to be the best time to study."

What is memory and how does it function?

- Information we actively process is permanently etched into the brain, but it is not always readily available for retrieval. The challenge is to recall information when we need it, and the key to effective recall is learning material in a way that makes recall easy.

- Forgetting is essential to permit us to disregard unimportant details and focus on what is important.

Why might I have problems with memory, and how can I deal with those problems?

- The problems we have with memory are mostly related to the inability to recall or retrieve information when it is needed. However, if information is rehearsed carefully, you can usually recall it more easily.

- Memory can be improved through careful preparation, by selecting in advance the pieces of information that are worthy of memorization and rehearsal.

- Another key to effective memorization is linking new information to information that is already in memory.

What are some techniques I can use for memorizing information?

- Many memory techniques are available to improve memorization. Rehearsal is a primary one, as is the use of mnemonics such as acronyms, acrostics, and rhymes.

- Other memory techniques are the keyword technique, the method of loci, the peg method, visualization, and the use of multiple senses while learning new material.

- Overlearning is a basic principle of memorization.

- Memory takes some time—days or even longer—to reach the point of consolidation, at which the physical links between brain cells that represent memory become stable. The need for consolidation explains why cramming is ineffective for long-term recall.

Key Terms and Concepts

Resources

On Campus

If you have considerable difficulty in memorizing material compared with your classmates, it's possible that you might have a learning disability. If you suspect this, visit the college learning disabilities office or counseling center.

In Print

Harry Lorayne's and Jerry Lucas's *The Memory Book* (Ballantine, 1996) offers a simple system for improving memory. Carol Turkington's *12 Steps to a Better Memory* (Arco, 1996) is helpful if you wish to have a better memory for lists and other difficult-to-remember material. Finally, *Memory Power: Memory Building Skills for Everyday Situations* (Barrons, 1997), by Jonathan Hancock, provides an overview of memory techniques.

On the Web

The following sites on the World Wide Web provide the opportunity to extend your learning about the material in this chapter. (Although the Web addresses were accurate at the time the book was printed, check the P.O.W.E.R. Learning Web site [http://mhhe.com/power] for any changes that may have occurred.)

http://www.coun.uvic.ca/learn/program/hndouts/map_ho.html
This site aids in concept mapping, an effective memory aid that improves recall by building meaning structures around key concepts.

http://www.coun.uvic.ca/learn/program/hndouts/mnemon.html
In this site, you'll find some good examples of mnemonics.

http://www.mindtools.com/memory.html
This site provides several methods for improving memory. It includes examples of how each technique can be applied to such topics as remembering lists and foreign languages.

Taking It to the Net

1 Practice the rehearsal technique for storing information in memory. Go to Yahoo (**www.yahoo.com**) and click on "Regional" and again on "U.S. States." Click on your state, then on "Government," and finally on "elected officials" to find the names of your state's U.S. Senators. Repeat the names several times. Now explore another, unrelated site on the Web. After a few minutes, write down the names of your state's U.S. Senators from memory. How did you do?

2 Practice the visualization memory technique. Go to the Web site listing the top 50 moneymaking movies (**http://movieweb.com/movie/alltime. html**). Try to memorize the top ten movies by creating weird visual images based on the titles.

The Case of . . .

Remember the Alamo

For Kyle Roteena, history had always been a hard subject. Although he had no trouble learning general historical trends and concepts, he had difficulty keeping names, dates, and places sorted out.

Consequently, when his American History instructor, Ms. Teeler, announced that a major history exam was coming up, Kyle panicked. He hadn't even finished all the assigned reading, and here he was expected to learn what seemed to be virtually everything there was to know about the U.S. western expansion during the 1800s. Ms. Teeler had said that the test would focus in particular on the Battle of the Alamo and its significance in U.S. history. When Kyle couldn't even recall where the Alamo was located, he knew he'd better get started memorizing. But where to begin?

1. How should Kyle prepare for the history exam? Should he simply get the history text and start reading? Why or why not?

2. How can Kyle prevent the facts of history from appearing to be a jumble of random words and numbers? How should he use his existing knowledge to structure historical information? Why might this become easier the more often Kyle does it?

3. Suppose Kyle is expected to remember the names of several officers in the two armies involved in the Battle of the Alamo, names that seem unusual to him and very hard to remember. Which memory technique is likely to be most effective? How would it work?

4. To remember lists of events in the western expansion movement, what technique would you recommend that Kyle use? How would it work?

5. How could Kyle use multiple senses while learning about the western expansion and the Battle of the Alamo?

Making Decisions That Are Right for You

10

For Rich Rinkowski, the moment of truth was fast approaching. He had to make up his mind and decide what he was going to do when he graduated.

Throughout his college career he had intended to go to law school, and he had even majored in criminal justice. He had taken the LSAT, the pre-law standardized test, at the beginning of his senior year and had done pretty well. He had applied to law schools and been accepted at a fairly decent one. It seemed that his future in law was well in hand.

Except for one thing: He was no longer sure he wanted to be a lawyer.

The reason for his indecision was an internship that he had spent at Columbia Pictures during the summer between his junior and senior years. Although he was just a glorified gofer on a film that starred Marisa Tomei, the director caught his attention. Directing looked like terrific fun, and the idea of becoming a film director had taken hold of him. Rich had spoken to the director, who had told him that it was a terrific, although high-stress, job. He also told Rich that the sooner he started working in the film industry, the better.

Rich couldn't shake the idea that he might be able to build a career in the movie industry. However, his girlfriend and family were dead set against the idea. His father argued that Rich should consider working in the film industry only after he got his law degree. But Rich was unconvinced; he didn't want to give up the idea of becoming a director in Hollywood.

As his last semester went by, Rich knew he had to make up his mind. But what was the right decision?

Looking
Ahead

Like Rich, all of us face important decisions in our lives at one time or another. How can we make the right decisions and avoid making the wrong ones? The best way is to employ some systematic, basic techniques that can help improve the quality of our decision making.

This chapter will give you a sense of what decision making is and is not, and it discusses a structured process that can help make your decisions the right ones. We'll also consider the related issue of problem solving. You'll confront a variety of problems as you proceed through college, and solving them is often challenging. We'll look at a number of proven techniques for approaching and ultimately solving problems.

Of course, making decisions and solving problems is never easy. Sometimes the best decision or solution to a problem is one that doesn't initially occur to us because of the mental blind spots we all have. The best problem solvers and decision makers have learned how to use critical thinking to see around these blind spots. Consequently, we'll examine some common problems that can affect our thinking and discuss several biases that can make us jump too quickly to conclusions.

In sum, after reading this chapter you'll be able to answer these questions:

- **How can I improve the quality of my decisions?**

- **What strategies can I use for problem solving?**

- **What are some problems that affect critical thinking, and how can I avoid them?**

Making Good Decisions: A Framework

Making choices is a constant part of everyday life. **Decision making** is the process of deciding among various alternatives. Whether you are trying to decide between buying a Ford or a Honda; between renting an apartment that is close to your job and farther from campus or renting one that is close to campus but farther from work; or simply between having a hamburger or pizza—every one of these choices requires a decision. Some decisions are easily made and have few consequences, but others, such as whether to major in music composition or follow a pre-med course of study in college, can be heart-wrenching and involve the deepest examination of our beliefs and values.

Whatever the decision, however, it is possible to map out a strategy for making the decision that is best for you. Even though some decisions require more thought than others, every decision can benefit from systematically thinking through the options involved, based on the P.O.W.E.R. Plan illustrated on the right below.

P repare: Identifying Your Goals

Every decision starts with the end: what you wish to accomplish by making the decision. You must ask yourself why a decision is necessary and what you wish to achieve by making it.

For example, suppose you are trying to decide between two alternative careers: either being a sales representative for a sporting goods manufacturer or working in and eventually running your own sporting goods store.

In such a case, the only way to make an appropriate decision is to know your goals. You need to consider both short- and long-term goals. For instance, becoming a sales representative would provide good benefits, such as health insurance, a company car, and a bonus plan. It would also allow you to meet colleagues with similar goals and interests and provide both opportunities to attend formal training programs as well as the ability to work your way up the corporate ladder.

On the other hand, although you might have a lower starting salary and fewer benefits working in a sporting goods store, there would probably be more job security. Even more important, it would give you the opportunity to achieve your long-term goal of learning how to run your own business. Both jobs might at first be equally rewarding in terms of satisfaction—new jobs tend to be exciting just because they are new—but one may grow stale, while the rewards of the other might continue to increase over the course of a career. In short, you need to consider both the short term and the long term when identifying your goals.

Thinking about the goals involved in decisions is an important process. Identifying the goals that underlie decisions

PREPARE

Identify your goals to help make decisions

ORGANIZE

Consider and assess the alternatives

WORK

Make and carry out the decision

EVALUATE

Consider the outcomes

RETHINK

Reconsider your goals and options

P.O.W.E.R. Plan

ensures that we make our decisions in the context of our entire lives and not just to provide short-term answers to immediate problems.

Organize: Considering and Assessing the Alternatives

Every decision is based on weighing various alternatives. Determining what those alternatives are, and their possible consequences, is often the most difficult part of decision making. Here's a process to help make sure you've considered all the alternatives.

Develop a List of Flexible Alternatives   It's important not only to think thoroughly about the obvious alternatives, but also to consider alternatives that are less obvious. For instance, if you are trying to obtain additional funds to support your college theater group, you might consider the alternatives of raising ticket prices for productions, holding a raffle to raise funds, or asking for sponsorship from a local business. After additional thought, though, you might reframe the issue as one of how to best place pressure on the college administration to increase funding for your group.

In short, the way you develop and frame alternatives is critical to the solution that you ultimately reach. The more alternatives you have, and the more ways that you conceptualize those alternatives, the better able you will be able to come to a good solution.

How can you be sure that you've considered all the alternatives? You can't. But using the freewriting technique described in Chapter 8 can help you maximize your efforts to develop reasonable alternatives.

In *freewriting*, one writes continuously for a fixed period of time, perhaps 5 or 10 minutes. During this period, the idea is to write as many different alter-

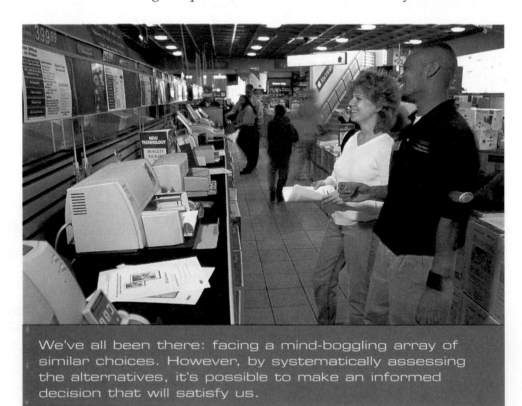

We've all been there: facing a mind-boggling array of similar choices. However, by systematically assessing the alternatives, it's possible to make an informed decision that will satisfy us.

Try It! 1

Use Freewriting

Use freewriting to think of as many answers as you can to one or more of the following questions. The ground rules are that you should spend three minutes on each question, generating as many ideas as possible—regardless of whether they are feasible or not. To give yourself maximum freedom, write each answer on a separate page.

1. What should I consider in deciding whether to take four versus five courses next term?

2. How can someone get from the 3rd floor to the 20th floor of a building?

3. What should you do if you suspected that one of your instructors was a space alien?

4. What would happen if the average life span was extended to 125 years of age?

After generating ideas, go back and evaluate them. How many were actually feasible or realistic? Do you think the ground rules of freewriting led to the production of more or fewer ideas than you would have come up with if you hadn't used the process? Did the quality of ideas change as a result of the use of freewriting? After you have answered the questions above using freewriting, form a group of classmates and compare your answers with those of others. Try to identify the best answers from those produced by each individual group member.

natives as possible, without stopping. It makes no difference if the alternatives are good or bad or even if they make sense. All that matters is that you let yourself brainstorm about the topic for a while and get it down on paper.

With freewriting, evaluating the worth of the ideas you've generated comes later. After you have produced as many possibilities as you can, then you go back and sift out the reasonable alternatives from those that are truly unlikely or just plain wacky. Even though you may delete quite a few alternatives from your list, that's OK; the processes of brainstorming and freewriting are likely to have liberated some truly reasonable alternatives that you might not otherwise have come up with. (Try the technique in the "Use Freewriting" exercise—see Try It 1.)

Teaching Tip: Point out that writing can serve to help students organize their ideas, which, in turn, can lead to better decision making.

Assess Alternatives Once you have generated as extensive a list of alternatives as possible, assess them. You need to follow three key steps when assessing each alternative:

1. *Determine the possible outcomes for each alternative.* Some outcomes are positive, some negative. Consider as many as you can think of. For example, if you are considering ways for solving transportation problems, one alternative might be to purchase a car. That alternative produces several potential outcomes. For example, you know that it will be easier to get wherever you want to go, and you might even have a better social life—clearly positive outcomes. But it is also true that buying and owning a car will be expensive, or you might get into an accident—both negative outcomes.

2. *Determine the probability that those outcomes will take place.* Some outcomes are far more likely than others. To take this into account, make

My Decision Crossroads

Have you ever made a decision that proved to be of great importance in terms of the direction your life would take? For example, perhaps you broke off a romantic relationship, or decided to quit a sports team because practice took up so much time, or participated in a deliberate act of civil disobedience during a protest rally. Reflect on that decision by answering these questions:

1. What was an important decision that you made that had significant effects on your life?

2. In what ways did that decision change your life?

3. What have been the main benefits (for yourself and others) that you derived from the decision?

4. What have been the main disadvantages (for yourself and others) of the decision?

5. Considering both the benefits and disadvantages of the decision, how would you judge your decision?

6. To what extent did you anticipate the effects the decision would have on your life?

7. Every decision to do something is also a decision not to do other things. What did your decision keep you from doing?

8. If you had it to do over again, would you make the same choice?

a rough estimate of the likelihood that an outcome will come to pass, ranging from 100 percent (it is certain that it will occur) to 0 percent (it is certain that it will never occur). For instance, consider these possible outcomes to buying a car:

Alternative: Purchase car

Outcome	Probability
Easier transportation	100%
Greater expense	100%
Greater opportunities for part-time job	50%
Improve social life	30%
Get in accident	5%

Obviously, the probabilities are just guesses, but going through the exercise of estimating them will make the outcomes more real and will permit you to compare the various alternatives against one another more easily.

3. *Compare the alternatives, taking into account the potential outcomes of each.* After assessing the potential outcomes for the first alternative you're considering and the probability that they will occur, do the same thing for the next alternatives, repeating the process for as many alternatives as you have devised. Finally, systematically compare each of the alternatives. Then ask yourself the key question: Which alternative, on balance, provides the most positive (and most likely) outcomes?

Obviously, not every decision requires such an elaborate process. In fact, most won't. But when it comes to major decisions, ones that potentially will have a major impact upon you and your life, it's worthwhile to follow a systematic process.

Take a look at Career Connections on page 250 for another process that you can follow to help you make a career decision.

Work: Making and Carrying Out the Decision

Working through the previous steps will lead you to the point of decision: choosing one of the alternatives you've identified. Having carried out the steps will make the actual decision easier, but not necessarily easy.

Choosing among Alternatives The reason that important decisions are difficult is that the alternatives you have to choose from carry both benefits and costs. Choosing one alternative means that you have to accept the costs of that choice as the price for obtaining the benefits. And not choosing other alternatives means that you have to give up the benefits of the other alternatives, even though you have also avoided their costs.

What if, after going through the steps of the process laid out here, you still can't make up your mind? Try these strategies:

- **Give the decision time.** Sometimes waiting helps. Time can be an ally by giving you a chance to think of additional alternatives. Sometimes the situation will change, or you'll have a change in viewpoint. If you are having great difficulty making up your mind about something, decide to give the decision some time.

- **Make a mental movie, acting out the various alternatives.** Many of us have difficulty seeing ourselves in the future and envisioning how various options would play out. One way to get around this difficulty is to cast yourself into a series of "mental movies" that have different endings depending on the decision you make. Working through the different scripts in your head makes potential outcomes far more real and less abstract than they would be if you simply left them as items on a list of various options.

- **Toss a coin.** This isn't always as crazy or escapist as it sounds. If each alternative seems equally positive or negative to you, pull out a coin and assign each of the two alternatives to either side. Then flip it.

    The real power of the coin-toss strategy is that it sometimes will help you find out your true feelings. It may happen while the coin is in the air or it may be that when you see the result of the coin toss, you won't like the outcome and will say to yourself, "No way." In such a case, you've just found out how you *really* feel about which alternative to choose.

- **Learn to view indecision as a decision.** Sometimes we spend so much time making a decision that our indecision becomes a decision. It works like this: Suppose a friend asks you to help her work on a student government task force that is studying the use of alcohol on campus. You'd like to participate, but, because you'll have to commit to a term-long series of meetings, you're worried about the expenditure of time it will take.

    Because the first meeting isn't going to occur for a few weeks, you have some time to make up your mind. But you just can't seem to decide,

If all else fails, toss a coin to decide what alternative to follow. Tossing a coin at least brings you to a decision. Then, if you find you're unhappy with the result, you'll have gained important information about how you really feel regarding a particular choice.

IM Link: "Teaching the Text," Chapter 10, Sections IV and VIII—Values Continuum Activity.

Discussion Prompt: What connection exists between indecision and personal values?

Career Connections

Weighing Career Possibilities

Some of the most important decisions you'll ever make concern choosing a career. Here's one method that can help you choose between different possible careers:

- **Generate a selection of choices for you to consider after graduation.** Make a list of possibilities—including work possibilities (e.g., computer programming, banking, teaching, law, business, insurance, computer software development, etc.), study possibilities (e.g., graduate school, business school, school, etc.), and even some dream possibilities (e.g., jazz musician, circus performer).

- **Determine life-satisfaction considerations that are important to you.** Generate a list of factors to use in assessing after-graduating possibilities. For instance, you might want to consider how the following factors will affect your degree of satisfaction with what you are doing:

  The benefit to society of what you are doing.

  Good income.

  Parents' opinions.

  Friends' opinions.

  Interest in the activity.

  Prestige.

  Job Security.

  Good vacations.

  Spare time.

  Likelihood of success.

  Everyday working conditions.

- **Determine how well a particular option fulfills each of the life-satisfaction factors you consider important.** By systematically considering how a potential career fulfills each of the factors important to you, you'll be able to compare different career options against one another. One easy way to do this is to create a chart like the one in Table 10.1 (which shows an example of how computer programming might fulfill the various life-satisfaction considerations).

- **Compare different choices.** Using the chart, evaluate which of your possible choices provides the most life-satisfaction considerations. Keep in mind that this is just a rough guide and that it's only as accurate as (a) the degree to which you know what is important to you and (b) your understanding of a given choice. Use the results in conjunction with other things you find out about careers—and yourself.

Table 10.1

Making Career Decisions

Life-Satisfaction Considerations	Possible Choice #1 *Computer programming*	Possible Choice #2	Possible Choice #3	Possible Choice #4
Desire to benefit society	✓			
Good income	✓			
Parents' opinions	✓			
Friends' opinions				
Interest in the activity	✓			
Prestige of job				
Job security				
Good vacations				
A lot of spare time				
Likelihood of success	✓			
Working conditions				
Other:				
Other:				
Other:				
Other:				
Other:				

even though you think about the pros and cons every once in a while. Finally, it's the day of the meeting, and you still don't know what to do.

The truth is, you've made the decision: You don't really want to be on the committee. Your indecision is telling you that—bottom line—you don't have sufficient interest to make the commitment. In some cases, then, viewing your own behavior gives you the response to your question.

- **Go with your gut feeling.** Call it what you like—gut feeling, intuition, superstition—but sometimes we need to go with our hearts and not our minds. If you've thought rationally about a decision and have been unable to determine the best course of action but have a gut feeling that one choice is better than another, then follow your feelings.

> "Each of us has the right and the responsibility to assess the roads which lie ahead and . . . if the future road looms ominous or unpromising . . . then we need to gather our resolve and . . . step off . . . into another direction."
>
> Maya Angelou, poet.

Following a gut feeling does not mean that you don't need to consider the pros and cons of a decision rationally and carefully. In fact, generally our "intuitions" are best when informed by the thoughtfulness of a more rational process.

Teaching Tip: Refer back to the discussion about learning styles in Chapter 3. What connection exists between learning styles and decision-making styles?

Carrying Out the Decision Ultimately, decisions must move from thought to action—they need to be carried out. Consequently, the final stage in making a decision is to act upon it. You need to turn what you've decided on into behavior.

E valuate: Considering the Outcomes

Did you make the right decision?

Even if you've spent time and mental effort in thinking through a decision, you still need to consider the results. Even well-considered decisions can end up being wrong, either because you neglected to consider some aspect or alternative or because you or the situation has changed.

For instance, suppose you were trying to decide between a major in management or biology. If you decide to go into management, it means that you'll be taking more courses related to finance and economics than if you had decided on a biology major. As you take these courses, you will be finding out whether you're enjoying them and how comfortable you feel with them. If you find you are consistently unhappy with these courses (and therefore your choice of major), you should allow yourself to re-evaluate your decision and reconsider the alternatives. It's not too late to change your mind about your decision.

> "Nothing is more difficult, and therefore more precious, than to be able to decide."
>
> Napoleon I, *Maxims* 15.

In fact, even major decisions are often reversible. That's why it's so important to evaluate your choices. If you chose the wrong alternative, reverse course and reconsider your options.

It's not bad to change your mind. In fact, admitting that a decision was a mistake is often the wisest and most courageous course of action. You don't want to be so rigidly committed to a decision that you're unable to evaluate the consequences objectively. Give yourself permission to be wrong.

R ethink: Reconsidering Your Goals and Options

We can get to most places by multiple routes. There's the fastest and most direct route, which will get us to our destination in the least amount of time. Then there's the longer, more scenic route, where the trip itself provides pleasure. You can "take the long way home," as the song goes.

Is one route better than the other? Often not. Both take us to our destination, so we've succeeded no matter which way we've chosen. However, the experience of reaching our goal will have been very different.

Decisions are similar to traveling down different routes. There's often no single decision that is best for us, just as there's often no single road to a particular place. Consequently, it's important to periodically reconsider the major decisions that we've made about our lives.

Ask yourself these questions:

- Are my decisions still producing the desired consequences?

- Are my decisions still appropriate, given my circumstances and changes in my life?

Discussion Prompt: Ask your students to answer these questions relating to their test preparation habits.

Chapter 10 Making Decisions That Are Right for You

- Are my decisions consistent with what I want to get out of life?

- Do my decisions fit with my mission statement (a written guiding philosophy of life, discussed in Chapter 3)?

Periodically taking stock like this is the best way to make sure that your decisions are taking you where you want. Taking stock also helps you to be more effective in making future decisions that affect your life.

Problem Solving: Applying Critical Thinking to Find Solutions

Two trains are approaching one another, each moving at 60 miles an hour. If the trains continue moving at the same speed, how long will it be before . . .

If this is what comes to mind when you think of problem solving, think again. **Problem solving** encompasses more than the abstract, often unrealistic situations portrayed in math texts. It involves everyday, commonplace situations: How do we divide the grocery bill so that each person pays a fair share? How do I keep my one-year-old from tumbling down the stairs when there seems to be no way to fasten a gate at the top? How can I stop a faucet from dripping? How do I manage to study for a test and complete a paper the same evening?

While decision making is most focused on *choosing* among various alternatives, the central issue in problem solving is *generating* alternatives. Since many problems require that decisions be made regarding alternatives, decision making and problem solving are often related.

Problem solving
The process of generating alternatives and finding solutions

What's the Problem?

The first step in solving any problem is to be as clear as you can about what the problem is. This may sound easy, but often it isn't. In fact, it may take some time to figure out just what is being asked. The reason is that some problems are big and hard to define, while others are quite precise, such as mathematical equations or the solution to a jigsaw puzzle. Determining how to stop the nuclear arms race between India and Pakistan and finding peace in the Middle East are big, ill-defined problems. Simply determining what information is required to solve such problems can be a major undertaking.

It's also necessary to determine what's important in coming to a solution. To determine what is critical in solving a problem, ask yourself these questions:

1. What is the initial set of facts?

2. What is it that you need to solve?

3. Which parts of the problem appear to be most critical to finding a solution?

4. Is there some information that can be ignored?

As you clarify what the problem is, you may find that you have encountered similar problems before. Your experience with them may suggest the means to the solution of the current problem. For example, consider the

Teaching Tip: Take any newspaper article about a world event and ask your students to "identify the problem." Ask them to practice this skill daily.

problem of the trains rushing toward one another. If you have worked on this kind of problem before and you know how quickly each train is moving and their starting points, there's a fairly simple equation you can write to determine how long it will take before they meet. On the other hand, to solve most of the problems we face in our daily lives, we have to do more than reach into our memories of prior situations. Instead, we need to devise novel approaches. How do you do this? There are several strategies you might use.

Strategies for Working on Life's Messier Problems

- **Trial and error.** Although it's a fairly primitive strategy, trial and error sometimes works. For instance, to invent a workable light bulb, Thomas Edison needed a good filament, the part of the bulb that actually glows. He tried out one material after another for the filament until he finally found one that worked.

- **Break the problem down into smaller, more-manageable pieces.** Break a problem down into a series of subgoals. As you reach each subgoal, you get closer to your overall goal of solving the problem. For example, if your goal is to spend your junior year in your school's program in Leningrad, a subgoal would probably be to learn some basic Russian. By reaching this subgoal, you move closer to reaching your ultimate goal—a year abroad in a country that interests you.

> "Problems are only opportunities in work clothes."
>
> Henry J. Kaiser, *Maxim.*

- **Work backward.** Sometimes you know the answer to the problem, but not how to get there. Then it's best to work backward. A **working backward** strategy starts at the desired solution or goal and works backward, moving away from the goal. For example, consider this problem:

  > Water lilies on a certain lake double in area every 24 hours. From the time the first water lily appears until the lake is completely covered takes 60 days. On what day is it half covered?

  It's impossible to solve this problem by breaking it down into subgoals, but most people solve it almost immediately if they work backwards. Here's a hint: If the pond is fully covered on day 60, how much is it covered the day before? Because the water lilies double each day, there had to be half as many the day before day 60. The answer, then, is that half the lake is covered on day 59. Only by moving backward could one see the solution clearly.

- **Use a graph, chart, or drawing to redefine the problem.** Transforming words into pictures often can help us to devise solutions that otherwise would elude us. One good example is this problem:

  > A man climbs a mountain on Saturday, leaving at daybreak and arriving at the top near sundown. He spends the night at the top. The next day, Sunday, he leaves at daybreak and heads down the mountain, following the same path that he climbed the day before. The question is this: Will there be any time during the second day when he will be at exactly the same point on the mountain as he was at exactly that time on the first day?

Working backward

The strategy of starting at the desired solution or goal and working toward the starting point of the problem

Discussion Prompt: What kinds of concerns do your students believe fit into the category of "messy problems"?

Chapter 10 Making Decisions That Are Right for You

Trying to solve the problem through the use of algebra or words is quite difficult. However, there's a simpler way: drawing the two paths. As you can see from Figure 10.1, the drawing provides a clear solution.

- **Consider the opposite.** Problems can sometimes be solved by considering the opposite of the problem you're seeking to solve. For example, in order to define "good mental health" you might try to define "bad mental health."

- **Use analogies.** Some problems can be solved through the use of **analogies,** comparisons between concepts or objects that are alike in some respects, but dissimilar in most others. For instance, if you liken a disastrous experience attending summer camp to a voyage on the *Titanic*, you're using an analogy.

    Analogies may help us gain additional insight into the problem at hand, and they may provide an alternative framework for interpreting the information that is provided. For instance, manufacturers of Pringles potato chips found that they could cut packaging costs if they slightly moistened the chips before packaging them—an idea that came when researchers noticed that dry tree leaves, which normally crumble easily, could be packed together tightly if they were wet.

- **Take another's perspective.** By viewing a problem from another person's point of view, it is often possible to obtain a new perspective on the problem that will make the problem easier to solve.

- **Forget about it.** Just as with decision making, sometimes it's best simply to walk away from a problem for a while. Just a few hours or days away from a problem may give us enough of a break to jar some hidden solutions from the recesses of our minds. The idea of "sleeping on it" also sometimes works; we may wake up refreshed and filled with new ideas.

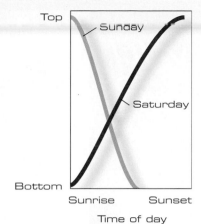

Figure 10.1

Up and Down the Mountain: The Paths to a Solution

Analogy

A comparison between concepts or objects that are alike in some respects, but dissimilar in most others

IM Link: "Teaching the Text," Chapter 10, Section VII, Goal 3, #2; characters from a novel provide a way to practice thinking about an issue through another person's perspective.

Assessing Your Potential Solutions

If a problem clearly has only one answer, such as a math problem, this step in problem solving is relatively easy. You should be able to work the problem and figure out if you've been successful. In contrast, messier problems have several possible solutions, some of which may be more involved and costly than others. In these cases, it's necessary to compare alternative solutions and choose the best one. For example, suppose you want to surprise your best friend on her birthday. She is working in Omaha, about 90 miles from you, and you need to find a way to get there. Perhaps you could rent a car, take a bus, or find some other way. Money is an issue. You will want to figure out how much each alternative costs before choosing one as your solution to the problem. Since every penny you spend getting there is a penny less that you will have to celebrate, you will want to weigh the options carefully.

Finally, spend a bit of time seeing if there is a way to refine the solution. Is the solution you've devised adequate? Does it address all aspects of the problem? Are there alternative approaches that might be superior? Answering these questions, and refining your solution to address them, can give you confidence that the solution you've come up with is the best. For example, if

Student Alert: As with writing papers or reading books, many first year students will not embrace the "refinement" process. Once they have done it/decided it, they are often reluctant to revisit it. Stress the importance of this part of the P.O.W.E.R. process.

Try It!
2

Exercise Your Problem-Solving Skills

Working in a group, try to solve these problems.[1] To help you devise solutions, a hint regarding the best strategy to use is included after each problem.

1. One cold, dark, and rainy night, a motorist has a flat tire on a deserted stretch of country road. He pulls onto the shoulder to change it. After removing the four lug nuts and placing them into the hub cap, he removes the flat tire and takes his spare out of the trunk. As he is moving the spare tire into position, his hand slips and he upsets the hub cap with the lug nuts, which tumble off into the night where he can't find them. What should he do? (*Hint:* Instead of asking how he might find the *scattered* lug nuts, reframe the problem and ask where else he might find other lug nuts.)

2. A worker paving a walk needs to add water quickly to the concrete she has just poured. She reaches for her pail to get water from a spigot in the front of the house, but suddenly realizes the pail has a large rust hole in it and cannot be used. As the concrete dries prematurely, she fumbles through her toolbox for tools and materials with which to repair the pail. She finds many tools, but nothing that would serve to patch the pail. The house is locked and no one is home. What should she do? (*Hint:* When is a pail not a pail?)

3. What day follows the day before yesterday if two days from now will be Sunday? (*Hint:* Break it up, or draw a diagram.)

4. A caterpillar has to climb up the muddy wall of a well that is 12 feet deep. Each day the caterpillar advances four feet, but each night as he sleeps he slips back two feet. How many days will it take him to get out? (*Hint:* Draw it.)

5. A man has four chains, each three links long. He wants to join the four chains into a single, closed chain. Having a link opened costs two cents and having a link closed costs three cents. How can he have the chains joined for 15 cents? (*Hint:* Can only end links be opened?)

6. What is two-thirds of one-half? (*Hint:* Reverse course.)

7. I have three separate large boxes. Inside each large box are two separate medium-sized boxes, and inside each of the medium boxes are four small boxes. How many boxes do I have altogether? (*Hint:* Draw it.)

After working to solve these problems, consider these questions: Which problems were the easiest to solve, and which were the more difficult ones? Why? Were the hints helpful? Do you think there was more than one solution to any of the problems? Did your initial assumptions about the problem help or hinder your efforts to solve it? (*Note:* Answers to the problems are found at the end of the chapter on page 260.)

you're trying to get to Omaha, you might decide to try to find a ride with someone going to Omaha that day, using the ride board at your school. Maybe her family is going to be driving in and could pick you up. Maybe your friend's family could lend you a car for the trip.

Reflect on the Process of Problem Solving

It's natural to step back and bask in the satisfaction of solving a tough problem. That's fine—but take a moment to consider your success. Each time we solve a problem we end up a couple steps ahead the next time around, but only if we've thought about the process we went through to solve it.

Go back and consider what it took to solve the problem and your emotional reactions along the way. Can the means you used to come up with your solution be applied to more-complex kinds of problems? If you arrived at a solution by drawing a chart, would this work on similar problems in the future? Taking a moment to rethink your solution can provide you with an opportunity to become an expert problem solver and, more generally, to improve your critical thinking skills. Don't let the opportunity slip away.

Don't Fool Yourself: Avoiding Everyday Problems in Critical Thinking

As you have probably noticed already, the quality of the thinking you do regarding problems and decisions plays a crucial role in determining how successful you are. Being able to think clearly and without bias is the basis for critical thinking.

Unfortunately, it is sometimes the alternative you *didn't* think of that can end up being the most satisfactory decision or solution. So how can we learn to think critically and avoid blind spots that hinder us in our decision making and problem solving? We can start by considering the common obstacles to critical thinking.

IM Link: "Teaching the Text," Chapter 10, Section VII, Goal 1; the roommate visit can be a great activity for becoming aware of biases or problems with labeling.

Here are some of the decision-making and problem-solving pitfalls to look out for. Avoiding them will improve your critical thinking greatly.

- **Don't assume that giving something a name explains it.** The mere fact that we can give an idea or problem a name doesn't mean we know its causes and can explain it. Yet we often confuse the two.

    For instance, consider the following sequences of questions and answers:

    Q. Why do I have so much trouble falling asleep?
    A. Because you have insomnia.

    Q. Why is he so unsociable?
    A. Because he's an introvert.

    Q. Why did the defendant shoot those people?
    A. Because he's insane.
    Q. How do you know he's insane?
    A. Because only someone who was insane would shoot people in that way.[2]

    It's clear that none of these answers is satisfactory. All use circular reasoning, in which the explanation for the behavior is simply the use of a label. But labels don't explain anything; they merely provide a convenient name.

- **Don't accept vague generalities dressed up as definitive statements.** Read the following personality analysis and think about how well it applies to you:

  > You have a need for other people to like and admire you and a tendency to be critical of yourself. You also have a great deal of unused potential that you have not turned to your advantage, and although you have some personality weaknesses, you are generally able to compensate for them. Nonetheless, relating to members of the opposite sex has presented problems to you, and while you appear to be disciplined and self-controlled to others, you tend to be anxious and insecure inside.

  If you believe that these statements provide an amazingly accurate description of your unique qualities, you're not alone: Most college students believe that the descriptions are tailored specifically to them.[3]

  But how is that possible? It isn't. The reality is that the statements are so vague that they are virtually meaningless. The acceptance of vague but seemingly useful and significant statements about oneself and others has been called the *Barnum Effect*, after showman and circus master P.T. Barnum, who coined the phrase "there's a sucker born every minute."

- **Don't confuse opinion with fact.** Opinions are not fact. Although you may be aware of this simple formula, almost all of us can be fooled into thinking that someone's opinion is the same as a fact. Sometimes it occurs when we listen to so-called authorities. For instance, the fact that a person has a distinguished title, such as "Doctor" or "Professor," doesn't mean that his or her statements are facts, as opposed to opinions.

  A fact is information that is proven to be true. In contrast, an opinion represents judgments, reasoning, beliefs, inferences, or conclusions. If we accept some bit of information as a fact, we can use it to build our opinions. But if we are presented with an opinion, we need to determine the facts on which it is built in order to judge its reliability.

  The difference between fact and opinion can sometimes be subtle. For instance, compare these two statements:

  1. Every college student needs to take a writing course during the first term of college.

  2. Many college students need to take a writing course during the first term of college.

  The first statement is most likely an opinion, because it is so absolute and unqualified. Words such as "every," "all," and "always" are evidence of opinion. On the other hand, the second statement is more likely a fact, since it contains the qualifier "many." In general, statements that are qualified in some way are more likely to be facts.

  Try "Fact versus Opinion" (see Try It 3) to see the difficulties in sometimes distinguishing between the two.

- **Avoid jumping to conclusions.** Read this riddle and try to answer it:

  > A father and his son were driving along the interstate highway when the father lost control of the car, swerved off the road, and crashed into a telephone pole. The father died instantly, and his son was critically injured. An ambulance rushed the boy to a nearby hospital. A prominent surgeon was summoned to provide immediate treatment. When the surgeon ar-

Try It! 3

Fact versus Opinion

Read the following statements and try to determine which are facts and which are opinions.

1. College students should get at least seven hours of sleep every night.

2. The average college student sleeps less than seven hours a night.

3. Nikes offer better styling and comfort than any other brand of shoe.

4. Two out of five sports figures surveyed preferred Nikes over Converse shoes.

5. The U.S. government spends too much money on guns and missiles and not enough money on education.

6. Government figures show spending is much higher for guns and missiles than for education.

7. In general, U.S. high school students receive less classroom instruction in foreign languages than their counterparts in Europe and Asia.

8. No student in the United States should graduate without having studied a language other than English for at least four years.

9. Michael Jordan is the most outstanding, most exciting, and certainly most successful basketball player who ever stepped onto a court.

---

rived and entered the operating room to examine the boy, a loud gasp was heard. "I can't operate on this boy," the surgeon said. "He is my son."[4]

How can this be?

If you find this puzzling, you've based your reasoning on an assumption: that the surgeon is a male. But suppose you had assumed that the surgeon was a female. Suddenly, the riddle becomes a lot easier. It's far easier to guess that the surgeon is the son's *mother* if we don't leap to embrace a faulty assumption.

Why is it so easy to jump to conclusions? One reason is that we sometimes aren't aware of the assumptions that underlie our thinking. Another is our reliance on "common sense."

- **Don't believe in the myth of common sense.** Much of what we call common sense makes contradictory claims. Which are we to believe? For example, if you subscribe to the notion "Absence makes the heart grow fonder," you may assume that your high school girlfriend, now in college across the country from you, will arrive home at Christmas even more in love with you than before. But what about "Out of sight, out of mind," which suggests a less positive outcome?

Truisms, as such statements are called, are not factually true. Sure, being away from a loved one for a few days or a week can make you aware of just how important that person is to you and make it seem as if your heart has grown fonder. But living away from someone for an extended period of time is frequently more likely to produce distance than romance.

Discussion Prompt: Ask students to think alone for 2–3 minutes about a time when they have jumped to a conclusion. Then ask them to share with a classmate why they did so, and what the outcome was. What would they do differently in the future?

Chapter 10 Making Decisions That Are Right for You

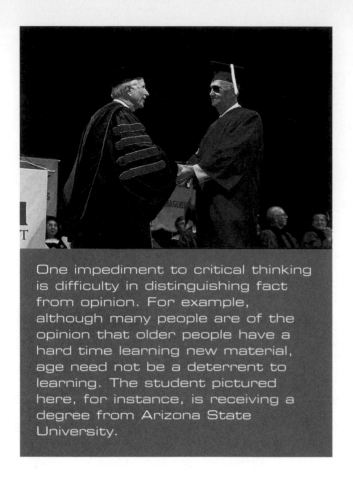

One impediment to critical thinking is difficulty in distinguishing fact from opinion. For example, although many people are of the opinion that older people have a hard time learning new material, age need not be a deterrent to learning. The student pictured here, for instance, is receiving a degree from Arizona State University.

Student Alert: False assumptions lead to many faulty conclusions. Ask your students when they have relied on similar faulty correlations.

Take a look at the commonsense truisms in Try It 4, "The Myth of Common Sense," and see if you can come up with their opposites.

- **Don't assume that just because two events occur together one causes the other.** Just because two events appear to be associated with one another—or, in the language of social science, are *correlated* with one another—we cannot conclude that one event has caused the other to occur. It's a basic rule: *Correlation does not prove causation.*

  For example, suppose you read that a study showed that 89 percent of juvenile delinquents use marijuana. Does this mean that smoking marijuana *causes* juvenile delinquency? No, it doesn't. It is pretty safe to say that 100 percent of juvenile delinquents grew up drinking milk. Would you feel comfortable saying that milk causes delinquency? With correlations such as marijuana use and delinquent behavior, it is very likely that there's some third factor—such as strife among family members—that causes people both to (a) try drugs and (b) engage in illegal acts. The bottom line: We don't know anything other than the fact that many young people charged with crimes said they had smoked marijuana. We do not know the cause of the correlation.

  In short, we need to be careful in assuming causality. Even if two events or other kinds of variables occur together, it does not mean that one causes the other. (To apply what we've been discussing to some actual situations, complete "What's Wrong with This Picture?" in Try It 5 on page 262.)

Answers to Try It 2 problems:

1. Remove one lug nut from each of the other three tires on the car and use these three to attach the spare tire. This will hold until four more lug nuts can be purchased. 2. Dump the tools out of the toolbox and use it as a pail. 3. Thursday. 4. Five days; on the fifth day the caterpillar will reach the top and will not have to slide down again. 5. Open all three links on one chain (cost = 6 cents) and use them to fasten the other three chains together (cost = 9 cents; total cost = 15 cents). 6. It is the same as one-half of two-thirds, or one-third. 7. 33 boxes (3 large, 6 medium, 24 small).

Try It!
4

The Myth of Common Sense

Read the list of proverbs—which represent the common sense of our culture—and see if you can recall another proverb that advises exactly the opposite course of action. Which of the opposing views of common sense is really sensible? Clearly, for any given situation, only hindsight can tell us.

1. A stitch in time saves nine.

   Opposite: _____

   _____

2. He who hesitates is lost.

   Opposite: _____

   _____

3. Birds of a feather flock together.

   Opposite: _____

   _____

4. You're never too old to learn

   Opposite: _____

   _____

5. It's no use beating a dead horse.

   Opposite: _____

   _____

6. A taste of honey is worse than none at all.

   Opposite: _____

   _____

Answers:

1. Haste makes waste. 2. Look before you leap. 3. Opposites attract. 4. You can't teach an old dog new tricks. 5. If at first you don't succeed, try, try again. 6. 'Tis better to have loved and lost than never to have loved at all.

Try It! 5

What's Wrong with This Picture? Identify the Faulty Reasoning

Each of the statements and situations below illustrates a failure of critical thinking. Analyze each of them and state why the conclusion might be wrong.

1. When asked why she often engages in shoplifting, Marian says, "I can't help it. I'm a kleptomaniac."

2. Zack reads in a newspaper horoscope that he "will have good luck toward the end of the week, especially in matters of chance, with a sharp downturn possible by early next week." He immediately buys 10 lottery tickets for Friday's drawing.

3. A political candidate makes this statement: "My party is 10 times more concerned about the lives and fortunes of the working person than is the opposing party."

4. Two students in a large lecture class—one evidently Asian and the other not—wait as their math professor grades their papers. The professor notes that Jackie Lee has done very well, while Dexter Roberts has not. As she finishes grading, the professor gives the good paper to the Asian-looking student and the other paper to the student who doesn't look Asian. The students look at the papers, and exchange them to the rightful owner.

Can you identify the faulty logic for each of the four scenarios? Do you think the people making the statements or taking the action are aware of their faulty thinking? Can you think of any instances in which you displayed similar faulty logic?

Speaking of Success

Name: *Colin Powell*

Education: *City College of New York, B.A.; George Washington University, M.S.*

Home: *McLean, Virginia*

Few who knew Colin Powell when he was growing up would have guessed that he would become a great general and the highest-ranking military commander in the United States as Chairman of the Joint Chiefs of Staff.

The son of Jamaican immigrants, Powell characterizes himself as lacking drive while growing up in a poor South Bronx neighborhood in New York City. As he describes himself, "I was a happy-go-lucky kid, amenable, amiable, and aimless."[5]

Although his parents, who had high educational expectations, urged him to transfer from his neighborhood high school to a more demanding school, his guidance counselor advised against it, citing his previous indifferent academic performance. Powell ended up maintaining a C average in his neighborhood school, where simply showing up was largely what it took to pass.

But Powell's parents encouraged him to continue his education and apply to college. Bowing to their pressure, he entered City College in New York, starting as an engineering major, and later switching to geology. Most important, though, Powell found a passion: participation in the college ROTC program, which provided train-

ing that allowed students to become officers in the military upon graduation. ROTC training provided him with a grounding, a sense that he had found what he was looking for in life.

When Powell graduated, he immediately entered the Army, distinguishing himself early on as a military leader. But he also came to feel he needed more education. He enrolled in a masters degree program in Government and Business Administration at George Washington

University in Washington, D.C., earning nearly straight A's.

Returning to the Army after receiving his master's degree, Powell moved up rapidly through the ranks, ultimately moving into the highest military post in the country. During his career, he won numerous awards, including the Defense Distinguished Service Medal, a Bronze Star Medal, a Purple Heart, the Presidential Medal of Freedom, and even an honorary knighthood.

As a highly visible and successful African-American, Powell understands that he is seen as a role model, particularly by young blacks. In his own words, "The message I give to young people as I talk in high schools essentially says, 'Do not let the fact that you're a minority or that you come from a different background or that you are trapped structurally somewhere serve as an anchor to keep you down. You've got to swim against it, you've got to climb against it.' The only thing I can do is tell them to reach down inside."[6] He certainly took his own advice.

How can I improve the quality of my decisions?

- A structured process of decision making can clarify the issues involved, expand our options, and improve the quality of our choices.

- Good decision making begins with understanding your short- and long-term goals.

- Decision making is improved if you have a large number of alternatives.

- For difficult decisions, strategies include giving the decision time, acting out alternatives, tossing a coin to test our feelings, understanding that indecision is often a decision itself, and acting on gut feelings.

What strategies can I use for problem solving?

- Problem solving entails the generation of alternatives to consider.

- We need to first understand and define the problem and to determine the important elements in coming to a solution to a problem.

- Approaches to generating solutions include using trial and error, breaking problems into pieces, working backward, using pictures, considering the opposite, using analogies, taking another's perspective, and "forgetting" the problem.

- Problem solving ultimately requires the evaluation and refinement of the solutions that have been generated.

What are some problems that affect critical thinking, and how can I avoid them?

- Several types of obstacles pose threats to critical thinking.

- Awareness of the biases that may affect our thinking can help us avoid them.

Key Terms and Concepts

Analogy (p. 255)
Decision making (p. 245)

Problem solving (p. 253)
Working backward (p. 254)

Resources

On Campus

Some colleges offer courses in critical thinking, and they are a good bet to help increase decision-making and problem-solving skills. In addition, courses in logic and philosophy will help improve critical thinking skills.

If you are having a personal problem that is difficult to solve, you can turn to staff at the campus counseling center, mental health center, or residential life office. Even if the person with whom you speak initially is not the right one, he or she can direct you to someone who can help.

In Print

If you have trouble making good decisions, the H.W. Lewis book *Why Flip a Coin? The Art and Science of Good Decisions* (Wiley, 1997) is for you. The book shows how to make a rational decision based on the information at hand. Dean Juniper's *Making Decisions: How to Develop Effective Skills for Making Good Decisions* (How To Books Ltd., 1998) also is a helpful guide to decision making. For more information on the biases that bedevil our thinking, read David Levy's *Tools of Critical Thinking* (Boston: Allyn & Bacon, 1997).

On the Web

The following sites on the World Wide Web provide the opportunity to extend your learning about the material in this chapter. (Although the Web addresses were accurate at the time the book was printed, check the P.O.W.E.R. Learning Web site [http://mhhe.com/power] for any changes that may have occurred.)

http://www.psychwww.com/mtsite/index.html
This Web site offers links to other sites that can help one with setting goals, time management, and stress control, and to numerous other helpful sites. It also includes shareware for setting up life plans.

http://nz.com/webnz/checkers/GoalSetting.html
This page is part of the Web site ABCheckers, an English language consultant group that was set up by a group of teachers. It contains pages designed to help students develop effective study skills.

http://www.kcmetro.cc.mo.us/longview/ctac/corenotes.htm
Core concepts in critical thinking are presented with exercises and examples. The site contains a short history of logic and answers the question: "What is the point of studying critical thinking?"

http://www.geodex.com/decmak.html
This site provides a general outline of steps to follow in helping you to make better decisions.

Taking It to the Net

1 Making good decisions can depend on distinguishing legitimate appeals (good reasons) from fallacious appeals (bad reasons). Go to this web site: **http://www.sjsu.edu/depts/itl/graphics/adhom/appeal.html**

After reading the description of the different kinds of fallacious appeals, do the related exercises.

2 Locate three problem-solving strategies on the Internet. Possible strategy: Go to Yahoo! (**www.yahoo.com**) or AltaVista (**www.altavista.digital. com**), and enter the key phrase "problem solving." Search the results until you find at least three different problem-solving strategies. Are these strategies similar to the ones described in the book? If not, how are they different?

The Case of . . .

Left Holding the Lease

Erica had a problem.

In the spring of her first year of college, she and her friend Jeri had found a two-bedroom apartment to share for the upcoming school year. The apartment was on the expensive side, but they had decided that it was worth it because it was so close to campus. She and Jeri had jointly paid the security deposit on the apartment. However, because Jeri hadn't been around when it came time to sign the lease, only Erica had signed it. Consequently, Erica was legally responsible for fulfilling the terms of the lease.

Now, only two weeks before the start of the fall term, Jeri told Erica that she had realized she couldn't afford the rent on the apartment and that she had decided she had to live with her parents. Jeri was simultaneously furious with Erica and panicky at the thought of having to pay the rent herself, which she simply couldn't afford.

How was she going to deal with the problem?

1. Is the problem a purely financial and legal one, or are there personal and social considerations that should be taken into account in solving the problem?

2. Is the problem solely Erica's problem, or should Jeri take responsibility for solving it as well?

3. What alternatives does Erica have for dealing with the situation?

4. How should Erica go about evaluating the outcomes for each alternative?

5. Based on your analysis of the problem, what advice would you give Erica for dealing with the situation?

Choosing
Your
Courses
and Major

"Mathematics for Poets."

The course title jumped out at Gwen Izell. Although she had managed to do well in math in high school, she had never liked it. In fact, when she began thinking about going to college, she'd vowed to look for a school that didn't have a math requirement. St. Ignatius College fit the bill; she would not be required to take a math class.

But she was intrigued by this course title. Here was a class that seemed designed with her in mind. "Mathematics for Poets," the description read, "presents the links between the arts and mathematics. The mathematical basis for several art forms will be explored. No previous background in mathematics is expected."

"Well, I need one more course," she said to herself. "I love poetry, and maybe this will give me a way to understand it better." Furthermore, she had heard from a friend that the course instructor was excellent. She decided to take a chance and enroll in the class.

It turned out to be one of the best decisions she ever made; she loved the course. The instructor was terrific, making math seem fascinating. She found that not only did she begin to like math, but she was good at it.

Gwen was hooked on math, and she actually took several other math courses. And during her senior year she found herself in an interview with a middle school principal, telling him—a bit to her surprise—that she could easily teach eighth-grade math.

Looking
Ahead

Our academic and professional careers are propelled by many forces, not the least of which is chance. Gwen Izell, like many other students, found a new direction while leafing through the St. Ignatius course list. Although she never would have predicted at the start of college that she would end up taking a variety of math courses and then teaching math, her willingness to take an academic chance led to a new passion and to a career opportunity.

In this chapter we focus on choosing an academic course of study, one of the central challenges of college. Not only do the choices we make color our entire college experience, but they also may determine the path we follow once we graduate.

This chapter begins by considering the many choices you'll have to make as a routine part of attending college, including the choice of courses, instructors, and especially majors—each of which has long-term implications. You'll learn ways to select courses that meet your needs and ensuring you get the courses you want.

Ultimately, the degree to which your college education benefits you is in your hands. By learning various strategies, you can act decisively to get the most out of your college experience. After reading this chapter, you'll be able to answer these questions:

- **How can I prepare for the academic choices that college demands?**

- **What is the best way to choose courses and ensure I'm getting the most out of my studies?**

- **How can I choose a major?**

- **How can I deal with academic success and failure?**

Making Academic Choices

It's a moment filled with promise.

A list of courses for the upcoming term lies on the table in front of you. Many of them sound interesting. Each offers the possibilities of new knowledge, new ideas, and new information and therefore has the potential for changing your life in significant ways.

As you leaf through the course catalog and begin to make your decisions, you will likely be feeling a wide range of emotions: anticipation over what you'll learn; hope that the course can bring you closer to your dreams; fear that you won't be able to do well; and excitement that you're proceeding with your college career, taking one more of the number of small steps that will eventually add up to your complete journey through college.

Choosing the right set of courses can be intimidating. But if you approach the problem thoughtfully, your final choices will make the best of the possibilities offered. Let's consider how to proceed, using the P.O.W.E.R. system as a guide (see the P.O.W.E.R. Plan).

Prepare: Becoming Familiar with Your Options and Requirements

PREPARE
Become familiar with your options and requirements

ORGANIZE
Examine what you have done and what you need to do

WORK
Choose the next term's courses

EVALUATE
Decide whether you are in the classes you need

RETHINK
Learn what you love and like what you learn

P.O.W.E.R. Plan

Choosing which courses to take requires that you take several significant preparatory steps before you jump in. These include the following:

Familiarize Yourself with Your College Catalog Think of your college catalog as a kind of mail-order catalog. Like a mail-order catalog, it provides you with information about the merchandise that's offered, its cost, and the steps you need to take in placing an order. In this case, though, instead of a new pair of pants or a rug, the merchandise offered in the catalog is a college degree.

College catalogs are actually legal documents that offer you a contract. If you are admitted to the college and you fulfill certain requirements (such as taking a particular set of courses, maintaining a certain level of grades, and—let us not forget—paying your tuition bills on time), you'll get something in return. That something is a college degree.

Because they outline contractual obligations, college catalogs are important documents. They provide an outline of what your institution expects and offers in a number of areas:

1. **Academic regulations.** Every college has strict rules, requirements, and policies; these are all spelled out in the college catalog. For example, in order to continue in college, you must maintain a particular grade average in all your courses; to drop a course, you need to do so

Student Alert: Most students do not realize how much valuable information can be found in a college catalog. Have students bring it to class and give them assignments or ask questions that will ensure that they read it.

by a certain date in the term; and to graduate, you need a certain number of courses or course credits.

2. **Academic programs.** Most of the college catalog is a description of the major areas of study offered by the school—its academic departments and majors, and the requirements for each major.

Requirements generally fall into two or three categories. First, typically, are collegewide requirements that every student enrolled in a college must fulfill. Second are specific requirements for each particular major. A **major** is a specialization in a particular subject area, requiring a set course of study; to major in an area, you must take a specific number of courses or credits in that area. Finally, if the major falls within a broader academic unit (such as a school of education), that broader entity may have its own requirements for a degree.

For instance, a psychology major might be required to fulfill collegewide requirements that apply to all students enrolled in the college, such as several English, writing, math, and science courses. Then, because the Department of Psychology may be housed in a more-general Division of Social Sciences, there may be divisional requirements to fulfill (perhaps a course in social science methodology or a foreign language requirement). Finally, the Department of Psychology will have its own separate requirements for its majors to complete, such as taking no fewer than six psychology courses.

The college catalog also provides information for students who have transferred from another college. For instance, transfer students may be permitted to receive credit for only a certain number of courses or credits earned at their first institution. Or they may be required to take particular courses even if they already took them at their previous school.

3. **Course listings.** The college catalog lists all the courses the school offers, even though not all of them may be offered every term. Courses are listed by department, and the descriptions typically include the course name, the number of credits it provides, and a short description. Some courses have **prerequisites**—requirements that must be fulfilled before one can enroll in them. If the course has a prerequisite, this will also be stated. Sometimes the description will also name the instructors who teach the course and the time and place the class meets, although this information may be published separately.

Make an Appointment with Your College Advisor Your **college advisor**'s job is to give you good, clear-headed advice. Your advisor will be someone who knows the ins and outs of the college's regulations, and whose experience in working with other students provides a good deal of knowledge in

Major
A specialization in a particular subject area, requiring a set course of study

Prerequisites
Requirements that must be fulfilled before a student may enroll in a course or discipline

College advisor
An individual who provides students with advice about their academic career

College advisors can play an important role in your academic career, providing valuable advice, helping you to overcome problems, and making sure that you meet all the requirements needed to graduate.

other areas as well. Advisors can help you figure out what classes to take, how to overcome academic bureaucracies, whom to go to about a problem, and generally how to prepare yourself for graduation and beyond. They can even provide information on extracurricular activities, volunteer opportunities, and part-time jobs. Advisors are usually very busy at the beginning of each term, so find out their office hours, schedule an appointment early, and be sure to keep your scheduled appointment.

Your advisor can be a tremendously valuable resource. Take some time to get to know your advisor—and to let him or her get to know you. To get a better sense of who your own advisor is, complete Try It 1, "Get to Know Your College Advisor," on page 272.

If you find that you and your advisor aren't a good match and you know of another advisor who is willing and qualified to advise you, you might consider making a switch. Just be sure you have given your original advisor a chance. It is not your advisor's fault, for example, that you missed your only chance this year to take astronomy. Similarly, even though you may not like your advisor's message ("You still need to take a science course"), this doesn't mean that he or she doesn't have your best interests at heart. If you feel you can trust and speak with your advisor frankly, you and your college career will have gained a valuable ally.

Teaching Tip: TRY IT! 1 is a good way for students to get to know their advisor. You may also want to invite an advisor to your class, or schedule a tour of your institution's advising center.

> "It can be no dishonor to learn from others when they speak good sense."
>
> Sophocles, *Antigone.*

> "Choosing courses can make or break you in college. The better you are at it, the better your grades and the less your aggravation."
>
> Junior, University of Colorado.[1]

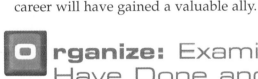

Organize: Examining What You Have Done and What You Need to Do

Where Are You?   If you've prepared well, you have a basic understanding of the courses you have already taken that fulfill the requirements for the degree you are seeking. To figure out what you need to do, you'll need to organize a list of the requirements you must fulfill in order to graduate. Try It 2 on page 273, "Create a List of Course Requirements," provides a form that you can complete if your college doesn't provide one for you. Even if you have yet to decide on a major, you will probably be taking some courses that may satisfy one of the requirements for a major you are considering. Noting this on your list will help you plan as your college career progresses.

If this is just the start of your college career, you'll probably have completed only a few of the requirements. Don't let the blanks on the form get you down; this is typical, and the credits have a way of adding up quickly.

If you are further along in your college career, you may find that you have already fulfilled a significant number of requirements. In fact, you may not remember everything you've already done. If you have trouble remembering what courses you've taken, get a copy of your transcript from the **registrar,** the official designated to oversee the scheduling of courses, the maintenance of grades and transcripts, and the creation and retention of other official

Registrar
The college official designated to oversee the scheduling of courses, the maintenance of grades and transcripts, and the creation and retention of other official documents

Try It!
1

Get to Know Your College Advisor

It is helpful to get a feel for who your advisor is, so schedule an appointment with him or her. Before you meet with your advisor, do some background research by looking at your college catalog. College catalogs usually provide information on the background of faculty and staff, listing their titles, where they went to college and graduate school, what departments they teach in, and what their areas of academic interest are. In addition, you can search the Web; some instructors have their own home pages that describe their background.

To further your knowledge of your advisor, cover some of these topics when you meet:

Philosophy of college advising:

Words of advice:

Things to try at college:

Things to avoid at college:

Before you leave, be sure to thank your advisor for his or her time. After you have met with your advisor, consider the following questions: Do you have a better sense of your advisor as an individual? What things did you learn that can help you? How can you use the responses to take better advantage of what your college has to offer?

Transcript
An official record of courses taken and grades received by students

documents. A **transcript** is the official record of the courses you've taken and the grades you received in them.

As you're recording the courses you've taken, remember that meeting graduation requirements may not be the same as meeting your major's requirements. For instance, some schools not only require that you take and pass cer-

Try It! 2

Create a List of Course Requirements

Use the form below to list all of your course requirements. The form covers both prerequisite courses (i.e., courses you must take before you can take other requirements) and requirements imposed by your college, the division of which your department is a part, and your department. In addition, the form allows you to indicate both credit requirements and grade requirements.

List of Course Requirements

Type of Course	Credits Required	Credits Completed	Grade Required	Grade Achieved	Whose Requirement?		
					College	Division	Department
I. Prerequisite Courses							
Total Prerequisite Courses							
II. Required Courses							
Total Required Courses							

What does the information in the chart tell you? How can you use it to plan your future course selections? What courses do you wish to take that are not requirements? How much leeway do you have to take nonrequired courses?

tain courses; sometimes you have to achieve a certain minimum grade in your courses as a whole. Or you may have to get a grade of C or better in a course for it to be counted toward your major. In this case, if you received a C– in the course, you'd still get credit toward graduation, but the course wouldn't count toward the number of credits you need in your major.

Teaching Tip: Your institution may have forms such as the one above specifically designed for your majors that can be picked up at an advising center, department, or on the university Web site. Have students bring a copy to class.

Confusing? You bet. That's why it's important to keep track of where you stand from the very start of your college career. (It's a good idea to keep all relevant information together in a file folder or even a shoebox.) There's no worse surprise than finding out a month before you thought you'd be graduating that you lack some critical requirement. Don't count on others to keep track of this information for you. No one knows more about what you've done—or is more interested in it—than you.

Where Are You Going?   You also need to determine what requirements you've yet to fulfill. Use this information to help determine which courses you should take in the upcoming term. Once you have declared a major you can add those requirements to your record.

Now that you know where you are and where you are going, you are ready to start selecting courses to take you there.

W ork: Choosing the Next Term's Courses

IM Link: "Teaching the Text," Chapter 11, Section V—this P.O.W.E.R. process includes good activities for teaching this part of the chapter.

The course listings for the next term are published in a *course schedule* that lists course offerings for the next term. It is organized by department, with each course in the department having a number, such as "History 204: The French Revolution." Generally, the higher the number, the more advanced the course. The course catalog will tell you when and where the class meets (for large introductory courses there may be several sections) and whether there are any prerequisites for the course—requirements that must be fulfilled before a student may enroll in a course or discipline.

Go with What You Know   Chances are, you already know of at least one or two courses you need to take in a given term. Perhaps this is the term you plan to fulfill your natural science or your foreign language requirement. There may be some courses you have been waiting to take, since some courses are only taught once a year. A good place to begin is to find out when these courses are given and where.

Draft a Personal Schedule for the Term   First, write down when the courses you absolutely have to take are scheduled. If, as is the case for many introductory courses in large colleges, you have a choice of times, choose one you prefer. In choosing times, take into consideration if you are a "morning person" who is at your best first thing in the morning, or if you usually must drag yourself out of bed in the morning and don't fully function until 11:00 A.M. This will be the beginning of your time management for the upcoming term.

Next, choose courses that are not required. Keep in mind broad considerations about the kinds of courses you need to take for your major and for graduation. But also explore possible courses that simply sound interesting to you. College offers the opportunity to discover who you are and what you like and do best, but the only way that can happen is by taking intellectual risks.

To get started in deciding what courses to take for the upcoming term, complete Try It 3, "Choose Your Courses."

Choose Your Courses

Try It! **3**

Use the form below to make your course selections for the coming term. The form will permit you to verify that you are meeting course requirements, avoiding schedule conflicts, and signing up for instructors you want.

Course Selections

Term: _____

Course Name and Number	Credits	Required Course or Just for Fun?	Prereq- uisites Met?	Grade Required	Meeting Days and Time	Schedule Conflicts	Instructor	Instructor OK?

After completing the chart, answer these questions: How does the next semester shape up for you? Will you be able to take the courses you *want* to take, as opposed to those you *need* to take? Have you made any choices that open you to new intellectual possibilities?

Register for Courses After laying the groundwork of course selection, the rest of the actual work of choosing courses for your classes consists of completing the college's paperwork to become formally enrolled in your chosen classes.

Meeting with your advisor is an essential step. Sometimes, in fact, it's mandatory, and you won't be allowed to register without your advisor's signature. But even if it's not required, it's a good idea to go over your proposed course of studies. You may have overlooked something, or your advisor may be able to suggest some alternative courses that will work better for you.

Remember, though, that the ultimate responsibility for taking the right courses rests with you. Not only can advisors sometimes make mistakes and overlook a requirement, but only you ultimately know what's right for you.

After meeting with your advisor, your next step will be to actually **register,** the formal act of enrolling in courses. Course registration varies significantly from one school to another. In some cases, it's a matter of listing course numbers on a form, along with some alternatives.

Student Alert: Remind students to consider their learning styles when planning their schedule. Have they scheduled their hardest classes at times when they learn best?

Register
To enroll formally in courses

_____

Figure 11.1

Telephone Course Registration Worksheet

Before you begin your telephone call, fill in this entire worksheet, listing all courses you wish to add, drop, or change including laboratory and discussion sections, and the appropriate "action codes" you will enter. Be sure to fill in all boxed areas properly and to enter '##' at the end of your call.

1. Call the system at (555) 444-3214 (From On-Campus, call 4-3214)

2. Enter your student ID number 1 2 6 - 0 4 - 9 8 1 1

3. Enter your branch code 1 (Undergraduate = 1, Graduate = 2)

4. Enter your personal ID number (PIN) 6 7 7 5

5. If the Schedule Confirmation you receive in the mail instructs you to get from your advisor a Registration Approval Code before

   add/drop, enter that code ☐ ☐ ☐ ☐

6. For each add, drop, or change you want to make, enter the appropriate action code from the list below and the schedule number for the course you want affected by that action.

Action Code*	Schedule Number of Course Requested	Dept	Course #	Section #	Crd	Day/Time
1 0	7 8 2 8 4 0	Psych	102	1	3	T-T 11:15-12:30
1 0	6 7 2 9 9 7	Engl	231	1	3	M-W-F 9:05-9:55
1 0	2 6 0 4 6 3	Phed	102	2	1	M 4:00-4:50
1 0	1 2 0 3 0 9	Latn	124	1	3	T-T 9:00-10:15
1 0	8 8 0 1 8 1	Hist	102	1	3	M-W-F 10:10-11:05
1 0	7 2 4 9 6 2	Phys	101	3	3	T-T 2:30-3:45
☐☐	☐☐☐☐☐☐					
☐☐	☐☐☐☐☐☐					
☐☐	☐☐☐☐☐☐					
☐☐	☐☐☐☐☐☐					

7. After entering your course requests, enter # # instead of an action code to terminate your call.

*Action Code	Action
10	ADD a course or Swap between sections of a course (To SWAP, simply add the new section; the old section will automatically be dropped from your schedule.)
30	ADD a course with Pass/Fail option or CHANGE existing course to Pass/Fail
90	DROP a course
80	REMOVE Pass/Fail or Audit option from existing course
50	CHANGE variable credit for an existing variable credit course
40	ADD a course with AUDIT grading option or CHANGE existing course to AUDIT grading
60	LIST your course schedule (press any key to end listing)
*	ERASE an entry error before completion
	Note: Action Codes 30 and 80 are not available to graduate students. 40 is not available to undergraduates.

Student Alert: Course availability is an issue on most college campuses. Encourage students to plan ahead and to meet with an advisor early. Students should get answers to all of their questions well in advance of registration time, and, always have a back-up plan!

In some larger schools, you will be expected to register for your courses over the telephone or through the World Wide Web. If your college uses a telephone registration system, you will be given a specific time period in which to call. When you do call, you'll receive voice prompts to enter your course choices using your telephone's touch-tone key pad (see Figure 11.1).

If your college uses the newest form of registration, the World Wide Web, you will be prompted to enter course information on a Web form, and your registration will be accomplished completely on-line.

E valuate: Deciding Whether You Are in the Classes You Need

Picture this horror story:

You receive your grade report from the previous term. You're excited because you know you've done well. You're especially looking forward to seeing your Spanish grade because you know you were on the borderline between an A– and a B+. Instead you're astounded to see that not only is there no grade listed for the Spanish class, but you've received an F in a French class that you didn't even take. That F pulls down your grade average, and at the bottom of your grade report is an announcement that you are on academic probation.

Here's the explanation: Because of an error during registration, you were never formally enrolled in the Spanish course, even though you actually spent the entire term attending classes in the course. To compound the mistake, your instructor never noticed that you weren't on her class roster. At the end of the term, when she was filling out her grade report, she didn't notice that your name wasn't listed. So no grade was reported for Spanish.

At the same time, the instructor of the French class in which you were erroneously enrolled had to give you a grade at the end of the semester. Because you never completed any assignments or took any tests, your average for the semester was 0—warranting an F for the term. That F is what appeared on your grade report.

The situation—which is far more likely to occur at a large university than a small college—might be seen as a comedy of errors if it weren't so painful. Fortunately, if this were actually your story, it would most likely have a happy ending—eventually. You would go to your college registrar, who would be able to tell you what to do to get the F erased and the appropriate grade added. Still, undoing the cascade of errors would take time and a considerable amount of effort. Difficulties such as these are encountered by a surprising number of students every term. Many problems, however, can be avoided with a bit of "due diligence" on the part of the student. One key is to evaluate your success in registering.

Before the term starts, your school will provide you with a list of courses in which you are enrolled for the upcoming term. Immediately look it over. Use the following checklist to determine how successful your efforts to register have been:

- Are the courses to which you are assigned the ones you wanted?

- Are the times accurate? Are there any conflicts?

- Have any substitutions been made?

- Are you registered for the number of credits that you wanted to be registered for?

If there are any problems, try to correct the situation immediately. If there has been a clerical error, you should pay a visit to the registrar's office. Sometimes, though, you'll find that there was no mistake. Class sizes are almost always limited, and not every student who wants to enroll can do so, either because of physical limitations (the room can hold only a certain number of

Teaching Tip: While academic planning usually focuses on what courses students need to take for graduation, we need to encourage students to consider taking a few courses just for fun that may enrich their lives but that don't fall into any required category.

students) or because of educational considerations (learning may be maximized when only a small number of students are in the class).

When a course is overbooked, you have several alternatives. One is to sign up for another section of the course that is not overbooked. Another is to attempt to register for an entirely different course.

Finally, you may appeal directly to the course instructor. Instructors sometimes will permit particularly interested or motivated students to enroll in the class, even if the official capacity has been reached. You may find that approaching an instructor with a polite request may yield you a slot in the course after all.

If none of these alternatives works, you will have to add a course to the ones you have already registered for. How do you add courses after the registration period has ended? Typically, you'll need to complete a special form. Depending on the timing of your request, the form may require the signature of the instructor whose course you are adding.

IM Link: "Teaching the Text," Chapter 11—Sections IV and VIII. Have students complete the four-year plan activity. Even if they do not stay with that specific major, the process will give them a sense of how essential it is to plan ahead.

"Help—I Can't Get into the Courses That I Need in Order to Graduate!"

For some students, their efforts to register result in utter disaster. Sometimes most or all of their first choices are unavailable, and they end up enrolled in only a few of the courses they had requested. Or perhaps they cannot get into the one crucial course required for graduation.

Whatever the problem, there are several steps you can take to improve the situation:

- **Don't despair—act!** There is virtually no academic problem that can't be solved in some way. Focus your energies on finding a creative solution to the problem.

In distance education, you can take classes at another institution without physically having to be on that campus. Although taking courses online can help you fulfill graduation requirements, make sure before you register that your own college will accept the course credits. What do you think the future of distance education will be?

- **Identify classes that are still available and enroll in them.** There are probably many classes offered at your college that are still available. Registrars or departments often maintain lists of classes that have many openings.

- **Talk with your advisor.** Perhaps what you think of as an absolute requirement can be waived or appealed. Or maybe some other course can substitute for a particular required course.

- **Speak with individual course instructors.** It may be that the instructor of the course you need will make an exception and permit you to enroll, given that you must take the course for some pressing reason.

- **Consider taking a must-have, required course at another college.** If you live in an area where there are other schools in the vicinity, it may be possible to enroll in a course that you simply *must* take at another school. It also may be possible to take the course using distance learning. In **distance learning,** courses are taught at some other institution, and students participate via either video technology or the World Wide Web.

   Before you take a course offered by a college other than your own, make sure that you'll receive credit for the course at your school. Also keep in mind that you'll probably have to pay for courses offered by other schools over and above what you've already spent for your own school's tuition.

Distance learning
The teaching of courses at another institution, with student participation via video technology or the World Wide Web

R ethink: Learning What You Love and Liking What You Learn in College

Take one step back. No, make that two steps back.

Stepping back and taking stock of where you are in your course of studies and where you're headed are absolutely essential tasks. In fact, they are among the most important things you can do during your college career. They can spell the difference between plodding through your courses, focused only on day-to-day deadlines and tribulations, and, alternatively, gaining a sense of satisfaction as you progress toward your own goals and see yourself growing as a person.

Taking stock of your course of studies is not something you need to do every day, or once a week, or even once a month. But you should do it, without fail, at least once every term. Circle a date on your calendar so you'll be sure to do it, and treat it no differently than any other deadline you simply can't miss.

When you do take stock, answer the questions in Try It 4 on page 280. If you're satisfied with your answers, feel affirmed in the choices you've made. You're on the right track, and you should feel secure in the knowledge that you're getting from college what you wish and aspire to.

On the other hand, if you're less than satisfied with the answers you come up with, take action. Choose courses in the future that better match your goals. Consider changing your major to one that more closely reflects what you want to get out of college. And, if you're truly unhappy with the way your college career is proceeding, consider changing colleges.

Whichever course you choose, don't accept being dissatisfied with your college career. There are few times in our lives when we have the opportunity to partake of an experience that has the potential to raise us to new intellectual

Discussion Prompt: So much emphasis is placed on academic planning and career choice—moving through life expeditiously, making a good living, etc. that we often lose sight of the value of loving what we do. Have your students share their dreams for the future with their classmates.

Try It! 4

Working in a Group
Reflect on Your College Experience

As you proceed in college, it's a good idea to take a few moments at regular intervals (e.g., once a term, once a year) to rethink your entire college experience. With a small group of classmates, discuss your reactions to the following topics and questions:

Course Work

- Are my courses moving me toward my educational, career, and personal goals?

- Are the classes I'm taking helping me to meet my short- and long-term goals?

- Are the classes I'm taking meeting my expectations?

Personal Commitment

- Am I working hard to get the most out of the classes I'm taking?

- Am I doing my best in every class?

- Am I keeping the goal of learning—apart from doing well in classes—in mind as I progress through my classes?

Personal Growth

- What personal growth am I experiencing?

- Am I becoming closer to the person I want to be?

- Are my critical-thinking abilities growing?

College

- Is my school providing me with the best educational experience possible?

- Am I learning not only in the classroom but outside the classroom?

- Am I learning from my fellow students as well as my instructors?

Changes

- Is there anything (my course selections, my major, or my college) that I should consider changing?

- Have I made the best choices in the past, and how can I remedy mistakes that I have made?

and emotional heights. College should be intellectually enlightening and exciting. We should be able to see how our education is preparing us for the rest of our lives. The worst thing we can do is let the time slip away without being confident that our college experience is the best experience possible.

Taking stock of your choice of courses and academic career also helps you with another important choice you will have to make: Choosing your major.

Choosing a Major

You attend a family gathering and encounter relatives you haven't seen for a while. What's the first question they ask when you say you're attending college? You can bet on it: "What's your major?"

Teaching Tip: Service learning is an excellent way to help students focus on potential majors. You may want to do a service project as a class activity. Remember that it is important to assign and evaluate students' written reflections of the experience.

Although one could argue that there are lots of other important questions that you could be asked—"What interesting things have you learned?" comes to mind—having a major focus of study *is* an important part of college. A major, a field of specialization requiring a particular course of study, is important because it focuses what we study, leading us to become experts in a specific area.

Some students know what they wish to major in when they begin college. In contrast, other students don't have a clue what they wish to major in when they start college. That's fine. No one says you should know.

In fact, using your first year in college to explore a range of possibilities is a very good idea. You might find after taking a civics course that you have a passion for legal studies. Or a physics class may lead you to consider a major in engineering. College is meant to be a time of exploration, and leaving yourself open to the future—and the unknown—is a completely reasonable thing to do. (To begin your own exploration of majors, complete Try It 5 on page 282, "Identify Major Attractions.")

But what if you don't have any idea which major you wish to pursue? If you are still in your first year of college, you have plenty of time to make up your mind. But here are some approaches that should help. You may also want to review the discussion of decision making in Chapter 10 as the time to declare a major (usually by the end of your sophomore or the beginning of your junior year) draws nearer.

1. **Celebrate your indecision.** If you don't have to make a decision for some time, take advantage of the situation. Enjoy the fact that you're uncommitted and that you have an uncommon degree of freedom.

2. **Focus on your interests.** Take a long look inward, paying attention to what your interests are. What do you most like to do in life? What are your strengths and weaknesses? What do you want to get out of life? The more you know about yourself, the easier it will become to narrow down the choices for a major.

3. **Seek the help of others.** College campuses provide many resources to help their students choose a major (and also to help narrow the

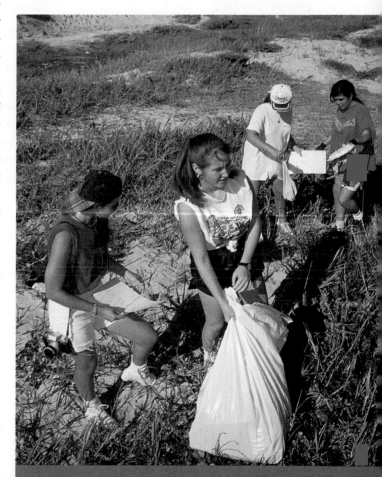

If you're having trouble choosing a major, one strategy is to consider the kinds of activities you most like doing outside the academic arena. For example, if you've enjoyed doing community service work as a volunteer, you might want to consider a major such as education, psychology, or social work that would permit you to work with underprivileged populations.

Identify Major Attractions

The following chart is meant to focus your thinking on the kinds of courses and educational experiences that typify several potential fields of study. While this list is not exhaustive, it may lead you toward some unexplored territory. You should also feel free to add areas of academic study not mentioned here but offered in your college catalog. The third column is for you to check off characteristics that appear to suit you.

Field of Study	Characteristics	Is This Me?
Arts (e.g., dance, drama, music, art, creative writing)	• High interest in creative expression. • Appreciation of nonverbal communication. • Understanding of aesthetics. • Commitment to perfection. • Ability to manipulate form and shape.	
Business	• Interest in organization and order. • Ability to lead and manage people. • Interest in practical problem solving. • Ambition and interest in financial incentives. • Can-do attitude. • Ability to simplify complexity.	
Engineering sciences (e.g., engineering, computer science)	• Intense interest in solving real problems. • "Tinkerer" mentality a plus. • Extreme ability to focus on minute details. • Commitment to exactness and perfection. • Strong logical ability. • Ability to work alone for long stretches.	
Helping professions (e.g., nursing, counseling, teaching, and many areas of medicine)	• Interest in people. • Desire to solve real human problems. • Commitment to people more than to money. • Tolerance of "messy" situations with multiple, partial solutions. • Insight and creativity. • Ability to work with people.	
Humanities (e.g., English literature, history, theater, film)	• Interest in human emotions and motivations. • Interest in cultural phenomena. • Ability to integrate broad areas of study and inquiry. • Good skills of human observation. • Interest in the panorama of human life.	

choices for potential careers). Talk to other students majoring in areas that interest you. Find out what they like and don't like about the field and its requirements. You will probably find your interest in the major grows or diminishes depending on how you feel about the issues they mention.

Speak with your advisor. If you've gotten to know your advisor, he

Field of Study	Characteristics	Is This Me?
Languages and linguistics	• Interest in words, word origins, and speech. • View of language as a science. • View of literature as human expression. • Appreciation of cultural differences as scientific phenomena.	
Physical education	• Interest in physical performance. • Enjoyment of sports and athletics. • Commitment to helping others appreciate physical activity. • Patience and perseverance. • Commitment to perfection through practice.	
Physical, biological, and natural sciences (e.g., physics, astronomy, chemistry, biology, some areas of medicine)	• Enjoyment of research questions; high level of curiosity about natural phenomena. • Quantitative thinking a requirement; high comfort level with mathematics and statistics. • Minute problem-solving skills; attention at great level of detail. • Strong logical ability. • Ability to work with others.	
Social sciences (e.g., psychology, communications, sociology, education, political science, economics)	• Interest in people as individuals or groups. • Ability to think quantitatively and qualitatively. • High comfort level with mathematics and statistics. • High level of creativity and curiosity. • Ability to work with others. • Interest in theory as much as problem solving.	
Spiritual and philosophical studies	• Interest in the inner life. • Interest in highly theoretical questions. • Ability to think rigorously about abstract matters. • Appreciation of the human search for meaning.	

After you complete the chart, consider how you can use the information. Did you learn anything new about yourself or about various courses of study? Do your responses direct you toward a particular major? Do they direct you away from any major?

or she can often provide reasonable, helpful information. For instance, you may be able to find out about the strengths and weaknesses of various departments.

You can also turn to your college counseling or career center. Most colleges have offices that can provide information about the different majors, including information about career opportunities typically available to graduates with the various majors. Sometimes it's possible to take tests that will help focus your choices, pinpointing your strengths and weaknesses.

4. **Consider double-majoring—or inventing your own major.** Although it's not easy to double-major or to develop your own specialized major, each of these two options can provide the solution if you know clearly what you want to do, but find it doesn't fit a single existing major.

> "He who hesitates is sometimes saved."
>
> James Thurber, author.

A **double major** is a course of study that fulfills all the requirements for each of two majors. If you can't decide between two majors, or if you are interested in a career that overlaps two majors, this is a reasonable solution. The down side: It can be an awful lot of work. Because both majors usually carry a number of their own requirements, you may have very little freedom to pick courses other than those directly relating to one of the two majors.

Another option that some, although not all, colleges permit is the creation of a unique major geared to your own needs. Again, this is not an easy road to take because you must put together a cohesive set of courses that center upon a discipline not normally offered through a major. Furthermore, you must also get the support of a faculty member or a committee of faculty members to oversee the process.

If double-majoring or inventing a major seems too daunting, there's another option that may resolve the difficulty of choosing between two majors: majoring in one field and minoring in another. A **minor** is a secondary specialization in a discipline different from one's major. Typically students must take at least four courses in a discipline for their study to qualify as a minor.

5. **Be career-oriented, but not *too* career-oriented.** If you have a good idea about what career you wish to embark upon once you graduate,

Double major
A course of study that fulfills all the requirements for two majors

Minor
A secondary specialization in a discipline different from one's major

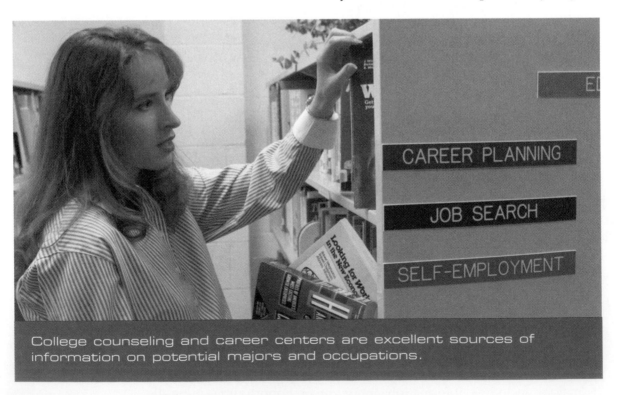

College counseling and career centers are excellent sources of information on potential majors and occupations.

you can easily find out what skills are required to be successful in that field. Knowing what you'll need to gain entry into a field can help you determine a good major that will set you on the road toward your desired profession.

Don't narrow your options too much, however. Students sometimes fear signing up for classes that don't seem to lead directly toward a career. Or they may avoid courses that seem to point them in the direction of a career that would be "unacceptable" to their parents or friends. One of the greatest sources of indecision in choosing a major stems from the mistaken notion that when you choose your major, you're also choosing a career.

Don't fall into that trap. Follow your heart—not always your head —and pursue courses without regard to how they may broaden or narrow your future job opportunities. You may discover a passion— and an aptitude—that you never knew you had.

6. **Always keep in mind that education is a lifelong enterprise.** Educational opportunities will continue to present themselves not just through the undergraduate years, but for the rest of your life.

Consequently, no matter what your choice of major, you're not precluding the possibility of taking courses in other areas in the future. You may eventually end up in a graduate school pursuing a masters degree, a doctorate, or an M.D. You also may take courses periodically at local colleges even after you graduate, enrolling in them because they will help you advance in your career or simply because they interest you.

In short, choosing a major is not a decision that sets your life on a set, unchangeable course. Instead, it's one step in what can be a lifetime of learning.

Focus on Your Interests

The following questions are intended to lead you to explore areas of personal preference and interest that should inform your choice of a major. These questions are informal and designed to be answered briefly; more-extended and formal "interest inventories" are available in your college's counseling office. You may want to explore your interests further through the use of one of those inventories.

1. Do you think you would enjoy being told exactly what to do and how to do it, or would you rather work things out by yourself, without extensive instructions or supervision? What implications might your answer have for a choice of majors?

2. Do you think you would enjoy helping other people more than earning money? Why or why not? What implications might your answer have for a choice of majors?

3. Are you ambitious and success-oriented and not ashamed to admit that you'd like to earn a lot of money, or are success and money of secondary importance to you? What implications might your answer have for a choice of majors?

4. Do you like exploring open-ended problems that probably will never be entirely resolved, or do you prefer exploring problems that offer a real chance of a practical solution? What implications might your answer have for a choice of majors?

5. Are you the artistic type and do you enjoy performing, creating, and viewing/listening to artistic works, or is art of relatively little interest to you? What implications might your answer have for a choice of majors?

6. Do you enjoy working with others, or do you prefer to work on your own? What implications might your answer have for choice of majors?

Career Connections

Choosing a Job That's Right for You

It's a question no parent can resist asking, and one that you've probably asked yourself: What kind of work are you going to do when you graduate?

Happily, it's a question you don't have to answer, at least not yet. Many students—perhaps most—don't decide what career they want until late in their academic career. After all, one of the reasons you are in college is to expose yourself to the universe of knowledge. In one sense, keeping your options open is a wise course. You don't want to prematurely narrow your options and discard possibilities too early.

In the Career Connections boxes in previous chapters, we've discussed various strategies for exploring future professions. Here, in summary, are some steps to take to identify a career:

1. **Clarify the goal of your search.** There's no single perfect career choice. Some people search for the ideal career, assuming that they need to identify the one, and only one, career for which they have been destined. The reality is, though, that there are many careers that they could choose that would make them equally happy and satisfied.

    Start with what you already know about yourself. You've already done a lot of mental work toward narrowing down a profession. Do you hate the sight of blood? Then you're probably well aware you're not cut out to be a surgeon or a veterinarian. Does the sight of a column of numbers bring an immediate yawn? Count out accounting and statistics.

    Awareness of your likes and dislikes already puts you on the road to identifying a future career. Knowing what you *don't* want to do helps identify what you *do* want to do and to narrow down the kinds of occupations for which you're more suited.

    The goal of your search is to identify several careers that would fulfill your needs and talents. Knowing that you're not seeking a single career will make the search more manageable.

2. **Gather information.** The more you know about potential careers, the better. Examine career-planning materials, read industry profiles, and visit relevant Web sites. Talk with career counselors. Discuss your options with people who work in professions in which you're interested. Find out how they chose their career, how they got their current job, and what advice they'd have for you. In addition, consider participating in an internship in a profession that you think might be attractive. As an intern, you'll gain first-hand experience—probably college credit as well—for the work that you do.

3. **Narrow down your choices.** Once you've gathered enough information to give yourself a reasonable comfort level, narrow down the choices. If it's early in your college career, you don't need to make up your mind. If it's late and you feel the pressure to choose, then make the decision. Just do it. Remember, there's no single, absolutely correct decision; there are many right decisions. And even if you make the wrong decision, there's nothing to prevent you from shifting careers later.

    Whatever it is you ultimately choose as a career, think of it only as a first step. As the average life span continues to lengthen due to advances in medical technology, most people will pass through several careers during the course of their life. By periodically taking stock of where you are and considering the things you wish for your life, you'll be in a position to make career changes that bring you closer to your ideal. In short, any career choice you make now is likely to be just the first of many.

Dealing with Academic Failure—and Success

Experiencing failure is not easy. If we take a course and fail it, it hurts, though we may pretend for a moment it doesn't. But even if you feel tempted to shrug it off publicly, don't make that mistake privately. It's important to take responsibility for and accept our failures.

However, there's a difference between accepting failure and blaming ourselves. When we fail, it's reasonable to seek to understand what went wrong. It's helpful to figure out how we can do better in the future and to take steps to avoid further failure.

On the other hand, it's not useful to spend time and energy blaming ourselves. Self-criticism, denunciation, and rebuke directed at ourselves are behaviors that don't take us forward; they keep us mired in the past.

It's important, then, to forgive ourselves for our failures. When friends and family members make a mistake, we forgive them. In the same way, we need to forgive ourselves. Our value as individuals does not decline because we've tried something and failed at it. In fact, the very act of taking on a challenge—regardless of whether the outcome is success or failure—is the true mark of our success as individuals.

> "Far and away the best prize that life offers is the chance to work hard at work worth doing."
>
> President Theodore Roosevelt

At the same time, we should not make failure a part of our lives. It's important to learn from it. We need to consider why a failure occurred, to analyze what we could have done—or avoided doing—to prevent it, and to seek ways of preventing a similar outcome in the future. Real failure occurs when we don't learn from our mistakes.

Dealing with Success   Some people have as much trouble dealing with academic success as they do dealing with failure. As we first noted in Chapter 1, fear of success is a very real factor in some people's lives. They feel that somehow they're not worthy of success—that their success is a fluke and totally undeserved.

It's simply not true. All of us deserve success, and when we achieve it, we should celebrate it. If you're doing well academically, it's not an accident. It's because you've worked hard and put your intellectual capacities to full use. Success is not something that only happens to the rich and famous. It can happen to the most inconspicuous and unknown among us.

Success occurs because we want it to and because we've worked to make it happen. It can happen every day if we allow it. Success is not just reaching an endpoint, such as when we're handed our diploma. Success is a process. Any achievement that brings us closer to fulfilling our goals and dreams should be counted as a success.

But in the same way that we need to learn from failure, we also need to learn from success. We need to consider what we did and didn't do to achieve success. We need to think about how we might repeat successful behaviors in the future—such as using a study strategy that works for us—and how we can

Teaching Tip: A critical part of academic planning is teaching your students about academic policy. Be sure to include information about calculating GPA, understanding academic "good standing," repeat policies—every institutional rule that pertains to academic progress and retention.

Speaking of Success

Name: Vincent J. Iodice

Education: Nassau Community College, Garden City, New York, Associate Degree; Touro College, Dix Hills, New York, pursuing joint bachelor's and master's degree in occupational therapy

Home: Lindenhurst, New York

Academic success comes from a number of sources. For Vincent Iodice, his sense of who he is, coupled with strong self-discipline, is the key to college success.

Iodice, whose goal is to achieve a master's degree in occupational therapy within the next few years, uses a number of strategies to achieve success. For example, before exams he tries to relax, focusing his mind. "I talk positively to myself and coach myself," he says. Furthermore, he believes strongly in meditation: "It relaxes my mind so I can absorb a lot more material in school."

A true believer in the power of positive thinking, Iodice feels that high self-esteem is closely linked to success in college. "I reward myself when I do well on an exam, and if I don't do as well as I hoped, I look at my mistakes and try to do better the next time."

But Iodice's success isn't only attributable to a positive outlook and self-confidence. He also puts in hard hours of study time.

"I try to write my notes on index cards in an outline format," he says.

"I also try to review the material every day, whether I have an exam coming up or not. I review the material once in the morning before school, again when I get home from school, and sometimes in the evening before I go to bed. For me it's always been important to reinforce what I've learned."

Iodice's success is all the more impressive because of the major obstacle he was forced to overcome: a head injury that forced him to relearn much of what he had known. But the experience left him even more motivated to succeed.

"I love to learn," Iodice says. "I work very hard and usually succeed because I have faith in my abilities," he concludes.

elaborate and extend the strategy to make the likelihood of achieving success even higher.

Finally, we need to keep in mind that life is not an either/or proposition; we're not either successes *or* failures. Even as we fail in one area, we're succeeding in others. And even as we succeed in one domain, there are other areas in which our lives may not be going so well. Keeping success and failure in perspective is a critical aspect of doing our best in both academic and nonacademic realms.

Looking
Back

How can I prepare for the academic choices that college demands?

- Making course choices involves finding out as much as possible about what your college has to offer. The college catalog is the best initial source of this information.

- The most personal source of information and guidance in college are college advisors, who have training and experience in advising students on courses, instructors, requirements, and regulations.

What is the best way to choose courses and ensure I'm getting the most out of my studies?

- In choosing courses, you should check out their selections with your academic advisor and then register for the courses. You should be prepared to choose different courses or course sections if your initial selections are unavailable.

- You should verify that you have received your chosen courses, that the schedule of courses makes sense, and that your course schedule will help provide the number of credits needed to graduate.

- Be prepared to deal with errors during registration or to cope with the unavailability of courses that you need to take.

- Reflect on your college experience regularly, verifying that course choices, academic performance, personal growth, choice of major, and your overall educational experience are satisfactory.

How can I choose a major?

- Choosing a major first involves accepting a period of indecision, finding out more about yourself, seeking the help and advice of others, considering going beyond the traditional structure of your college major, trying out unusual courses, and taking career plans into account.

How can I deal with academic failure and success?

- Failure and success are part of everyone's life.

- We need to learn to take responsibility for both our failures and our successes.

Key Terms and Concepts

College advisor (p. 270)
Distance learning (p. 279)
Double major (p. 284)
Major (p. 270)
Minor (p. 284)

Prerequisites (p. 270)
Register (p. 275)
Registrar (p. 271)
Transcript (p. 271)

Resources

On Campus

The obvious choice for information about courses is your advisor. Sometimes your advisor will be associated with a general program, such as liberal arts; sometimes with a particular department, such as English or Sociology; or sometimes with a collegewide academic advising center. Your course instructors also can often give good advice about what future courses to sign up for. Finally, don't forget about your fellow students; they can be an excellent source of information about the most interesting and exciting courses. In fact, some colleges publish students' course evaluations, which can provide valuable insights about particular courses and instructors.

In Print

The third edition of Richard Blumenthal and Josepha Despres's *Major Decisions: A Guide to College Majors* (Wintergreen, 1996) provides a good overview of college majors. To get help in deciding what to major in, consult Linda Andrew's *How to Choose a College Major* (VGM Career Horizons, 1997). Probably the most popular guide to careers is *What Color Is Your Parachute* (Ten Speed Press, 1999). In it you'll find ways to make decisions about choosing (and changing) professions, as well as ways to obtain a job.

On the Web

The following sites on the World Wide Web provide the opportunity to extend your learning about the material in this chapter. (Although the Web addresses were accurate at the time the book was printed, check the P.O.W.E.R. Learning Web site [http://mhhe.com/power] for any changes that may have occurred.)

www.collegeedge.com/CM/

This site offers an enormous amount of information related to choosing a course of study, as well as a career. You can find information on choosing the right major, as well as interviews with students in popular majors. Get the inside scoop on how to expand your college and university options. You can even get help selecting a career that matches your goals and interests.

www-osf.wesleyan.edu/deans/sophmajor.html

Guide to Choosing a Major. This site is maintained by Wesleyan University to help students through the process of deciding on a major. Though some of the information is tailored specifically to Wesleyan, many of the ideas are helpful for students at any college or university. Even if you've already decided on a major, this site can help you to examine and reevaluate your academic priorities.

www.uic.edu/depts/advisenet/stunet.htm

This site is maintained by the University of Illinois at Chicago with university undergraduate students in mind. Its purpose is to provide students with useful links on the Internet that can help them assess themselves, choose a course of study, or even prepare for getting a job.

Taking It to the Net

1 Colleges usually have a set of core courses that each student must take in order to fulfill the liberal arts education requirement. Visit a college Web site and see if you can determine the core requirements for that school. How many science courses are required? How many math courses? Are any other types of courses required?

2 Use different search engines to help you locate information about selecting classes or majors. Go to Excite (**www.excite.com**), Yahoo! (**www.yahoo.com/**), and AltaVista (**www.altavista.digital.com/**) and type in the key words "choosing college classes." Look over the first few pages in each search. Did they offer any helpful information on choosing classes or majors? Are there any common tips that are offered by most or all of the sites?

The Case of . . .

Major Problems

As Chen Lee began his junior year, he still was unsure which major to choose. He had come to college as an "undeclared major," and that was still his official designation—although he thought "clueless major" would be a more accurate label.

Chen had thought seriously about several possibilities, including communications and marketing, but none seemed to offer just what he was looking for. Part of the trouble was, of course, that he really didn't know what he was looking for. In fact, he was a lot clearer about what he *didn't* want to major in than what he *did* want to major in.

The clock was ticking away, and he felt lost. His parents offered many suggestions, but that just seemed to increase the pressure. And now he was getting warnings from the school that he had to make a decision.

1. What seems to be Chen's main problem in coming to grips with the choice of a major?

2. How can Chen's prior consideration of majors such as communications and marketing help him move closer to a decision?

3. How would you advise Chen to make use of his understanding of what he *doesn't* want to major in?

4. How can Chen find out more about himself? Why is this important in choosing a major?

5. Do you think Chen is taking this decision too seriously or not seriously enough? What advice would you give him about the importance of the choice of a major?

Getting Along with Others

12

ablinasian.

That's the word coined by star golfer Tiger Woods to describe his racial heritage. "Cablinasian" means a mix of Caucasian, Black, Indian, and Asian, and it was a label he didn't find on forms asking for his racial identity when he began college.

But Woods did not want to fit himself into some arbitrary racial category. His mother is from Thailand and his father is an African-American, and none of the standard racial categories were appropriate to describe him.

But to Woods, it didn't matter. His background is less important than who he is now and where he is going in the future. "I'm just who I am," he told one interviewer, "whoever you see in front of you."[1]

Looking
Ahead

Whether you have skin that is black or white or brown, are Jewish or Muslim or Greek Orthodox, were born in Cuba or Vietnam or Boise, are able-bodied or physically challenged, college presents new opportunities with regard to diversity and your relationships with others. Because almost every college draws students from a wider sphere than the average high school, college permits you to encounter people with very different backgrounds from your own. If you take the opportunity to form relationships with a wide variety of individuals, you will stretch your understanding of the human experience and enrich your life.

In this chapter, we consider how social diversity and relationships affect your college experience. We examine the increasing diversity of U.S. society and college campuses and consider the meanings and social effects of race, ethnicity, and culture. We look at practical strategies for acknowledging—and shedding—prejudice and stereotypes and for being receptive to others on their own merits.

Next we discuss relationships from a broader perspective, exploring ways that you can build lasting friendships with others. Finally, the chapter discusses the conflicts that can arise between people and what you can do to resolve them.

In short, after reading this chapter you'll know the answers to these questions:

- **Why is the increasing racial, ethnic, and cultural diversity of society important to you?**

- **How can you become more at ease with differences and diversity?**

- **How can you build lasting relationships and deal with conflict?**

Becoming Comfortable In a World of Diversity

No matter where we live, our contacts with others who are racially, ethnically, and physically different from us are increasing. The Internet and World Wide Web are bringing people from across the globe into our homes, as close to us as the computer sitting on our desk. Businesses now operate globally, so co-workers are likely to come from many different countries and cultures. Being comfortable with people whose backgrounds and beliefs may differ from our own is not only a social necessity, but it is virtually a requirement for career success.

By the mid-twenty-first century, the percentage of people in the United States of African, Hispanic, Asian, and Arabic ancestry will be greater than the percentage of those of white European ancestry—a profound statistical shift. College enrollments will mirror these changes, as what once were considered minority populations turn into the majority. You can examine the diversity of your own campus by completing Try It 1, "Determine the Diversity of Your Campus Community" on page 296.

Student Alert—What backgrounds do your students bring to the classroom? Ask them to describe their high schools, families, and home communities. See the Journal Reflection on p. 299. Compare this to the information you discover in Try It 1.

Race, Ethnicity, and Culture

Are you African-American or black? Caucasian or white or Euro-American? Hispanic or Latino? American Indian or Native American?

The language we use to describe our ethnic and racial group membership, and those of other people, is in constant flux. And what we call people matters. The subtleties of language affect how people think about members of particular groups, and how they think about themselves.

One of the difficulties in understanding diversity is that many of the terms we use are ill-defined and often are overlapping. The term **race** is generally used to refer to obvious physical differences that set one group apart from others. According to such a definition, whites, blacks, and Asian Americans

Race
Biologically determined physical characteristics that distinguish one group from others

Our cultural heritage plays an important role in shaping who we are.

Try It!

1

Determine the Diversity of Your Campus Community

Try to assess the degree of diversity that exists at your college, and the overall attitude toward diversity on your campus, by answering these questions. When thinking of diversity, remember to include the many different ways in which people can be different from one another, including race, ethnicity, culture, sexual orientation, physical challenges, and so on.

Overall, how diverse would you say your campus is?

What is the nature of your college's student diversity in terms of statistics regarding student membership in different racial, ethnic, or cultural groups?

What is the nature of your college's faculty diversity in terms of statistics regarding faculty membership in different racial, ethnic, or cultural groups?

Are many courses available that directly address diversity as an issue? (A good place to check is your college catalog listing of courses in the social sciences and humanities.)

Does your college have an explicit statement of policy and principles relating to diversity and/or the avoidance of discrimination?

Was diversity discussed during your orientation to the campus?

Look back at your answer to the first question ("Overall, how diverse would you say your campus is?") and answer the question again. Did your response change?

are typically thought of as different races, determined largely by biological factors.

Ethnicity refers to shared national origins or cultural patterns. In the United States, for example, Puerto Ricans, Irish, and Italian Americans are categorized as ethnic groups. However, ethnicity—like race—is very much in the eye of the beholder. For instance, a Cuban American who is a third-generation citizen of the United States may feel few ties or associations to Cuba. Yet whites may view her as "Hispanic," and blacks may view her as "white."

Ethnicity
Shared national origins or cultural patterns

Finally, **culture** comprises the learned behaviors, beliefs, and attitudes that are characteristic of an individual society or population. But it's more than that: Culture also encompasses the products that people create, such as architecture, music, art, and literature. Culture is created and shaped by people, but at the same time it creates and shapes people's behavior.

Race, ethnicity, and culture shape each of us to an enormous degree. They profoundly influence our view of others, as well as who we are. They affect how others treat us, and how we treat them in turn. They determine whether we look people in the eye when we meet them, how early we arrive when we're invited to dinner at a friend's house, and even, sometimes, how well we do in school.

Culture
The learned behaviors, beliefs, and attitudes—as well as the products people create—that are characteristic of an individual society or population

Cultural competence
Knowledge and understanding about other races, ethnic groups, cultures, and minority groups

Building Cultural Competence

We're not born knowing how to drive a car or cook. We have to learn how to do these things. The same is true of developing a basic understanding of other races, ethnic groups, cultures, and minority groups. Called **cultural competence,** this knowledge of others' customs, perspectives, background, and history can also teach us a great deal about ourselves.

The building of cultural competence proceeds in several steps, as outlined in the P.O.W.E.R. Plan to the right.

Discussion Prompt: Ask your students: What are the defining characteristics of your culture?

P repare: Accepting Diversity As a Valued Part of Your Life

In the title of her book on social diversity, psychologist Beverly Tatum asks, "Why Are All the Black Kids Sitting Together in the Cafeteria?"[2] She might just as well have asked a similar question about the white kids, the Asian-American kids, and so forth. It often appears as if the world comes already divided into separate racial, ethnic, and cultural groups.

It's more than appearances: We form relationships more easily with others who are similar to us than with those who are different. It's easier to interact with others who look the same as we do, who come from similar backgrounds, and who share our race, ethnicity, and culture because we can take for granted certain shared cultural assumptions and views of the world.

But that doesn't mean that easy and comfortable are good. We can learn a great deal more, and grow and be challenged, if we seek out people who are different from us. If you look beyond surface differences and find out what motivates other people, you can become aware of ways of thinking about family, relationships, earning a living, and the value of education that are very different from your own. It can in fact be

PREPARE
Accept diversity as a valued part of your life

ORGANIZE
Explore your own prejudices and stereotypes

WORK
Develop cultural competence

EVALUATE
Check your progress in attaining cultural competence

RETHINK
Understand how your own racial, ethnic, and cultural background affects others

P.O.W.E.R. Plan

Career Connections

Diversity in the Workplace

Diversity issues are a part of today's workplace. For example, in one California computer assembly company with 3,200 employees, 40 different languages and dialects are spoken among people representing 30 nationalities.[3] Furthermore, employers must deal with issues ranging from whether time off for religious holidays should count as vacation time to whether the partner of a gay or lesbian worker should be covered by the worker's medical insurance.

The gulf in the workplace between people with different cultural backgrounds may be wide. For instance, an immigrant from Japan might consider it the height of immodesty to outline his or her accomplishments in a job interview. The explanation? In Japan, the general cultural expectation is that people should stress their incompetence; to do otherwise would be considered highly immodest.

The increasing diversity of the workplace means that increasing your cultural competence will serve you well. It will help you perform on work-group teams that are composed of people of different races and ethnic backgrounds; it will help you supervise people whose native language and customs may be different from yours; and it will help you to work for a boss from another country and cultural background.

Equally important, gaining cultural competence will help you respond to the legal issues that surround diversity. It is illegal for employers to discriminate on the basis of race, ethnic background, age, gender, and physical disability. Cultural competence will help you deal not only with the letter of the law, but understand why embracing diversity is so important to getting along with others in the workplace.

liberating to realize that others may hold very different perspectives from your own and that there are many ways to lead your life.

Letting diversity into your own life may not be simple or easy, but it's incredibly helpful in and important to achieving your own growth and understanding. Understanding diversity also has very practical implications: As we discuss in Career Connections, "Diversity in the Workplace," learning to accept and work with people who are different from you is a crucial skill that will help you in whatever job you hold.

Organize: Exploring Your Own Prejudices and Stereotypes

Arab. Lesbian. African-American. Hispanic. Female.

Quick: What comes into your mind when you think about each of these labels? If you're like most people, you don't draw a blank. Instead, a collection of images and feelings comes into your mind, based on what you know, have been told, or assume about the group.

The fact that we don't draw a blank when thinking about each of these terms means that we already have a set of attitudes and beliefs about them and the groups they represent. Acknowledging and then examining these preexisting assumptions is a first step toward developing cultural competence. We need to explore our own prejudices and stereotypes to know where we're starting from.

Prejudice refers to evaluations or judgments of members of a group that are based primarily on membership in the group, rather than on an individual's particular characteristics. For example, the auto mechanic who doesn't expect a woman to understand the repair he is undertaking or the supervisor who finds it unthinkable that a father might want to take a child care leave are engaging in gender prejudice, evaluating individuals on the basis of their being a male or female and not on their own specific characteristics or abilities. Similarly, prejudice can be directed toward individuals because of their race, ethnic origin, sexual orientation, age, physical disability, or even degree of physical attractiveness.

Prejudice is maintained by **stereotypes,** beliefs and expectations about members of a group that are held simply because of their membership in the group. For example, do you think that women don't drive as well as men? Do you agree that "white men can't jump"? Do you believe that people raised in the jungles of South America are less intelligent than those raised in a Western society? Do you think that people on welfare are lazy? If you answered yes to any of these questions, you hold stereotypes about the group being referred to. It is the degree of generalization involved that makes stereotypes inaccurate. Some white men *can't* jump. But the fact is, many can—and do—and the stereotypes ignore this diversity.

In order to develop cultural competence, it's important to identify our prejudices and stereotypes and to fight them. Sometimes they are quite subtle and difficult to detect. For instance, a wealth of data taken from observation of elementary school classrooms shows that teachers often are more responsive to boys than to girls. The teachers don't know they're doing it; it's a subtle, but very real, bias.

Why does this happen? In part it's because we're exposed to stereotypes from a very young age. Parents and relatives teach them to us, sometimes unwittingly, sometimes on purpose. The media illustrate them constantly, and often in very subtle ways. For instance, African-Americans and Latinos are often portrayed as unemployed or as criminals, and women are less likely than men to be shown as employed.

But it's not only stereotypes that lead us to view members of other groups differently from those of our own. For most people, their own membership in a cultural or racial or ethnic group is a source of pride and self-worth. There's nothing

Journal Reflections

Thinking about Race, Ethnicity, and Culture

1. Were race and ethnicity discussed in your family? In what ways?

2. In what ways has your race or ethnicity affected your schooling?

3. In what ways has your race or ethnicity affected your social life?

4. If you are a member of a majority group, imagine yourself as a member of a minority group. In what ways would your childhood and adolescence have been different? If you are a member of a minority group, perform this exercise in reverse.

5. Are you proud of your ethnicity? Why? What traces of ethnicity do you show?

6. What are some cultural differences between you and members of *other* races or ethnicities?

7. How many "cultures" can you identify among your fellow students? Among your friends?

8. Have you taken steps to learn more about persons of another race, ethnicity, or culture? What steps might you take in the future?

Try It! 2

Check Your Stereotype Quotient

Do you hold stereotypes about other people? How pervasive do you think they are? Respond to the following informal questionnaire to get a sense of your susceptibility to stereotyping.

1. When you see five African-American students sitting together in the cafeteria, do you think that they are exhibiting racism? How is your reaction similar or different when you see five white students sitting together in the cafeteria?

2. When you are speaking with a person who has a speech-related disorder such as stuttering, are you likely to conclude that the person is less intelligent than a fluent speaker?

3. When an elderly woman can't remember something, do you assume her forgetfulness is because she is old or perhaps has Alzheimer's disease?

4. When an attractive blonde female student states an opinion in class, are you surprised if the opinion is intelligent and well expressed?

5. If a person with a mobility disorder turns down your offer for assistance, would you be offended and resentful?

Prejudice
Evaluations or judgments of members of a group that are based primarily on membership in the group, and not on the particular characteristics of individuals

wrong with this. However, these feelings can lead to a less desirable outcome: the belief that their own group is superior to others. As a result, people inflate the positive aspects of their own group and belittle groups to which they do not belong. The bottom line is continuing prejudice.

In order to overcome stereotypes and to develop cultural competence, we must first explore and identify our prejudices. To begin that process, complete Try It 2, "Check Your Stereotype Quotient."

W ork: Developing Cultural Competence

Stereotypes
Beliefs and expectations about members of a group that are held simply because of their membership in the group

Although it's neither easy nor simple to to increase your understanding of and sensitivity to other cultures, it can be done. Several strategies are effective:

- **Study other cultures and customs.** Take an anthropology course, study religion, or learn history. If you understand the purposes behind differ-

6. When you meet a student with a Hispanic or Asian last name, are you surprised if he or she speaks fluent, unaccented American English?

7. When an African-American student whom you don't know joins an athletic team you're on, are you secretly happy because you believe he or she will be a good athlete?

8. If you see a group of three large males walking toward you in the distance at night, are you more nervous if they're members of a different race from yours than if they're members of your own race?

9. If a male student and a female student ask you the same question about a technical topic you understand thoroughly, do you respond differently or in the exact same way?

Do you think you would have answered any of these questions differently five years ago? Do you think you will answer any of them differently five years from now? What experiences would make you change your responses? 🏃 Working in a group, compare your responses with those of your classmates. What similarities and differences do you see? Do you have the sense, not just from this exercise but from your general experience, that stereotypes are still prevalent?

ent cultural customs, attitudes, and beliefs, you will be able to understand the richness and meaning of other people's cultural heritage.

Many colleges offer workshops on diversity and prejudice reduction. These can help too. The important point is that understanding comes from knowledge, and you won't be able to fully appreciate others without learning about their background.

> **"Prejudice is the child of ignorance."**
> William Hazlitt, essayist.

- **Travel.** There is no better way to learn about people from other cultures than to see those cultures firsthand. College vacations offer you the time to travel, and relatively inexpensive charter flights can take you to Europe, Asia, and other places around the globe. Sometimes, in fact, it's cheaper to take a transoceanic flight than to travel to closer locations in the United States.

  If you can't afford air fare, take a car or bus ride to Mexico or Canada. In many parts of Canada, French is spoken and the culture is decidedly

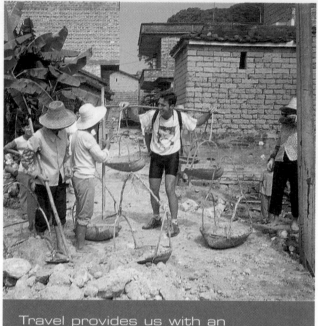

Travel provides us with an opportunity to become immersed in very different cultures and to see the world—and ourselves—through different eyes.

different from that in the United States (or the rest of Canada, for that matter). Travel needn't be international, however. If you are from the northern states, head south. If you are from California, consider heading east. No matter where you go, simply finding yourself away from home can aid your efforts to learn about other cultures by putting you in a new context.

- **Don't ignore people's backgrounds.** None of us is color blind. Or blind to ethnicity. Or to culture. It's impossible to be completely unaffected by people's racial, ethnic, and cultural backgrounds. So why pretend to be? Cultural heritage is an important part of other people's identity, and to pretend that their background doesn't exist and has no impact on them is unrealistic at best, and insulting at worst. It's important, though, to distinguish between accepting the fact that other people's backgrounds affect them and pigeonholing people and expecting them to behave in particular ways.

- **Don't treat people as representatives of the groups to which they belong.** If you're a member of a minority group, you've probably been asked how members of your group think, feel, or behave with respect to a particular issue. Somehow, as a member of the group, you're expected to know how every other member feels about a topic.

  Of course that's impossible; no single individual can speak for an entire group. Furthermore, group members are likely to display little uniformity on most issues and in most behaviors, and so this type of question is ultimately impossible to answer. In short, it makes little sense to treat others as if they were representatives of the racial, ethnic, and cultural group to which they belong.

- **Accept differences.** Different does not mean better. Different does not mean worse. Different just means not looking, acting, or believing exactly the same as you. We shouldn't attach any kind of value to being different; it's neither better nor worse than being similar.

  In fact, even people who seem obviously different on the surface probably share many similarities with you. Like you, they are students; they have fears and anxieties like yours; and they have aspirations and dreams, just as you do.

  The important point about differences is that we need to accept them. Think about some differences you may have with people who are similar to you. Perhaps you really can't stand classical music, yet one of your childhood friends has taken piano lessons since he was five and loves it. Chances are you both accept that you have different tastes and see this difference as part of who each of you is. All people want to be accepted for who they are—their abilities and talents, their attitudes and beliefs, their interests and accomplishments—not just because they are similar to you.

IM Link: "Teaching the Text," Section VII, Goals 2 and 3, offer suggestions for extending the discussion of "difference" beyond the classroom.

Evaluate: Checking Your Progress in Attaining Cultural Competence

Because cultural groups are constantly changing, developing cultural competence is an ongoing process. To evaluate where you stand, ask yourself the following questions:

- Do I make judgments about others based on external features, such as skin color, ethnic background, cultural customs, gender, weight, or physical appearance?

- Who are my friends? Do they represent diversity or are they generally similar to me?

- Do I openly express positive values relating to diversity? Do I sit back passively when others express stereotypes and prejudices, or do I actively question their remarks?

- Am I educating myself about the history and varying experiences of different racial, ethnic, and cultural groups?

- Do I give special treatment to members of particular groups, or am I evenhanded in my relationships?

- Do I recognize that, despite surface differences, all people have the same basic needs?

- Do I feel so much pride in my own racial, ethnic, and cultural heritage that it leads me to look less favorably upon members of other groups?

- Do I seek to understand events and situations through the perspectives of others and not just my own?

Teaching Tip: Films, lectures, novels and other outside readings are valuable activities for helping your students evaluate their cultural competence.

Rethink: Understanding How Your Own Racial, Ethnic, and Cultural Background Affects Others

If you are a member of a minority group, you probably don't need to be told that your race, ethnicity, and cultural background affects the way that others treat you. But even if you are a member of a majority group, the way in which others respond to you is, in part, a result of others' assumptions about the groups of which you are a part.

In short, both how we view others and how we ourselves are viewed are affected by the groups to which we—and others—belong. But keep this in mind: No matter how different other students are from you in terms of their race, ethnicity, and cultural background, they undoubtedly share many of the same concerns you do. Like all of us, they question themselves, wonder whether they will be successful, and fret about what they will do for the rest of their lives. Bridging the surface difference between you and others can result in the development of close, lasting social ties—a topic we consider next.

Building Lasting Relationships

IM Link: "Teaching the Text,"
Section V, Evaluation.

Few of us lead our lives in isolation. There's a reason for this: Relationships with others are a critical aspect of our sense of well-being. The support of friends and relatives helps us feel good about ourselves. In fact, studies have found that our physical and psychological health may suffer without friendships. The social support of others acts as a guard against stress and illness.

> "I have met the most amazing individuals and made the most incredible friends in such a short amount of time."
>
> Wittenberg University student.[4]

And if we do get sick, we recover more quickly if we have a supportive network of friends.

Our relationships with others also help us understand who we are. In order to understand our own abilities and achievements, we compare them with those of others who are similar to ourselves. Our attitudes, beliefs, and values are influenced—and shaped—by others. We are who we are largely because of the people with whom we come in contact. (To learn more about your views of friendship, complete Try It 3, "Define Friendship.")

Making Friends

Although some of us naturally make friends with ease, for others making friends is more difficult. But building relationships is not a mystery. Here are several ways to go about it:

Teaching Tip/IM Link: Try It 3
is an excellent tool for
evaluating your students and
providing feedback. See
Teaching the Text, Section IV,
Evaluation.

- **Invest time in others.** There's no better way to demonstrate that you are interested in being friends than investing time. Relationships need to be nourished by the commitment of time. You can't expect friendships to flourish unless you spend time with people.

- **Reveal yourself.** Good friends understand each other. The best way to make that happen is to let others get to know you. Be open and honest about the things you like and dislike. Talk about where you come from, what your family is like. Find out about the other person. Having a deeper understanding of where someone comes from not only helps build bridges between people of different racial and ethnic backgrounds, it also helps build friendships. By honestly communicating your beliefs and attitudes, you give others the chance to learn those things you have in common—which, despite surface differences, may be substantial when it comes to basic values and approaches to the world.

- **Let others know you like them.** It may seem scary, but don't be coy and try to pretend you are uninterested in the friendships of others. Take the risk of being rebuffed. You don't have to announce outright that you like someone. Instead, reveal your interest in a friendship by inviting the person to do something with you or simply by engaging in conversation, sharing something about your life. Your actions will speak louder than words.

- **Accept others as they are, not as you would like them to be.** One mark of friendship is acceptance of people the way they are, warts and all, and

Try It!
3

Define Friendship

Everyone has a personal understanding of what friendship is, but different people may define it differently. Answer the following questions to sharpen your personal definition of friendship.

1. How important are close personal relationships to you?

2. Approximately how much time do you spend on your friendships (being with, talking with, or corresponding with your friends)? Do you tend to initiate your contacts with your friends (e.g., are you the one to pick up the phone?), do your friends tend to initiate them, or is it about fifty-fifty?

3. How honest are you with your close friends? Do you have any friend with whom you would share even your most secret ideas, acts, and fantasies?

4. What is your style of making friends (e.g., just letting it happen or perhaps opening up to someone in the hope of reciprocation)? How do you know when an acquaintanceship has moved to a true friendship?

5. Has a friend of yours ever changed in a fairly substantial way during your friendship? What has been your reaction?

6. All things considered, how would you define *friendship,* and how would you describe what makes a good friend?

After completing these questions, ask yourself the following ones: Are you generally satisfied with your friendships? Would you like to change them in some way? Working in a group, compare your definitions of friendship, considering similarities and differences.

not the way you would like them to be. Do not impose conditions on accepting others. Keep in mind that no one is perfect and that everyone has both good and bad qualities.

- **Show concern and caring.** This is really the substance of friendship and the basis for the trust that develops between friends. Don't be afraid to show your interest in the fortunes of others and to share the sadness when they suffer some setback or loss.

- **Not everyone makes a good friend.** People who belittle you, consistently make you feel bad or unhappy, or behave in ways that violate your own personal standards are not friends, no matter what they may tell you. Choose your friends based on the good feelings you have when you are with them and the concern and caring they show for you. Friendship is a two-way street.

The R-Word: Relationships

Discussion Project: Few topics inspire college students more than relationships. Be prepared for lots of discussion, but try to direct it towards positive comments, and insist on good listening practice from non-speakers.

Relationships move beyond friendship. They occur when two people feel emotionally attached, fulfill each other's needs, and generally feel interdependent. When a true relationship exists, several components are present:

- **Trust.** Relationships must be built on a foundation of trust. We need to be able to count on others and feel that they will be open with us.

- **Honesty.** No relationship can survive if the partners are not honest with one another. Each partner must share a commitment to the truth. Your life does not have to be a completely open book—it's the rare individual who has no secrets whatsoever—but it is important to be honest about your fundamental beliefs, values, and attitudes. Those in good relationships accept one another, blemishes and all, and a relationship based on untruths or even half-truths lacks depth and meaning.

- **Mutual support.** Healthy relationships are characterized by mutual support. A partner's well-being should have an impact on you, and your well-being should affect your partner. In good relationships, the partners seek out what is best for each other, and they act as advocates for and defend each other.

- **Loyalty.** The mark of a good relationship is loyalty. Loyalty implies that relationship partners are supportive of each other, even in times of adversity and difficulty.

- **Acceptance.** Your best friend develops a love for the Dave Matthews Band and listens to their CDs seemingly without interruption. You can't stand to listen to them. Do you decide that you can no longer be friends? Of course not.

  In good relationships small annoyances don't get in the way of the deeper connection between you and another person. We don't have to like everything others do in order to maintain relationships with them. We don't even have to appreciate or approve of every aspect of their personality. What is crucial is the willingness to

What you *don't* say matters. Close, lasting relationships are often built on good listening skills.

accept others as they are, without constantly yearning for changes. All of us wish to be accepted by others as who we are, not as who they'd like us to be; we should offer the same approval to those with whom we maintain relationships.

- **Willingness to embrace change.** Change is part of everyone's life. As people grow and develop, they change. So do relationships.

  We need to accept change as a fundamental part of relationships and build upon that change. In fact, we need to welcome change. Although change brings challenges with it, it also helps us to understand ourselves and our own place in the world more accurately.

  It is only natural that some relationships will fade over time. People do outgrow one another. That's inevitable. What's important is not to live in fear that your relationship is so fragile that you have to avoid or ignore changes in who you and a partner are. Instead, both partners in a relationship should do their best to accept transformations in the relationship as a part of life.

Communicating in Relationships

Communicating well in personal relationships is a blend of talking and listening. Not only does it help to do both well, it is also important to know when it's time to listen and when it's time to speak up. Listening is an often overlooked skill in personal relationships. We may be so busy trying to communicate our feelings and interests, that we overlook the need of the other person to be heard. As friendships develop into personal relationships, simply talking isn't enough. How you express yourself, especially in moments of difficulty, can be very important to getting your message across.

Student Alert: Listening has become a lost art for many students. Their busy, electronic, multimedia world has not taught them the value of "supportive silence." Model this skill throughout the section and have students practice it in class.

Being a Good Listener: The Power of Supportive Silence

When it comes to building relationships, how you listen is sometimes more important than what you say. The silence involved in listening is a powerful force, one that can bind us more closely to others.

We've already discussed the art and science of listening as it applies to academic success in Chapter 7. The same principles that promote learning about lecture topics also promote learning about our friends. You

> "The reason why we have two ears and only one mouth is that we may listen more and talk less."
>
> Zeno of Citium.

can't call yourself a good friend without knowing what others are like and what they are thinking. Good listening is one of the ways to enhance your understanding of others.

When we are heard, we appreciate it because we get the message that our listeners care about us, not just about themselves. Similarly, when we listen, we show that we have respect for those who are speaking, are interested in their ideas and beliefs, and are willing to take the time to pay attention to them.

There are several ways you can improve your ability to listen:

1. **Stop talking!** Are you the kind of person who revels in telling stories about what happened to you? Do you wait eagerly for others to finish what they are saying so that you can jump in with a response? Do you even accidentally cut other people off or finish their sentences while they are speaking?

    No one likes to be interrupted, even in casual conversation. In more personal relationships, it really is a sign of not respecting what the other person has to say and, thus, is disrespectful of *them.*

    One way to break the habit of overtalking is to consciously slow the conversation down. Wait several seconds (mentally count to three) before making a response.

2. **Demonstrate that you are listening.** Linguists call them "conversational markers"—those nonverbal indications that we're listening. They consist of head nods, uh-huh's, OK's, and other signs that we're keeping up with the conversation. Eye contact is important too. Listening this way shows that we're paying attention and are interested in what the other person is saying.

3. **Use reflective feedback.** Carl Rogers, a respected therapist, developed a very useful way to lend support to someone and draw him or her out. In **reflective feedback,** a listener rephrases what a speaker has said, trying to echo the speaker's meaning. For example, a listener might say, "as I understand what you're saying . . . ," or "you seem to feel that . . . ," or "in other words, you believe that . . . ."

    In each case, the summary statement doesn't just "play back" the speaker's statements literally. Instead, it is a rephrasing that captures the essence of the message in different words.

    Reflective feedback has two big benefits. First, it provides speakers with a clear indication that you are listening and taking what they're saying seriously. Second, and equally important, it helps ensure that you have an accurate understanding of what the speaker is saying. If your reflective feedback is inaccurate, you can be certain that the speaker will attempt to correct your erroneous impression.

4. **Ask questions.** Asking questions shows that you are paying attention to a speaker's comments. Questions permit you to clarify what the speaker has said, and they can move the conversation forward. Further, people feel valued when others ask them about themselves.

5. **Admit when you're distracted.** We've all had those moments: Something is bothering you and you can't get it out of your mind, or you've simply got to finish something and don't really have time to chat. If at the same time someone wants to engage you in conversation, your distraction will undoubtedly show, making the other person feel you are not interested in her or him.

    The way to deal with this situation is to admit that you're distracted. Simply saying, "I'd love to talk, but I've got to finish reading a chapter" is enough to explain the situation to a classmate who wants to talk about his date. If you don't say anything, you will probably feel resentment, anger, or some other negative emotion, which will surely be conveyed to your friend.

Reflective feedback

A technique of verbal listening in which a listener rephrases what a speaker has said, trying to echo the speaker's meaning

Loneliness

Loneliness is a subjective state: We can be totally alone and not feel lonely, or we can be in the midst of a crowd and feel lonely. Loneliness occurs when we don't experience the level of connection with others that we desire. There are also different types of loneliness. Some of us feel lonely if we lack a deep emotional attachment to a single person, which can occur even if we have many friends. Others feel loneliness because they believe they don't have enough friends or relatives.

Although people may feel lonely because they have an insufficient number of relationships, the reality is that there is no standard that indicates the "right" number of relationships. Is it enough to have one or two close friends? Does having many acquaintances replace having a single enduring, close relationship? Obviously, there are no hard-and-fast rules, and you shouldn't think that there's a single standard against which to measure yourself and the number, and kind, of relationships that you have. It's something you need to decide.

What is clear is that certain situations produce loneliness. First-year college students almost always report higher degrees of loneliness than students in subsequent years of study.

On the other hand, loneliness is not inevitable. Several strategies for dealing with loneliness follow:

- **Become involved in campus activities.** Join a club. Volunteer to help some social organization. Try out for a play. You'll soon get to know others who have similar interests.

- **Find a study partner.** Ask one of your classmates to study with you. You can review your class notes, work together on a project, or study for tests together. Working together will not only help you to master the class material, it will also help you make what can become an important social connection.

- **Understand how certain circumstances lend themselves to feeling lonely.** Why are first-year students lonely? It's because they haven't had time to meet people and become well-enough acquainted with anyone to develop a true friendship. Furthermore, many of the people whom they may have relied on previously are no longer present. The combination of no new friends and unavailable old friends can easily lead to loneliness. Simply knowing the reasons for your loneliness can help you deal with it.

- **Know that you're not alone in your loneliness.** If you're feeling lonely, you may find yourself looking at your classmates and noticing groups of people engaged in social activities. This can make you feel even more isolated. Don't be fooled by such social illusions into believing that you are the only one experiencing loneliness. Remember that for every person you notice who is socializing, there are others who are not doing so.

- **Take advantage of orientation and first-year student social events.** Even if you don't consider yourself particularly good at socializing, it's

Teaching Tip: Throughout the term, you're talking about building community and about having your students become part of this academic community. This is a good check point. If students in your class still feel lonely, more serious intervention may be warranted.

Participating in campus activities is a good way to meet people with similar interests, and to avoid the loneliness that is sometimes a part of college life.

important to make the effort. If you're shy—and even if you're not—consider it a social success if you meet just one new person at such an event.

- **Take a job on campus.** Campus jobs provide not only income, but social connections as well. Through work you can meet members of the college staff and make connections with other students.

- **Remember that loneliness is a subjective—and typically temporary—state.** Whether you experience isolation depends on how you interpret your current state. If you interpret your feelings of isolation as due to your personal failings ("I'm alone because I'm not a very likable or interesting person"), you'll experience loneliness. On the other hand, if you view your isolation as a consequence of temporary, short-term factors ("Everyone has a lot of work this semester and there are few opportunities to socialize"), you're less likely to feel loneliness. In short, try to pinpoint why you're feeling lonely, and don't blame yourself for your sense of loneliness.

What if your feelings of loneliness are extreme and you experience a sense of complete isolation and alienation from your classmates? If the feeling persists, it's wise to talk to someone at your college counseling center, a health service provider, or your advisor. Although everyone feels isolated at times, such feelings shouldn't be extreme. Counselors can help you deal with them.

It's Not Just Talk: Avoiding and Handling Conflicts in Relationships

Discussion Prompt: Ask your students to describe how they deal with conflict. Before you teach new strategies for dealing with conflict, it's important to assess students' past experiences and attitudes towards conflict.

Listening communicates a great deal in personal relationships, but, as discussed previously, it is also important to put yourself forward. Generally, close relationships are built on good communication, so day to day there may be no problem in this regard. But when misunderstandings or conflicts occur—as

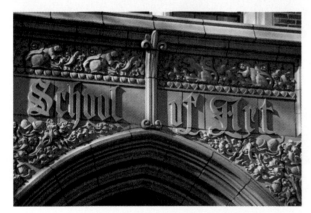

they definitely will from time to time—communication can fall apart. In these situations your ability to communicate in words is tested, and more-sensitive listening and more-careful ways of saying what you think and feel are needed.

The Subject Is "I," and Not "You"

Suppose a close friend says something with which you disagree: "All you guys are the same—you expect to get everything your way!" You might respond by directing anger at the other person, directly or indirectly accusing them of some imperfection. "You never have any ideas! You're just looking for something to complain about!" Such responses (and, as you will notice, the initial statement) typically include the word *you*. For instance, consider these possible responses to indicate disagreement: *"You really don't understand"*; *"You're being stubborn"*; and "How can *you* say that?"

The problem with such statements is that each includes the word you, putting the speaker on the defensive. These types of statements cast blame, make accusations, express criticism, and make assumptions about what's inside the other person's head. And they lead to defensive replies that will probably do

Try It! 4

Working in a Group
Switch "You" to "I"

Working in a group or in pairs, turn the following "you" statements into less aggressive "I" statements.

You Statements

1. You just don't get it, do you?

2. You never listen to what I say.

3. You don't see where I'm coming from.

4. You don't really believe that, do you?

5. You never try to see my point of view.

6. Please stop interrupting me and listen to what I'm saying for a change.

7. Stop changing the subject!

8. You're not making sense.

9. You keep distorting what I say until I don't even know what point I'm trying to make.

10. You use too many "you" statements. Use more "I" statements when you're talking to others.

little to move the conversation forward: "I do so understand"; "I'm not being stubborn"; and "I can say that because that's the way I feel."

A far more reasonable tactic is to use "I" statements. **"I" statements** cast responses in terms of yourself and your individual interpretation. Instead of saying, for example, "You really don't understand," a more appropriate response would be, "I feel we have a misunderstanding." "You're being stubborn" could be rephrased as "I feel as though you're acting in a stubborn way." And "how can you say that" becomes "I don't understand why you're saying that." In each case, "I" statements permit you to state your reaction in terms of your perception or understanding, rather than as a critical judgment about the other person. (Practice using "I" statements in Try It 4.)

"I" statements
Statements that cast responses in terms of oneself and one's individual interpretation

Chapter 12 Getting Along with Others

311

Resolving Conflict: A Win–Win Proposition Even with careful attention to putting our own feelings forward instead of making accusations, whenever two people share their thoughts, concerns, fears, and honest reactions with each other, the chances are that sooner or later some sort of conflict will arise.

Conflict is not necessarily bad.

Often, people are upset simply by the fact that they are having a conflict. It is as though they believe conflicts don't occur in "good" relationships. In fact, however, conflict is helpful in some very important ways. It can force us to say what is really on our minds. It can allow us to clear up misconceptions and miscommunications before they begin to undermine the relationship. It can even give us practice at resolving conflicts with others with whom we might not share such good relations.

Like anything else, though, there are good ways to resolve conflict, and there are bad ways. Good ways move people forward, defining the problem and promoting creative problem solving. Bad ways make the situation worse, driving people apart rather than bringing them together. The following are some fundamental principles of conflict resolution that you can use when conflict occurs in personal and professional relationships:

Teaching Tip: This is an excellent place to make career connections. Much of workplace success is based on an individual's ability to incorporate win–win attitudes and practices in everyday working situations.

- **Stop, look, and listen.** In the heat of an argument, all sorts of things that otherwise would go unsaid get said. If you find yourself making rash or hurtful statements, stop, look at yourself, and listen to what you and the other person are saying.

  Stopping works like a circuit breaker that prevents a short circuit from causing a deadly fire. You've probably heard about counting to 10 when one is angry. Do it. Take a break and count to 10 . . . or 20 . . . or more. Whether you count to 10 or 100, stopping the action gives you time to think and not react.

- **Defuse the argument.** Anger is not an emotion that encourages rational discourse. When you're angry and annoyed with someone, you're not in the best position to evaluate logically the merits of various arguments or excuses others may offer. It may feel exhilarating to get our fury off our chests in the heat of an argument, but you can bet it isn't taking anyone any closer to resolving the problem.

  Don't assume that you are 100 percent right and the other person is 100 percent wrong. Make your goal *solving the problem* rather than winning an argument.

- **Get personal.** Perhaps you've heard others suggest that you want to avoid getting personal in an argument. In one sense that's true: You don't want to accuse people you're arguing with of having character flaws that make some aspect of their behavior unacceptable.

  At the same time, you should be willing to admit personal responsibility for at least part of the conflict. The conflict would not exist without you, so you need to accept that the argument has two sides and that you are not automatically blameless. In a way this creates a little piece of ground you and the other person can work from.

- **Listen to the real message.** When people argue, what they say is often not the real message. There's typically an underlying communication— a meta-message—that is the source of the conflict.

It's important, then, to dig beneath what you're hearing. If someone accuses you of being selfish, the real meaning hidden in the accusation may be that you don't give anyone else a chance to make decisions. Remember, arguments are usually about behavior, not underlying character and personality. What people *do* is not necessarily synonymous with what they *are*.

If you rephrase the person's statement in your own mind, it moves from an insult ("You're a bad person") to a request for a change of behavior ("Let me participate in decision making"). You're much more likely to respond reasonably when you don't feel that your personal essence is under attack.

- **Show that you're listening.** It's not enough only to listen to the underlying message that someone is conveying. You also need to acknowledge the message. For example, saying something like "OK. I can tell you are concerned about sharing the burden on our group project, and I think we should talk about it" acknowledges that you see the issue and admit that it is worthy of discussion. This is a far more successful strategy than firing back a countercharge each time your partner makes a complaint.

- **If you are angry, acknowledge it.** Don't pretend that everything is fine if it isn't. Ultimately, relationships in which the partners bottle up their anger may suffer more than those in which the partners express their true feelings. If you're angry, say so.

- **Ask for clarification.** As you're listening to another person's arguments, check out your understanding of what is being said. Don't assume that you know what's intended. Saying something like "Are you saying . . ." or "Do you mean that . . ." is a way of verifying that what you *think* someone means is really what is meant.

- **Make your requests explicit.** If you're upset that your roommate leaves clothes lying around your apartment or dorm room, remarking that he or she is a "pig" shows more than that you are angry. It also shows that your intent is to hurt rather than to solve the problem.

  It's far better to be explicit in your concerns. Say something like "It would make me feel better if you would pick up your clothes from the floor." Couching your concern in this way changes the focus of the message from your roommate's personality to a specific behavior that potentially can be changed.

- **Always remember that life is not a zero-sum game.** Many of us act as if life were a **zero-sum game,** a situation in which when one person wins, the other person automatically loses. It's what happens when you make a bet: If one person wins the bet, the other person loses.

  Life is not like that. If one person wins an argument, it doesn't mean that others automatically have to lose it. And if someone loses an argument, it doesn't mean that others have automatically won. In fact, all too often conflict escalates so much that the argument turns into a lose–lose situation, where everyone ends up a loser.

  However, life can be a win–win situation. The best resolution of conflict occurs when both parties walk away with something they want. Each may not have achieved *every* goal they had, but they at least have enough to feel satisfied. (For practice in resolving conflict, do Try It 5.)

IM Link: Teaching the Text, Section VII, Goal 1. Residence life is often the first place students in your class encounter these ideas. Look at the tools residence life professionals use to teach these skills by inviting a speaker to class.

Zero-sum game
A situation in which when one person wins, the other person automatically loses

Try It! 5

Resolve That Conflict

Try to find and resolve as many conflicts as you can in the following discussion:

Todd: Wait a minute. There should be a semicolon there, not a comma.

Megan: What are you talking about? That's just a slight pause in the sentence, not a complete stop. A semicolon is too brusque. It interrupts the flow.

Todd: What are *you* talking about? Pause, brusque, flow—what *are* you, a musician or a journalist? You don't know the first thing about grammar.

Gerry: Todd's right, Meg. That pause business is just a smokescreen. With that comma, that's just a plain old lousy run-on sentence. It needs at least a semicolon, if not a period.

Sara: You guys are always picking on Megan. She's about the most creative writer on this stupid newspaper. Leave her alone and let her write. Quit taking out the old "grammar hammer" and beating her on the head with it.

Todd: Creative? Fine, she's creative. But who says you can't be creative and use good English at the same time? At least she should *try* to be literate. This is supposed to be a newspaper article, not some trashy slop overflowing with emotionalism. Let's stick with the rules of the language, okay?

Megan: Oh, don't hide behind rules. You're just into a power trip because you got the title of editor-in-chief. The truth is you and the other males on this paper can't wait to get your blue pencils out and start "correcting" every word that every woman writer puts on paper.

Gerry: Oh brother—or should I say, oh sister! Here we go with the women's movement stuff again. Let's all empower ourselves and express ourselves any way we want. Great. And let's forget everything we ever learned about journalism while we're at it. Like it or not, journalists live by principles, and English—the *mother* tongue—lives by rules.

Sara: Here come the rules again, as if grammar were some set of macho laws set in stone and handed down to Moses on the mountain. You guys are so hung up on rules you can't even communicate any more. Who's our audience—English professors? If you want rigid rules, go play football or hockey or some other hierarchical, male pastime, and leave the writing to those who can express themselves.

Can you think of several approaches for resolving each of the various conflicts? Which of the resolution possibilities you've devised do you think would work best? Are there any approaches that should be avoided?

Changing Relationships:
Surviving Endings

Not all relationships last a lifetime. Sometimes they just wind down, as the two people involved slowly lose interest in maintaining their partnership. At other times, they break apart, as disagreements build and there is not a strong enough bond to hold the two parties together. Or there may be an abrupt rupture if some event occurs that destroys one partner's feeling of trust.

Caring for others is rewarding, but risky. When relationships don't work out, their endings can be painful, even devastating, for a time. Even when re-

Speaking of Success

Name: *Kari Smith*
Education: *B.A. in English from University of California at Santa Barbara*
Home: *Santa Cruz, California*

ari Smith thought she knew what she wanted to pursue when she entered the University of California at Santa Barbara as a first-year student. "I started out as a computer science major," said Smith. "But I really didn't know what it entailed until I went through my first courses." By the end of her first year, she knew she had made a mistake. But she had no idea how to remedy the problem.

Luckily, she got some good advice from her older sister. "She told me something very simple: to experiment and take courses that seemed interesting, without regard to whether they fit in with a potential major. So the next year I took a course in Shakespeare with a fabulous professor. As a result, I was turned on to the world of literature."

"I took a series of courses on world literature, Milton, and Chaucer, and on modern literature and modern drama," Smith noted. "I began to see the connections between literature and everything else. There was a bit

UCSB

UNIVERSITY OF CALIFORNIA
SANTA BARBARA

of history, psychology, sociology, and a lot of human nature in all the literature courses I was taking."

As an added—and important—benefit, she found people on campus with whom she shared common academic interests. "As a result of taking these literature courses, I fell in with

a great group of people, and we became lasting friends," Smith added. Her friendships significantly enriched her college experience and played a central role in her development as an individual.

"I believe you have to try new things in order to find courses—and people—that you really believe in. A good basic education at the undergraduate level is the key to achieving what you want."

Although Smith had no inkling of it at the time, her future career would rely substantially on the combination of academic and interpersonal skills she developed in college. Today she works as a publisher's sales representative for McGraw-Hill, Inc., blending her love of books with her ability to relate well to customers and colleagues. For Smith, it represents a perfect combination.

we can learn to become more sensitive and emotionally aware of others. Finally, Stewart Levine's *Getting to Resolution: Turning Conflict into Collaboration* (Berrett-Koehler, 1998) suggests a variety of practical approaches to resolving conflict.

On the Web

The following sites on the World Wide Web provide the opportunity to extend your learning about the material in this chapter. (Although the Web addresses were accurate at the time the book was printed, check the P.O.W.E.R. Learning Web site [http://mhhe.com/power] for any changes that may have occurred.)

http://www.nadm.org/
　Sponsored by the National Association for Diversity Management (NADM), this Diversity Resources Online site provides a platform for disseminating information and a comprehensive resource center for aspects of diversity in education, human resources, the public sector, and the society at large. It also provides opportunities for professional networking, research, and global dialogue.

http://www.cmhc.com/psyhelp/chap13/chap13m.htm
　As a portion of the Mental Health Net's Psychological Self-Help site, this is a good starting point for developing skills in conflict resolution.

http://www.ncbe.gwu.edu/links/langcult/
　Part of the National Clearinghouse for Bilingual Education (NCBE), this site provides language and education links dealing with culture, diversity, and multiculturalism. Connect to everything from the American Folk Life Center to worldwide ethnology resources.

Taking It to the Net

1 Explore cultural differences using the Internet. Go to Yahoo! (**www.yahoo.com**), choose "Society and Culture" and then "Cultures and Groups." Click on "Cultures" and type a topic that you find interesting into the search field. Make sure to limit your search to just this category. How many pages did you find? Read and compare the information from different cultural groups.

2 Use the Internet to help find a volunteer organization that sounds interesting to you. Using either Yahoo! (**www.yahoo.com**) or AltaVista (**www.altavista.com**), enter "volunteer organizations" into the search field. Examine the volunteer organizations listed and write down the ones that sound interesting to you.

The Case of . . .

Answering for ALL

Jace Kinkaid stood out in any crowd. With his six-foot-eight height, he towered above most of his classmates. Even when he was seated at a desk, he looked huge. And since he was an African-American, his skin color set him apart from his classmates, almost all of whom were white.

Although, by and large, people were polite and nice enough to him, Jace felt isolated from most of his peers and instructors. While he had one or two good friends from high school with whom he kept in touch, he was not close to many people on campus. His isolation came to a head, however, in the most public of places: his English literature class. It happened when his instructor, a white man, was leading a discussion on *The Fire Next Time,* a novel by noted black writer James Baldwin. The instructor turned to Jace and asked him to comment on a passage from the novel.

"Does it ring true to you, Jace, as an African-American?" asked his instructor, who then went on to inquire "What do African-Americans think about the perspective that Baldwin is taking?"

Jace was taken aback. What was he supposed to say? He hardly felt like a representative of every black person. He barely knew how *he* felt, let alone everyone else who was African-American. What an absurd situation to be placed in—his instructor asking him to answer for millions of other people. He felt awful—embarrassed, upset, and angry at his instructor for putting him on the spot.

1. Why was the instructor's question so troubling to Jace? If the instructor really wanted Jace's opinion about the passage, what should he have said?

2. Would the question have had a different effect if the instructor had also been African-American? Why or why not?

3. What are some cultural assumptions that the instructor is making about Jace? About African-Americans? About white people?

4. What response might Jace make in this situation to make his feelings clear without causing excessive conflict?

Money Matters

13

David Marcheschi didn't like the taste of coffee or soda, but he needed something that would help him to stay awake while he studied late at night. He needed something else, too—a way to support himself while he attended college.

The solution to both his problems came when Marcheschi asked himself, "Why couldn't plain water be caffeinated?" After consulting with a chemist, Marcheschi discovered that it was possible to keep the clean taste of spring water while adding caffeine—and "Water Joe" was born. A bottle of Water Joe produces the same jolt as an eight-ounce cup of coffee.

As soon as it hit the market, Water Joe was a success, selling half a million bottles in its first year of sales. Customers ranged from college students to athletes seeking to boost their energy, and Water Joe is now distributed around the world.

Money problems aren't often solved as readily as they were for David Marcheschi. And, even under the best of circumstances, our finances present us with challenges that affect many facets of our lives. Money often plays a large role in where we go to school, where we live, and what jobs we take. It is the source of many of our problems and stress, forcing us to find a balance between what we need and what we want.

This chapter will show you how to manage your money. It begins by discussing the process of preparing a budget and identifying your financial goals—the basis for money management. The chapter goes on to examine ways you can keep track of your expenditures and estimate your financial needs and resources, and it discusses ways to exercise control over your spending habits and save money.

Education is one of the largest financial expenditures anyone encounters in life. Knowing the best ways to meet the costs of a college education—finding loans, grants, and scholarships—can give your finances a big boost and help you avoid graduating with thousands of dollars of debt. You will also learn what to do if your personal finances get out of control and how to stop the downward spiral of unpaid bills, defaulted loans, and unfavorable credit ratings. The chapter ends by suggesting ways to develop a financial philosophy.

In sum, after reading this chapter you'll be able to answer these questions:

- **What purpose does a budget serve and how can you prepare and stick to one?**

- **What help is available to pay for your college education?**

- **What can you do if you fall into financial difficulty?**

Managing Your Money

Do you never have quite enough cash to purchase the things you want? Do you spend more than you think you should? Do you know where your money goes?

Answering these questions and understanding the role money plays in your life is the first step of wise money management. To begin getting a grip on your finances, complete the Journal Reflections on page 325.

If you have money problems—and there's virtually no one who doesn't have at least *some* concerns about finances—the solution is to develop a budget. A **budget** is a formal plan that accounts and plans for expenditures and income. Taking your goals into account, a budget helps determine how much money you should be spending each month, based on your income and your other financial resources. Budgets also help prepare for unexpected occurrences that would reduce your income, such as the loss of a job or an illness, or for sudden, unanticipated expenses, such as a major car repair.

Budget
A formal plan that accounts for expenditures and income

> "There was a time when a fool and his money were soon parted, but now it happens to everybody."
>
> Adlai Stevenson.

Although all budgets are based on an uncomplicated premise—expenditures should not exceed income—budgeting is not simple, particularly when you are a student. There are several times during the year that require especially large expenditures, such as the start of a semester, when you must pay your tuition and purchase books. Furthermore, income is erratic; it is often lower during the school year and higher during the summers. But a budget will help you deal with the ups and downs of income and expenditures, smoothing the curves and extending your view toward the horizon. Learning budgeting skills also helps prepare you for the world of work, of which budgeting is an important aspect, as discussed in Career Connections on page 324.

Most of all, a budget provides security. It will let you take control of your money, permitting you to spend it as you need to without guilt because you

Discussion Prompt: What history and experience do your students bring to this subject? Were they involved in financial discussions in their families? Do they have any idea about their family income? Have they ever lived on a budget? Held a job? Had a checking account? Finding out the answers to these questions will help you determine your approach to this chapter.

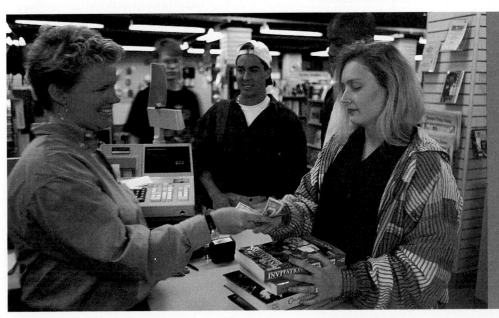

Keeping to a budget is a constant balancing act. For example, even though you know you'll need to purchase books at the start of each semester, you can't predict exactly how much they'll cost.

Career Connections

Budgeting on the Job

If you've ever held a job, the salary you received was determined, in part, by your employer's budget.

Although they may not always be accessible to every employee, budgets are part of the world of work. Regardless of who the employer is—be it a small dry-cleaning store or the massive federal government—the organization undoubtedly has a budget outlining anticipated income and expenditures. Managers are expected to keep to the budget, and if their expenditures exceed what is budgeted, they are held accountable.

For this reason, the ability to create and live within a budget is an important skill to acquire. Not only will it help keep your own finances under control, but it will prepare you to be financially responsible and savvy on the job—qualities that are highly valued by employers.

have planned for the expenditure. It also makes it easier to put money aside because you know that your current financial sacrifice will be rewarded later, when you can make a purchase that you've been planning for.

Developing a Budget

Budgeting is very personal: What is appropriate for one person doesn't work for another. For a few people, keeping track of their spending comes naturally; they enjoy accounting for every dollar that passes through their hands. For most people, though, developing a budget—and sticking to it—does not come easily.

However, if you follow several basic steps, the process of budgeting is straightforward. These steps include the following:

- **Identify your financial goals.** Your first reaction when asked to identify your financial goals may be that the question is a no-brainer: You want to have more money to spend. But it's not that simple. You need to ask yourself *why* you want more money. What would you spend it on? What would bring you the most satisfaction? Purchasing a CD player? Paying off your debt? Saving money for a vacation? Starting a business? Paying for college rather than taking out loans?

  Until you determine your short- and long-term financial goals, you simply won't be able to develop a budget that will work for you. To determine them, use Try It 1, "Identify Your Financial Goals," on page 326.

- **Find out where your money is going.** Do you open your wallet for the 10 dollars that was there yesterday and find only a dollar? Spending money without realizing it is a common affliction.

  There's only one way to get a handle on where your money is going: Keep track of it. To get an overview of your expenditures, go through any records you've kept to identify where you've spent money for the last year—old checks, rent and utility receipts, and previous college bills can help you.

  In addition, keep track of everything you spend for a week. *Everything.* When you spend 50 cents for a candy bar from a vending machine, write it down. When you buy lunch for $2.97 at a fast-food restaurant, write it down. When you buy a 20-cent postcard, write it down.

  Record your expenditures in a small notebook that you carry with you all the time. It may be tedious, but you're doing it for only a week.

And it will be eye-opening: Almost everyone is surprised at how much they spend on little items without thinking about it.

Finally, make a list of everything you think you'll need to spend over the next year. Some items are easy to think of, such as rent and tuition payments, because they occur regularly and the amount you pay is fixed. Others are harder to budget for, because they can vary substantially. For example, the price of gasoline changes frequently. If you have a long commute, the changing price of gasoline can cause substantial variation in what you pay each month. Similarly, the cost of books varies considerably from one term to another. (Use Table 13.1 on page 328 to estimate your expenditures for the coming year.)

- **Determine your income sources.** You probably have a pretty good idea of how much money you have each month. But it's as important to list each source of income as it is to account for everything you spend.

  Add up what you make from any jobs you hold. Also list any support you receive from family members, including occasional gifts you might get from relatives. Finally, include any financial aid (such as tuition reductions, loan payments, or scholarships) you receive from your college. Use Table 13.2 on page 329 to record this information. When you do, be sure to list the amounts you receive in terms of after-tax income.

- **Add it up.** Here's the acid test. Add up your list of expenses, and add up your sources of income. Which number is bigger?

  Don't be surprised if your expenditures are larger than your income. After all, if you had plenty of excess cash, you probably wouldn't be bothering to make a budget in the first place.

  Knowing the extent of the difference between income and expenses is important. For one thing, it gives you a sense of the seriousness of

My Sense of Cents

Answer the following questions about your financial sense.

1. How much money do you now have in your pockets and wallet? (Guess first, then look.) How close did you come? Explain how your answers reflect the importance of money in your life.

2. Do you know how much money you typically spend in a month on all expenditures, including food, lodging, and other items?

3. How much money do you estimate is needed each term for your college expenses, including tuition and books?

4. How would you rate yourself with regard to your ability to manage your money responsibly? What improvements are needed in this area?

5. What methods do you use to plan for future expenses? How effective have these methods been for you?

6. What are your short-term and long-term financial goals?

7. What immediate strategies would you use if you suddenly found yourself in a financial crisis and didn't have enough money to meet your obligations?

Identify Your Financial Goals

STEP 1: Use the planning tool below to identify and organize your financial goals.

Short-Term Goals

What would you like to have money for in the short term (over the next three months)? Consider these categories:

Personal necessities (such as food, clothes, household supplies, shelter, transportation, loan payments, debts, medical expenses):

Educational necessities (such as tuition, fees, books, educational tools, computer hardware and software, office hardware):

Social needs (for example, getting together with family, friends, and others; charitable contributions; clubs; teams; entertainment):

Lifestyle improvements (for example, optional but desirable personal or educational tools, computer hardware and software, living space improvements, transportation improvements, clothing "upgrades"):

Other:

Midrange goals

What would you like to have money for soon, but not immediately (from three months to a year out)? Use the same categories:

Personal necessities:

Educational necessities:

Social needs:

Lifestyle improvements:

Other:

Long-Range Goals

What would you like to have money for more than a year, but less than three years, from now? Use the same categories:

Personal necessities:

Educational necessities:

Social needs:

Lifestyle improvements:

Other:

STEP 2: *Now put each of your lists in* <u>priority</u> *order, arranging items in each list across the categories.*

Short Term Priorities:

Midrange Priorities:

Long-Range Priorities:

After you've completed prioritizing your financial goals, consider these questions: What does the list tell you about what is important to you? Did you find any surprises? Would you classify yourself as a financial risk taker or someone who values financial security? Working in a group, compare your priorities with those of your classmates. What similarities and differences do you find, and what can you learn from others' priorities?

Table 13.1

Estimated Expenditures Next 12 Months

	Now to 3 months from now	3–6 months from now	6–9 months from now	9–12 months from now
Personal Necessities				
Food				
Clothing				
Shelter (rent, utilities, etc.)				
Household supplies				
Transportation (car payments, gas, repairs, bus tickets, etc.)				
Loan and debt payments				
Medical expenses				
Other				
Educational Necessities				
Tuition and fees				
Books				
Tools and hardware				
Computer costs				
Other				
Social Needs				
Relationships				
Clubs and teams				
Charitable contributions				
Other				
Entertainment				
Movies and shows				
Trips				
Recreation and sports				
Other				
Lifestyle Improvements				
Educational				
Living space				
Computer				
Transportation				
Clothing				
Other				
TOTAL				

your financial situation. By looking at how you spend your money, you can probably find some areas where cutting back is possible, so you can adjust your budget to ensure that expenditures do not exceed income.

- **Modify your budget.** If you spend more than you make, there are only two things to do: decrease your spending or increase your income. It's of-

Table 13.2

Estimated Income Next 12 Months

	Now to 3 months from now	3–6 months from now	6–9 months from now	9–12 months from now
Wages				
Family support				
Financial Aid				
Tuition reductions				
Loan income				
Scholarship payments				
Other				
Interest and dividends				
Gifts				
Other				
TOTAL				

ten easiest to decrease expenditures because your expenses tend to be more under your control. For instance, there are many things you can do to save money, including the following:

Control impulse buying. If you shop for your groceries, always take a list with you, and don't shop if you're hungry.

Make and take your own lunch. Brown-bag lunches can save you a substantial amount of money over purchasing your lunches, even if you go to a fast-food restaurant or snack bar.

Read the daily newspaper and magazines at the library. College libraries subscribe to virtually every daily newspaper and magazine that you could want.

Check bills for errors. Computers make mistakes, and so do the people who enter the data into them. So make sure that your charges on any bill are accurate.

Cut up your credit cards and pay cash. Using a credit card is seductive; when you take out

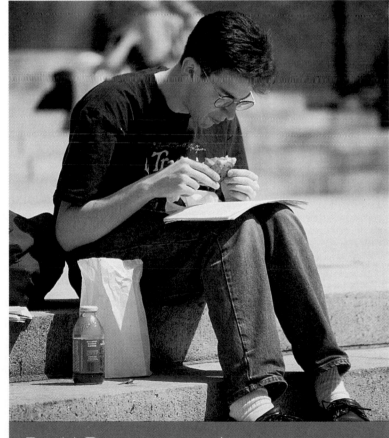

Bag it! One way to cut down on expenditures is to reduce everyday expenses, such as by making your own lunch, rather than grabbing a bite at a campus snack bar. Even small savings like this can add up fast.

your plastic, it's easy to feel as if you're not really spending money. If you use cash for purchases, you'll see the money going out.

Make major purchases only during sales. Plan major purchases so they coincide with sales.

Share and trade. Pool your resources with friends. Car pool, share resources such as computers, and trade CDs.

Live more simply. Do you really need a cellular phone or beeper? Is cable TV an absolute necessity? Is it really necessary to eat out once a week? Do you buy clothes because you need them or because you want them?

Do well in your classes. One of the best ways to save money is to get good grades, because you avoid the hidden costs of poor performance. If you receive a low final grade in a class, you may be forced to repeat the class or you may have to take another course in the future as a substitute, and that may be an added expense. Doing well avoids the possibility of additional tuition costs.

There are as many ways to save money as there are people looking to save it. But keep in mind that saving money should not necessarily be an end in itself. Don't spend hours thinking of ways to save a dime, and don't get upset about situations where you are forced to spend money. The goal is to bring your budget into balance, not to become a tightwad who keeps track of every penny and feels that spending money is a personal failure. To start the process, work on Try It 2, "Save Money."

Finally, it's important to remember that budgets may be brought into balance not only by decreasing expenditures, but also by increasing income. The most direct way to increase income is to get a part-time job if you don't already have one.

Many students work during college. Although it adds to the time-management challenges you will face, working does not mean that your grades will necessarily suffer. In fact, many students who work do better in school than those who don't work, because those with jobs need to be more disciplined and focused. It often helps to take a part-time job on campus because on-campus employers are often more sympathetic to the demands of college. On the other hand, an off-campus job may prove to be helpful in getting a job after you graduate.

Considering part-time work is often a better strategy for dealing with budget shortfalls than taking out a loan. Because student loans are relatively easy to take out, it's simple to use them as a crutch. Loans can be a help in an emergency or if you couldn't afford to attend college without them. Don't take out loans without regard to the fact that someday you'll be paying them back.

Student Alert: Freshman are often unaware of job opportunities on campus. The benefits are many—extra cash, a sense of belonging, a source of personal references, a broader sense of responsibility. Find out what resources are available on your campus, and share the information with the class, through guest speakers, student presentations, or a campus tour.

Credit Cards

"Congratulations! You've been preapproved for a Gold credit card! Just send us your signature on the enclosed authorization form, and we'll rush you your card."

Have you ever gotten such a letter in the mail? If so, you're far from the only one: Millions of people in the United States are regularly enticed to receive credit cards in just such a manner, and college students are especially at-

Try It! 2

Save Money

Use the following organizer to list ways you might reduce your monthly expenditures. Enter adjustments you could make in your daily life to decrease your expenses. Consider the amount of savings each adjustment would bring and weigh the importance that you attach to the expenditure against the size of the savings you might realize.

Expense Item	Estimated Savings per Month If Eliminated	How Important Is the Item to You? 1 = Unimportant 2 = Moderately Unimportant 3 = Moderately Important 4 = Important			
		1	2	3	4

After you have completed the list, consider whether there are other places where you could reduce spending. How much could you save by reducing these expenditures? Would the decrease in expenditures result in a significant change in your lifestyle? Could you live with this change? Can you come up with any substitutes for high-cost expenses and so reduce expenses without giving up so much?

tractive targets. In many cases, it doesn't even matter if you have income; the mere fact that you're a college student is sufficient to win you approval to receive a card.

Credit cards are not necessarily bad. In fact, used appropriately, they can help get you through brief periods when you must make a purchase—such as a car tire to replace an unexpected flat—but temporarily don't have enough money to do so. But there are several questions you should ask when deciding whether to get and use a credit card:

Try It! 3

Maintain Your Interest

Suppose you saw a $275 television set on sale "for a limited time" for $240. Suppose also that you don't really *need* a TV because your roommate has one, but the $35 discount tempts you. The trouble is you don't have $240 to spare. But you *do* have a credit card—and you decide to buy the TV with the card and pay it off over time.

The advantages of this strategy are that you get the discount and have immediate use of the television set. The main disadvantage is that you will end up paying more than the $240 figure that you have in mind as the bargain price for the TV. In fact, depending on how high your credit card's interest rate is, how long you take to pay your bill in full, and how large each monthly payment is, you may wipe out most or all of the $35 savings that caused you to make the purchase in the first place.

Suppose you have a card with an interest rate of 12 percent compounded monthly. First, because of the compounding factor, the actual annual rate is 12.68 percent. Second, because the monthly interest ($\frac{1}{12}$ of the annual interest) is calculated on the unpaid balance that remains each month, the more slowly you pay off the loan, the more money you pay for the television set.

In fact, at the end of a year, assuming you pay $10 per month toward the $240 purchase, you will have paid $120 and still have $143.61 to pay. If you wrote a check for $143.61 after the 12th month, you would have paid $263.61 for the TV, meaning your actual discount wasn't $35, but only $11.39. Would you have bought the television set if it had been marked down only $11, from $275 to $264?

If you decided to continue your $10 monthly payments for a second 12-month period, you would end up paying $35 in interest on top of the $240 purchase price—in other words, you would have driven the discount purchase price right back up to the original selling price of $275!

The 12-month calculation is illustrated in the first table on the next page. To see how much of a factor the interest rate is, complete the second table, which shows the same purchase on a credit card with a 20 percent annual (approximately 1.67 percent monthly) interest rate, compounded monthly (actual compounded annual interest rate is 21.94 percent).

1. **Is there an annual fee?** Many cards charge an annual fee, ranging from $20 a year to $100 a year, although some are free. You need to determine if the advantages of the card are worth the cost of an annual fee.

2. **What is the interest rate?** Interest rates—the percentage of the unpaid balance you are charged on credit cards—vary substantially. Some interest rates are as low as 12 percent per year, while some are as high as 25 percent per year. If the rate is 25 percent, you may be charged $250 each year if you owe an average of $1,000. Furthermore, although some interest rates are *fixed*, meaning that they don't vary from month to month, others are *variable*, which means they change each month. How much they change is tied to various factors in the overall economy. To get a better sense of how interest rates add up, consider Try It 3, "Maintain Your Interest."

3. **Do I need a credit card?** There are good reasons for getting a credit card, and bad reasons.

Teaching Tip: Consider bringing play money to class to demonstrate the point made in Try It 3. It will be more dramatic with dollars changing hands among class members.

How much would the $240 TV set cost if you bought it with this card, paying $10 per month for 12 months and then paying the remaining balance by check? How does this compare to the original purchase price of $275?

Credit Card Payments: 12% Interest, Compounded Monthly (1% per month)

	Month 1	2	3	4	5	6	7	8	9	10	11	12
Unpaid balance	$240.00	$232.40	$224.72	$216.97	$209.14	$201.23	$193.24	$185.18	$177.03	$168.80	$160.49	$152.09
Plus interest of	2.40	2.32	2.25	2.17	2.09	2.01	1.93	1.85	1.77	1.69	1.60	1.52
Minus payment of	10.00	10.00	10.00	10.00	10.00	10.00	10.00	10.00	10.00	10.00	10.00	10.00
Balance Due	$232.40	$224.72	$216.97	$209.14	$201.23	$193.24	$185.18	$177.03	$168.80	$160.49	$152.09	$143.61

Credit Card Payments: 20% Interest, Compounded Monthly (approx. 1.67% per month)

	Month 1	2	3	4	5	6	7	8	9	10	11	12
Unpaid balance	$240.00	$234.01	$227.92	$221.72	$215.42							
Plus interest of	4.01	3.91	3.81	3.70								
Minus payment of	10.00	10.00	10.00	10.00	10.00	10.00	10.00	10.00	10.00	10.00	10.00	10.00
Balance Due	$234.01	$227.92	$221.72	$215.42								

The Pluses of Credit Cards

- **Establishing a good credit history.** If you've ever owed money to a bank or your college, a computer file exists describing your payment history. If you have never missed a loan payment and always pay on time, you have a good credit history. If you haven't paid on time or have missed payments, your history has negative marks against it. Negative information can stay in a file for seven years, so it's important to establish and keep a clear credit history. Using a credit card moderately, never exceeding your credit limit, and paying on time will help you establish a good credit history. (You can get a copy of your credit report; complete Try It 4, "I Know What You Did Last Summer" on page 335.)

- **Emergency use.** Few of us carry around enough cash to deal with emergencies. A credit card can be a life saver if we're on a trip and the car breaks down and needs emergency repairs.

Student Alert: How many students in your class carry credit cards? Are these issued in their names or their parents'?

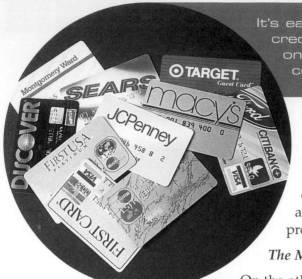

It's easy for most college students to get credit cards, and even easier to use them once they have them. The hard part comes later—paying the bills.

- **Convenience.** Sometimes it's just easier to make purchases using a credit card. For instance, we can make mail-order purchases from catalogs over the telephone if we have a credit card. Furthermore, credit cards not only provide a record of purchases, but they also give us consumer protection should a product prove to be defective and we seek a refund.

The Minuses of Credit Cards

On the other hand, there can be significant drawbacks to the use of credit cards. Potential problems include the following:

- **Interest costs can be high.** As you saw earlier, the interest rate on credit card purchases can be significant. Unless you pay off your entire balance each month, your account will be charged interest, which can mount up rapidly.

- **It's too easy to spend money.** Credit cards are so convenient to use that you may not realize how much you're spending in a given period. Furthermore, spending can become addictive or can be viewed as a recreational activity. Unless you're careful, you can end up exceeding your budget by a significant amount.

- **If you're late in making your payments or exceed your credit limit, your credit rating will be damaged.** Credit card companies have long memories, and any mistakes you make will be reflected in your credit record for close to a decade. That may prevent you from buying a car or house in the future and jeopardize your ability to take out student loans.

> "It is difficult to learn the meaning of fiscal responsibility, especially when you've got a new VISA and there's a great-looking sweater in the shop window. It's even harder when the sweater is on sale."
>
> Lauren Pass, Grossmont Community College.[1]

Discussion Prompt: Why does our culture support the notion of living on borrowed credit? Why are we not better savers?

Paying for College

Tuition costs vary greatly from one school to another, but they are substantial everywhere. It costs just over $1,500 per year in tuition at the average public community college; more than $3,000 per year at the average four-year public college; and almost $14,000 per year at the average private college.[2] If you live on campus, count on another five or six thousand dollars for room and board.

Nothing about college is cheap. It takes enormous expenditures of three often-scarce commodities to attend college: energy, time, and money. Many find that, of these, the easiest to find is—perhaps surprisingly—money. So

P O W E R

Try It! 4

I Know What You Did Last Summer: Learn What Your Credit History Shows

Big Brother is alive and well, at least in terms of your credit history. If you've ever had a credit card in your own name, taken out a student loan, or sometimes just received an unsolicited offer for credit in the mail, there's probably a computer file describing who you are, where you live, and your financial history. It shows how big your credit lines are on every credit card you have, if you've ever been late on a payment, and a considerable amount of additional information.

Even worse: Many people's credit histories are riddled with errors. That's why it's important to periodically check the record. To get a copy of your credit file, write a letter stating that you would like a complimentary copy of your credit report. Include your name, address, social security number, your birth date, your prior addresses for the past five years, and other names (like a maiden name) you may have gone by. You should also include a copy of your driver's license, a copy of a utility bill with your name and address, and a copy of your social security card (if you don't have one, a medical insurance card with the number, a W2 form, a tax return, or a bank statement will do). Then send the letter to TRW, P.O. Box 2106, Allen, TX 75002. [If they are unable to provide a copy, there are two other agencies to contact, but they charge. For information call Equifax at (800) 685-1111 or Trans Union at (800) 916-8800.]

Once you get your credit report, check it carefully. If you find any mistakes, contact the credit bureau and explain the error. They are legally responsible for investigating the report and correcting the file. It's also a good idea to check your file at least once a year.

many sources of aid for education exist that no one should feel that he or she can't afford college.

While it's not simple to get financial aid and no one is going to walk up to you and offer you an all-expenses-paid scholarship, it is a fact that if you are persistent, you can find many sources of funding for your education.

To find money to attend college, you will need to spend ample amounts of the other two scarce commodities: time and energy. The entire process of securing financial aid takes a considerable amount of preparation: You need to first identify potential sources of funds and then apply for them. You should assume the process will take from several weeks to as long as several months, depending on the type of aid you're applying for. The steps you need to take to find funding are summarized in the P.O.W.E.R. Plan on page 336.

> **IM Link:** Teaching the Text, Chapter 13, Sections IV and VIII. The "Cost of Higher Education" activity in the IM is a very efficient way to make a point about the cost of a college education.

P repare: Identifying the Different Types of Funding Available

Funding for college comes in three basic categories: loans, grants, and scholarships. Although each supplies you with funds for college, they do so in very different ways.

> **Loan**
> Funds provided by a bank, credit union, or other agency that must be repaid after a specified period of time

- **Loans.** When you receive a **loan,** a bank, credit union, or other agency provides funds that must be repaid after a specified period of time. A loan

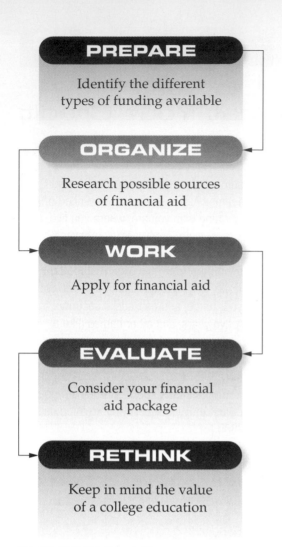

PREPARE

Identify the different types of funding available

ORGANIZE

Research possible sources of financial aid

WORK

Apply for financial aid

EVALUATE

Consider your financial aid package

RETHINK

Keep in mind the value of a college education

P.O.W.E.R. Plan

Principal

The stated amount of a loan

Term

The length of time for which money is lent

carries a particular interest rate, which is stated as an annual percentage rate. The interest rate is the cost of borrowing. Think of a loan as renting money: As long as you have the use of someone else's money, you have to pay them "rent" for the privilege. Banks and other lending agencies make money through the interest they charge on loans, just as credit card companies do.

For example, suppose a bank gives you a $5,000 loan that has an interest rate of 8 percent per year. Not only must you pay back the $5,000 over a specified period, but you must pay the bank interest of 8 percent on the balance that you owe on the loan. Obviously, the higher the interest rate, the more you are paying for the privilege of borrowing the bank's money.

Three factors must be considered when you receive a loan: the stated amount of the loan (called the **principal**), the interest rate (stated as a percentage), and the length of the loan (referred to as the **term** of the loan). All three factors are important because they determine how much your payments will be when you pay the loan back.

Many loans for college have an enormous advantage over loans you'll take out for other purchases, such as a car or house, because payments on college loans are deferred. *Deferred payments* means that you can defer paying back the loan for some specified period; it is often not necessary to start paying back the loan until you graduate and (presumably!) begin to earn an income. Depending on the type of loan you take out, interest on the loan is either paid for by the government while you are enrolled in college or is deferred until you graduate.

There are several national loan programs, sponsored by the federal government, that lend money to students. The major ones include the following:

Stafford loans. Stafford loans are available to any student who is registered at least half time and is a U.S. citizen or permanent resident. They provide from just over $2,600 to $5,500 a year.

Stafford loans come in two types: subsidized and unsubsidized. *Subsidized Stafford loans* are awarded through colleges on the basis of student financial need. For subsidized loans, the government pays interest until repayment begins, typically after the student graduates.

Unsubsidized Stafford loans do not require demonstration of financial need. Interest is not paid by the government; instead it accumulates while the student is in college. However, the student doesn't have to make any payments until after graduation, when both principal and accumulated interest must be repaid over a specified period, which is up to 10 years.

PLUS loans. If your parents support you and claim you as a deduction on their income tax return, they may take out a PLUS loan. PLUS loans can cover up to the full amount of a student's cost of college attendance and can be paid back over a 10-year period.

Perkins loans. Perkins loans have a low interest rate. They are awarded on the basis of exceptional financial need, as determined by a student's college. The loans are made by a school's financial aid office.

- **Grants.** A **grant** is money that does not have to be repaid. Obviously, it's more advantageous to receive a grant than a loan. And not surprisingly, it's harder to qualify for grants than loans. Harder—but not impossible. Several grant programs exist that can help reduce the amount you'll need to pay for college. They include the following:

Grant
An award of money that does not have to be repaid

Pell grants. Based on need, Pell grants are provided to undergraduate students who have earned no previous degrees. They are awarded by college financial aid offices, which follow a formula provided by the federal government. Every student who meets certain need criteria is eligible for a Pell grant, ensuring that the neediest students receive some support.

> "Interest works night and day, in fair weather and in foul."
>
> Henry Ward Beecher, author.

Student Alert: Every college campus has its own packaging formula designed to conform to state and federal guidelines. Encourage students who are applying for aid to find out about your institution's policy.

Federal Supplemental Educational Opportunity Grants (FSEOG). The government supplies a limited number of FSEOGs to every college, which can provide these grants to needy students. Unlike Pell grants, which are guaranteed to every eligible student, FSEOGs are in limited supply. Once a college awards its allotment for a given year, no other awards are possible.

Work-study grants. Work-study grants provide jobs for undergraduates with financial needs. The jobs are typically related to a student's course of study, and the salary is subsidized by the government. Because a work-study position is often part of a student's total package of financial aid, it is generally considered a grant, even though work is required.

© 1999 Michael Maslin from cartoonbank.com. All Rights Reserved.

- **Scholarship.** Scholarships are support awarded by colleges and other organizations. Like a grant, a scholarship is money that does not have to be repaid. Most scholarships are based primarily on a student's financial need, although some are based on merit. For instance, students with exceptional academic or athletic abilities may receive a scholarship even though they wouldn't necessarily qualify under typical need-based measures.

Scholarship
An award of money to a student based on need or merit

The most frequent source of scholarships is one's own college, which may give money to reduce tuition and fees. But there are literally thousands of organizations that provide scholarships, ranging from companies such as Microsoft to nonprofit groups such as the Boy Scouts and Girl Scouts.

The federal government also provides some scholarships to students whose family income does not rise above certain levels. These include the following:

Hope Scholarship. The Hope Scholarship is a tax credit that helps free up funds for college. Students receive a 100 percent tax credit for the first $1,000 of tuition and required fees, and a 50 percent credit on the second $1,000.

Lifetime Learning Tax Credit. This tax credit is targeted to older students who are going back to school, changing careers, or taking courses to upgrade their skills, as well as to juniors and seniors in four-year colleges. Families can receive a 20 percent tax credit for the first $5,000 of tuition and fees, and the amount will increase in future years.

O rganize: Researching Possible Sources of Financial Aid

As you can see, there are many types of financial aid. The biggest problem is finding them.

Your first stop on your search for sources of financial aid: your college financial aid office. Every college has one, and it tends to be one of the busiest places on campus.

Most student aid offices contain a great deal of information about possible sources of aid. But that's only a starting point. The library and World Wide Web also contain many types of information that can direct you to specific possibilities. One place to get started is the Federal Student Aid Information Center in Washington, which can be reached at 1-800-4-FED-AID (1-800-433-3243) or on the Web at **www.ed.gov/prog_info/SFA/StudentGuide**. The center will send you *The Student Guide,* which describes programs that account for almost three-fourths of all financial aid awarded to students.

Keep in mind, however, that where money is involved, there are scams. Do not pay money to someone who offers to identify obscure scholarships that will yield you thousands of dollars. It's unlikely that anyone could find sources that you couldn't find yourself through careful research. Be especially wary of Web sites that ask for a credit card number in order to provide you with on-line information. The results are likely to be disappointing. (The Web sites we provide at the end of the chapter are completely reputable.)

Whatever the potential source of financial aid, you'll be asked to bare your financial soul. There will also be forms galore. Before actually completing the forms, it will be important to gather the information you will need. Much of it may have to come from your parents, if you are being supported by them, and they will have to complete some of the forms.

Keep track of deadlines! If you miss a deadline for applying for financial aid, you'll be out of luck; no exceptions are made. You'll just have to wait for another aid cycle.

Finally, make sure you know what your needs are. The typical costs of college include not only tuition but also fees, books, and supplies, as well as associated costs, such as transportation, housing, food, and child care.

W ork: Applying for Financial Aid

It may seem that for every dollar in aid you get, there is a different line to complete on a complicated form. Prepare yourself for a blizzard of paperwork.

Following are the steps in applying for financial aid:

- **Speak with a financial aid counselor at your school.** Because the best source of financial aid is your own college, make an appointment to discuss your needs with a campus financial aid counselor or officer. In addition to giving you the most up-to-date information about possible sources of aid, the college financial aid officer can provide you with the forms you need to fill out and a list of the deadlines you need to meet.

- **Decide how much aid you need.** It's important to ask for just the right amount of aid, neither too little nor too much. If you ask for too little aid, you may be strapped for funds during the school term. It's much more difficult to get aid in the middle of a term than it is to do so during the normal application period.

  At the same time, don't apply for more financial aid than you actually need. First there is an issue of equity: What you get in aid may reduce the pool for others, and if you receive surplus aid you may be preventing other students from getting their fair share. Further, you don't want to load yourself up with unnecessary debt. Most graduates pay from $150 to $175 a month to pay off their student loans; you don't want to end up with so much debt that your loan payments are even higher than this.

- **Fill out your college's application for financial aid.** Colleges have their own forms to apply for financial aid. Carefully fill the form out, making sure you file it before the required deadline. In fact, the earlier you get the form in, the better: Most schools have a limited pool of funds, and the earlier you get your application in, the higher your chances of getting an appropriate share of the financial aid pie.

- **Write a personal letter to accompany your application.** If you think there are factors affecting your ability to pay for college that are not adequately reflected in the application, write a letter to the financial aid officer describing them.

"Good day, Madam. I'm working my son's way through college."

© The New Yorker collection 1974 J. B. Handelsman from cartoonbank.com. All Rights Reserved.

- **Complete a Free Application for Federal Student Aid (FAFSA) and Financial Aid PROFILE.** The FAFSA and Profile are standard forms used to assess a student's financial capabilities and determine how much the student and family can be expected to contribute toward college expenses. One or both of the forms are used by almost every college. They require a great deal of information, including past, present, and expected income from all sources. Copies of several tax returns from prior years are also required.

  Be scrupulously honest when you complete the forms. If you fail to include a source of income that is later discovered by a financial aid provider, you may be required to repay immediately any aid that you have received. In addition, you may face disciplinary measures that put your education in jeopardy; in the worst case, you may even face legal charges.

- **Wait.** It takes time for loan applications to be processed and financial aid decisions to be made. Be prepared to wait, and consider contingency plans for various possibilities.

Student Alert: Deadlines are critical! Many sources of aid are available on a first come, first serve basis. Do not delay! Also, summer school aid is often considered separately from aid available for the academic year. Check out the policies on your campus.

Evaluate: Considering Your Financial Aid Package

Some time later, when the college has had time to consider your application for aid, you will receive an official response. This will most likely be in the form of a "package"—a combination of loans, grants, scholarships, and, perhaps, an offer of an on-campus job. This is the time for a thorough evaluation of the offer. Consider the various elements of the package carefully to determine whether, taken together, they will fully meet your financial needs.

What if the package doesn't seem sufficient? The most important thing is not to give up. A polite call or visit to the financial aid office is in order.

Discussion Prompt: Direct the conversation to the discussion about the value of a college education presented in Chapter 1.

When you speak to someone from financial aid, lay out your difficulty with the package. If the aid is so low that you won't be able to attend college, let the financial aid office know. If you had noted special circumstances in a letter, ask if they were taken into account. (Sometimes letters and other vital pieces of information get overlooked.) Ask if there is a formal appeal process and, if there is, ask how to begin it. Your main goal is to get the financial aid office to take a second look at your application. By being polite and to the point in your dealings with the office, you stand a better chance of having them reevaluate your application.

What if the school is unable to come up with a greater level of support? The first step is to ask the staff of the financial aid office for advice. They may be able to suggest an approach that you initially overlooked. The second step is to redouble your research efforts. You may be able to take out a loan to make up the deficit. Finally, consider alternatives to full-time college attendance. It may be preferable to attend school part-time while working than to give up college altogether or to get so much into debt that it will be hard to pay off your loans.

Above all, don't give up! You will find some way to support your efforts to get an education.

Rethink: Keeping in Mind the Value of a College Education

Our present focus on paying for college has led us, of necessity, to concentrate on the dollars-and-cents aspect of education. But it is important to reflect on what the money we spend on education buys us: a better understanding of the world and its people, insight into who we are, better job opportunities, and a chance to befriend people who share the common goal of becoming well-educated citizens of a global society. It would be terribly shortsighted to put a price tag on education, deciding, in effect, that if you must pay a lot you won't bother with an education. You may need to choose your school according to the tuition it charges and financial aid package it offers you, but that's not the same as choosing to skip becoming educated because it is going to be financially stressful. An experience that will permit us to reach the potential that lies within us is worth everything.

If Financial Disaster Strikes

You lose your job and can't afford to pay next semester's tuition.

Your roommate moves out and leaves you with an $800 phone bill. You don't have $800.

Your parents, who have promised to pay for your education, run into financial difficulties and say they can't afford to pay your college costs any longer.

Your car breaks down, and repairing it will cost $1,500. If you don't have a car, you can't get to campus. But if you pay for repairs, you can't afford tuition.

All of us face financial difficulties at one time or another. Sometimes it happens suddenly and without warning. Other times people sink more gradually into financial difficulties, each month accruing more debt until they reach a point at which they can't pay their bills.

However it happens, finding yourself with too little money to pay your bills requires action. You need to confront the situation and take steps to solve the problem. The worst thing to do is nothing. Hiding from those to whom you owe money makes the situation worse. Your creditors—the institutions and people to whom you owe money—will assume that you don't care, and they'll be spurred on to take harsher actions.

These are the steps, summarized in Table 13.3, to take if you do find yourself with financial difficulties:

- **Assess the problem.** Make a list of what you owe and to whom. Look at the bottom line and figure out a reasonable amount you can put toward each debt. Work out a specific plan that can lead you out of the situation.

- **Contact each of your creditors.** Start with your bank, credit card companies, and landlord, and continue through each creditor. It's best to visit personally, but a phone call will do.

    When you speak with them, explain the situation. If the problem is due to illness or unemployment, let them know. If it's due to overspending, let them know that. Tell them what you plan to do to pay off your debt, and show them your plan. The fact that you have a plan demonstrates not only what you intend to do, but also that you are serious about your situation and capable of financial planning.

    If you've had a clean financial record in the past, your creditors may be willing to agree to your plan. Ultimately, it is cheaper for them to accept smaller payments over a longer time than to hire a collection agency.

- **See a credit counselor.** If you can't work out a repayment plan on your own, visit a credit counseling service. These are nonprofit organizations

Student Alert: Caution students about hidden costs like phone bills and parking tickets. These are two areas that constantly cause financial woes for students.

Assess the problem	Make a list of what you owe and to whom.
	Figure out a reasonable amount you can put toward each debt.
	Work out a specific plan.
Contact each of your creditors	Start with your bank, credit card companies, and landlord.
	Explain the situation.
	Show them your plan to pay off debt.
See a credit counselor	If you cannot work out a repayment plan on your own, visit a credit counseling service.
Stick to the plan	Once you have a plan make a commitment to stick to it.
	Your bank or creditor can help you identify a credit counselor.

Table 13.3

Steps in Dealing with Financial Difficulties

Working in a Group: Discover Your Personal Financial Philosophy

Begin to create a personal financial philosophy by completing this exercise.

A. Attitudes toward Money

	Strongly Disagree	Disagree	Neutral	Agree	Strongly Agree
1. Money is essential for happiness.					
2. Having money guarantees happiness.					
3. Money makes no difference to one's happiness.					
4. More money equals more happiness.					
5. Beyond having enough to live modestly on, money doesn't make much of a difference.					
6. I frequently worry about money.					
7. I frequently daydream about having a lot of money.					
8. If I suddenly had to live on very little money, I could adjust easily.					
9. If I suddenly won a lot of money, I would go on a spending spree.					
10. If I suddenly won a lot of money, I would share it with my relatives.					
11. If I suddenly won a lot of money, I would give a large percentage to charity.					
12. If I found a substantial amount of cash in a bag, I would try hard to find its rightful owner.					
13. If I could carry only a briefcase full of $100 bills or my pet dog out of a burning building, I would take the dog.					
14. I plan to make a lot of money in my career.					
15. I plan to make only enough money to live in reasonable comfort.					
16. It's great to have money.					
17. Money is a necessary evil.					
18. Money is the root of all evil.					

that help people who find themselves in financial trouble. Your bank or a creditor can help you identify one, or you can call the National Foundation for Consumer Credit at 1-800-388-2227 or visit their Web site at **http://www.nfcc.org**.

B. Sources of Satisfaction

1. Which activities that you engaged in over the last five years have given you the greatest satisfaction?

2. How much money did those activities cost?

3. How would you spend your time if you could do anything you chose?

4. How much money would this cost each year?

C. Personal Financial Philosophy

Consider your attitudes toward money and the sources of your satisfaction. Sum up your personal financial philosophy here:

After you've completed these questions, separate into small groups and compare your answers with those of other students. How does your financial philosophy compare to that of other students? What are the major similarities and differences, and how do you think they came about?

- **Stick to the plan.** Once you have a plan to get yourself out of debt, follow it. Unless you diligently make the payments you commit to, you'll find your debt spiraling out of control once again. It's essential, then, to regard your plan as a firm commitment and stick to it.

Teaching Tip: Try It 5 is a useful summary exercise and a good source for evaluation.

Show Me the Money: Building a Financial Philosophy

It's hard to forget the famous line from *Jerry McGuire,* the movie in which Tom Cruise plays a sports agent: "Show me the money." That direct statement—however crude—might be used to illustrate one financial philosophy: Life revolves around money.

Many would disagree. For instance, authors Vicki Robin and Joe Dominguez argue in their book *Your Money or Your Life*[3] that, while most people find money to be a controlling force in their lives and, consequently, their major source of stress, it needn't be. Yes, the authors concede, acquiring and spending money can become an obsession, and when this is the case the simple pleasures of life are lost. But Robin and Dominguez outline an alternative approach in which we reprioritize our values, live frugally, and ultimately achieve financial independence.

Whether you choose to follow the path of Jerry McGuire or that of Vicki Robin and Joe Dominguez, the important thing is to develop your own personal financial philosophy. You can get a start in developing your financial philosophy by completing Try It 5, which can help assess how money affects your life. It will help you consider the role that money plays in your life. How much does money motivate what you do? Are you interested in becoming rich, or do you tend to think more in terms of simply having enough to have a comfortable life, without lots of luxuries? What activities bring you the greatest satisfaction in life? Do those activities require a certain level of income?

Ultimately, consider how college relates to issues involving finances. College is undoubtedly one of the biggest investments that you'll ever make. If you only think of it in terms of its eventual financial payoff—getting a better job and leading a more affluent life—you'll be missing some central aspects of the process of educating yourself.

Looking Back

What purpose does a budget serve and how can you prepare and stick to one?

- Concerns about money can be significantly lowered through the creation of a budget by which expenditures and income can be planned, accounted for, and aligned with your goals.

- Budgets provide security by helping you control your finances and avoid surprises.

- The process of budgeting involves identifying your financial goals, keeping track of current expenses and estimating future expenses, and making the necessary adjustments to keep income and expenditures in balance.

Speaking of Success

Name: *Solomon Trujillo*
Education: *B.A., M.B.A., University of Wyoming*
Occupation: *President and chief executive officer, US West*
Home: *Denver, Colorado*

As the highest-ranking Hispanic in American business and the chief executive officer of the biggest company in Colorado, Solomon Trujillo has certainly had his share of extraordinary success. President of US West, Trujillo presides over a company with 67,000 employees and revenues of more than $11 billion annually.

But his success was hardly predetermined. His parents, married when they were 14 and 16 years old, never finished high school, and Trujillo grew up in poverty. His father worked for the Union Pacific railroad in Cheyenne, Wyoming, and Trujillo says, "All I knew was that I sure didn't have a lot of things that other people had."[4]

But he actually knew something more: that college represented the road to success. Working several jobs—including playing trumpet in a mariachi band—while putting himself through college at the University of Wyoming, Trujillo earned high grades. He still managed time for regular pickup games of basketball, which helped him stay in shape and relieved the pressures of school.

Trujillo's grades were so good that he was accepted into a master's in business administration (MBA) program. Because he could only afford one year of postgraduate college, he convinced the graduate program to permit him to complete his degree in just one year, rather than the regular two. Not only did he manage to earn nearly straight A's, but he also held down three jobs at the same time. He became the school's first student to complete the two-year program in just one year.

After graduating, Trujillo joined Mountain Bell as an economic forecaster. He quickly moved up the company ranks, becoming a senior manager by the time he was 32 years old. He became president of US West when he was in his early 40s.

Trujillo's philosophy of success? He believes in "always striving, because things never come easy . . . valuing diversity, looking to be inclusive rather than exclusive . . . and innovating and enjoying a change in the game." He adds, "I am a believer in a performance-based orientation. Results speak louder than words. Wherever you are, if you deliver results, it will serve [you] well."[5]

What help is available to pay for your college education?

- Loans for education are available with reasonable interest rates and conditions, especially the ability to defer paying the loans back until after graduation. Several federal programs offer loan guarantees, interest subsidies, and lower interest rates.

- Grants offer money without requiring repayment. They are harder to receive than loans because they are typically reserved for people with exceptional financial need.

- Scholarships are usually awarded by colleges and other institutions based on either financial need or academic, athletic, or other abilities.

What can you do if you fall into financial difficulty?

- If financial difficulties arise, contact your creditors and arrange a plan for paying off the debt. If you need help in designing a repayment plan, nonprofit credit counselors can help.

Key Terms and Concepts

Budget (p. 323)   Principal (p. 336)
Grant (p. 337)   Scholarship (p. 337)
Loan (p. 335)   Term (p. 336)

Resources

On Campus

The bursar's or treasurer's office handles money affairs. Not only do they collect money owed for tuition, but they may perform other services such as cashing checks.

If you are receiving financial aid, there is usually a particular office devoted to the complexities of scholarships, loan processing, and other forms of aid. The personnel in the office can be very helpful in maximizing your financial aid package as well as in solving financial problems related to your schooling. If you have a problem with your finances, see them sooner rather than later.

In Print

Judy Lawrence's *The Budget Kit: The Common Cents Money Management Workbook* (Dearborn, 1997) offers a clear path to getting all your finances under control. *Paying for College* (Time Life, 1997), by Marc Robinson, includes many practical tips for finding ways to finance a college education. Finally, *The Student Guide* (U.S. Department of Education, 1999) is the most complete resource on student financial aid, providing up-to-date and thorough explanations of financial aid programs. You can get a free copy by calling 1-800-4-FED-AID.

On the Web

The following sites on the World Wide Web provide the opportunity to extend your learning about the material in this chapter. (Although the Web addresses were accurate at the time the book was printed, check the P.O.W.E.R. Learning Web site [http://mhhe.com/power] for any changes that may have occurred.)

http://www.cashe.com/

The home page for College Aid Sources for Higher Education (CASHE) is a valuable, time-saving tool for students and their parents who are trying to identify sources of funds to pay for college. Through this service you can receive information about scholarships, fellowships, grants, work study, loan programs, tuition waivers, internships, competitions, and work cooperative programs.

http://www.finaid.org/calculators/

This site offers loads of online calculators including: College Cost Projector, Savings Plan Designer, Financial Aid Estimation Form, Loan Payment Calculator, and Student Loan Advisor (Undergraduate).

http://www.finaid.org/finaid.html

This site provides a free, comprehensive, independent, and objective guide to student financial aid. It was created by Mark Kantrowitz, author of *The Prentice Hall Guide to Scholarships and Fellowships for Math and Science Students*.

Taking It to the Net

1 Find four sources of financial aid. One possible strategy: Go to Yahoo! (**www.yahoo.com**) and choose "education," and then "financial aid." Click on "grants" or "Scholarship programs" and examine what is available. What are the differences between scholarships and grants?

2 Discover three new ways to save money. Possible strategy: Using a search engine (**www.yahoo.com** or **www.altavista.com**), enter the keyword "saving money." Examine the sites for tips you can use for saving money.

The Case of . . .

Overdrawn, Overwrought, and Over Her Head

Her life was a house of cards, and someone had just pulled one out from the bottom.

At least that's what it felt like to Tara Kenko. The month had started out badly when Tara found that she had made a mistake in her checking account and had only $439, instead of the $939 she thought she had. After paying her share of the rent— $210—there wasn't enough money left to make her car payment. So she just put the bill aside, figuring that she'd take care of it later in the month when she got paid.

Things went from bad to worse two days later when her car refused to start. She had to have it towed to a mechanic, who told her that it would cost about $350 to get it fixed. She didn't have that, either, but she figured she could put it on her credit card even though her unpaid balance was already pretty high. But later, when she went to pick up her car and pay for the repair, which turned out to be closer to $400 than the $350 she expected to pay, her card was rejected. She called the credit card company from the repair shop and was told that she had exceeded her authorized credit limit and that her card was frozen. Because the mechanic wouldn't let her take her car until she paid for the repairs, she was forced to leave it and catch a bus to campus.

The final straw came in her chemistry class. The instructor announced that students in the class would have to buy yet another book in order to do the latest assignment. Having already spent $150 for books in that class alone, Tara was both angry and dismayed. She had no idea how she was going to find the money to pay for the book, let alone her regular car payment and the car repairs. She was in financial trouble, and she didn't know what to do.

1. What should Tara do now to start addressing her problem?

2. Can you suggest some approaches Tara can take to deal with the problem of the new book for her chemistry class?

3. How do you think the mistake may have occurred in Tara's checking account? What advice would you give her to avoid a similar mistake in the future?

4. Given that Tara does not have a lot of leeway in her finances for multiple disasters such as the ones that befell her this month, what general course would you advise her to take as a way to plan her expenditures more effectively?

5. What steps might Tara take to decrease her expenses? What might she do to increase her income?

Enjoying Health and Wellness

14

One step at a time. One step at a time. That's how Greg Vadisch got himself through the last mile of the 10-mile race. Although he was in agony, with a blister on his foot that caused searing pain each time he stepped down, he methodically moved forward, repeating to himself the phrase, "One step at a time. One step at a time."

It was a personal challenge just to finish the race. Greg didn't care about his time; just finishing would be reward enough—for the extraordinary thing about Greg was that, only a year earlier, the idea of entering a race had never even entered his mind. Fairly inactive, Greg had never made exercise a priority. But then he'd had a routine physical, and his physician had told him that he was 20 pounds overweight and his cholesterol count was sky-high—at age 26. It was a wake-up call.

Greg embarked on an exercise program, the centerpiece of which was jogging three times a week. To his surprise, he found himself enjoying it. After a few months, he was running 3 and occasionally 4 miles.

When a friend first suggested he enter a 10-mile race sponsored by the American Cancer Society to raise money for research, Greg was dubious and at first refused. But the idea began to take hold, and one day he decided to take the plunge. He registered for the race, which was scheduled to take place in a few months, and he began to train seriously for it. He knew he'd never come close to winning, but his goal was just to finish the race.

So there he was, fighting his way toward the finish line. The pain was awful, but he found some inner strength and pulled himself forward. When he crossed the finish line, he collapsed, physically drained and in agony. But the pain was something he accepted; he was filled with pure joy over his achievement.

Looking Ahead

For Greg Vadisch, running took on a significance far beyond mere exercise. It brought him a sense of accomplishment, a feeling of pride in what he had been able to do for himself.

Keeping your body healthy is one of the challenges that college students face. The many demands on your time can produce a feeling that there's always something else that has to be accomplished. This pressure produces wear and tear on your body and mind, and it's easy to fall prey to stress and ill health.

However, stress and ill health are not inevitable outcomes of college. In fact, by deciding to make health a conscious priority, you can experience a sense of health and well-being that will make you feel good both physically and mentally.

This chapter covers the ways you can keep fit and healthy by offering suggestions on how you can improve your diet, get enough exercise, and sleep better. You will get a chance to figure out why you experience stress and how you can control it. Finally, the chapter helps you consider threats to mental and physical health including alcohol and drugs, pregnancy, sexually transmitted diseases, and rape.

In sum, after reading this chapter you'll be able to answer these questions:

- **What is involved in keeping fit and healthy, and why is it important for me to do so?**

- **What is stress and how can I control it?**

- **What are the main threats to my health and well-being?**

- **What are the components of sexual health?**

Keeping Well

Eat right. Exercise. Get plenty of sleep.

Pretty simple, isn't it? We learn the fundamentals of fitness and health in the first years of elementary school.

Yet for millions of us, wellness is an elusive goal. We eat on the fly, stopping for a bite at the drive-in window of a fast-food restaurant. Most of us don't exercise enough, either because we feel we don't have enough time or because it's not much fun for us. And as for sleep, we're a nation in which getting by with as little sleep as possible is seen as a badge of honor.

> "The first wealth is health."
> Emerson.

You can buck the trends, however; you can begin to eat more properly, exercise effectively, and sleep better by following several basic rules. They include the following:

Teaching Tip: Does your institution have a Wellness Center? Consider having your students keep a nutrition log and asking the staff of your center to evaluate your students' logs. They may be amazed at their eating habits.

Eating Right

- **Eat a variety of foods.** Strive to eat a range of different foods. If you make *variety* your goal, you will end up eating the right foods.

- **Eat plenty of fruits, vegetables, and grain products.** Enough said.

- **Avoid foods that are high in sugar and salt content.** Read labels on supermarket packages carefully and beware of hidden sugars and salts. Many ingredients that end in *-ose* (such as dextrose, sucrose, maltose, and fructose) are actually sugars; salt can lurk within any number of compounds beginning with the word *sodium*. Your best bet is to trust the nutrition labels that the U.S. government requires food manufacturers to put on their products.

- **Seek a diet low in fat and cholesterol.** The fat that is to be especially avoided is saturated fat—the most difficult for your body to rid itself of.

- **Less is more.** You don't need to walk away stuffed from every meal. Moderation is the key. To be sure you don't eat more than your body is telling you to eat, pay attention to internal hunger cues.

- **Schedule three regular meals a day.** Eating should be a priority—

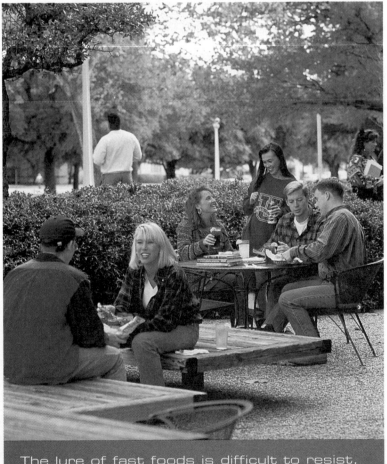

The lure of fast foods is difficult to resist, and eating a balanced, nutritious diet is a challenge for most college students.

a definite part of your daily schedule. Avoid skipping any meals. Breakfast is particularly important; get up early enough to eat a full meal.

- **Be sensitive to the hidden contents of various foods.** Soda and chocolate can contain substantial quantities of caffeine, which can disrupt your sleep and, along with coffee, become addictive. Many cereals—even those labeled "low fat"—contain a substantial amount of sugar or salt. Pay attention to labels.

- **Beware of eating disorders.** Between 1 and 4 percent of college-age women, and a smaller percentage of men, suffer from an eating disorder. Those with *anorexia nervosa* may refuse to eat, while denying that their behavior and appearance—which can become skeletonlike—are unusual. Some 15 to 20 percent of those with anorexia literally starve themselves to death. *Bulimia* is a disorder in which individuals binge on incredibly large quantities of food, such as a gallon of ice cream and a whole pie, but later feel so much guilt and depression that they induce vomiting or take laxatives to rid themselves of the food. Eating disorders represent serious threats to health and require aggressive medical intervention.

Discussion Prompt: Many students have had experience with eating disorders, either personally or with friends. Encourage them to talk about this subject in class.

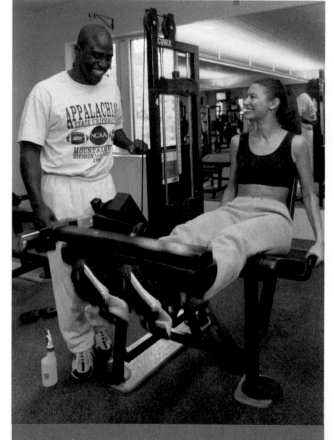

In order to maintain the habit of exercising, you need to choose an activity you enjoy doing. In addition, working out with others, as these students at Appalachian State University's fitness center are doing, turns exercise into a social activity and gives you social support, increasing the chances you'll stick with an exercise regimen.

Making Exercise a Part of Your Life

Exercise produces a variety of benefits. Your body will run more efficiently, you'll have more energy, your heart and circulatory system will run more smoothly, and you'll be able to bounce back from stress and illness more quickly.

- **Choose a type of exercise that you like.** Exercising will be a chore you end up avoiding if you don't enjoy what you're doing.

- **Incorporate exercise into your life.** Take the stairs instead of elevators. Leave your car at home and walk to campus or work. Join an intramural team. When you're on campus, take the longer way to reach your destination.

- **Make exercise a group activity.** Exercising with others brings you social support and turns exercise into a social activity. You'll be more likely to stick to a program if you have a regular "exercise date" with a friend.

- **Vary your routine.** You don't need to do the same kind of exercise day after day. Choose different sorts of activities that will involve different parts of your body and keep you from getting bored.

One note of caution: Before you begin an exercise program, it is a good idea to have a physical checkup, even if you feel you're in the peak of health. This is especially true if you're starting an exercise program after years of inactivity. You also might consult a trainer at the gym to set up a program that gradually builds you up to more vigorous exercise.

Getting a Good Night's Sleep

Do you feel as if you don't get enough sleep? You probably don't. Most college students are sleep-deprived, a condition that causes them to feel fatigued, short-tempered, and tense. Insufficient sleep also leads to declines in academic and physical performance. You can't do your best at anything if you're exhausted—or even tired.

Often the solution to the problem is simply to allow yourself more time to sleep. Most people need around eight hours of sleep each night, although there are wide individual differences. In addition to sleeping more, there are also some relatively simple changes you can make in your behavior that will help you to sleep better. They include the following:

- **Exercise during the day.** Regular exercise will help you sleep more soundly at night, as well as help you cope with stress that might otherwise keep you awake.

- **Have a regular bedtime.** By going to bed at pretty much the same time each night, you give your body a regular rhythm and make sleep a habit.

- **Use your bed for sleeping and not as an all-purpose area.** Don't use your bed as a place to study, read, eat, or watch TV. Let your bed be a trigger for sleep.

- **Avoid caffeine after lunch.** The stimulant effects of caffeine (found in coffee, tea, and some soft drinks) may last as long as 8 to 12 hours after it's consumed.

- **Drink a glass of milk at bedtime.** Your Mom was right: Drinking a

Journal Reflections

Experiences with Exercise

How successful we are at exercising depends in large part on our past experiences with exercise. Examine your own feelings about, and personal history of, exercise.

1. Overall, how do you feel about exercise?

2. How would you rate yourself in terms of your success at engaging in an appropriate amount of exercise each week?

3. What obstacles stand in the way of your obtaining adequate exercise?

4. Describe your past experiences with exercise. Would you say your history with exercise has been good or bad? Why?

5. What is your favorite form of exercise? What do you like about it?

6. What is your least favorite form of exercise? What is it that you dislike about it?

7. What steps could you take in the future to ensure that you get an adequate amount of exercise?

Student Alert: Communal living in a residence hall usually changes students' sleeping habits. What coping mechanisms have your students discovered?

glass of milk before you go to bed will help you get to sleep. The reason: Milk contains a natural chemical that makes you drowsy.

- **Avoid sleeping pills.** Despite advertisements to the contrary, you're better off not taking sleeping pills. Although they may be temporarily effective, in the long run they impair your ability to sleep because they disrupt your natural sleep cycles.

- **Don't try to force sleep on yourself.** Although this advice sounds odd, it turns out that one of the reasons that we have trouble sleeping is that we try too hard. To follow this advice, try to relax when you go to bed—and don't try to go to sleep. If you're awake after 10 minutes or so, get up and do something else. Only go back to bed when you feel tired. Do this as often as necessary. If you follow this regimen for several weeks—and don't take naps or rest during the day—eventually getting into your bed will trigger sleep.

Living with Stress

Stress
The response to events that threaten or challenge us

Stressed out? Tests, papers, due dates, job demands, roommate problems, political activities, committee work . . . It's no surprise that each of these can produce stress. But it may be a surprise to know that so can graduating from high school, starting your dream job, falling in love, getting married, and even winning the lottery.

Virtually *anything*—good or bad—is capable of producing stress if it in some way presents us with a challenge. **Stress** is the physical and emotional response we have to events that threaten or challenge us. It is rooted in the primitive fight or flight response wired into all animals—human and nonhuman. You see it in cats, for instance, when confronted by a dog or other threat: Their backs go up, their hair stands on end, their eyes widen, and, ultimately, they either take off or attack. The challenge stimulating this revved-up response is called a *stressor*. For humans, stressors can range from a first date to losing our chemistry notes to living through a flash flood.

Because our everyday lives are filled with events that potentially can be interpreted as threatening or challenging, stress is commonplace in most people's lives. There are three main types of stressors:

Cataclysmic events
Sudden, powerful events that occur quickly and affect many people simultaneously

1. **Cataclysmic events** are sudden, powerful events that occur quickly and affect many people simultaneously. Tornadoes, hurricanes, and plane crashes are examples of cataclysmic events. Although they may produce powerful immediate consequences, ironically they produce less stress than other types of stressors. The reason? Cataclysmic events have a clear end-point, which can make them more manageable. Furthermore, because they affect many people simultaneously, their consequences are shared with others, and no individual feels singled out.

Personal stressors
Major life events that produce stress

2. **Personal stressors** are major life events that produce a negative physical and psychological reaction. Failing a course, losing a job, and ending a relationship are all examples of personal stressors. Sometimes positive events—such as getting married or starting a new job—can act as personal stressors. Although the short-term impact of a personal stressor can be difficult, the long-term consequences may decline as people learn to adapt to the situation.

3. **Daily hassles** are the minor irritations of life that, singly, produce relatively little stress. Waiting in a traffic jam, receiving a tuition bill riddled with mistakes, and being interrupted by noises of major construction while trying to study are examples of daily hassles. However, daily hassles add up, and eventually they can produce even more stress than a single larger-scale event. (Figure 14.1 indicates the most common daily hassles in people's lives.[1])

Daily hassles
The minor irritants of life that, by themselves, produce little stress, but that can add up and produce more stress than a single larger-scale event

Figure 14.1
Daily Hassles

Teaching Tip: Stress is one of the leading reasons college students visit an infirmary or a counseling center on college campuses. Spend time talking about the "daily hassles" identified in Figure 14.1 in an effort to determine ways to develop a healthy lifestyle.

Figure 14.1 — Daily Hassles

Daily Hassle	Percentage of people experiencing
Not enough time	~88
Too many things to do	~78
Troubling thoughts about the future	~76
Too many interruptions	~72
Misplacing or losing things	~70
Health of a family member	~53
Social obligations	~52
Concerns about standards	~51
Concerns about getting ahead	~50
Too many responsibilities	~50

Percentage of people experiencing

What Is Happening When We are Stressed Out

Stress does more than make us feel anxious, upset, and fearful. Beneath those responses, we are experiencing many different physical reactions, each placing a high demand on our body's resources. Our hearts beat faster, our breathing becomes more rapid and shallow, and we produce more sweat. Our internal organs churn out a variety of hormones. In the long run, these physical responses wear down our immune system, our body's defense against disease. We become more susceptible to a variety of diseases, ranging from the common cold and headaches to strokes and heart disease. In fact, surveys have found that the greater the number of stressful events a person experiences over the course of a year, the more likely it is that he or she will have a major illness (see Try It 1, "Assess Your Susceptibility to Stress-Related Illness," on page 356).

Handling Stress

Stress is an inevitable part of life. In fact, a life with no stress at all would be so boring, so uneventful, that you'd quickly miss the stress that had been removed.

That doesn't mean, though, that we have to sit back and accept stress when it does arise. **Coping** is the effort to control, reduce, or tolerate the threats that lead to stress. Using the P.O.W.E.R. principles we can ward off stress and actively deal with it.

Coping
The effort to control, reduce, or tolerate the threats that lead to stress

Try It!
1

Assess Your Susceptibility to Stress-Related Illness

Are you susceptible to a stress-related illness? The more stress in your life, the more likely it is that you may experience a major illness.

To determine the stress in your life, take the stressor value given beside each event you have experienced and multiply it by the number of occurrences over the past year (up to a maximum of four), and then add up these scores.[2]

87 Experienced the death of a spouse

77 Getting married

77 Experienced the death of a close family member

76 Were divorced

74 Experienced a marital separation

68 Experienced the death of a close friend

68 Experienced pregnancy or fathered a pregnancy

65 Had a major personal injury or illness

62 Were fired from work

60 Ended a marital engagement or a steady relationship

58 Had sexual difficulties

58 Experienced a marital reconciliation

57 Had a major change in self-concept or self-awareness

56 Experienced a major change in the health or behavior of a family member

54 Became engaged to be married

53 Had a major change in financial status

52 Took on a mortgage or loan of more than $10,000

52 Had a major change in use of drugs

50 Had a major conflict or change in values

50 Had a major change in the number of arguments with your spouse

50 Gained a new family member

50 Entered college

50 Changed to a new school

50 Changed to a different line of work

Teaching Tip: Do not forget to give some attention to those college students who do not feel stress in their life. Sliding through life, always taking the easy way out, and never expecting the best of ourselves is certainly not the answer to stressful living.

P repare: Readying Yourself Physically

Being in good physical condition is the primary way to prepare for future stress. Stress takes its toll on your body, so it makes sense that the stronger and fitter you are, the less negative impact stress will have on you. For example, a regular exercise program reduces heart rate, respiration rate, and blood pres-

Chapter 14 Enjoying Health and Wellness

49 Had a major change in amount of independence and responsibility

47 Had a major change in responsibilities at work

46 Experienced a major change in use of alcohol

45 Revised personal habits

44 Had trouble with school administration

43 Held a job while attending school

43 Had a major change in social activities

42 Had trouble with in-laws

42 Had a major change in working hours or conditions

42 Changed residence or living conditions

41 Had your spouse begin or cease work outside the home

41 Changed your choice of major field of study

41 Changed dating habits

40 Had an outstanding personal achievement

38 Had trouble with your boss

38 Had a major change in amount of participation in school activities

37 Had a major change in type and/or amount of recreation

36 Had a major change in religious activities

34 Had a major change of sleeping habits

33 Took a trip or vacation

30 Had a major change in eating habits

26 Had a major change in the number of family get-togethers

22 Were found guilty of minor violations of the law

Scoring: If your total score is above 1,435, you are in a high-stress category and therefore more at risk for experiencing a stress-related illness. However, a high score does not mean that you are sure to get sick. Many other factors determine ill health, and high stress is only one cause. Other positive factors in your life, such as getting enough sleep and exercise, may help to prevent illness. Still, having an unusually high amount of stress in your life is a cause for concern, and you may wish to take steps to reduce it.

sure at times when the body is at rest—making us better able to withstand the negative consequences of stress. Furthermore, vigorous exercise produces *endorphins,* natural painkilling chemicals in the brain. Endorphins produce feelings of happiness—even euphoria—and may be responsible for the "runner's high," the positive feelings often reported by long-distance runners following long runs. Through the production of endorphins, then, exercise can help our bodies produce a natural coping response to stress.

Discussion Prompt: What makes us feel good? For a few minutes have your class write down as many healthy ideas as they can think of—then share them with the class.

If you now drink a lot of coffee or soda, a change in your diet may be enough to bring about a reduction in stress. Coffee, soda, chocolate, and a surprising number of other foods contain caffeine, which can make you feel jittery and anxious even without stress; add a stressor, and the reaction can be very intense and unpleasant. Simply reducing the amount of caffeine you take in can make you better prepared to deal with stress.

Eating right can alleviate another problem: obesity. Around one-third of people in the United States are *obese,* defined as having body weight more than 20 percent above the average weight for a person of a given height. Obesity can bring on stress for several reasons. For one thing, being overweight drags down the functioning of the body, leading to fatigue and a reduced ability to bounce back when we encounter challenges to our well-being. In addition, feeling fat in a society that acclaims the virtues of slimness can be stressful in and of itself.

Organize: Identifying What Is Causing You Stress

Student Alert: Identifying the factors that cause stress is more difficult than it seems, and what is stressful to one person is not always stressful to someone else. Help your students (or let them help each other) find the real causes of their stress.

You can't cope effectively with stress until you know what's causing it. In some cases, it's obvious—a series of bad test grades in a course, a roommate problem that keeps getting worse, a job supervisor who seems to delight in making things difficult. In other cases, however, the causes of stress may be more subtle. Perhaps your relationship with your boyfriend or girlfriend is rocky, and you have a nagging feeling that something is wrong.

Whatever the source of stress, you can't deal with it unless you know what it is. To organize your assault on stress, then, take a piece of paper and list the major circumstances that are causing you stress. Just listing them will help put you in control, and you'll be better able to figure out and apply strategies for coping with them.

> ### Sources of Stress
> 1. Government professor talks so fast that notetaking is nearly impossible
> 2. Difficulty paying rent this month.
> 3. Not enough time to study for Tuesday's psych test

Work: Developing Effective Coping Strategies

A wide variety of tactics can help you deal with stress. Among the most effective approaches to coping are these:

- **Take charge of the situation.** Stress is most apt to arise when we are faced with situations over which we have little or no control. Take charge of the situation and you'll increase your sense of mastery and reduce the experience of stress. For example, if several assignments are all due on the same day, you might try negotiating with one of your instructors for a later due date.

- **Don't waste energy trying to change the unchangeable.** There are some situations that you simply can't control. You can't change the fact that you have come down with a case of mono, and you can't change your performance on a test you took last week. Don't hit your head against a brick wall and try to modify things that can't be changed. Use your energy to address the situation as a problem to be solved: Seek out ways to improve the situation, not to rewrite history.

> "A smooth sea never made a skillful mariner."
>
> English proverb.

IM Link: Teaching the Text, Chapter 14, has several activities to assist you in teaching this part of the chapter.

- **Look for the silver lining.** Stress arises when we perceive a situation as threatening. If we can change how we perceive that situation, we can change our reactions to it. For instance, if your computer science instructor requires you to learn a difficult spreadsheet program in a very short time, the saving grace is that you may be able to use the skill to your advantage in getting a future job. (You can practice finding the silver lining in Try It 2 on page 360.)

- **Talk to your friends. Social support,** assistance and comfort supplied by others, can help us through stressful periods. Turning to our friends and family and simply talking about the stress we're under can help us tolerate it more effectively. Even anonymous telephone hotlines can provide us with social support. (The U.S. Public Health Service maintains a "master" toll-free number that can provide telephone numbers and addresses of many national groups. You can reach it by calling 800-336-4794.)

Social support

Assistance and comfort supplied by others in times of stress

- **Relax.** Because stress produces constant wear and tear on the body, it seems possible that practices that lead to the relaxation of the body might lead to a reduction in stress. And that's just what happens. Using any one of several techniques for producing physical relaxation can prevent stress. Among the best relaxation techniques:

    Meditation. Though often associated with its roots in the ancient Eastern religion of Zen Buddhism, **meditation,** a learned technique for refocusing attention and producing bodily relaxation, is practiced in some form by members of virtually every major religion. Meditation reduces blood pressure, slows respiration, and in general produces relaxation in the body.

Meditation

A learned technique for refocusing attention and producing bodily relaxation

How do you meditate? The process is actually rather simple. As summarized in Table 14.1 (p. 361), it includes sitting in a quiet room with eyes closed or focused on a point about six feet away from you and paying attention to your breath. Though the specifics of what you do may vary slightly, meditation works by helping you concentrate on breathing deeply and rhythmically, sometimes murmuring a word or sound repeatedly.

Teaching Tip: Do a relaxation activity in class (see above IM Link and Try It 3) or invite a colleague from your counseling center to do this with your class. You may want to schedule this activity near exam period at the end of the semester.

Progressive relaxation. Progressive relaxation does some of the same things that meditation does, but in a more direct way. To use progressive relaxation, you systematically tense and then relax different groups of muscles. For example, you might start with your lower arm, tensing it for five seconds and then relaxing it for a similar amount of

Try It! 2

Look for the Silver Lining

Consider the following list of potentially stressful situations. Try to find something positive—a silver lining—in each of them. The first two are completed to give you an idea of where to look for the silver lining.

Situation	Silver Lining
1. Your car just broke down and repairing it is more than you can afford right now.	1. This is the perfect time to begin exercising by walking and using your bicycle.
2. Your boss just yelled at you and threatened to fire you.	2. Either this is a good time to open an honest discussion with your boss about your job situation, OR this is a good time to get a more interesting job.
3. You have two papers due on Monday and there's a great concert you wanted to go to on Saturday night.	3.
4. You just failed an important test.	4.
5. You're flat broke, you have a date on Saturday, and you wanted to buy some things beforehand.	5.
6. Your last date went poorly and you think your girlfriend/boyfriend was hinting that it was time to break up.	6.
7. Your parents just told you that they can't afford to pay your tuition next semester.	7.
8. You just got cut from a sports team or club activity you loved.	8.
9. Your best friend is starting to turn weird and seems not to enjoy being with you as much as before.	9.
10. You just realized you don't really like your academic major, and you're not even sure you like your college much any more.	10.

time. By doing the same thing throughout the parts of your body, you'll be able to learn the "feel" of bodily relaxation. You can use the technique when you feel that stress is getting the better of you. (Use Try It 3 on page 362 to experience progressive relaxation for yourself.)

- **Remember that wimping out doesn't work—so keep your commitments.** Suppose you've promised a friend that you'll help out on moving day and yourself that you'll spend more time with your children. You've also been elected to the student body governing board, and you've made a commitment to bring more speakers to campus. Now you are facing all the demands connected to these commitments and feeling stressed.

You may be tempted to cope with the feeling by breaking some or all of your commitments, thinking, "I just need to sit at home and relax in front of the television!" This is not coping. It is escaping, and it doesn't reduce stress. Ducking out of commitments, whether to yourself or to

Discussion Prompt: What does keeping your promises, keeping your commitments, really mean? The current generation of college students sometimes is accused of not knowing what it means to be committed, to keep a promise. Ask them to defend themselves.

Table 14.1

Methods of Meditation

Step 1. Pick a focus word or short phrase that's firmly rooted in your personal belief system. For example, a nonreligious individual might choose a neutral word like *one* or *peace* or *love*. A Christian person desiring to use a prayer could pick the opening words of Psalm 23. *The Lord is my shepherd;* a Jewish person could choose *Shalom.*

Step 2. Sit quietly in a comfortable position.

Step 3. Close your eyes.

Step 4. Relax your muscles.

Step 5. Breathe slowly and naturally, repeating your focus word or phrase silently as you exhale.

Step 6. Throughout, assume a passive attitude. Don't worry about how well you're doing. When other thoughts come to mind, simply say to yourself, "Oh, well," and gently return to the repetition.

Step 7. Continue for 10 to 20 minutes. You may open your eyes to check the time, but do not use an alarm. When you finish, sit quietly for a minute or so, at first with your eyes closed and later with your eyes open. Then do not stand for one or two minutes.

Step 8. Practice the technique once or twice a day.

others, will make you feel guilty and anxious, and will be another source of stress—one without the satisfaction of having accomplished what you set out to do. Keep your promises.

 valuate: Asking If Your Strategies for Dealing with Stress Are Effective

Just as the experience of stress depends on how we interpret circumstances, the strategies for dealing with stress also vary in effectiveness depending on who we are. So if your efforts at coping aren't working, it's time to reconsider your approach. If talking to friends hasn't helped ease your stress response, maybe you need a different approach. Maybe you need to see the silver lining or cut back on some of your commitments. If one coping strategy doesn't work for you, try another. What's critical is that you don't become paralyzed, unable to deal with a situation. Instead, try something different until you find the right combination of strategies to improve the situation.

ethink: Placing Stress in Perspective

It's easy to think of stress as an enemy. In fact, the coping steps outlined in the P.O.W.E.R. Plan at the right are geared to overcoming its negative consequences. But consider the following two principles, which in the end may help you more than any others with understanding how to deal with stress:

PREPARE
Ready yourself physically

ORGANIZE
Identify what is causing you stress

WORK
Develop effective coping strategies

EVALUATE
Ask yourself if your strategies for dealing with stress are effective

RETHINK
Place stress in perspective

P.O.W.E.R. Plan

Try It! 3

Use Progressive Relaxation

You can undertake progressive relaxation almost anywhere, including the library, a sports field, or a classroom, since tensing and relaxing muscles is quiet and unobtrusive. Although the following exercise suggests you lie down, you can use parts of it no matter where you are.

1. Lie flat on your back, get comfortable, and focus on your toes.

2. Become aware of your left toes. Bunch them up into a tight ball, then let them go. Then let them relax even further.

3. Now work on your left foot, from the toes to the heel. Without tensing your toes, tighten up the rest of your foot and then let it relax. Then relax it more.

4. Work your way up your left leg all the way to your groin, first tensing and then relaxing each part. You may move up as slowly or as quickly as you wish, using big leaps (e.g., the entire lower leg) or small steps (e.g., the ankle, the calf, the front of the lower leg, the knee, etc.).

5. Repeat the process for the right leg.

6. Now tense and relax progressively your groin, buttocks, abdomen, lower back, ribs, upper back, and shoulders.

7. Work your way down each arm, one at a time, until you reach the fingers.

8. Return to the neck, then the jaw, cheeks, nose, eyes, ears, forehead, and skull.

By now you should be completely relaxed. In fact, you may even be asleep—this technique works well as a sleep-induction strategy.

To vary the routine, play with it. Try going from top to bottom, or from your extremities in and ending with your groin. Or target any other part of your body to end up at, and take the most circuitous route you can think of.

IM Link: Teaching the Text, Chapter 14, Sections IV, VII and VIII, for helpful activities in teaching this chapter.

- **Don't sweat the small stuff . . . and it's all small stuff.** Stress expert Richard Carlson[3] emphasizes the importance of putting the circumstances we encounter into the proper perspective. He argues that we frequently let ourselves get upset about situations that are actually minor. So what if someone cuts us off in traffic, or does less than his or her share on a group project, or unfairly criticizes us? It's hardly the end of the world, and the behavior of the other people involved in such situations reflects negatively on them, not us. One of the best ways to reduce stress, consequently, is to maintain an appropriate perspective on the events of your life, sorting out what is and is not important.

- **Make peace with stress.** Think of what it would be like to have no stress—none at all—in your life. Would you really be happier, better adjusted, and more successful? The answer is "probably not." A life that presented no challenges would probably be, in a word, boring. So think about stress as an exciting, although admittedly sometimes difficult, friend. Welcome it, because its presence indicates that your life is stimulating, challenging, and exciting—and who would want it any other way?

Drug Abuse

For better or worse, drugs are part of all of our lives. It's virtually impossible to be unaware of the extent of the U.S. and international problem of illegal drug use, which involves millions of individuals who have used illegal substances at least once. Patterns of drug use and the ability to avoid abusing drugs are often established in college. These patterns can have a big impact on your college career and your life, so it is a good idea to learn what you can now, before negative patterns of abuse, and in some cases, addiction, take hold.

Teaching Tip: Before you begin this final section of the chapter, get specific facts about drugs and alcohol use on your campus. This will give you more credibility when talking to your students who think they know this information already.

Alcohol and Its Allure

The drug most likely to be found on college campuses is alcohol. It may surprise you to know that though it initially seems to raise your spirits, alcohol is actually and ultimately a depressant. As the amount of alcohol one consumes increases, its depressive effects become more obvious. You've probably seen its other negative effects: Drinkers show poor judgment, their memory is impaired, and their speech becomes slurred and eventually incoherent. If you drink enough, you'll pass out. And if you consume enough alcohol in a short period, you can die of alcohol poisoning.

> **"I set some limits for myself, and my transcript thanked me for it from then on."**
>
> Betty Baugh Harrison, University of North Carolina.[4]

The potential negative consequences of drinking have done little to prevent the use of alcohol on college campuses. More than 75 percent of college students say they've had a drink within the last 30 days, and the average person over the age of fourteen drinks 2½ gallons of pure alcohol over the course of a year—some 200 drinks, on average, per person. (To assess alcohol use on your campus, complete Try It 4 on page 365.)

Some students drink even more, and the extent of alcohol consumption can reach astonishing levels. Half of all male college students and 40 percent of all female college students have engaged in **binge drinking,** defined as having at least four (for females) or five (for males) drinks in a single sitting. Such heavy drinking doesn't just affect the drinker. Most college students report having had their studying or sleep disturbed by drunk students. Further, around a third of students have been insulted or humiliated by a drunk student, and 25 percent of women have been the target of an unwanted sexual advance by a drunk classmate.

Binge drinking
Having at least four (for females) or five (for males) drinks in a single sitting

Close to 20 million people in the United States are alcoholics, and college students make up their fair share of the total. **Alcoholics,** individuals with serious alcohol-abuse problems, become dependent on alcohol, experiencing a physical craving for it. They continue to drink despite serious consequences. Furthermore, they develop a tolerance for alcohol and must drink increasing amounts in order to experience the initially positive effects that alcohol brings about.

Alcoholics
Individuals with serious alcohol-abuse problems who become dependent on alcohol and continue to drink despite serious consequences

The long-term consequences of high levels of alcohol consumption are severe. Heavy drinking damages the liver and digestive system, and can even affect brain cells. In fact, virtually every part of the body is eventually affected by heavy alcohol use.

Anticipating Job Stress

Students are not the only ones who have to cope with stress. It's also one of the prime hazards of the world of work. Illnesses related to job stress result in costs of $150 *billion* each year.

Consequently, taking potential stress into account should be an important consideration when choosing a profession. Asking yourself the following questions can help you identify the factors that may induce stress on the job:

- How much control over working conditions will I have? The more control an employee has in day-to-day decision making, the lower the level of stress.

- What are the demands of the job? Will I face constant demands to do more work and to work more quickly? Higher work demands create a more stressful work environment.

- What is the tolerance for error? Some occupations, such as that of air traffic controller, have no margin for error, while others, such as in many white-collar professions, give workers a second chance if they make a mistake.

- How closely do my abilities and strengths match the requirements of the job? A good match between one's abilities and the demands of a job is the best insurance against an unduly stressful work environment.

- How well do I cope with stress? If your coping skills are good, you may be suited for entering a high-stress occupation. But if you have difficulty dealing with stress, choosing a career in a field that produces less stress makes more sense.

Nicotine

Despite the multi-billion-dollar tobacco settlements between the various governmental bodies and manufacturers of cigarettes, smoking remains a significant health problem. Smoking causes lung damage and increases the risks of developing cancer, emphysema, and a host of other diseases.

Why do people smoke, when the evidence is so clear about its risks? They start to smoke for a variety of reasons. Smoking is sometimes viewed as a kind of initiation into adulthood, a sign of growing up. In other cases, teenagers see smoking as "cool," a view glorified by movies and television.

The problem is that, no matter what the reason a person tries out a few cigarettes, smoking usually quickly becomes a habit because a major ingredient of tobacco—nicotine—is an addictive drug. An *addictive drug* produces a biological or psychological dependence. The absence of the drug leads to a craving for it that may be nearly irresistible.

Smoking is one of the hardest addictions to break. Among the suggestions for quitting are the following:

- **Remain smoke-free one day at a time.** Don't think to yourself about not smoking tomorrow, or next week, or for the rest of your life. Instead, think of what you're doing as not smoking for the rest of the day. You can worry about tomorrow . . . tomorrow.

- **Visualize the consequences of smoking.** Visualize blackened, rotting lungs filled with smoke. Then think about the fresh, pink lungs that you'll have after you've stopped smoking.

- **Exercise.** The all-purpose antidote, exercise, will make you feel better physically and take your mind off smoking.

- **Use nicotine patches or nicotine gum.** "The Patch" and nicotine gum can provide enough nicotine to satisfy your craving for the drug, while permitting you to stop smoking. Physicians can also sometimes prescribe drugs that help reduce the craving for nicotine.

Try It!
4

Assess Alcohol Use on Campus

What is the alcohol situation on your campus? Is liquor legal or illegal? Free-flowing or hard to come by? Available on campus or do drinkers have to go off campus?

How tough is your college administration about the use of alcohol on campus?

Would you characterize your school as a party school? About what percent of the students who are on campus on Friday night consume several drinks?

Does the partying start on Friday? Thursday? Earlier?

Do you know people who drink only to get drunk?

Have you ever suspected any of your friends or acquaintances of being alcoholics? If so, do you know what to do about it?

Have you ever witnessed a scene in which drunkenness played a part in violence? Obnoxious behavior? Abuse of women?

Are you aware of offices or people on your campus who can help with problems related to alcohol abuse?

- **Avoid smokers.** It's nearly impossible to avoid the urge to smoke when others are lighting up. If you're trying to quit, stay away from people who are smoking.

- **Enlist the social support of family and friends.** Tell others that you're trying to quit, and accept their encouragement and praise.

- **Reward yourself.** Every few days, give yourself some kind of reinforcement for spending a period of time smoke-free. Go to a movie, buy a CD. Think about how you can afford these more easily since you aren't buying cigarettes anymore.

- **Join a quit-smoking program.** Many college health services hold periodic programs to help students who wish to stop smoking. By enrolling in one, you'll receive the support of others who are in the same boat as you are.

- **Keep trying.** If after quitting you start smoking again, just consider that lapse as part of the process of quitting. Many people quit several times before they manage to quit for good.

Illegal Drugs

Student Alert: Who enforces the laws regarding illegal drug use on your campus? Local or campus police? Have students research campus drug policies and bring this information to class.

"Just say 'no.'"

If it were only so easy. Decisions about drugs are quite a bit more complicated than simplistic antidrug slogans would have you believe. They involve complex decisions about your body, peer pressure, and your personal values.

Several things are clear, however. Despite the prevalence of illicit drug use among college students—surveys show that around a third of college students report having used an illegal drug at least once in the previous year—the benefits of drug use are difficult to enumerate. Apart from a temporary high, the advantages of using drugs are nil, and the use of illegal drugs is among the riskiest activities in which people can engage. Not only does drug use make you vulnerable to arrest, it also poses short- and long-term health risks. The escape from one's responsibilities that drugs provide is likely to make it even harder to later deal with those responsibilities—which aren't going to go away.

> "Every form of addiction is bad, no matter whether the narcotic be alcohol or morphine or idealism."
>
> —Carl Jung

Not all illegal drugs are the same, and they produce widely varying effects and consequences (see Table 14.1). But they all share a common result: a reduction in your awareness of what is happening around you and an escape from the realities of life.

People often fall into drug use without much thought. But doing so is still a personal choice. Preaching and slogans are not going to help you to make a sensible decision. You need to employ every critical thinking skill you can to determine exactly what you wish—and don't wish—to introduce into your body. Give some thought to why escape is attractive and consider seeking counseling instead. Allow yourself to consider the long- and short-term effects of drug use—both the physical effects as well as the potential effects on your own aspirations and dreams. Let yourself think about the legal consequences of drug use. A drug conviction can lead to expulsion from college and refusal

Table 14.1

Common Drugs

Drug	Street Name	Effects	Withdrawal Symptoms	Adverse/Overdose Reactions
Stimulants				
Cocaine	Coke, blow, toot, snow, lady, crack	Increased confidence, mood elevation, sense of energy and alertness, decreased appetite, anxiety, irritability, insomnia, transient drowsiness, delayed orgasm	Apathy, general fatigue, prolonged sleep, depression, disorientation, suicidal thoughts, agitated motor activity, irritability, bizarre dreams	Elevated blood pressure, increase in body temperature, face-picking, suspiciousness, bizarre and repetitious behavior, vivid hallucinations, convulsions, possible death
Amphetamines				
Benzedrine	Speed			
Dexedrine	Speed			
Depressants				
Barbiturates				
Nembutal	Yellowjackets, yellows, reds	Anxiety reduction, impulsiveness, dramatic mood swings, bizarre thoughts, suicidal behavior, slurred speech, disorientation, slowed mental and physical functioning, limited attention span	Weakness, restlessness, nausea and vomiting, headaches, nightmares, irritability, depression, acute anxiety, hallucinations, seizures, possible death	Confusion, decreased response to pain, shallow respiration, dilated pupils, weak and rapid pulse, coma, possible death
Seconal				
Phenobarbital				
Alcohol	Booze			
Narcotics				
Heroin	H, hombre, junk, smack, dope, horse, crap	Anxiety and pain reduction, apathy, difficulty in concentration, slowed speech, decreased physical activity, drooling, itching, euphoria, nausea	Anxiety, vomiting, sneezing, diarrhea, lower back pain, watery eyes, runny nose, yawning, irritability, tremors, panic, chills and sweating, cramps	Depressed levels of consciousness, low blood pressure, rapid heart rate, shallow breathing, convulsions, coma, possible death
Morphine	Drugstore dope, cube, first line, mud			
Hallucinogens				
Cannabis	Bhang, Kif, ganja, dope, grass, pot, smoke, hemp, joint, weed, bone, Mary Jane, herb, tea	Euphoria, relaxed inhibitions, increased appetite, disoriented behavior	Hyperactivity, insomnia, decreased appetite, anxiety	Severe reactions are rare but include panic, paranoia, fatigue, bizarre and dangerous behavior, decreased testosterone over long term; immune-system effects
Marijuana				
Hashish				
Hash oil				
LSD	Electricity, acid, quasey, blotter acid, microdot, white lightning, purple barrels	Fascination with ordinary objects; heightened aesthetic responses; vision and depth distortion; heightened sensitivity to faces and gestures; magnified feelings; paranoia; panic; euphoria	Not reported	Nausea and chills; increased pulse, temperature, and blood pressure; trembling; slow, deep breathing; loss of appetite; insomnia; longer, more intense "trips"; bizarre, dangerous behavior
Phencyclidine (PCP)	Angel dust, hog, rocket fuel, superweed, peace pill, elephant tranquilizer, dust, bad pizza	Increased blood pressure and heart rate; sweating; nausea; slowed reflexes; altered body image; altered perception of time and space; impaired memory	Not reported	Highly variable and possibly dose-related; disorientation; loss of recent memory; bizarre, violent behavior; hallucinations and delusions; coma

by many employers to hire you. Furthermore, random drug tests are increasingly a part of corporate life, and your ability to get and keep a job may be placed at risk if you use drugs—even only occasionally.

Drugs that produce addiction, such as cocaine and heroin, present a further set of problems. The lives of people with drug addictions become centered on the drug. They enter into a pattern of alternating highs—when on the drug—and lows. During their lows, much of their thinking is centered on obtaining the drug and looking forward to their next high.

Addiction's Warning Signs Addictions to drugs—and alcohol—can begin subtly, and you may not be aware of the extent of the problem. Here are some signs that indicate when use becomes abuse:

- Feeling you need to be high to have a good time.
- Being high more often than not.
- Getting high to get yourself going.
- Going to class or work high.
- Missing class or work because you are high.
- Being unprepared for class because you were high.
- Feeling regret over something you did while you were high.
- Driving while high.
- Having a legal problem due to being high.
- Behaving, while high, in a way you wouldn't otherwise.
- Being high in nonsocial, solitary situations.
- Thinking about drugs or alcohol much of the time.
- Avoiding family or friends while using liquor or drugs.
- Hiding drug or alcohol use from others.

Any one of these symptoms indicates that you have a drug or alcohol problem. If you do have a problem, seek professional help. Addictions to illegal drugs or alcohol are extremely difficult to deal with on your own. No matter how good your intentions, almost no one can overcome the cravings brought about by an addiction to a particular substance without help.

Here are some places to which you can turn:

1. **College health services, counseling centers, and mental health centers.** Most colleges provide services to help you overcome an addiction. They can evaluate the extent of the problem and refer you to the proper place for further help. (To learn about your own campus resources, complete Try It 5.)

2. **Drug treatment centers and clinics.** Sometimes located in hospitals and sometimes independently run, drug treatment centers or clinics can provide help. You can also check your telephone book for a local listing of Alcoholics Anonymous or Narcotics Anonymous.

3. **Government hotlines.** The federal government provides extensive information about drug and alcohol use. For starters, call The National Clearinghouse on Alcohol and Drug Information at 1-800-729-6686. For alcohol difficulties in particular, call the National Council on Alco-

Teaching Tip: Denial of behavior remains a big part of the problem in dealing with drug and alcohol abuse. Encourage students to keep a journal. They may find it easier to face their thoughts in private than in public.

Try It! 5

Tap Campus Resources

Complete the following chart to identify the campus office locations and their services that deal with alcohol and drug problems.

Campus Resource	Where Is It?	What Service Does It Provide?	How Do You Get in Touch?
Health Center			
Mental Health Center			
Campus Chaplain			
Drug and Alcohol Education Center(s)			
Counseling Center			
Residential Life Office			
Ombudsman			
Campus Security Services			
(add other office here)			
(add other office here)			
(add other office here)			
(add other office here)			

holism at (800) 622-2255. For drug problems, you can call the National Institute on Drug Abuse at (800) 662-4357. Finally, you can write to the National Council on Alcoholism and Drug Dependence, 12 West 21 Street, New York, NY 10010, for help with alcohol and drug problems.

Sexual Health and Decision Making

Relationships. Contraception. AIDS. Rape.

Sexual health relates to a host of issues, involving not just your body but your heart and mind as well. In fact, it is often said that our most important sexual organ is our brain. It determines what we view as sexually arousing, and it's what we use to make decisions and choices about our sexuality.

Although the focus of the brief discussion of sexual health here is on strategies for protecting yourself (from pregnancy, sexually transmitted diseases, and rape), sexual decisions are also a reflection of your basic values. You can't make responsible decisions about sex without knowing what is important to you and how you view yourself. So you don't want to wait until a sexual encounter begins before thinking through your views of sexuality and what is and is not right for you.

Preventing Unwanted Pregnancy

There is one and only one totally effective means of preventing pregnancy: Don't have sexual intercourse. **Abstinence**, refraining from intercourse, only works, however, if you practice it without fail—something that many people find difficult. But it certainly is possible. Despite the folklore that insists "everybody's doing it," they're not. In fact, if you think critically about what others say about their sexual activity, you'll conclude that the possibility of misrepresentation of sexual activity is high.

Those who do want to have a sexual relationship can still avoid pregnancy. A variety of possibilities exists, including the following:

- **Birth control pills.** Composed of artificial hormones, birth control pills are among the most effective ways of preventing pregnancy—as long as they are taken as prescribed. Except for women with particular medical conditions, the side effects are minimal.

- **Implants.** One of the newest forms of birth control, implants work through a simple surgical procedure in which a small capsule is inserted into a woman's upper arm. Implants last for five years, preventing pregnancy for the entire period. With few side effects, implants are highly effective, but they are only practical for women who wish to avoid pregnancy for extended periods.

- **Intrauterine device, or IUD.** IUDs are small pieces of plastic inserted by a medical practitioner into a woman's uterus. Although highly effective, some have been found to produce unacceptable side effects, including infections and scarring that can make it impossible for a woman to get pregnant when she wants to.

- **Diaphragms and cervical caps.** Diaphragms and cervical caps are circular, dome-shaped pieces of thin rubber that a woman inserts into her vagina, covering the cervix. A sperm-killing cream or jelly must be used simultaneously, and the diaphragm and cervical cap must be removed after sexual intercourse. Although side effects are few, the risk of pregnancy is somewhat higher than with the other forms of birth control we've discussed; some 18 percent of women using them become pregnant.

- **Condoms.** Condoms are thin sheaths that fit over the penis. By preventing sperm from entering the vagina, they are highly effective in preventing pregnancy, if used properly and consistently. If they are used

Relationships and sexuality raise substantial issues, involving your attitudes, beliefs, values, and emotions, as well as your body, in a complex intermix. Making responsible decisions requires that you know who you are and what's important to you.

Abstinence
The avoidance of sexual contact

Chapter 14 Enjoying Health and Wellness

with a contraceptive jelly that kills sperm and are positioned properly, condoms are highly effective.

- **Contraceptive sponge.** The sponge, shaped like a large mushroom cap, is inserted into the vagina. It can be left in place for 24 hours, during which time it can be used for multiple acts of intercourse. Although it has few side effects, it has a failure rate of between 17 and 25 percent.

- **Rhythm.** The only form of birth control that involves no chemical or mechanical intervention, rhythm consists of refraining from intercourse during times in a woman's menstrual cycle when pregnancy is possible. With a failure rate of 20 percent, rhythm requires close scrutiny of calendars, body temperature, or cervical mucus—all of which can be indicators of the time of the month to avoid intercourse.

- **Withdrawal and douching: ineffective birth control.** Withdrawal, in which a man removes his penis from a woman's vagina before climaxing, and douching, flushing the vagina with a liquid, just don't work. They should not be used for birth control because they are so ineffective.

- **Sterilization.** Sterilization is a surgical procedure that causes a person to become permanently incapable of having children.

What You Can Do to Avoid Sexually Transmitted Diseases

Right now, one out of five people in the United States is infected with some form of **sexually transmitted diseases (STDs)**—medical conditions acquired through sexual contact. At least one out of four will eventually contract an STD at some point in life (see Table 14.2 on page 372).

There are many varieties of STDs, although all share a similar origin: sexual contact. Depending on the type of disease, symptoms may include warts in the genital area, pelvic infection, painful urination, infertility, blindness, and even death.

The STD that has had the greatest impact in the last decade is **acquired immune deficiency syndrome (AIDS)**. Although it started as a disease that most often affected homosexuals, AIDS quickly spread among heterosexuals. Some populations are particularly affected, such as intravenous drug users. Worldwide, more than six million people have already died from the disease. Some estimates suggest that 40 million people now carry the AIDS virus.

Although AIDS is the best-known STD, the most common is *chlamydia*, a disease that if left untreated can cause sterility in some victims. *Genital herpes* is a virus that appears as small blisters or sores around the genitals. Although the sores heal after several weeks, the disease can remain dormant and reappear periodically. Other STDs, although somewhat less common, also afflict millions of people. (See Table 14.2 for a summary of the common STDs.)

It's no secret how to avoid AIDS and other STDs: Abstinence—the avoidance of sexual contact—is completely effective. However, many people are unwilling to make such a choice. Several alternative approaches, called "smart sex" practices, reduce the risk of contracting STDs. They include the following:

- **Know your sexual partner—well.** You should not have sexual contact with a person who is only a casual acquaintance. You want to know the person well enough to have a discussion with him or her in which you both talk about your sexual histories.

Sexually transmitted diseases (STDs)
Medical conditions acquired through sexual contact

Acquired immune deficiency syndrome (AIDS)
A lethal, sexually transmitted disease that causes the destruction of the body's immune system

Table 14.2

Common Sexually Transmitted Diseases (STDs)

	Cause	Transmission	Symptoms
AIDS—HIV	Human immuno-deficiency virus (HIV)	Coming in direct contact with infected blood, semen, or vaginal secretions. Anal or vaginal intercourse, being born to an infected female, receiving infected blood or blood products, or sharing needles and syringes with someone infected with the HIV virus.	In early stages of infection with HIV there typically are no symptoms. As the disease progresses the following are usual symptoms: Chronic or swollen glands. Weight loss of more than 10 pounds. Flu-like symptoms that persist. Purple spots on the skin and inside the mouth, nose, or rectum. Unusual susceptibility to parasitic, fungal, bacterial, and viral infections or certain cancers.
Chlamydia	Bacteria	Vaginal or anal intercourse or oral sex with someone who is infected.	Many infected people have no symptoms, but when present the most common are the following: Pain, burning or "itching" sensations with urination. Vaginal infections may be associated with abnormal discharge. Oral infections may be exhibited by a sore throat but usually have no symptoms. Penile infections may be associated with a yellowish discharge.
Gonorrhea	Bacteria	Vaginal or anal intercourse or oral sex with someone who is infected.	Many infected people have no symptoms but are still contagious. Most common symptoms are the following: Pain, burning or "itching" sensations with urination. Vaginal infections may be associated with abnormal discharge. Oral infections may be exhibited by a sore throat but usually have no symptoms. Penile infections may be associated with a yellowish discharge.
Hepatitis A	Virus	Spread through contaminated feces and anal–oral contact during sexual activity.	Symptoms for hepatitis A and B will be similar: nausea, vomiting, diarrhea, fatigue, lack of appetite, dark urine, light stools, and/or abdominal tenderness.
Hepatitis B	Virus	Spread via blood by sexual contact or via an injection with a contaminated needle.	Symptoms for hepatitis A and B will be similar: nausea, vomiting, diarrhea, fatigue, lack of appetite, dark urine, light stools, and/or abdominal tenderness.
Genital Herpes	Herpes simplex virus (HSV)	Contact with virus in infected blisters or within virus being shed from the site of previous infections that may have no symptoms.	Cluster of tender, painful blisters, ulcers, or sores typically on or around the lips, mouth, genitals, or anus. Symptoms may be very mild or not present at all, but people are still infected and contagious. Blisters, ulcers, and sores last one to three weeks during initial outbreaks. Lesions heal, but person still has herpes. Lesions commonly recur without being re-exposed to the disease.
Genital Warts	Human papilloma virus (HPV)	Vaginal or anal intercourse or oral sex with someone who has the virus.	Small bumpy "cauliflower" looking warts that are usually painless and appear on or around the genitals or anus. Itching and burning around the lesions may occur, but such symptoms are rare. Infections without symptoms are common.

- **Prevent the exchange of bodily fluids during all sex acts.** Avoid semen and unprotected anal intercourse and oral sex.

- **Use condoms.** Condoms not only prevent the spread of AIDS and other STDs, but they also prevent pregnancy.

- **Be faithful to a single partner.** People in long-term relationships with only one other individual are less likely to contract AIDS and other STDs than those with multiple sexual partners.

Date Rape

We usually think of rape as a rare crime, committed by strangers. Unfortunately, not only is rape surprisingly common, but rapists usually know their victims. In a national survey conducted on college campuses, one out of eight women reported having been raped. In about half the reported cases, the rapists were first dates, casual dates, or romantic acquaintances—situations categorized as **date rape.** Overall, then, women are far more likely to be raped by someone they know than by a stranger. There is a 14 to 25 percent chance that a woman will be the victim of rape during her lifetime. Although we'll focus on date rape because it is the more-common type on campus, it is no different from any other form of rape, except for the victim's acquaintance with the rapist.

What leads to rape? Most often, rape has less to do with sex than with power and anger. Rapists use forced sex to demonstrate their power and control over the victim. The rapist's pleasure comes not so much from sex as from forcing someone to submit. Sometimes sexual behavior is a demonstration of the rapist's rage at women in general.

In addition, rapes sometimes are brought about by the common—but untrue—belief that when women offer resistance to sex, they don't really mean it. If a man holds the view that when a woman says no to sex, she really means yes, he is likely to ignore the woman's protests that she doesn't want sex, resulting in rape. Some men may even believe that it is unmasculine to accept no for an answer, perhaps because they feel it is a rejection of them as men.

Whatever the causes, rape is devastating to the victim. Victims experience extreme anxiety, disbelief, fear, and shock. These reactions may linger for years, and rape victims may experience suspiciousness and a fear of entering into relationships.

Both men and women must be sensitive to the issue of date rape. Among the suggestions for reducing its incidence are the following:

- **Set limits.** Women have the right to set firm limits, and these should be communicated clearly, firmly, and early on.

- **No means no.** When a partner says no, it means nothing other than no.

- **Be assertive.** You should never passively accept being pressured into an activity in which you don't want to engage. Remember that passivity may be interpreted as consent.

- **Communicate.** Women and men should talk about their views of sexual behavior and what is and is not permissible.

- **Keep in mind that alcohol and drugs cloud judgment.** Nothing hinders communication more than alcohol and drugs.

Date rape
Forced sex in which the rapist is a date or romantic acquaintance

Discussion Project: The issue of violence in relationships of college-aged students is a difficult but important one. Open the floor to your students and encourage them to share their views.

Speaking of Success

Name: *Justin McCarthy*
Education: *Washington College, Chestertown, Maryland; senior majoring in political science*
Home: *Ardmore, Pennsylvania*

Justin McCarthy was an all-around athlete in high school—he wrestled and played football, soccer, and lacrosse, and was a good student, too, but things changed when he became a freshman at Washington College.

"Sports always played a huge role in my life," McCarthy says. "In high school I could play sports and do my work, but in college I found both to be much more demanding. I had almost convinced myself that studying and sports were no different in college, but soon I was struggling at both."

McCarthy attributes his problems, and the stress he felt, to his living situation in college. He shared a residence with an all-male, all-athlete group, and it proved the wrong mix for him.

"We all just hung out and procrastinated. Wasting time was our biggest problem," he says. "We were all so happy to be in college, but we didn't understand that to stay there we had to commit ourselves and discipline ourselves to the work."

The results of his freshman year were not good. McCarthy turned in a dismal 1.75 grade point average, and it became clear that something had to give. College wasn't fun anymore; it was becoming a highly stressful experience.

"My mother would tell me that if I

put half the effort into my studies that I put into sports, I would be fine," McCarthy recalls. "I heard her, but I never listened. But that summer I realized I had to make some changes and reevaluate my priorities."

McCarthy made two major changes when he returned to campus as a sophomore. First, he changed his living situation, and second, he got organized.

"I went from living with all these guys who weren't sure what they wanted to do, to a more controlled environment. I moved in with some of my best friends who were organized and motivated," he says. "I started to take notes, to highlight reading assignments. I noted when tests and papers were due, established a rapport with my teachers, and, instead of sitting in the back of the class, I started to sit up front.

"I've completely evolved into this person who is constantly organized and dedicated to his goals. Now I'm willing to sacrifice and study that extra hour. I didn't know what success was like before."

At the end of his sophomore year McCarthy turned in a grade point average of 3.1. He is committed to doing well and knows how to go about it.

"I've brought my total grade point average up, and I know I can do better," he notes. "My whole outlook and perspective have come full circle since my freshman year. I know if I try a little harder I can attain the goals that I set for myself."

What is involved in keeping fit and healthy, and why is it important for me to do so?

- For all people, keeping fit and healthy is both essential and challenging. It is vital to learn to eat properly, especially by eating a variety of foods on a regular schedule and by restricting your intake of fat, cholesterol, and salt.

- Exercise is valuable because it improves health and well-being. Choosing exercises that we like, making everyday activities a part of exercise, and exercising with others can help form the habit of exercise.

- The third key element of good health is sleeping properly. Good exercise and eating habits can contribute to sound sleep, as can the development of regular sleeping habits and the use of sleep-assisting practices.

What is stress and how can I control it?

- Stress is a common experience, appearing in three main forms: cataclysmic events, personal stressors, and daily hassles. Excessive stress is not only unpleasant and upsetting, it also has negative effects on the body and mind.

- Coping with stress involves becoming prepared for future stress through proper diet and exercise, identifying the causes of stress in one's life, taking control of stress, seeking social support, practicing relaxation techniques, training oneself to redefine and reinterpret stressful situations, and keeping one's promises.

What are the main threats to my health and well-being?

- One of the major threats that college students (and others) face is the improper use of drugs. The most commonly abused drug is alcohol, which is a depressant (despite an initial reduction of inhibitions and feeling of euphoria) and can lead to a physical or psychological dependence. Nicotine is the second most commonly abused drug.

- The use of illegal drugs presents not only potential dangers related to law-breaking and prosecution, but short- and long-term health risks as well. Drugs cause a reduction in awareness and involvement in life, and some drugs can be dangerously addictive.

What are the components of sexual health?

- Sexual health is as important as other forms of health. People must make their own individual decisions about their sexuality and how they will express it.

- Many forms of contraception are available, ranging from abstinence to surgical implants. Each form has different procedures, risks, and effectiveness.

- The incidence of sexually transmitted diseases (STDs) is high in the United States, with about 25 percent of the population experiencing an STD at some point in life.

- Rape is a surprisingly common crime, with most victims knowing the rapist—often in a circumstance known as date rape.

Key Terms and Concepts

Abstinence (p. 370)
Acquired immune deficiency
   syndrome (AIDS) (p. 371)
Alcoholics (p. 363)
Binge drinking (p. 363)
Cataclysmic events (p. 354)
Coping (p. 355)
Daily hassles (p. 355)

Date rape (p. 373)
Meditation (p. 359)
Personal stressors (p. 354)
Sexually transmitted diseases
   (STDs) (p. 371)
Social support (p. 359)
Stress (p. 354)

Resources

On Campus

Your college health service/medical provider is the first line of defense if you become ill. The staff can provide you with advice and often medical care. Furthermore, colleges often have health education offices that help educate students on safer sex practices, on how to eat in healthier ways, and generally on how to increase wellness. Finally, colleges sometimes offer stress reduction workshops to help students cope more effectively.

In Print

The title says it all: *The New York Times Book of Health: How to Feel Fitter, Eat Better, and Live Longer* (Times Books, 1998), by Jane Brody, provides an up-to-date, commonsense guide to living well. *Why Zebras Don't Get Ulcers: An Updated Guide to Stress, Stress-Related Diseases, and Coping* (W. H. Freeman, 1998), by Robert M. Sapolsky, offers an entertaining guide to both the reasons we experience stress and ways of coping with it. Jeffery Nevid's *Choices: Sex in the Age of STDs* (Allyn & Bacon, 1997) offers clear-headed and accurate advice on decisions relating to sexual behavior.

On the Web

The following sites on the World Wide Web provide the opportunity to extend your learning about the material in this chapter. (Although the Web addresses were accurate at the time the book was printed, check the P.O.W.E.R. Learning Web site [http://mhhe.com/power] for any changes that may have occurred.)

http://www.amwa-doc.org/publications/WCHealthbook/dietamwa-ch03.html
   The American Medical Women's Association Web site offers suggestions on healthy eating and dieting. Sections include choosing and preparing foods, the health risks of obesity, and dietary myths.

A page on coping with stress from the Canadian Mental Health Association's Web site. It includes numerous subsections covering such areas as physical exercise, easy ways to take pressure off yourself, the effects of stress on health, and mental skills using meditation.

http://www.mirror-mirror.org/eatdis.htm

A guide to eating disorders. Definitions, coping strategies, links to related organizations, and personal messages from survivors can all be found among the information related to eating disorders presented here.

http://www.healthywomen.org/qa/contraception.html

A concise presentation and discussion of various methods of contraception is provided here by the National Women's Health Resource Center.

http://www.state.ma.us/dph/commdis.htm

This site provides information on the prevention and control of sexually transmitted diseases. It also includes links to fact sheets and publications containing further information.

Taking It to the Net

1 Find two stress reduction techniques. Possible strategy: Go to AltaVista (**www.altavista.com**) and enter "stress+reduction+techniques" into the search field. Examine the sites located until you find two stress reduction techniques. Try each of the techniques. Do you feel less stressed and more relaxed? Which of the techniques works best for you?

2 Locate the most-recent statistics on drug use by U.S. students. One possible approach: Go to Yahoo! (**www.yahoo.com**) and enter the phrase "drug statistics government." Examine the results and consider how they compare to your own perceptions of the extent of drug use.

The Case of . . .

Two Perspectives

It started out innocently, as a date to study for an exam. And then it turned wrong. Here's what Bob had to say:

Patty and I were in the same statistics class. She usually sat near me and was always very friendly. I liked her and thought maybe she liked me, too.

Last Thursday I decided to find out. After class I suggested that she come to my place so we could study for midterms together. She agreed immediately, which was a good sign.

That night everything seemed to go perfectly. We studied for a while and then took a break. I could tell that she liked me, and I was attracted to her. I was getting excited. I started kissing her. I could tell that she really liked it.

We started touching each other and it felt really good. All of a sudden she pulled away and said "Stop." I figured she didn't want me to think that she was "easy" or "loose. . . ."

I just ignored her protests and eventually she stopped struggling. I think she liked it but afterwards she acted bummed out and cold.

Patty, on the other hand, had a very different view of their encounter. Here's her description:

I knew Bob from my statistics class. He's cute and we are both good at statistics, so when a tough midterm was scheduled, I was glad that he suggested we study together. It never occurred to me that it was anything except a study date.

That night everything went fine at first. We got a lot of studying done in a short amount of time, so when he suggested we take a break, I thought we deserved it.

Well, all of a sudden he started acting really romantic and started kissing me. I liked the kissing, but then he started touching me below the waist. I pulled away and tried to stop him but he didn't listen. After a while I stopped struggling; he was hurting me and I was scared. He was so much bigger and stronger than me. I couldn't believe it was happening to me. I didn't know what to do.

He actually forced me to have sex with him. I guess looking back on it I should have screamed or done something besides trying to reason with him, but it was so unexpected. I couldn't believe it was happening. [5]

1. Was Bob being dishonest in setting up the study date? Was he dishonest during the sexual encounter? Is he still being dishonest?

2. What should Bob have done when Patty first said "Stop"?

3. What could Patty have done when Bob began acting romantically?

4. Was Bob right to interpret Patty's initial responsiveness to his romantic advances as acceptance of a sexual relationship? Was Patty "leading him on"? Did Patty's initial responsiveness justify his pursuing sex beyond the point at which she said "Stop"?

A Final Word

Throughout this book you've seen how the principles of P.O.W.E.R. Learning can be applied to a variety of situations, ranging from reading and writing to coping with stress. You can use the framework in any situation where you need to organize your thinking and behavior in a systematic way. It's a tool you can call on throughout life.

College is the beginning of a journey through adulthood. This book has been designed to help you with the immediate demands and challenges of college, but at the same time to prepare you for life after school. It has tried to show you that it is you who must make things happen to fulfill your own aspirations and goals to attain success.

Ultimately, however, there are some key ingredients to success that no book can teach you, and that only you can provide: integrity and honesty, intellectual curiosity, and love. I hope this book will help you as you consider what your contribution to the world will be and work to make that contribution.

Endnotes

Chapter 1

1. Higher Education Research Institute, University of California at Los Angeles. (1998). *The American Freshman: National Norms for Fall 1997*. Los Angeles: Higher Education Research Institute, UCLA.

2. Tyler, S. (1997). *Been there should've done that!* Haslett, MI: Front Porch Press. p. 214.

3. Gottesman, G. (1994). *College survival*. New York: Macmillan. p. 70.

4. Adapted from Good, L.R., & Good, K.C. (1973). An objective measure of the motive to avoid success. *Psychological Reports, 33*, 1009–1010.

Chapter 2

1. Adapted, in part, from Ferner, J.D. (1980). *Successful time management*. New York: Wiley. p. 33.

2. Adapted from Ferner, J.D. (1980). *Successful time management*. New York: Wiley. p. 33.

3. Gottesman, G. (1994). *College survival*. New York: MacMillan. p. 61.

Chapter 3

1. Sternberg, R.J. (1997). *Thinking styles*. Cambridge, England: Cambridge University Press.

2. Rosenberg, M. (1979). *Conceiving the self. New York*: Basic Books.

3. Maslow, A.H. (1987). *Motivation and personality* (3rd ed.). New York: Harper & Row.

4. **http://www.benjerry.com**

5. Bolles, R.N. (1999). *The 1999 what color is your parachute?* Berkeley, CA: Ten Speed Press.

6. Waldron, C. (1988, August 29). How college education enriched lives of stars. *Jet*, 16–18.

7. Herbert, S.J., & Hill, G.H. (1990). *Bill Cosby*. Danbury, CT: Grolier. p. 38.

8. Ibid., p. 40.

Chapter 4

1. Gottesman, G. (1994). *College survival*. New York: Macmillan. p. 92.

2. Gregory, H. (1998). *Public speaking for college and career*. N.Y.: McGraw-Hill.

2. Davidson, J.W., Gienapp, W.E., Heyrman, C.L., Lytle, M.H., & Stoff, M.B. (1996). *Nation of nations. A concise narrative of the American republic*. New York: McGraw-Hill. p. 540.

Chapter 5

1. Pauk, W. (1974). *How to study in college*. Boston: Houghton Mifflin.

2. Tyler, S. (1997). *Been there should've done that!* Haslett, MI: Front Porch Press. p. 117.

3. Based on McPherson, J.M. (1988). *Battle cry of freedom: The Civil War era*. New York: Ballantine Books. pp. 504–510.

4. Tyler, S. (1997). *Been there should've done that!* Haslett, MI: Front Porch Press. p. 114.

5. Telander, R. (1995, March 20). The Post with the Most. *Sports Illustrated*.

6. Lobo, R.A., & Lobo, R. (1996). *The home team: Of mothers, daughters & American champions*. New York: Kodansha International.

7. Ibid.

8. Ibid.

9. Ibid.

Chapter 6

1. Tyler, S. (1997). *Been there should've done that!* Haslett, MI: Front Porch Press. p. 126.

2. Tyler, S. (1997). *Been there should've done that!* Haslett, MI: Front Porch Press. p. 128.

Chapter 7

1. Bransford, J.D., & Johnson, M.K. (1972). Contextual prerequisites for understanding: Some investigations of comprehension and recall. *Journal of Verbal Learning and Verbal Behavior, 11*, 171–221.

2. Quotes from Irving, J. (December 11, 1995). Slipped away: At fifty-three, the novelist remembers his first love: wrestling. *The New Yorker*, pp. 70–77; and Gussow, M. (April 28, 1998). John Irving: *A novelist builds out from fact to reach the truth*. **http://www.nytimes.com/lbirary/books/042898 irving-novel.html.**

Chapter 8

1. Elbow, P. (1998). *Writing with power* (2nd ed.). New York: Oxford University Press.

2. The American freshman: National norms for fall 1998, Los Angeles Higher Education Research Institute: American Council on Education and University of California.

3. Wydro, K. (1985) *Think on your feet: The art of thinking and speaking under pressure*. Englewood Cliffs, NJ: Prentice Hall.

Chapter 9

1. Smith, M.U. (1992). Expertise and the organization of knowledge: Unexpected differences among genetic counselors, faculty, and students on problem categorization tasks. *Journal of Research in Science Teaching, 29*, 179–205.

2. Halpern, D.F. (1996). *Thought and knowledge: An introduction to critical thinking*. Mahwah, NJ: Erlbaum. p. 48.

3. Gottesman, G. (1994). *College survival*. New York: Macmillan. p. 59.

4. Abel, T., Alberini, C., Ghiradi, M., Huang, Y.Y., Nguyen, P., & Kandel, E.R. (1995). Steps toward a molecular definition of memory consolidation. In D.L. Schacter (Ed.), *Memory distortions: How minds, brains, and societies reconstruct the past*. Cambridge, MA: Harvard University Press.

Chapter 10

1. Adapted from Halpern, D.F. (1996). *Thought and knowledge: An introduction to critical thinking* (3rd ed.). Mahwah, NJ: Erlbaum.

2. Ibid.; and Bransford, J.D., & Stein, B.S. (1993). *The ideal problem solver* (2nd ed.). New York: W.H. Freeman.

3. Adapted from Levy, D.A. (1997). *Tools of critical thinking*. Boston: Allyn & Bacon. p. 20.

4. Forer, B. (1949). The fallacy of personal validation: A classroom demonstration of gullibility. *Journal of Abnormal and Social Psychology, 44*, 118–123.

5. Byrne, D., & Kelley, L. (1981). *An introduction to personality* (3rd ed.). Englewood Cliffs, NJ: Prentice-Hall. p. 304.

6. Roberts, S.V., Auster, B.B., & Barone, M. (1993, September 20). Colin Powell, superstar: Will America's top general trade his uniform for a future in politics? *U.S. News & World Report*.

7. Ibid.

Chapter 11

1. Tyler, S. (1997). *Been there should've done that!* Haslett, MI: Front Porch Press.

2. Ibid.

Chapter 12

1. Nolan, M.F. (1997, April 26). Tiger's racial multiplicity. *Boston Globe*, A11.

2. Tatum, B.D. (1997). *"Why are all the black kids sitting together in the cafeteria?" And other conversations about race*. New York: Basic Books.

3. Malone, M.S. (1993, July 18). Translating diversity into high-tech gains. *The New York Times*, B2.

4. Sponholz, M., & Sponholz, J. (1996). *The Princeton Review college companion*. New York: Random House. p. 24.

5. Farber, B.A., Brink, D.C., & Raskin, P.M. (Eds.). (1996). *The psychotherapy of Carl Rogers: Cases and commentary*. New York: Guilford Press; Rogers, C.R. (1951). *Client-centered therapy*. Boston: Houghton Mifflin.

Chapter 13

1. Gottesman, G. (1994). *College survival*. New York: Macmillan. p. 206.

2. The College Board (1998, August 28). Cited in "Average college costs, 1997–1998." *Chronicle of Higher Education, 38*.

3. Dominguez, J., & Robin, V. (1993). *Your money or your life: Transforming your relationship with money and achieving financial independence*. New York: Penguin USA.

4. Rex, R. (1998, March/April). Sol Trujillo. *Emerging Markets*, 26–28.

5. Russell, J. (1998, October). Empire in the West. *Hispanic Business*, 82.

Chapter 14

1. Chamberlain, K., & Zika, S. (1990). The minor events approach to stress: Support for the use of daily hassles. *British Journal of Psychology, 81*, 469–481.

2. Source of table: Marx, M.B., Garrity, T.F., & Bowers, F.R. (1975). The influence of recent life experience on the health of college freshmen. *Journal of Psychosomatic Research, 19*, 87–98. (Questionnaire p. 97.)

3. Carlson, R. (1997). *Don't sweat the small stuff . . . and it's all small stuff*. New York: Hyperion.

4. Gottesman, G. (1994). *College survival*. New York: Macmillan. p. 160.

5. Adapted from Hughes, J.O., & Sandler, B.R. (1987). *"Friends" raping friends: Could it happen to you?* Washington, DC: Association of American Colleges.

Acknowledgments

Pp. 4, 9, 40, 93, 234, 334, 363: Excerpts from Gottesman, G. (1994). *College Survival*. Reprinted by permission of Macmillan USA.

P. 3: Fig. 1.1 from *The American Freshman: National Norms for Fall 1997*. Reprinted by permission of UCLA Higher Education Research Institute.

P. 20: Adapted from Good, L. R., & Good, K. C. (1973). An objective measure of the motive to avoid success. *Psychological Reports, 33*, 1009–1010. © Psychological Reports 1973. Adapted by permission.

P. 21: Logo of the University of Massachusetts. Reprinted by permission of the University of Massachusetts.

P. 27: Cartoon © 1999 William Haefeli from cartoonbank.com. All Rights Reserved.

P. 29: Cartoon © 1999 Michael Maslin from cartoonbank.com. All Rights Reserved.

P. 48: Logo of Creighton University. Reprinted by permission of Creighton University.

P. 63: Cartoon © The New Yorker Collection 1991 William Steig from cartoonbank.com. All Rights Reserved.

P. 67: Rosenberg, M. (1979). *Conceiving the Self*. Reprinted by permission of The Morris Rosenberg Foundation.

P. 68: Cartoon, CALVIN AND HOBBES © 1992 Watterson. Reprinted with permission of UNIVERSAL PRESS SYNDICATE. All rights reserved.

P. 72: Figure 3-2: Maslow, Abraham (1970). MOTIVATION AND PERSONALITY, 3rd ed. Copyright 1954, 1987 by Harper & Row Publishers, Inc. Copyright 1970 by Abraham H. Maslow. Reprinted by permission of Addison-Wesley Education Publishers, Inc.

P. 78: Logo of Temple University. Reprinted by permission of Collegiate Licensing Company and Temple University.

P. 87: Innovative Interfaces, Inc. Copyright 1999. Reproduced by permission.

P. 90: Cartoon © The New Yorker Collection 1998 Arnie Levin from cartoonbank.com. All Rights Reserved.

P. 103: Cartoon © The New Yorker Collection 1998 Ed Fisher from cartoonbank.com. All Rights Reserved.

Pp. 104–105: Excerpt from Gould, S. J. (1991). The streak of streaks. *Bully for brontosaurus: Reflections in natural history by Stephen Jay Gould*, 466–467. Copyright © 1991 by Stephen Jay Gould. Reprinted by permission of W. W. Norton & Company, Inc.

P. 105: Excerpt from Marshall, Ian, & Zohar, Danah, with contributions by F. David Peat (1997). General relativity. *Who's afraid of Schrödinger's cat?*, 170–171. Text Copyright © 1997 by Ian Marshall and Danah Zohar. By permission of William Morrow and Company, Inc.

P. 107: Logo of Florida State University. Reprinted by permission of Florida State University.

Pp. 120, 129, 150, 151, 271: Excerpts from Tyler, Suzette (1997). *Been There, Should've Done That.* © 1997 by Suzette Tyler. Reprinted by permission of Front Porch Press, Lansing, MI.

P. 123: Excerpt from McPherson, J. M. (1988). *Battle cry of freedom: The Civil War era,* 504–510. Reprinted by permission of Oxford University Press.

P. 133: Logo of the University of Connecticut. Reprinted by permission of the University of Connecticut.

P. 153: Cartoon, PEANUTS by Charles Schulz. Reprinted by permission of United Feature Syndicate, Inc.

P. 163: Logo of Austin Community College. Reprinted by permission of Austin Community College.

P. 171: Excerpt from Bransford, J. D., & Johnson, M. K. (1972). Contextual prerequisites for understanding: Some investigations of comprehension and recall. *Journal of Verbal Learning and Verbal Behavior, 11,* 717–721. Reprinted by permission of Academic Press.

P. 174: Cartoon, PEANUTS by Charles Schulz. Reprinted by permission of United Feature Syndicate, Inc.

P. 189: Excerpt from Irving, John (1995). Slipped away: At fifty-three, the novelist remembers his first love: wrestling. *The New Yorker,* 12/11/95, 70–77. © 1995 Garp Enterprises, Ltd. Reprinted by permission.

P. 189: Logo of the University of New Hampshire. Reprinted by permission of University of New Hampshire.

P. 215: Cartoon © 1999 Leo Cullum from cartoonbank.com. All Rights Reserved.

P. 217: Logo of Mount Holyoke College. Reprinted by permission of Mount Holyoke College.

P. 228–229: Exercise from Halpern, Diane F. (1996). *Thought and knowledge: An introduction to critical thinking,* 3rd edition, 48. Reprinted by permission of Lawrence Erlbaum Associates, Inc., Mahwah, NJ.

P. 239: Logo™ of Virginia Commonwealth University. Reprinted by permission of Virginia Commonwealth University.

Pp. 256, 266: Exercise adapted in part from Bransford, J. D., & Stein, B. S. (1993). *The Ideal Problem Solver,* 2/e. © 1993, 1984 by W. H. Freeman & Company. Used with permission. And adapted in part from Halpern, Diane F. (1996). *Thought and knowledge: An introduction to critical thinking,* 3rd edition, 48. Reprinted by permission of Lawrence Erlbaum Associates, Inc., Mahwah, NJ.

P. 263: Logo of City College of New York. Reprinted by permission of The City College of New York/CUNY.

P. 263: Excerpt from Roberts, S. V., Auster, B. B., & Barone, M. (1993). Colin Powell, superstar: Will America's top general trade his uniform for a future in politics? *U. S. News and World Report,* 9/20/93. Copyright, September 20, 1993, U.S. News and World Report. Visit website at www.usnews.com for additional information.

P. 288: Logo of Nassau Community College. Reprinted by permission of EGC Group and Nassau Community College.

P. 315: Logo of the University of California at Santa Barbara. Reprinted by permission of the Regents of the University of California.

P. 337: Cartoon © 1999 Michael Maslin from cartoonbank.com. All Rights Reserved.

P. 339: Cartoon © The New Yorker Collection 1974 J. B. Handelsman from cartoonbank.com. All Rights Reserved.

P. 345: Excerpt from Russell, J. (1998). Empire in the West. *Hispanic Business* (October), 82. Reprinted by permission of Hispanic Business Inc., Santa Barbara, CA.

P. 345: Logo of the University of Wyoming. Reprinted by permission of the University of Wyoming.

Pp. 356–357: Exercise from Marx, M. B., Garrity, T. F., & Bowers, F. R. (1975). The influence of recent life experience on the health of college freshmen. *Journal of Psychosomatic Research, 19*, 87–98. Copyright 1975. Reprinted with permission from Elsevier Science.

P. 367: Table 14-1: Chamberlain, Kerry, & Zika, Sheryl (1990). The minor events approach to stress: Support for the use of daily hassles. *British Journal of Psychology, 81*, 469–481. © The British Psychological Society. Reprinted by permission of the publisher and authors.

P. 374: Logo of Washington College. Reprinted by permission of Washington College.

P. 378: Excerpt from Hughes, J. O., & Sandler, B. R. (1987). *Friends raping friends: Could it happen to you?* National Association for Women in Education, Washington, DC. Reprinted by permission of Bernice R. Sandler.

Photo Credits

p. 1, Tom Stewart/Stock Market

p. 17, Lyndon B. Johnson Space Center/NASA

p. 21, Courtesy Normaris Gonzales

p. 25, George Haling/Photo Researchers

p. 31, Mark Gamba/Stock Market

p. 41, John Henley/Stock Market

p. 47, Jim Steinberg/Photo Researchers

p. 48, Courtesy Jennifer Schulte

p. 53, Paul S. Howell/Liaison International

p. 55, Nicholas Devore III/Photographers/Aspen

p. 61, Tom Stewart/Stock Market

p. 69, James D. Wilson/Gamma Liaison

p. 78, Dennis Cook/AP Photo

p. 83, Kenneth Gabrielsen/Liaison International

p. 89, Index Stock

p. 100, Oscar Chavez/Courtesy Pasadena City College

p. 107, Courtesy LeAlan Jones

p. 113, Tom & Deeann McCarthy/Stock Market

p. 117, Kaluzny & Thatcher/Tony Stone

p. 121, Robert Ullman/Monkmeyer

p. 126, Richard Pasley/Stock Boston

p. 133, Bob Galbraith/AP Photo

p. 139, Jose L. Pelaez/Stock Market

p. 143, Gary A. Conner/PhotoEdit

p. 149, Stephen Frisch/Stock Boston

p. 157, Index Stock

p. 163, Courtesy Theresa Winebrenner

p. 167, Richard Shock/Liaison International

p. 176, L. Kolvoord/Image Works

p. 186, Mary Steinbacher/PhotoEdit

p. 188, Randy Duchane/Stock Market

p. 189, Kagan/Gamma Liaison

p. 193, Sotographs/Liaison International

p. 196, EsbinAnderson/Image Works

p. 213, David Shopper/Stock Boston

p. 217, Courtesy ThaoMee Xiong

p. 221, Robert Smith/Picture Cube

p. 226, Chuck Savage/Stock Market

p. 232, Frank Siteman/Monkmeyer

p. 237, John Touscany/Picture Cube

p. 239, Courtesy Lamar Heckstall

p. 246, Porter Gifford/Gamma Liaison

p. 249, Fred Lyon/Photo Researchers

p. 260, Tim Trumble/Courtesy Arizona State University

p. 263, Mark Reinstein/Image Works

p. 267, George Zimbel/Monkmeyer

p. 270, Will & Deni McIntyre/Photo Researchers

p. 278, Wojnarowicz/Image Works

p. 281, Bob Daemmrich/Stock Boston

p. 284, Carl J. Single/Image Works

p. 288, Courtesy Vincent J. Iodice

p. 293, Gaye Hilsenrath/Picture Cube

p. 295, John Henley/Stock Market

p. 302, Sonda Dawes/Image Works

p. 306, Bill Aron/PhotoEdit

p. 309, Richard Pasley/Stock Boston

p. 315, Courtesy Kari Smith

p. 321, Chuck Savage/Stock Market

p. 323, Tom Stewart/Stock Market

p. 329, Margot Granitsas/Image Works

p. 334, Pat O'Leary/PhotoEdit

p. 345, Douglas C. Piza/AP Photo

p. 349, Mark A. Johnson/Stock Market

p. 351, Jeff Zaruba/Stock Market

p. 352, Mike Rominger/Courtesy Appalachian State University Public Affairs

p. 370, David Hanover/Tony Stone

p. 374, Courtesy Justin McCarthy

Index